W9-BXN-961

Divine
Sovereignty

Divine
Sovereignty

The Origins of Modern State Power

Daniel Engster

NORTHERN ILLINOIS UNIVERSITY PRESS • DEKALB

© 2001 by Northern Illinois University Press

Published by the Northern Illinois University Press, DeKalb, Illinois 60115

Manufactured in the United States using acid-free paper
All Rights Reserved
Designed by Julia Fauci

Library of Congress Cataloging-in-Publication Data

Engster, Daniel

Divine sovereignty: the origins of modern state power/Daniel Engster.

  p.   cm.

Includes bibliographical references and index.

ISBN 0-87580-275-3 (alk. paper)

1. State, The—History—16th century. 2. State, The—History—17th century.

3. Political science—France—History—16th century. 4. Political science—France—

History—17th century.

JC139 .E54 2001

 320.1—dc21

2001030463

CONTENTS

ACKNOWLEDGMENTS

This book was originally written as a dissertation under the guidance of Bernard Manin, Constantin Fasolt, Lloyd Rudolph, and Stephen Holmes. I would like to thank them for their advice and support during the early stages of this project. I would also like to thank all those who have read and commented upon chapters of this manuscript. I am especially grateful to Zachary Schiffmann, Susan Rosa, Jay Smith, Ann Davies, and Susan Liebell.

I received financial support for the early stages of this project from the Mellon Foundation and the Department of Political Science at the University of Chicago. A faculty research award from the University of Texas at San Antonio allowed me to finish work on this manuscript.

I owe my deepest debt to Kate, who has provided me with love, friendship, and support throughout the long process of writing this book.

I am grateful for permission to reprint earlier versions of two chapters. A partial and earlier version of chapter 1 appeared in the *Journal of the History of Ideas* 59 (1998): 625–50 (© The Johns Hopkins University Press). A partial and earlier version of chapter 2 appeared in *History of Political Thought* 17 (winter 1996): 469–99 (© Imprint Academic).

*T*his work concentrates on sixteenth- and seventeenth-century European political thinkers. Most of the thinkers studied here assumed that state rulers would be and should be male. This is especially true of writers in France, where women were legally excluded from the crown. Consistent with these facts, I have chosen to use male pronouns throughout this study to refer to the sovereign ruler. It seemed there was little to be gained by imposing a false gender neutrality upon the thought of these writers. Whenever these theorists made reference to humanity at large, however, I have tried to use gender-neutral language. Suffice it to say that I have remained conscious of my use of pronouns throughout this study and have used gender-neutral language whenever I believed it appropriate.

I have tried to make this study accessible to scholars outside of the area of early modern political thought. As such, I have used generally available texts and translations whenever possible. All other translations are my own.

Divine
Sovereignty

Introduction

his is the story of the development of modern state power. It traces the genealogy of the key concepts of modern state theory back to their origins in sixteenth- and seventeenth-century French and English thought. It thus explores the emergence of one of the central modes of organizing political power during the modern period: the state. The purpose is to highlight the historical and philosophical peculiarity of the modern state as well as to explain some of the problems associated with modern state legitimacy.

The modern state began to emerge during the later Middle Ages in Europe. It reached maturity during the sixteenth and seventeenth centuries, when sovereign rulers asserted their supreme authority over the people within their territorial jurisdictions. Numerous articles and books have been written about the development of the sovereign state.[1] The institutional development of the state has been attributed to war making, taxation policies, and alliances between kings and town elites.[2] The theoretical development of the state has been traced to the rebirth of a distinct "language of politics" during the twelfth and thirteenth centuries.[3] This book is an examination of the last crucial stage in the theoretical development of the early modern state, when the central principles of modern state theory were articulated and legitimized. These principles may be briefly summarized as follows:

> —legislative sovereignty: state rulers asserted their supreme and un-
> limited authority to make and change the laws for all individuals
> within their jurisdictions
> —reason of state/executive prerogative: state rulers claimed the moral

authority to carry out seemingly immoral or illegal actions for the sake of the public interest
—state regulatory powers: state rulers declared their right to regulate and discipline all areas of social life for the good of the people
—rationalistic rule: the proper conduct of state officials came to be associated with an impersonal and instrumental ethic[4]

At the beginning of the sixteenth century, none of these principles were considered morally legitimate; by the end of the seventeenth, all were widely accepted as necessary and good. How did this important transitional development come about? How did the central principles of modern state theory come to be accepted as legitimate modes of organizing and exercising power?

While existing scholarship provides a good background survey of the ideas and trends that contributed to the development of state theory, it has failed to provide a satisfactory account of the arguments used by early modern statesmen and theorists to explain and justify the new principles of state power. The main purpose of this book is to fill this gap in the literature by examining the ideology or language that early modern writers employed to define and legitimize the principles of legislative sovereignty, executive prerogative, state regulatory powers, and rationalistic rule.[5] The arguments of these writers may be dubbed an ideology not because they were formulated to serve the narrow interests of the ruling class—even though they may have had this effect—but because they established a cogent discursive paradigm in which the sovereign state came to appear as a necessary and good institution.[6]

There are several reasons for studying the ideology of the early modern state. Historically, this ideology was instrumental in establishing the new state paradigm. At the beginning of the sixteenth century, European rulers did not yet have available to them a coherent language to explain and justify their right (that is, if they even imagined they possessed such a right) to carry out broad legislative, executive, and administrative actions and to govern in an impartial and instrumental manner. These principles were explained and justified only over the course of the sixteenth and seventeenth centuries. The state ideology made it possible for rulers to justify actions in 1700 that would have been considered tyrannical and immoral in 1500. Of course, the state ideology never gained a complete hold over the people within any country. It was aimed primarily at the nobility and elites, and even among these groups it never achieved total acceptance. Throughout the sixteenth and seventeenth centuries, some elites continued to appeal to traditional political ideals while others began to develop new political ideologies to challenge the state. The point is simply that the state ideology provided theorists and statesmen with a conceptual framework that made it easier to explain and justify the exercise of state powers.

Another important reason for studying the state ideology is to gain a fuller picture of state-building processes in early modern Europe. While historians once envisioned the development of state powers in terms of a conflict between kings and the nobility, recent studies have shown that there actually existed a good deal of cooperation between kings and nobles in state-building activities. Kings used patronage and persuasion to win over local nobles while local nobles looked to the king to solidify their power and privileges.[7] Given this new historical perspective, it now seems plausible to bring ideology back into discussions of state-building.[8] For insofar as kings had to rely upon persuasion to win over the nobility and elites to institute new power arrangements, then ideology may be said to have played some role in state-building processes. Part of state-building consisted of the monarchy's efforts to explain to the nobility, elites, and (to a lesser extent) the people why they ought to support the state's efforts to expand and redefine governmental powers.

A third important reason for studying the state ideology is to gain insight into the nature of modern state theory itself. The central principles of modern state theory were all legitimized during the early modern period by drawing upon a particular set of ideological assumptions. These assumptions were not merely justifications for state principles but constitutive of them: they defined the nature and purpose of the state. While later theorists disavowed many of the elements of the early modern ideology and amended the principles of early modern state theory, they never entirely broke away from them. As a result, they confronted irresolvable problems when they attempted to establish the legitimacy of modern state powers. A central contention of this book is that the legitimacy of legislative sovereignty, executive prerogative, state regulatory powers, and rationalistic rule cannot be sustained apart from a set of ideological assumptions very similar to those articulated by early modern theorists. By studying the ideology of the early modern state, this book elucidates some of the forgotten premises behind modern state theory and explains some of the deep problems associated with modern state legitimacy.

This book focuses primarily on early modern French and English state theory. The focus on French thinkers is explained by the fact that they were chiefly responsible for defining and legitimizing the principles of modern state theory. The chapter on English state theory charts the development of state principles in the Anglo-American tradition. While many of the theorists and statesmen studied in this book are commonly known as "absolutist" or "absolute state" theorists, this designation can be misleading.[9] "Absolutist" theorists did not support arbitrary or unrestrained powers for the king. They were certainly not "totalitarians" in the modern sense of the term. They merely advocated greater powers for the state than earlier writers had considered legitimate, and they favored a greater concentration of power than later writers deemed prudent. It is only in this highly qualified sense that "absolutist" is used here. The term "state" is used throughout this study, in turn, to designate the central governing apparatus of a country, and more specifically, a type of governmental apparatus organized around the principles of legislative sovereignty, executive prerogative, regulatory powers, and rationalistic rule.[10] It is, however, at times impossible to avoid using "state" in the older sense of the term, as when writers such as Richelieu or Louis XIV use the term to designate the whole body of society.

This study examines the canonical texts of writers such as Bodin and Hobbes as well as the pamphlets and advice books of practical statesmen such as Richelieu and Louis XIV. This mixture of "high" and "practical" theorists is dictated by the topic: the legitimacy of the modern state was established not only by the grand philosophers of the state but also by many lesser thinkers. In fact, lesser theoreticians played a seminal role in formulating and legitimizing the principles of executive prerogative, administrative regulation, and rationalistic rule. Their ideas are also useful in helping us to understand philosophers such as Bodin and Hobbes, because they fill out the intellectual context in which these writers developed their ideas.[11] Nonetheless, many of these lesser-known works deserve attention on their own merits. The political theories of some of the practical statesmen studied here—especially Richelieu and Louis XIV—are quite coherent and interesting in themselves. Even within a traditional framework of political philosophy, their works deserve more attention than they have thus far received.

The argument of this book may be briefly summarized as follows. Early modern theorists and statesmen legitimized the new powers of the state by appealing to an ideology based on two broad assumptions. The first related to what modern scholars have dubbed the "disappearance" or "breakdown" of the medieval idea of order[12]—the dominant political paradigm during the later Middle Ages.[13] This paradigm posited the existence of immanent divine and natural order within the temporal world that extended into political society. The most famous expression of this belief was the "great chain of being."[14] Medieval thinkers almost universally maintained that God had organized the universe into a vast hierarchical order stretching from the heavens down to the lowest earthly substance. He placed angels above human beings, human beings above animals, animals above plants, and plants above inanimate objects. God was believed to have organized human society in a similar manner. He placed priests and kings at the top of the social hierarchy, the nobility in the middle ranks, and peasants and craftspeople at the bottom. Just as the chain of being established a perfect harmony throughout the universe, so it also established a perfect harmony within human society. Individuals were called upon to fulfill the positions and duties that God had assigned them in order to maintain the divine and natural social order—"For it is sufficient," Christine de Pizan wrote in the *Book of the Body Politic*, "to speak of the manner in which everyone ought to do his own part in the order that God has established, that is, nobles do as nobles should, the populace does as it is appropriate for them, and everyone should come together as one body of the same polity, to live justly and in peace as they ought."[15] Medieval legal theories embodied this same ideal of order. Medieval thinkers widely assumed that God's eternal law pervaded all things in the universe. "Every motion and every act in the whole universe is subject to the Eternal Law," St. Thomas Aquinas wrote.[16] The divine law, natural law, law of nations, canonical law, Roman law, customary law, and positive law were all assumed to derive from the eternal law and to provide merely more particular expressions of it. Political authorities were exhorted to respect and maintain these laws because they were part of the immanent divine and natural order of the universe; to act contrary to the law was to expose oneself to corruption and disorder. All of the universe, according to mainstream medieval thought, was subject to a universal and eternal, static and harmonious moral order.

Over the course of the sixteenth and seventeenth centuries, this medieval idea of order was challenged and eventually replaced by a more dynamic and contingent worldview. This development has been carefully studied in Renaissance Italy.[17] During the fifteenth and sixteenth centuries, the universal and static framework of medieval political thought was replaced with a more dynamic vision of social order emphasizing fortune and contingency and the constructive powers of human virtue. A similar development occurred during the sixteenth and seventeenth centuries in the rest of Europe in response to a number of technological, religious, and economic innovations. The Protestant Reformation shattered the medieval ideal of Christian unity. The religious wars of the later sixteenth century caused civil strife and warfare throughout much of European society. Price inflation and the growing wealth of merchants undermined traditional social hierarchies. Reflecting upon the social changes taking place in English society, John Donne wrote at the beginning of the seventeenth century:

> 'Tis all in pieces, all coherence gone;
> All just supply, and all relation:
> Prince, subject, father, son, are things forgot,
> For every man alone thinks he hath got
> To be a phoenix, and that then can be
> None of that kind of which he is, but he.[18]

Donne's writings provide only one example of an attitude that was becoming prevalent by the early seventeenth century.[19] Writers commented with increasing frequency upon the change and uncertainty of social and temporal affairs. The medieval vision of a static and harmonious world was giving way to a more contingent and dynamic understanding of human and temporal affairs.

Intellectual developments further contributed to the breakdown of the medieval paradigm. One important development was the rise of voluntarist theologies.[20] William Ockham and Duns Scotus first proposed voluntarist theologies during the later Middle Ages, arguing that God ruled the universe not though a rational eternal law but through his omnipotent and unfettered will. Over the course of the sixteenth and seventeenth centuries,

Protestant and Catholic writers alike increasingly adopted this theology. They argued that the course of human and temporal affairs was entirely dependent "from moment to moment" upon God's will. They rejected the notion of "order as immanent, grounded in the very natures or essences of things" in favor of a view of "order as external to things, imposed, as it were, [by God] from the outside."[21] The result was a much more contingent understanding of human and temporal affairs. God was portrayed as unknowable, unpredictable, and unconstrained by nature and reason, while human beings were said to be entirely dependent upon his will for their well-being.[22]

Another important intellectual development contributing to (as well as reflecting) the breakdown of the medieval idea of order was the rise of skepticism.[23] Richard Popkin traced the rise of skepticism in early modern Europe to the Reformation. Luther's challenge to Church authority raised fundamental questions about the nature of religious truth and certainty. With the revival of Greek Pyrrhonism in the middle of the sixteenth century, skepticism spread from religious questions to all branches of knowledge, including political and social thought. Michel de Montaigne was a central figure in this movement. He argued that human reason was too weak to comprehend the universal principles of moral and natural law. Different societies defined the natural law in different ways at different times. "What am I to make," Montaigne famously asked, "of a virtue that I saw in credit yesterday, that will be discredited tomorrow, and that becomes a crime on the other side of the river?"[24] Openly challenging the assumptions of medieval moral and legal theory, Montaigne asserted that very few substantive principles of natural law were comprehensible to human beings. He rejected the medieval vision of a static and moral universe for one pervaded by fortune, contingency, and diversity.

Still other intellectual developments contributed to the breakdown of the medieval paradigm. The historical and philological studies of Italian and French humanists highlighted the historicity of social institutions and customs.[25] The "good old law" was discovered to be not so old and in many cases not so good, either. New scientific discoveries and theories further challenged fundamental assumptions of the medieval cosmology (for example, the geocentric universe).[26] Early modern state theorists drew upon these developments to legitimize modern state theory. Some explicitly endorsed voluntarist theologies. Some emphasized the indeterminateness of natural law. Others pointed to dislocations in the social hierarchy. All emphasized the extreme contingency, fluidity, and diversity of human and temporal affairs.

In *The Machiavellian Moment*, J. G. A. Pocock argued that modern republican theory emerged in concert with the development of modern historical thinking.[27] The same can be said about modern state theory. By insisting on the uncertainty and fluidity of temporal affairs, state theorists opened a new theoretical space for state action. They used the notion of contingency and change to justify more flexible and unlimited state powers. But state theorists revised the traditional humanist conception of temporal processes. Specifically, they portrayed temporal affairs as much more contingent and disorderly than the Italian humanists envisioned them. Their ideological perspective was marked by a radicalization of the Machiavellian notion of fortune and flux, and they used this radical vision to legitimize a more permanent and powerful state apparatus.

The second pillar of the statist ideology was a sacred vision of the nature and purpose of the state. Early modern statesmen and theorists portrayed the state as a metaphysically privileged institution responsible for instituting a static and universal political order within the contingent and disorderly temporal world. The central elements of this conception of the state may be traced back to the Middle Ages. The sacred theory of kingship, for example, was standard to medieval political thought.[28] Kings were said to rule *dei gratia* (by the grace of God) for the temporal and spiritual well-being of their subjects. They were described as the heads of the *corpus mysticum* of society, possessing a Christlike mortal and immortal nature. The Most Christian King of France was believed to possess the miraculous ability to heal scrofula by laying his hands upon his afflicted subjects. Early modern state theorists built upon the medieval tradition of sacred monarchy but magnified the grandeur and significance of the sovereign prince. By the sixteenth century, the king was being described as "God on earth" blessed with superhuman wisdom and an unblemished moral character. Moreover, he was no longer portrayed as merely one point of divine order within a world suffused with divine and natural order. He was portrayed as the lone point of divine order within an otherwise chaotic and contingent temporal world. The state authority was deified, in other words, as the temporal world was secularized. Just as God was responsible for imposing and maintaining order within the temporal world, the king or state became responsible for imposing and maintaining order within society.

State theorists further attributed a sacred purpose to the state. The purpose was not simply to establish a secular peace among individuals—the state was supposed to create a sanctified political order set apart from the contingent and corrupt "outside" world of temporal affairs. State theorists looked to the state to reproduce within territorial boundaries the static and universal order associated with the medieval paradigm. The state was charged with the task of establishing a harmonious and predictable social order and uniting individuals into a moral community organized around the principles of divine and natural law. In the *Legitimacy of the Modern Age*, Hans Blumenberg suggested that many modern concepts were formulated to "re-occupy" ideological positions left open by the collapse of the medieval cosmology.[29] These concepts fulfilled the "residual needs" of individuals who were still tied to a universal Christian framework. State theory arose in this same manner. Early modern theorists and statesmen proposed the core principles of modern state theory to reconstruct a sanctified political order in what they perceived to be a secular and disorderly temporal world. They played upon individuals' desire for a harmonious universal community in order to legitimize the awesome new powers of their mighty Leviathan.

This account challenges the widely held assumption that the development of modern state theory represented the triumph of secular realism over medieval idealism. Undoubtedly there was an important secular element in early modern state theory. State theorists argued that the realm of human and temporal affairs (that is, the *saeculum*) had fallen away from the universal order of God and nature and had come to be dominated by contingency and fortune. But they proposed and legitimized state theory in an effort to combat the contingency and disorder associated with this "secularism." They imagined the state as the great mediator between God and humanity responsible for entering into the corruption of human existence (like Jesus Christ himself) in order to save humanity from it. They legitimized the broad powers of the state by arguing that these powers were necessary to address the contingency and flux of temporal affairs and maintain the universal stability and morality associated with the good political community. To borrow a phrase from Ernst Cassirer, this was the "myth of the state"—the state was the metaphysically ordained source of order, morality, and unity in a disorderly temporal world.[30]

From the late seventeenth century onward, the state was increasingly desacralized and liberalized.[31] The foundations of state legitimacy were transferred from divine grace to popular consent. The king came to be seen as the first minister of state rather than the embodiment of God on earth. The legislative, executive, and judicial powers of the state were separated among different branches of government. Yet despite these reforms, liberal theorists never broke away entirely from the early modern state paradigm. They still organized their state theories around the principles of legislative sovereignty, executive prerogative, state regulatory powers, and rationalistic rule. While they no longer legitimized these principles in terms of divine or natural right, they devised a new metaphysical fiction to support them: "the people."[32] The state was no longer said to be the universal representative of God on earth but instead the universal representative of the people. Liberal theorists likewise continued to call upon the state to establish a moral and unified community standing apart from the outside temporal world. While the state was stripped of its overtly sacred veneer, it thus remained an exalted institution in form and purpose. Only the surface features of state theory were detached from their divine origins.

Early modern state theorists thus left an important paradigmatic legacy to modern political thought. They defined the fundamental principles and purposes of modern state theory. These origins explain some of the deep problems associated with modern state legitimacy. For the powers and purposes of the state never meshed very well with the more mundane and popularly based approaches to government outlined by Enlightenment thinkers. Rousseau was among the first writers to point out that the idea of a centralized and representative sovereign state was incompatible with the notion of popular sovereignty. Many other critics followed in his wake, arguing that liberal theories of state legitimacy based upon individual freedom, equality, and consent stand at odds with liberal theories of state power. In recent years, the problems of state legitimacy have been compounded by new social developments. Feminist and multicultural theorists have challenged the universalist claims of the sovereign state by arguing that it has never been the true representative of "the people."[33] Social theorists have pointed out that the state is no longer capable of monopolizing the organization of time and space amid the global flows of capital, goods, services, technology, communication, and information.[34] At the root of these problems is an antiquated political myth. The legitimacy of state powers rests upon a divine vision of politics.

This study is organized analytically and chronologically. The first chapter outlines the general development of the statist ideology by comparing the writings of Niccolò Machiavelli (1469–1527) and Michel de Montaigne (1533–1592). While Machiavelli is usually placed at the head of the statist tradition, this distinction more properly belongs to Montaigne. Montaigne self-consciously debunked Machiavelli's humanist approach to temporality and politics and laid out a new discourse that established the framework for the development of state theory. Montaigne, however, did not himself articulate a state theory. He only identified a few principles for establishing order within a highly contingent temporal world. In general, he was also more accepting of contingency and change than later state theorists. The last part of this chapter thus discusses the ideas of two writers who outlined more complete state theories: Justus Lipsius (1547–1606) and Pierre Charron (1541–1603). Both articulated ideas very similar to Montaigne's, but described more complete state theories designed to impose a static order upon contingency and change. By studying Montaigne, Lipsius, and Charron, the general background to the development of the state paradigm is elucidated.

Each of the next three chapters examines the development and legitimization of one of the core principles of modern state theory. Chapter 2 looks at the development of the principle of legislative sovereignty in the writings of Jean Bodin (1529/30–1596). While Bodin is often identified as the inventor of the modern principle of legislative sovereignty (and hence as the founder of modern state theory), scholars have for the most part overlooked the moral cosmology underlying his political philosophy. Bodin adhered to a view of the universe replete with angels, demons, and witches and marked by an incessant struggle between good and evil, order and chaos. This chapter links Bodin's political theory to his cosmological views, demonstrating that he proposed his theory of legislative sovereignty as a means to institute a universal moral order amid what he feared was becoming a corrupt and secularized social environment.

The third chapter looks at the development of the principle of executive prerogative in the writings of French *raison d'état* theorists, focusing on the writings of Cardinal Richelieu (1585–1642) and some of his most important

supporters, including Jéremie Ferrier, Jean Louis Guez de Balzac, Jean de Silhon, Daniel de Priézac, Gabriel Naudé, and the Duke de Rohan. While Italian and Spanish thinkers had previously set forth "reason of state" theories,
Richelieu and his supporters were the first writers fully to develop and legitimize this concept. They argued that the king was justified in carrying out
even the most seemingly immoral and illegal actions when necessary for
the "interests of the state." Building upon the ideas of Montaigne, Lipsius,
and Charron, they also took important steps toward developing a new governmental ethic based upon impersonal and instrumental rule.

Chapter 4 examines the development of the theory of state regulatory
powers in the writings and propaganda of Louis XIV (1638–1715), Colbert
(1619–1683), Bossuet (1627–1704), and several other figures from the
epoch of the Sun King. Drawing upon the state ideology developed by
Bodin, Richelieu, and others, Louis XIV and his cohorts legitimized the extension of state regulatory powers and surveillance over a wide variety of
social activities that had previously been outside state control. It was only
by touching and directing all affairs, they claimed, that the king could
overcome the chaos of social affairs and integrate individuals into a harmonious community aligned with the providential order. Louis XIV and his
supporters also took the final steps toward establishing impartiality and rationality as the new governing ethic of the state.

In chapter 5, the analysis of state ideology is extended to English political thought. English political thought is often studied in isolation from
continental political theory, but at least in the case of state theory, this distinction is misguided. The ideas of James I, Filmer, and Hobbes all reveal a
close affinity to the state theories of French thinkers; in particular, they
were all intended to reinstitute the principles of the traditional medieval
idea of order within what was perceived to be an inherently disorderly and
contingent social environment. This chapter especially challenges the traditional image of Hobbes as a strictly secular political philosopher and of his
"Leviathan" as a strictly secular political institution.

The conclusion summarizes the new insights that this book contributes
to existing accounts of the development of modern state theory and brings
these insights to bear on the contemporary crisis of the state. The emergence of global economic markets, new communication and transportation
technologies, and multicultural and transnational political movements
have all undermined the ability of states to fulfill their traditional functions. The state is no longer able to protect society from "outside" contingencies or even very credibly portray itself as the universal representative of
the people. The powers and purposes of the state are increasingly incongruous with the perceived realities of the contemporary world. At the center of
this crisis is our conception of the state. By understanding the origins of
state powers and purposes, we can better understand the current crisis and
recognize some of the necessary steps for reforming and restoring legitimacy to contemporary politics.

CHAPTER ONE

The Montaignian Moment

*I*n his classic work *The Machiavellian Moment,* J. G. A. Pocock traced the development of modern republican theory to a conceptual breakthrough in historical consciousness.[1] Whereas medieval Christian thinkers subsumed temporal affairs within a providential framework, Italian humanists emphasized their contingency and flux.[2] They also outlined an activist approach to establishing political order within time that differed markedly from medieval political theories.[3] These innovations reached their culmination in the writings of Niccolò Machiavelli. "The Machiavellian moment," Pocock wrote, "is a name for the moment in conceptualized time in which the republic was seen as confronting its own temporal finitude, as attempting to remain morally and politically stable in a stream of irrational events conceived as essentially destructive of all systems of secular stability."[4] Machiavelli responded to the challenge of fortune and contingency, according to Pocock, by articulating a political theory that "left an important paradigmatic legacy" to modern political thought. He stands at the head of the modern republican tradition, emphasizing the importance of "concepts of balanced government, dynamic virtù, and the role of arms and property" in establishing order within time.[5]

Pocock's thesis has been criticized on a number of grounds.[6] Above all, scholars have charged that he overstated the importance of republican themes within Machiavelli's thought while downplaying the despotic elements. "For if Machiavellism is a rhetoric for conceptualizing and responding to the realm of contingency," Victoria Kahn wrote, "it includes not only republicanism but also tyranny; it involves the use of force and fraud not only to advance one's self interest but also to serve the commonwealth."[7]

Kahn's point is well taken. Machiavelli was not a doctrinaire proponent of the republican ideology but interested more broadly in exploring all the possibilities for taming fortune and flux. Nonetheless, Pocock's thesis remains useful. The Machiavellian moment still marks a fundamental breakthrough in theories of temporality and politics. Pocock's thesis needs merely to be broadened to encompass the variety of humanist strategies that Machiavelli proposed for maintaining political stability within a stream of irrational and contingent temporal events.

A second important breakthrough in early modern theories of temporality and politics was made by Michel de Montaigne (1533–1592). In his *Essays,* Montaigne extended and deepened Machiavelli's understanding of temporal contingency.[8] He also challenged the effectiveness of humanist strategies for establishing order within time, and proposed a new set of political principles based on the concept of "nature." No less than Machiavelli, Montaigne left an important paradigmatic legacy to modern political thought. Montaigne may be seen as a central transitional figure between the activist humanism of the fifteenth and early sixteenth centuries and the naturalistic and rationalistic state theories of the late sixteenth and seventeenth centuries. Or more succinctly, he may be seen as the intermediary between Machiavelli and Hobbes. The "Montaignian moment" marked a conceptual breakthrough in theories of temporality and politics that opened a new theoretical space for the development of modern state theory.[9]

Montaigne, however, was not himself a state theorist. He identified a few principles for establishing order within a contingent temporal world, but did not outline a systematic political philosophy. He stands at the head of the modern state tradition but not within it. Two writers who outlined more complete state theories are Justus Lipsius (1547–1606) and Pierre Charron (1541–1603), both of whom articulated cosmologies very similar to Montaigne's but formulated more detailed political strategies. By examining the philosophies of Lipsius and Charron in the latter part of this chapater, it will be demonstrated more precisely how the ideas associated with the Montaignian moment were used to establish the legitimacy of the modern theory of the state.

THE MACHIAVELLIAN MOMENT

In chapter 25 of the *Prince,* Machiavelli famously observed that although "fortune is arbiter of half of our actions . . . she leaves the other half, or close to it, for us to govern."[10] The virtuous prince could always build "dikes and dams" to stem fortune's course or "beat her and strike her down." In this chapter, Machiavelli concisely summarized one of the core assumptions of humanist political thought: the idea that "virtù vince fortuna (virtue triumphs over accidental luck)."[11] Quattrocento humanists widely believed that human beings possessed the ability to control and direct the outcome of temporal events through an activist and assertive virtue.[12] Machiavelli's major innovation was simply to reframe this activist humanism in more practical and amoral terms.[13] This can be seen in his redefinition of two central concepts of humanist political discourse: history and virtue.

Earlier humanists had looked to history to find praiseworthy examples of good conduct.[14] They believed history should be used primarily to inculcate moral and civic lessons from antiquity. In the opening pages of the *Discourses,* Machiavelli sharply criticized this historical method. He lamented the fact that his contemporaries more "admired than imitated" the examples of antiquity and attributed this to their "not having a true knowledge of histories, through not getting from reading them that sense nor tasting that flavor that they have in themselves."[15] At the root of his contemporaries' misguided approach to historical studies, Machiavelli suggested, was an ontological confusion. It was not "as if heaven, sun, elements, [and] men had varied in motion, order, and power from what they were in antiquity." It was therefore possible to make a much more concrete and practical use of history than earlier humanists had recognized.[16] Since the natural world and human nature were always the same everywhere, and the planets moved in regular patterns, human beings could extract precise rules from history and use this knowledge to manipulate present-day affairs (for example, "How Far Accusations May Be Necessary in a Republic to Maintain It in Freedom," "Whether When Fearing to Be Assaulted, It Is Better to Bring On or Await War"). As Mario Santoro has written, "The error of the humanists according to Machiavelli was their not having responsibly aimed to translate into political reality the lessons handed down from antiquity, of having limited imitation to the realm of rhetoric, art and speculation."[17] Machiavelli most clearly summarized his methodological assumptions in the following statement:

> Whoever considers present and ancient things easily knows that in all cities and in all peoples there are the same desires and the same humors, and there always have been. So it is an easy thing for whoever examines past things diligently to foresee future things in every republic and to take the remedies for them that were used by the ancients, or, if they do not find any that were used, to think up new ones through the similarity of accidents. But because these considerations are neglected or not understood by whoever reads, or, if they are understood, they are not known to whoever governs, it follows that there are always the same scandals in every time.[18]

Later in the *Discourses* Machiavelli noted with particular bitterness a recent instance in which the failure to appreciate lessons of the past had brought about an unnecessary defeat.[19] After first listing a number of examples from history demonstrating that a city should always negotiate with an enemy armed with superior forces, he noted that the Florentines had nonetheless refused to do just that when confronted with superior Spanish forces in 1512.[20] As a result, Prato was sacked, Florence was forced to surrender, the Florentine republic collapsed, and the Medici returned to power. Yet none of this would have happened, Machaivelli concluded, if the Florentines had simply studied the practical lessons of history.

Machiavelli did not of course believe that the lessons of history could be applied to contemporary affairs in a rigid or simpleminded fashion. While the universe and human nature may have remained constant over time, he was all too aware of the important cultural and religious changes that had taken place since antiquity. Because Christianity had inclined modern peoples to "esteem less the honor of the world," he observed that the examples of the ancients would have to be modified before they could be applied to present affairs.[21] He was also careful to note qualifications and exceptions to his general historical rules whenever they appeared, and always stressed the need for individuals to adapt historical rules to their own particular times and circumstances.[22] Nevertheless, Machiavelli clearly believed that history could provide human beings with an important resource for negotiating human and temporal affairs. Without a more scientific study of past events, human beings would lack an important tool in their struggle with fortune and their decisions would be left, unnecessarily, to chance.

Closely related to Machiavelli's new approach to history was his new definition of virtue.[23] Earlier humanists had equated virtue with the traditional Christian values. They assumed that what was good in a moral sense *(honestum)* would also be useful *(utile)*, contributing to political and temporal success. In his advice book to princes published in the 1470s, for example, Francesco Patrizi wrote that all of a prince's virtues would be powerless against fortune if he lacked the essential qualities of Christian piety, faith, liberality, mercy, and honesty.[24] In his infamous chapters 15 through 18 of the *Prince,* Machiavelli broke this traditional connection between virtue and Christian morality, declaring his intention of setting aside questions of "how one should live" in order "to go directly to the effectual truth of the thing."[25] He noted that although the qualities of liberality, mercy, love, and honor were sometimes useful to a prince, there were many situations in which these qualities might bring him to ruin. In these situations, the prince should not hesitate to depart from traditional morality and to do whatever was necessary to secure his power. True *virtù* consisted not of a rigid adherence to fixed moral precepts but in the ability of an individual to adapt to changing times and circumstances. Summarizing his position at the end of chapter 18, Machiavelli wrote: "And so [the prince] needs to have a spirit disposed to change as the winds of fortune and variations of things command him, and as I said above, not depart from good, when possible, but know how to enter into evil, when forced by necessity."[26] While still holding to the traditional humanist belief in the power of virtue, Machiavelli cut virtue loose from its traditional moral moorings and associated it with whatever qualities were necessary to conquer fortune and maintain power.

THE MONTAIGNIAN MOMENT

Machiavelli was among the last of the Italian humanists to claim that human beings possessed considerable control over fortune. Confronted with the repeated invasions of the Italian peninsula during the first part of the sixteenth century and Charles V's sack of Rome in 1527, Italian writers grew increasingly pessimistic about the ability of human beings to control their fate.[27] Even Machiavelli sometimes struck a more resigned note in this regard.[28] In a chapter from his *Discourses* entitled "Fortune Blinds the Spirits of Men When It Does Not Wish Them to Oppose Its Plans," he outlined an almost fatalistic account of fortune's powers.[29] "I indeed affirm it anew to be very true, according to what is seen through all the histories, that men can second fortune but not oppose it, that they can weave its warp but not break it." But even here at his most pessimistic, Machiavelli still concluded that "since [human beings] do not know [fortune's] end and it proceeds by oblique and unknown ways, they have also to hope and, since they hope, not to give up in whatever fortune and in whatever travail they may find themselves." Machiavelli counseled hope and action no matter how dire the circumstances. By contrast, in his *History of Italy* written in the 1530s, Francesco Guicciardini abandoned the optimism of his earlier writings and emphasized the numerous "calamities" and "frequent shifts of fortune" that dominated human and temporal affairs.[30] Felix Gilbert argued that the chief lesson of Guicciardini's *History* is "the helplessness and impotence of man in the face of fate" and the need to develop a more "philosophical attitude" toward temporal events.[31]

When we turn to Montaigne's *Essays,* we find these sentiments even more strongly pronounced.[32] Confronted with the nearly total breakdown of order caused by the religious and civil wars, Montaigne portrayed fortune as an almost all-pervasive and all-powerful force over human affairs. While he did acknowledge at several points the existence of a perfect providential and natural order underlying the course of affairs, he claimed this order was for the most part incomprehensible to human beings (I, 26, 116; I, 32, 159–61; II, 12, 343; II, 30, 538–39). Human beings were caught up in the "perennial movement" of nature, depriving them of any "firm footing" from which they might objectively catalogue or assess affairs (III, 2, 610–11). For all practical purposes, human beings were wholly immersed in a stream of contingent and unstable events beyond their complete knowledge or control.

Like Machiavelli and other earlier humanists, Montaigne dubbed the stream of temporal events by the name of "fortune," but he saw it as much more powerful and unpredictable than earlier humanists had.[33] Montaigne's central message was that fortune was extremely capricious and human prudence too weak to control it. He introduced this theme in the very first essay of book 1, "By Diverse Means We Arrive at the Same End" (I, 1, 3–5).[34] The topic of this essay was the Machiavellian question of what individuals should do to save themselves when they fall into the enemy's hands. Montaigne began by recounting various examples where acts of courage and defiance by defeated individuals had won over conquering princes. However, he noted that "weaker natures, such as women, children, and the common herd" often reacted better to pleas for mercy. Immediately after making this apparently helpful distinction, however, Montaigne then contradicted it. The Theban mob rejected Pelopidas's pleas for mercy and responded favorably to Epaminondas's haughty courage. "And directly contrary to my first examples," Montaigne continued, Alexander the Great was driven into a fit of rage by the insolent and haughty behavior of the enemy commander Betis. Montaigne's conclusion was that it was nearly impossible to identify any general rules or precepts of action from history. The diversity and contingency of human affairs rendered the means of achieving the same ends so diverse as to defy rational explanation: "Truly man is a marvelously vain, diverse, and undulating object. It is hard to found any constant and uniform judgment on him."

Montaigne sounded a similar theme in his essay ""Various Outcomes of the Same Plan" (I, 24, 90–97). He began this essay by noting that the Duke of Guise had recently pardoned a man who had plotted to assassinate him. He then observed that Caesar Augustus had once taken a similar action. Yet, whereas Augustus's action had won him a good reputation and served to quell future conspiracies, the duke of Guise was assassinated a few months later in another plot. Machiavelli had likewise noted a variety of cases where two individuals employing the same means had come to different ends, or alternatively had achieved the same end through different means. But he usually tried to account for these differences by identifying mitigating circumstances and he nearly always drew some general conclusion from his examples. Machiavelli identified "several reasons," for example, why Scipio conquered Spain through humanity and mercy while Hannibal took Italy through cruelty and violence, and then concluded generally that "most often whoever makes himself feared is more followed and more obeyed than whoever makes himself loved."[35] Montaigne, by contrast, argued that the only general rule one could draw from the diversity of outcomes was the supreme dominance of fortune over all human endeavors. "So vain and frivolous a thing is human prudence, and athwart all our plans, counsels, and precautions, Fortune still maintains her grasp on the results" (I, 24, 92). Montaigne considered history and prudence weak weapons in the struggle against fortune.

In the remainder of this essay, Montaigne went on to detail the tremendous role that fortune played in determining the outcome of medical operations, artistic endeavors, and military enterprises. He repeated these themes in his essays "Fortune Is Often Met in the Path of Reason" (I, 34, 163–65) and "Of the Uncertainty of Our Judgment" (I, 47, 205–9). After noting in this latter essay that there was much to be said "both for and against" a variety of different military strategies and that "there was no lack of examples on both sides," he concluded: "Thus we are wont to say, with reason, that events and outcomes depend for the most part, especially in war, on Fortune, who will not fall into line and subject herself to our reason and foresight." Montaigne's arguments here represented a total subversion of classical humanist rhetoric.[36] Earlier humanists had used the *in utramque partem* method (arguing on both sides of a question) to arrive at some approximation of the truth about human affairs. Montaigne instead used it only to demonstrate fortune's extreme capriciousness. One could argue on either side of almost every issue, he claimed, because human and temporal affairs were so wildly diverse and unpredictable. All the *in utramque partem* method really proved was the limited power of human beings to formulate general rules of conduct or determine the outcome of affairs.

Montaigne further departed from traditional humanist thought in describing the scope of fortune's powers. Machiavelli argued that individuals had a set of fixed dispositions inclining them to behave in consistent ways over time, concluding that good and bad fortune were largely determined by whether one's dispositions suited the times and circumstances.[37] Montaigne challenged this account of individual personality. He claimed human behavior was for the most part the product of circumstances. In his essay "Of the Inconsistency of Our Actions," he mocked writers who attempted to fashion "a consistent and solid fabric out of us" by interpreting all of an individual's actions in light of one overriding disposition (II, 1, 239–44). Individuals were comprised of a "patchwork" of "shapeless and diverse" feelings and dispositions that oscillated and changed "each moment." "That man whom you saw so adventurous yesterday, do not think it strange to find him just as cowardly today: either anger, or necessity, or company, or wine, or the sound of a trumpet, had put his heart in his belly. His was a courage formed not by reason, but by one of these circumstances; it is no wonder if he has now been made different by other, contrary circumstances." As this passage indicates, Montaigne did hold out the possibility that human beings might impose some consistency upon their actions through reason. But lacking an exerted effort, he claimed most individuals simply reflected the ever-changing circumstances of fortune.[38] "It is no wonder, says an ancient [Seneca], that chance has so much power over us, since we live by chance. A man who has not directed his life as a whole toward a definite goal cannot possibly set his particular actions in order" (II, 1, 243). In contrast to Machiavelli, Montaigne argued that individuals did not confront fortune simply as an external foe. Individual behaviors were themselves largely the product of fortune (I, 38, 172–74; II, 1, 239–44).

Even after the papal censors rebuked Montaigne for his excessive references to fortune in the first edition of the *Essays* (1580), he continued in later essays to invoke the pagan deity.[39] In "Of the Art of Discussion," for example, he portrayed fortune as a nearly all-powerful deity over human affairs: "Good and bad luck are in my opinion two sovereign powers. It is unwise to think that human wisdom can fill the role of Fortune. And vain is the undertaking of him who presumes to embrace both causes and consequences and to lead by the hand the progress of his affair" (III, 8, 713). In one of his last essays, "Of Physiognomy," Montaigne even directly revised Machiavelli's estimate of the relative powers of fortune and prudence over human affairs. After noting his own tendency to abandon himself to fortune, he wrote: "There have been some actions in my life the conduct of which might justly be called difficult, or, if you wish, prudent. Even of those, put it that one-third were my doing, truly two-thirds were richly her [Fortune's] doing" (III, 12, 812). Montaigne almost surely had Machiavelli in mind in asserting this arithmetic estimate of the relative powers of fortune and prudence over human affairs. While Machiavelli had argued that fortune was arbiter of only one-half of our actions, Montaigne declared that she controlled "richly" two-thirds of them. Human beings were by his estimation generally incapable of directing events toward their desired ends. For the most part, our lives were in fortune's hands.

More than in any of his particular essays, Montaigne best conveyed his sense of the extreme contingency and mutability of human existence through the organization of the *Essays*. Here his break with Machiavelli is especially clear. In the *Prince* and *Discourses,* Machiavelli still assumed that human and temporal affairs followed some regular patterns based upon the regular movements of the planets and the constancy of human nature and individual dispositions.[40] Accordingly, he organized these works around distinctive chapters designed to identify the general rules of conduct for manipulating affairs ("Whether It Is Better to be Loved or Feared," "How Much Artillery Should be Esteemed by Armies in Present Times"). In the *Essays,* by contrast, Montaigne moved from topic to topic, idea to idea, fluidly and lithely, making passing observations about an array of topics without apparent order or system. He even inserted thousands of additions into this work over the course of his life without correcting or revising his earlier views. Yet Montaigne was not a careless writer; nor was his work without a plan: his plan was to represent the perpetual motion and random change of human existence. His *Essays* were designed to record the flux and flow of his ever-changing existence within the contingent temporal world. If his reflections were sometimes disjointed or contradictory, it was because human life itself contained discrete and inconsistent moments.[41] In one of his most explicit discussions of the plan of his work, he wrote:

> I cannot keep my subject still. It goes along befuddled and staggering, with a natural drunkenness. I take it in this condition, just as it is at the moment I give my attention to it. I do not portray being: I portray passing. Not the passing from one age to another, or, as the people say, from seven years to seven years, but from day to day, from minute to minute. *My history needs to be adapted to the moment.* I may presently change, not only by chance, but also by

intention. This is a record of various and changeable occurrences, and of irresolute and, when it so befalls, contradictory ideas: whether I am different myself, or whether I take hold of my subjects in different circumstances and different aspects. So, all in all, I may indeed contradict myself now and then; but truth, as Demades said, I do not contradict. *If my mind could gain a firm footing, I would not make essays, I would make decisions;* but it is always in apprenticeship and on trial. (III, 2, 610–11; emphasis added)

Montaigne wrote *Essays* rather than *Discourses* for the simple reason that he could never very thoroughly "run through" *(discursus)* his subject matter. Because human existence was so deeply pervaded by the vicissitudes of fortune, he could only try *(essayer)* to record his ever-changing thoughts and feelings as they occurred to him "moment" to "moment."[42] Far from looking for continuity and patterns in history, Montaigne portrayed the flow of events as a rapidly changing series of discrete moments. If the "Machiavellian moment" represented the moment when human beings came to imagine their existence within a stream of contingent temporal events, the "Montaignian moment" thus signified the radicalization of this conceptual breakthrough. It was the moment when human beings came to imagine their existence within a stream of temporal affairs far more contingent and unstable than even Machiavelli had imagined them.

THE MONTAIGNIAN MOMENT AND MACHIAVELLIAN POLITICS

Montaigne made two important references to Machiavelli in the *Essays*.[43] Scholars have interpreted these passages in quite different ways. Some have seen them as morally based criticisms of Machiavelli's teachings. R. A. Sayce, for example, has claimed that these passages reveal Montaigne's "hatred of lying and cruelty . . . which may stand as a moral absolute for [him], or as near as he gets to it."[44] Alternatively, David Schaefer has argued that Montaigne's references to Machiavelli were not really critical at all, but reveal his general sympathy with the Florentine.[45] A better interpretation is to acknowledge that Montaigne was critical of Machiavelli's thought but not fundamentally for moral reasons. Rather, his criticisms stemmed from his new account of fortune. He claimed Machiavelli's political ideas were insufficient, or even counterproductive, for establishing order within time, because Machiavelli had failed to grasp the deeply contingent nature of temporal affairs.[46] His criticisms were intended to demonstrate the need to move beyond humanist ideas to develop a new approach for establishing order within time.

Significantly, both of Montaigne's criticisms of Machiavelli appear in his essay entitled "Of Presumption." The central theme of this essay was the "over-good opinion" human beings tend to have of their abilities and accomplishments (II, 17, 478). Montaigne contrasted these opinions with his own self-estimate. Highlighting his own deficiencies and failures, he proclaimed his own humility before fortune: "I foster as best I can this idea: to abandon myself completely to Fortune, expect the worst in everything, and resolve to bear that worst meekly and patiently" (488).

It was with these thoughts in mind that Montaigne commented on Machiavelli's political ideas. In his most explicit reference, he first observed that in political affairs generally there was always "a fine field open for vacillation and dispute" (497). What had succeeded in one set of circumstances often failed in another. He continued: "Machiavelli's arguments, for example, were solid enough for the subject, yet it was very easy to combat them; and those who did so left it no less easy to combat theirs. In such an argument there would always be matter for answers, rejoinders, replications, triplications, quadruplications, and that infinite web of disputes that our pettifoggers have spun out as far as they could in favor of lawsuits." Schaefer has suggested that Montaigne meant here only to criticize some of Machiavelli's substantive political rules.[47] Since Machiavelli himself had acknowledged that some of his maxims might require future revision, Schaefer has concluded that this statement hardly amounts to a criticism at all. Montaigne may actually have intended to praise Machiavelli covertly by saying his ideas were "solid enough for the subject." The problem with Schaefer's interpretation, however, is that it fails to take into account the general context of this passage. In the immediately ensuing sentences, Montaigne made plain that he intended not simply to amend some of Machiavelli's substantive precepts, but to challenge the very basis of these precepts: his historical methodology. Machiavelli had argued that "it is an easy thing for whoever examines past things diligently to foresee future things in every republic and to take the remedies for them that were used by the ancients, or, if they do not find any that were used, to think up new ones through the similarity of accidents."[48] Montaigne, by contrast, asserted that political precepts "have little other foundation than experience, and the diversity of human events offers us infinite examples in all sorts of forms." Drawing upon his account of fortune, he claimed that human experience was simply too diverse and variable to allow for the articulation of any meaningful historical maxims and laws. Every moment and each event were unique in themselves. This is why Machiavelli's arguments were "easy to combat." By attempting to fit the infinite range of human experiences into finite categories and patterns, Machiavelli had left his ideas forever open to "answers, rejoinders, replications, triplications, quadruplications," and an "infinite web of disputes" as later writers tried to amend his general principles to account for the full spectrum of particular accidents.[49] Machiavelli had founded his political philosophy upon a faulty and reductive understanding of fortune.

Montaigne took up this same theme in his final essay, "Of Experience." Writing here about the futility of attempting to create laws for every sort of contingency, he repeated his criticism of Machiavelli (whom he had earlier compared to lawyers and pettifoggers):

What have our legislators gained by selecting a hundred thousand particular cases and actions, and applying a hundred thousand laws to them? This number bears no proportion to the infinite diversity of human actions. Multiplication of our imaginary cases will never equal the variety of the real examples. Add to them a hundred times as many more: and still no future event will be found to correspond so exactly to any one of all the many, many thousands of selected and recorded events that there will not remain some circumstance, some difference, that will require separate consideration in forming a judgment. There is no relation between our actions, which are in perpetual mutation, and fixed and immutable laws. (III, 13, 815–16)

Although Montaigne's discussion here focused on political laws rather than historical precepts, his point was the same. From Montaigne's perspective, human and temporal affairs were simply too mutable and diverse to be accurately represented by any set of fixed laws. Even if we might sometimes perceive certain common features among different events, each event always remained distinctive in important ways. There was no way to relate what one individual did in one set of circumstances to what another did in another set of circumstances except by distorting and simplifying the facts.

As no event and no shape is entirely like another, so none is entirely different from another. An ingenious mixture on the part of nature. If our faces were not similar, we could not distinguish man from beast; if they were not dissimilar, we could not distinguish man from man. All things hold together by some similarity; every example is lame, and the comparison that is drawn from experience is always faulty and imperfect; however, we fasten together our comparisons by some corner. Thus the laws serve, and thus adapt themselves to each of our affairs, by some round-about, forced, and biased interpretation. (819)

For Schaefer, this statement reveals that Montaigne did in fact believe human beings could deduce general scientific maxims from particular empirical events.[50] But the thrust of Montaigne's concluding remark points in just the opposite direction: it was only "by some round-about, forced, and biased interpretation" that empirical events could ever be made to fit into any general categories or laws.[51] And just a few pages earlier, he compared the attempt to formulate general laws for human experience to the children's game of trying to divide quicksilver: "The more they press it and knead it and try to constrain it to their will, the more they provoke the independence of this spirited metal; it escapes their skill and keeps dividing and scattering in little particles beyond all reckoning" (816). Here, then, Montaigne directly repeated his criticism of "Machiavelli's arguments." The more human beings tried to explain and categorize their experiences in terms of fixed rules and laws, the more they opened themselves to "answers, rejoinders," and the "scattering" of their material into "little particles." Rather than helping to bring order to temporal affairs,

Machiavelli's misguided advice usually contributed to the disorder and confusion of the times.

Returning now to "Of Presumption," Montaigne closed his discussion of Machiavelli's historical methodology by ridiculing his claim that past events could be used to predict future outcomes.

> A learned person of our time says that where they say warm in our almanacs, if someone wants to say cold, and wet where they say dry, and always put down the opposite of what they forecast, and if he had to lay a wager on one or the other coming true, he would not care which side he took; except in cases that admit of no uncertainty, such as promising extreme heat at Christmas and the rigors of winter on Mid-summer's Day. I have the same opinion about these [Machiavelli's] political arguments: whatever part they give you to play, you have as good a chance as your opponent, provided you do not bump up against principles that are too plain and obvious. (II, 17, 497)

Although Montaigne did admit that there existed some general rules of politics, he indicated that these were "too plain and obvious" to merit serious attention. In his opinion, the more substantive maxims of Machiavellian politics were no more reliable than almanacs in predicting the weather. If they sometimes correctly predicted the outcome of events, they just as frequently proved wrong. They provided simple guesses about future affairs based upon past events that took place in entirely different and unique circumstances.

Montaigne's second criticism of Machiavelli pertained to his definition of virtue. After first expressing his own personal aversion to "this new-fangled virtue of hypocrisy and dissimulation," Montaigne next turned to consider its utility for political affairs. While Montaigne did not specifically mention Machiavelli in the following passage, the wording and content strongly point toward Machiavelli's ideas.

> Those who, in our time, in establishing the duties of a prince, have considered only the good of his affairs, and have preferred that to caring for his fidelity and conscience, would have something to say to a prince whose affairs Fortune had so arranged that he could establish them once and for all by a single breach and betrayal of his word. But that is not the way it goes. You often fall into the same sort of bargain again; you make more than one peace, more than one treaty, in your life. The gain that lures them to the first breach of faith . . . brings after it endless losses, casting this prince out of all relations and means of negotiation in consequence of this breach of faith. (II, 17, 492)[52]

Scholars have often maintained that Montaigne's argument here was motivated by moral concerns. He meant to show the practical pitfalls of treachery and deceit in order to guide princes back to moral action.[53] Yet, Montaigne was generally not so moralistic about politics. While declaring himself unable to perform evil deeds, he stressed: "I do not want to deprive deceit of its proper place; that would be misunderstanding the world" (III, 1, 604). Even in the above passage, moral concerns play little part. If a prince really could secure his fortune all at one stroke, as Machiavelli had believed, then Montaigne indicated he would be justified in using whatever means were necessary to achieve his ends. *"But that is not the way it goes."* Fortune does not work that way. Machiavelli had assumed that princes could manipulate fortune to such an extent that one "well used" evil could establish their safety and security for a long time to come.[54] Montaigne countered that fortune was neither so tame nor so pliable. It changed from moment to moment, event to event, problem to problem. It never offered princes the sort of life-altering moments envisioned by Machiavelli. No matter what actions a prince might take in the present times—no matter how shocking or ingenious—he would soon encounter fortune again in the form of new problems and difficulties. Then his past wickedness would rise up to haunt him. If he had deceived others in earlier negotiations, he would find himself at a disadvantage in later negotiations. Conversely, the prince who dealt honestly with others could establish a bond of trust with them and thereby establish some stability over his affairs. In an essay entitled "Of Giving the Lie," Montaigne observed: "Since mutual understanding is brought about solely by way of words, he who breaks his word betrays human society. It is the only instrument by means of which our will and thoughts communicate, it is the interpreter of our soul. If it fails us, we have no more hold on each other, no more knowledge of each other. If it deceives us, it breaks up all our relations and dissolves all the bonds of our society" (II, 18, 505). At least as a long-term policy, Montaigne concluded that honesty was usually the best policy. Since princes could not conquer fortune all at one stroke, but had to negotiate and bargain with others again and again, they could usually secure more advantages by remaining in good standing with their peers than by tricking them for short-term gains. Montaigne's criticism of Machiavelli was actually based upon his different understanding of fortune.

Montaigne summarized his policy on deceit and treachery in the following way:

> We must not always say everything, for that would be folly; but what we say must be what we think; otherwise it is wickedness. I do not know what people expect to gain by incessant feigning and dissimulating, unless it is not to be believed even when they speak truth. That may deceive people once or twice; but to make a profession of covering up, and to boast, as some of our princes have done, that they would throw their shirt in the fire if it were privy to their real intentions (which is a saying of the ancient Metellus of Macedon), and that a man who does not know how to dissemble does not know how to rule—this is warning those who have to deal with them that all they say is nothing but deceit and lies. (II, 17, 491)[55]

Montaigne did not believe that princes should naively tell the truth in all matters. This would be foolishness. But then again, he pointed out that dissimulation and treachery had only a very limited effectiveness. Although princes might achieve some short-term gains by wicked measures, they usually expended a great deal of political capital in the process. They announced their own untrustworthiness and undermined their ability to form bonds in future situations. Weighing the costs and benefits of these policies, Montaigne concluded that the only situation in which treachery and deceit were generally profitable was as a last resort to preserve the public peace (I, 23, 89; III, 1, 607). In this case, a prince had nothing to lose by lying or performing some great evil. But in all other situations, Montaigne claimed that "Machiavellian politics" usually just exposed a prince all the more to fortune and chance. They deluded him into believing he could conquer fortune all at one stroke when in fact he would have to engage with fortune time and time again during his entire life.

THE MONTAIGNIAN MOMENT AND THE PHILOSOPHICAL ORIGINS OF THE STATE

The "Montaignian moment" marked the origin not only of a new understanding of temporal processes, but also of a new approach to establishing order within time. The key to Montaigne's theory of order was his philosophy of nature. He alluded to this philosophy in his early essays but developed it most fully in the third book of his *Essays*.[56] "As I have said elsewhere," Montaigne wrote in the second to the last of his essays, "I have very simply and crudely adopted for my own sake this ancient precept: that we cannot go wrong by following Nature, that the sovereign precept is to conform to her" (III, 12, 811). Nature represented for Montaigne a true standard of order underlying the contingency of human affairs. He defined the term "nature" in three different senses throughout the *Essays*,[57] and based upon these definitions identified a number of interrelated strategies for establishing order within time.

In the first place, Montaigne associated nature with a perfect order comprising all the particular elements and motions within the universe. In this all-encompassing sense, he argued that nature was beyond human comprehension. Since we were immersed within nature, we could never gain a clear picture of the whole, but we could recognize our own limited place within that whole. Montaigne claimed this recognition represented the first step toward developing a natural morality. "Whoever considers as in a painting the greater picture of our mother Nature in her full majesty; whoever reads such universal and constant variety in her face; whoever finds himself there, and not merely himself, but a whole kingdom, as a dot made with a very fine brush; that man alone estimates things according to their true proportions" (I, 26, 116). Two important lessons followed from this understanding of nature. First, Montaigne claimed that we should moderate our beliefs since they were at best only one perspective on the whole, never authoritative or final. Secondly, he suggested we should moderate our actions and projects to reflect our limited power over temporal affairs.

Montaigne most clearly laid out this first lesson in his "Apology for Raymond Sebond." The ostensible purpose of this essay was to defend the natural theology of the fifteenth-century Spanish theologian Raymond Sebond. But Montaigne used the occasion to attack the presumption of human reason in general. Reason did "nothing but go astray" in religious matters (II, 12, 386). Human beings necessarily reduced or belittled God when they attempted to define or understand him: "Now nothing of ours can be likened or compared in any way whatsoever to the divine nature without staining and marking it with just that much imperfection" (389). Montaigne made a similar point about traditional natural law teachings. If there were substantive universal moral principles inscribed in our natures, as medieval Christian theologians contended, then surely these principles would have received "universality of approval." Yet Montaigne demanded: "Let them show me just one law of that sort—I'd like to see it" (437). There was nothing so varied or changing as human laws and moral beliefs. Every society defined its morality and laws differently and even changed those definitions over time: "What am I to make of a virtue that I saw in credit yesterday, that will be discredited tomorrow, and that becomes a crime on the other side of the river? What of a truth that is bounded by these mountains and is falsehood to the world that lives beyond?" (437). The lesson was that human beings should recognize the limitations of their religious and moral beliefs. All of our beliefs were faulty. None was deserving of our wholehearted commitment. The safest course was to follow the common opinions and customary routines without mortgaging oneself to them. Montaigne concluded this "Apology": "For to make the handful bigger than the hand, the armful bigger than the arm, and to hope to straddle more than the reach of our legs, is impossible and unnatural. Nor can man raise himself above himself and humanity; for he can see only with his own eyes, and seize only with his own grasp" (II, 12, 457). A proper understanding of nature dictated moderation and humility in all of our religious and moral beliefs.

Montaigne argued that such an understanding also dictated a relaxed or moderate approach to policies and actions.[58] It was beyond human capacities to conquer the flux and flow of nature: the whole of nature was flux and flow. "There is no existence that is constant," he wrote, "either of our being or of that of objects. And we, and our judgment, and all mortal things go on flowing and rolling unceasingly" (II, 12, 455). To live in harmony with nature meant to accept our position within the flux and flow of events. The natural way was, so to speak, to go with the flow: "Happy the people . . . who let themselves roll relaxedly with the rolling of the heavens" (II, 17, 498). Surrendering oneself to nature did not lead to a loss of order, Montaigne claimed, but actually contributed to a more peaceful existence. By reorienting their actions in accordance with the "true proportions" of things, human beings could do what was possible without needlessly involving themselves in affairs beyond their control.

Montaigne most clearly laid out this lesson in his essay "Of Physiognomy" (III, 12, 812–13). In this essay, he recounted how his neighbor appeared one day at his door claiming that he and his men had just been ambushed by enemy troops. Soon after, four or five of this man's soldiers arrived with a similar story, and a bit later still more arrived. After twenty-five or thirty men had gathered in front of his house, Montaigne became suspicious that all of this activity might be part of a plot to gain entry to his house and seize it from him—a suspicion that he later confirmed. But since there was nothing he could do at this point to stop these men—since the outcome of this affair was effectively beyond his control—he abandoned himself "to the most natural and simple course" and "gave orders for them to come in." He explained the logic of his action in the following passage, part of which was discussed above when contrasting Montaigne's and Machiavelli's conceptions of fortune and virtue:

> I am the sort of man who readily commits himself to Fortune and abandons himself bodily into her arms. For which I have up to now had more occasion to applaud myself than to complain; and I have found her both wiser and more friendly to my affairs than I am. There have been some actions in my life the conduct of which might justly be called difficult, or, if you wish, prudent. Even of those, put it that one-third was my doing, truly two-thirds were richly her doing. We err, it seems to me, in that we do not trust ourselves enough to heaven, and we expect more from our own conduct than belongs to us. That is why our plans so often go astray. Heaven is jealous of the extent we attribute to the claims of human wisdom, to the prejudice of its own; and the more we amplify them, the more it cuts them down. (812)

In this statement, Montaigne not only redefined Machiavelli's estimate of the powers of fortune and virtue, but also outlined a new approach to fortune. In a wildly contingent temporal world, he claimed it was not the virile and self-assertive man who usually succeeded in his affairs, but the more restrained and relaxed individual. The former usually just provoked fortune by attempting to manipulate affairs that were beyond his powers,[59] whereas the latter was usually able to avoid the whims of fortune and accomplish his goals by moderating his actions in accordance with his powers. The restrained individual did not provoke the wrath of heaven because he did not presume too much for his abilities.

After setting forth this general principle, Montaigne concluded his story by demonstrating how his "natural and simple" behavior had helped to bring about the happy resolution of this dangerous situation. By playing along with the plot, Montaigne so disarmed his neighbor that he lost his nerve to carry out his action. His neighbor ordered his men to remount their horses and rode away without doing anything. Montaigne thus actually regained some power over this affair by attempting to do so little. Had he tried to do more, he almost certainly would have provoked his neighbor into carrying out his plan. In another passage, Montaigne summed up his perspective: "I owe much to Fortune in that up to this point she has done nothing hostile to me, at least nothing beyond my endurance. Might it not be her way to leave in peace those who do not trouble her?" (III, 9, 763). From Montaigne's perspective, fortune afflicted primarily those individuals who overstepped the natural limits of their powers. By moderating one's actions and accepting one's place within "nature," one could avoid much uncertainty and enjoy a more orderly and safe existence.

Montaigne also associated "nature" with a minimal set of instincts common to human beings and animals. While he generally designated these instincts by the term "natural law," he distinguished his own definition from the medieval Christian theory. His notion of natural law was not "sublime," "high," and "sophisticated" (III, 13, 822). It did not consist of universal moral precepts universally approved by right reason (II, 12, 437). Instead, he maintained that the natural law was comprised of a number of prerational inclinations implanted in animals and human beings, including "an instinct for taking care of themselves and for their preservation," an instinct for looking after their young, and a tendency to seek "peace, repose, security, innocence, and health" (II, 8, 279; II, 12, 357; III, 12, 807). In his clearest statement on the subject, Montaigne distinguished his own theory of natural law from the medieval theory in the following way:

> The philosophers with much reason refer us to the rules of Nature: but these have no concern with such sublime knowledge. The philosophers falsify them and show us the face of Nature painted in too high a color, and too sophisticated, whence spring so many varied portraits of so uniform a subject. As she has furnished us with feet to walk with, so she has given us wisdom to guide us in life: a wisdom not so ingenious, robust, and pompous as that of their invention, but correspondingly easy and salutary. (III, 13, 821–22)

Montaigne derided in his "Apology for Raymond Sebond" not the natural law per se but only the philosophers' pompous portrait of it. Underlying these sophisticated and varied portraits of natural law was a simple and uniform set of natural principles fundamental to easy and salutary living.

In defining natural law as a set of minimal natural instincts, Montaigne contributed to the transition from the teleological natural law theory to the modern doctrine of natural rights.[60] As Brian Tierney has pointed out, this modern doctrine was not unknown to medieval thinkers,[61] but Montaigne's sharp distinction between the minimal principles of natural right and the more sophisticated moral deductions of natural law was original. While medieval thinkers regarded the natural instincts of animals and human beings as only one (and usually the least important) element of the natural law, Montaigne claimed the whole of natural law was composed of these natural instincts. Furthermore, he identified these minimal principles of natural right as the foundation of a more regulated and orderly existence. He thus presented a notion of "nature" that was to become highly influential in European political thought over the next century. He pointed the way to the natural rights theories of thinkers such as Hobbes and Rousseau. He argued, for example, that because the French peasantry lived in closer proximity to nature than members of polite society, they tended "to show greater regularity in their relations," more "constancy and endurance," and better "models of constancy, innocence, and tranquility" than the higher ranks of society ((I, 23, 77; II, 12, 438; II, 17, 501; III, 12, 795, 803). He argued similarly about the "cannibals" of the New World. The people of the New World were "wild, just as we call wild the fruits that Nature has produced by herself and in her normal course. . . . The laws of nature still rule them, very little corrupted by ours" (I, 31, 152–53). Montaigne later contrasted the tranquility of the cannibals' society with the disorder and inconstancy of European civilization: "Those who return from that new world which was discovered in our fathers' time by the Spaniards can testify to us how much more lawfully and regulatedly these nations live, without magistrates and without law, than ours, where there are more officers and laws than there are other men and actions" (II, 12, 367). Montaigne even asserted that the natural behaviors of animals provided a model for orderly government: "We hardly need any more offices, rules, and laws of living, in our community than do the cranes and ants in theirs. And nevertheless we see that they conduct themselves in a very orderly manner without erudition. If man were wise, he would set the true price of each thing according as it was most useful and appropriate for his life" (II, 12, 359). While Montaigne did not believe that "civilized" human beings could or should return to their more primitive existence, he did suggest that they would enjoy more order and tranquility in their lives if they more closely modeled their behavior upon the minimal principles of nature (III, 12, 803). Just as fortune usually did not bother those individuals who moderated their beliefs and actions, so also it did not harass those who organized their lives around the simple and minimal principles of natural right. Those principles defined the proper limits of human actions within nature.

The third way in which Montaigne defined nature was in terms of the ruling patterns of each individual soul. As indicated above, Montaigne did not conceive of these individual ruling patterns as robust personality traits. They did not invariably determine our actions or necessarily lend any consistency to our lives. Instead, they existed below the surface of our daily lives as a sort of "settled state" to which we returned during our unguarded moments. They represented the substance of our souls:

> As vicious souls are often incited to do good by some extraneous impulse, so are virtuous souls to do evil. Thus we must judge them by their settled state, when they are at home, if ever they are; or at least when they are closest to repose and their natural position. . . . Just consider the evidence of this in our

experience. There is no one who, if he listens to himself, does not discover in himself a pattern all his own, a ruling pattern, which struggles against education and against the tempest of the passions that oppose it. (III, 2, 615; see also I, 26, 109; II, 17, 499)

Despite the extremely minimal character of our internal ruling patterns, Montaigne claimed they nonetheless did provide a firm basis for ordering our lives. They were a natural substance that was impervious to fortune and flux.[62] They represented a source of constancy beneath the change and flux of our lives. By tapping into our ruling patterns, we could control fortune in our internal lives regardless of our external fate.

> Things in themselves may have their own weights and measures and qualities: but once inside, within us, [the soul] allots them their qualities as she sees fit. Death is frightful to Cicero, desirable to Cato, a matter of indifference to Socrates. Health, conscience, authority, knowledge, riches, beauty, and their opposites—all are stripped on entry and receive from the soul new clothing, and the coloring that she chooses—brown, green, bright, dark, bitter, sweet, deep, superficial,—and which each individual soul chooses; for they have not agreed together on their styles, rules, and forms; each one is queen in her realm. Wherefore let us no longer make the external qualities of things our excuse; it is up to us to reckon them as we will. Our good and our ill depend on ourselves alone. Let us offer our offerings and vows to ourselves, not to Fortune; she has no power over our character; on the contrary, it drags her in its train and molds her in its own form. (I, 50, 220)

In his earliest essays, Montaigne envisioned this process of imposing a form upon fortune in a classical stoical manner, suggesting that an individual ought to "prescribe and establish definite laws and a definite organization in his head" and "direct his life as a whole toward a definite goal" (II, 1, 240–43). But even in these early essays, he expressed doubts about the ability of most human beings to follow this advice (I, 37, 169; II, 1, 240, 242–43). In his later essays, he rejected this advice altogether: "It is existing, but not being, to keep ourselves bound and obliged by necessity to a single course. The fairest souls are those that have the most variety and adaptability" (III, 3, 621). By the 1580s, Montaigne adopted a more relaxed internal approach to fortune.[63] Rather than calling upon individuals to impose a predefined plan upon fortune, he suggested that they should allow their characters to emerge gradually through their interactions with fortune. By carefully observing their reactions to fortune, they would be able to identify the true substance of their souls behind their various changes. In this way, they would be able to discover the already existing order within their lives. Montaigne put forth his *Essays* as an example of this process of self-discovery and character formation (II, 18, 504).[64] By studying his own ever-changing self, his character had "to some extent grown firm and taken shape." He had discovered an order to his life simply by recording all his "little thoughts" and actions from day to day, moment to moment.

Scholars have traditionally seen the *Essays* as an apolitical or even antipolitical work.[65] Montaigne even announced at several points that his philosophy was best practiced outside the hustle and bustle of society and away from the entanglements of political life (III, 1, 599–600; III, 9, 756–60). Nonetheless, his philosophy did have important political implications. At the very least, he raised doubts about the effectiveness of existing political paradigms. Montaigne portrayed the ideas of earlier "activist" humanists, for example, as an important source of disorder. By overstating the powers of human virtue and underestimating the powers of fortune, they encouraged individuals to undertake activities beyond their abilities. Their advice was not only flawed but actually provoked fortune and contributed to disorder. This explains the rhetorical purpose behind Montaigne's incessant attacks on humanist commonplace thought. Montaigne regarded classical humanist teachings as not only misguided but dangerous. In the *Essays*, he meant to reorient human beings' understanding about their place in nature so that they might begin to behave in more regular and orderly ways. If only indirectly, his book was in this way an important political manifesto.

But Montaigne's political thought also had a more constructive side. Drawing upon his philosophy of nature, he suggested two revisions to contemporary political practices that contributed in important ways to the development of modern state theory. One was a new theory of law and legal obligation. The first step of this project consisted of his critique of contemporary understandings of custom (I, 23, 77–90; III, 9, 730–31; III, 13, 815–57). In sixteenth-century France, the customary laws were generally regarded as the "ancient and immemorial" foundations of the monarchy.[66] Montaigne, however, scorned this traditional understanding of custom. "Once, having to justify one of our observances, which was received with steadfast authority far and wide around us, and preferring to establish it, not as is usually done, merely by force of laws and examples, but by tracking it to its origins, I there found its foundation so weak that I nearly became disgusted with it, I who was supposed to confirm it in others" (I, 23, 84). Montaigne denounced also the general belief that customs represented more particular expressions of the divine and natural laws. "The common notions that we find in credit around us and infused into our soul by our fathers' seed, these seem to be the universal and natural ones. Whence it comes to pass that what is off the hinges of custom, people believe to be off the hinges of reason: God knows how unreasonably, most of the time" (I, 23, 83). Customs were neither ancient nor true. But neither were they without their merits. Having undercut the traditional foundations of custom, Montaigne proposed a new ground of legitimacy for them. Just because customary laws and practices were not immemorial or universal did not mean they were entirely without a natural foundation. Customs represented the primitive natural desire of all human beings for peace and preservation as it had developed through time. He explained his perspective most clearly in his essay "Of Husbanding Your Will," which contains the core of his positive political philosophy:

> If what Nature flatly and originally demands of us for the preservation of our being is too little—as indeed, there is no better way of expressing how little that is and how cheaply our life can be maintained than by this consideration, that it is so little as to escape the grasp and shock of fortune by its very littleness—then let us grant ourselves something further: let us also call the habits and condition of each of us nature; let us rate and treat ourselves according to this measure, let us stretch our appurtenances and our accounts that far. For in going thus far we certainly seem to me to have some justification. Habit *(l'accoustumance)* is a second nature, and no less powerful. What my habit *(coustume)* lacks, I hold I lack. And I would almost as soon be deprived of life as have it reduced and cut down very far from the state in which I have lived for so long. (III, 10, 772)

Customs were natural not in the sense that they mirrored the static and universal moral principles of nature, but rather in that they grew out of and gave substance to our original natural instincts, which were, in any case, "too little" to sustain us. They effectively completed our "nature" by giving concrete form to our instinctual desires in and through time: "By long usage this form of mine has turned into substance, and fortune into nature" (773).

Relating these observations to his theory of obligation, Montaigne argued that human beings generally ought to follow their existing customs not because they were "just" in any universal sense, but because they served our instinctual desires and sheltered us from fortune (I, 23, 86; III, 1, 604; III, 13, 821). As mere extensions of our natural instincts, they were "so little as to escape the grasp and shock of fortune." Just as Montaigne argued that individuals could avoid fortune by living according to their simple natural instincts, so also he claimed they could generally escape fortune by obeying their customs. For customs were merely an expression of human beings' natural instincts forged over time. As long as human beings obeyed their customs, they remained within the limits of their natural powers and avoided fortune's blows. But as soon as they challenged the existing laws and practices, they stepped beyond their natural limits and provoked fortune to enter into their affairs. "So I say that every one of us feeble creatures is excusable for considering as his own what is comprised under this measure [of custom]. But it is also true that beyond these limits there is nothing left but confusion. This is the broadest extent that we can grant our claims. The more we amplify our need and our possession, the more we involve ourselves in the blows of fortune and adversity" (773). Like the minimal principles of natural right, customs defined the proper scope of human actions within nature.

Most scholars have regarded Montaigne's theory of custom as deeply conservative. They have claimed he opposed political innovation and change because it threatened to undermine public order.[67] This interpretation is generally correct. However, Montaigne did identify one set of circumstances in which the reform of the customary laws was justifiable. It was possible, he noted, that the customary laws themselves could become overwrought and overextended. In this case, they could become a provocation to fortune and disorder. If this were to happen, Montaigne suggested that the customary laws might be legitimately reformed in order to bring them back into line with the minimal principles of nature. In France, for example, he claimed the lawyers and judges had so multiplied and complicated the customary laws that the legal system had become a source of disorder. "Our French laws, by their irregularity and lack of form, rather lend a hand to the disorder and corruption that is seen in their administration and execution. Their commands are so confused and inconsistent that they are some excuse for both disobedience and faulty interpretation, administration, and observance" (III, 13, 821). His solution was to trim back the laws in order to realign them with nature. "The most desirable laws are those that are rarest, simplest, and the most general; and I even think that it would be better to have none at all than to have them in such numbers as we have. Nature always gives us happier laws than those we give ourselves. Witness the picture of the Golden Age of the poets, and the state in which we see nations live which have no other laws" (816). In this passage, Montaigne may be said to have articulated the first modern appeal to the "state of nature" as a positive base for reforming the legal structure of the state. In his earlier essay "Of Cannibals," he had already compared the civilizations of the New World to the ideal civilizations of the "Golden Age" (I, 31, 153). Later, while discussing the advantages of a simple and natural existence, he observed that the French could learn much from the legal arrangements of the cannibals (II, 12, 367). Here, then, in his final essay, Montaigne pointed to the natural life of the cannibals as an example to follow in the reformation of French laws. By pruning back the laws and bringing them into closer conformity with the minimal principles of nature, he suggested that the French people could enjoy more peace and security than they presently did under the customary legal system.

The other important element of Montaigne's positive political theory was his ideal of princely rule. He presented this ideal, too, in his essay "Of Husbanding Your Will." He began this essay by reaffirming his commitment to a natural and simple introspective life. Nevertheless, when the electors of Bordeaux asked him to be mayor of their city, he accepted this charge. He explained that although one ought not actively to seek out public office, neither should one neglect one's duties. But he made clear from the outset that he had no intention of ruling in the manner of traditional public servants who placed the common good above their own, the love of their neighbors above themselves (III, 10, 769). He had seen his father adopt this selfless ethic to no good end. Instead, he announced that he would continue to live primarily for himself according to the dictates of nature: "The main responsibility of each of us is his own conduct; and that is what we are here for. Just as anyone who should forget to live a good and saintly life, and think he was quit of his duty by guiding and training others to do so, would be a fool; even so he who abandons healthy and gay living of his own to serve others thereby, takes, to my taste, a bad and unnatural course" (769–70).

While this pronouncement might not seem a very promising platform for political rule, Montaigne argued that his mode of governing was actually far superior to the traditional ideal. Because he did not allow himself to become personally wrapped up in political projects, he remained more flexible in dealing with fortune. Like his friend Henry IV, he maintained "a great nonchalance and freedom in his actions and countenance throughout very great and thorny affairs" (771). By contrast, the prince who zealously devoted himself to public affairs often became swept up in events and unnecessarily endangered himself and his people.

> He who employs in [public office] only his judgment and skill proceeds more gaily. He feints, he bends, he postpones entirely at his ease according to the need of the occasions; he misses the target without torment or affliction, and remains intact and ready for a new undertaking; he always walks bridle in hand. In the man who is intoxicated with a violent and tyrannical intensity of purpose we see of necessity much imprudence and injustice; the impetuosity of his desire carries him away. These are reckless movements, and, unless fortune lends them a great hand, of little fruit. (770)

Just as Montaigne maintained that individuals could accomplish more in their private affairs through moderate and flexible behavior, so he claimed a prince could do more to promote order and stability by remaining detached and easygoing. He suggested that not only the laws but also the actions of political rulers should be reoriented around "nature."

Montaigne concluded his defense of this governmental ethic by summarizing the criticisms of his service. "Some say about this municipal service of mine," he began, "that I went about it like a man who exerts himself too weakly and with a languishing zeal; and they are not at all far from having a case. I try to keep my soul and my thoughts in repose" (781). Montaigne conducted himself in public office much as he did in private affairs. He ruled himself and moderated his external endeavors. Yet, he quickly added, "one ought not to derive any proof of impotence" from this "natural langour." His conduct was not based upon an ideal of lassitude but represented a new positive ideal of action. He behaved with self-restraint and detachment because he believed this form of conduct was most natural and best suited for establishing order. He continued: "People also say that my administration passed without a mark or a trace. That's a good one! They accuse me of inactivity in a time when almost everyone was convicted of doing too much." The very reason France was immersed in civil wars was because too many people were engaged in civic activities beyond their natural concerns and abilities. What was needed in this situation was not a vigorous prince drawn on the Machiavellian model, but a self-restrained and detached ruler. In an erratic and unstable temporal world, self-restraint and self-regulation were the proper ideals of governmental action, not glory and honor. A public servant detached from his work and moderate in his policies was more likely to promote order and peace than a zealous or heroic prince. In short, Montaigne claimed the proper ethic of governmental rule was found not in the activist *virtù* of classical humanism or even in the moral principles of medieval natural law theory. The appropriate ethic of rule was based upon moderation, detachment, and restraint. If only in a preliminary way, his thought thus pointed toward a more rationalistic governmental ethic.

Montaigne was finally sick and tired of the political disorder and uncertainty that surrounded him:

> The conflicting invasions and incursions and the alternations and vicissitudes of fortune around me have up to now more exasperated than mollified the temper of the country, and burden me again and again with insuperable dangers and difficulties. I escape; but I dislike the fact that it is more by good luck, and even by my prudence, than because of justice; and I dislike being outside the protection of the laws and under another safeguard than theirs. (III, 9, 738)

The *Essays* were a first step toward restoring order and justice to this contingent and disorderly world. Montaigne suggested that individuals would enjoy more stability and order in their lives if they reoriented their actions around nature. On a personal level, this meant they should focus their attention inwardly on their characters, organize their lives around the minimal principles of natural law, and moderate their beliefs and external activities. Politically, it meant a general obedience to the laws, a willingness to reform the legal structure around the original principles of nature, and a more detached ideal of princely rule.

JUSTUS LIPSIUS AND PIERRE CHARRON

Montaigne's philosophy marked an important turning point in the development of political thought. Before Montaigne, the major political traditions were medieval legal theories and Italian humanism. Montaigne helped to open a new dimension to political inquiry. The Montaignian moment defined a new understanding of time and politics that challenged the efficacy of existing political paradigms and pointed toward a natural and rationalistic political philosophy as the key to stability and order. Of course, Montaigne never presented his ideas in anything like a programmatic fashion. Nor did he even begin to broach the thorny question of who should be responsible for reforming the laws or what (if anything) might be done to encourage individuals to show more moderation in their actions. In short, he did not articulate a state theory. Nonetheless, he did lay out a pattern of thought that later writers found extremely useful in defining and justifying the central principles of the state. Later state theorists drew upon Montaigne's account of temporal contingency to legitimize the expansion of the sovereign's law-making powers and to justify the development of prerogative powers for the king. Natural rights theorists drew upon Montaigne's minimal theory of natural law to define a new normative foundation for the state. Hobbes's state theory, for example, can be situated directly in a line of development from the "Montaignian moment." Hobbes not only emphasized the radical contingency of human affairs but also identified the minimal principles of natural law as the new foundation of stability and order within a contingent temporal world. Certainly Hobbes modified a number of Montaigne's ideas. He pared down Montaigne's rather broad definition of nature to the most basic desire of all human beings for self-preservation. He further argued that human beings should appoint an all-powerful sovereign ruler to coerce individuals into obeying this minimal natural law. Montaigne almost surely would have disapproved of these revisions. They represent a departure from the ambivalent, open, and genial character of his philosophy. Nonetheless, the broad outlines of Hobbes's philosophy as well as the ideas of other state theorists can be traced back to Montaigne's philosophy.

During the late sixteenth and early seventeenth centuries, two writers in particular developed the ideas associated with the Montaignian moment into a more substantial state theory: Justus Lipsius (1547–1606) and Pierre Charron (1541–1603).[68] Both of these men were close to Montaigne personally and intellectually. Montaigne and Lipsius corresponded through letters, traveled in the same intellectual circles, and greatly admired one another's works. Lipsius hailed Montaigne as "the French Thales" and observed in 1589 that "I have found no one in Europe whose way of thinking about things is closer to my own."[69] Montaigne reciprocated by writing that Lipsius was the "most learned man" alive (II, 12, 436). Montaigne and Charron, too, were personal acquaintances. Charron's biographer Gabriel Michel de la Rochemaillet reported that the two became intimate friends during the last years of Montaigne's life, although there is little independent evidence to confirm this claim.[70] What is beyond doubt is Montaigne's tremendous influence upon Charron. Charron copied large portions of Montaigne's *Essays* directly into his central moral and political work, *De la sagesse*. Yet while both Lipsius and Charron outlined philosophical ideas very similar to Montaigne's, they departed from him in two important respects. Both identified a universal essence to human nature and a special metaphysical purpose for the state. Based upon these important amendments to Montaigne's thought, they were able to legitimize a more substantial state theory. Lipsius and Charron's thought thus helps to explain how the Montaignian moment was transformed into a justification for modern state theory.

The similarity between Montaigne's and Lipsius's thought is evident in Lipsius's first major ethical work, *De Constantia* (1584).[71] Lipsius wrote this work as a dialogue between a younger fictionalized version of himself and his teacher Charles Langius. At the beginning of this dialogue, the fictional Lipsius explains that he has come to visit his teacher in Liège to escape from "the tempest of civil wars" afflicting his home country (C, I, 1, 72). Langius replies by questioning the wisdom of this action. "Thy country (I confess) is tossed and turmoiled grievously: What part of Europe is at this day free?" Between the Dutch revolt, the religious wars, and all the other smaller conflicts throughout Europe, the whole continent was immersed in disorder. Nor, according to Langius, were the present times unique. History was full of examples of wars, tyrannies, plagues, famines, and other disorders (C, II, 20–26, 181–200). "For these miseries do but wheel about continually, and circularly run about this circle of the world" (198). Indeed, Langius asserted that even the earth and elements themselves were in perpetual conflict:

> Behold also the earth which is taken to be immovable, and to stand steady of her own force: it faints and is striken with an inward secret blast that makes it to tremble. Somewhere it is corrupted by the water, other where by fire. For these same things do strive among themselves. Neither grudge thou to see war among men, there is likewise between the elements. (C, I, 16, 108)

Human beings could hardly expect tranquility in their own affairs, Langius argued, when the earth itself was known to tremble and quake.

Langius assured his pupil that there nonetheless did exist a solid foundation of order underlying the contingency and flux of the universe. All temporal affairs were actually guided by the perfect order of Providence (C, I, 13, 101–3). Langius noted that "chance and fortune" did not have any real existence at all. They were but were figments of human beings' incomplete understanding of the world. Earthquakes, plagues, wars, and tyranny all came from God. Everything that happened was necessary and even profitable to human beings in God's grand scheme of things.

Having described temporal affairs in much the same terms as Montaigne, Lipsius proceeded to outline a similar strategy for establishing order. He shared Montaigne's distrust of scientific precepts.[72] Whereas Machiavelli had attempted to raise politics to a "science" by identifying certain universal rules of prudence, Lipsius claimed this was impossible since human and temporal affairs were too contingent for rational classification.

> Now, if the things themselves are uncertain, Prudence itself likewise must of necessity be so, and so much the rather, because it is not only tied to the things themselves, but to their dependents, having regard unto the times, the places, and to men, and for their least change, she changes herself, which is the reason why she is not in all places alike, no nor the same in one and the selfsame thing. . . . And surely it is impossible for any man to reduce that which is uncertain, to certain and strict limits of precepts. (P, IV, 1, 60)[73]

Lipsius further rejected the *vir virtutis* of classical humanist thought (P, II, 15, 36–37). The sheer intractability of external events greatly limited the ability of human beings to control or direct affairs to their ends.

Lipsius instead argued that the best way to achieve order and stability was by following nature. God had placed in each of us a "spark" of "right reason." Through our reason we could attain "a true sense and judgement of things human and divine" (C, I, 4–5, 78–83). That is, we could gain a sense of the order of the whole. This, in turn, would allow us to endure the hardships and contingency of temporal affairs with perfect constancy. "Constancy," Lipsius wrote, "is a right and immovable strength of the mind, neither lifted up, nor pressed down with external and casual accidents" (C, I, 4, 79). Like Montaigne, Lipsius thus argued that although human beings could do very little to control external affairs, they could at least control their reaction to affairs. By fostering the "patience" necessary to suffer all accidents without resentment, they could rise above fortune and partake of the ruling order of the universe. "Thou shall be a king indeed, free indeed, only subject to God, enfranchised from the servile yoke of Fortune and affections. As some rivers are said to run through the sea and yet keep their stream fresh: So shall thou pass through the confused tumults of the world, and not be infected with any brinish saltiness of this Sea of sorrows" (I, 6, 83–84). The constant individual was unmoved by fortune and flux because he set his sights always on the perfect providential order of God and nature.

Despite the parallels between Lipsius's and Montaigne's thought, there were also important differences. Lipsius adhered more consistently to a classical stoical ethic than Montaigne. While Montaigne encouraged each individual to reflect upon his or her own unique nature, Lipsius suggested that individuals should strive to rise above their individual particularity and adhere to the divine spark of right reason residing within them.[74] They should all follow the one universal and homogeneous form of right conduct defined by right reason in order to achieve constancy. In contrast to Montaigne, Lipsius's approach to fortune thus involved the denial of what we might call the individual personality. He argued that individuals should attempt to separate themselves from the "filth" and "corruption" of the body and "contagion of the senses" in order to raise themselves above particularity and merge into the universal *nous* (C, I, 5, 81).

This different understanding of nature carried profound implications for Lipsius's political theory. Montaigne's philosophy precluded any sort of disciplinarian solution to the problem of fortune. He argued that the establishment of order necessarily entailed individual discovery and development. He believed governmental rulers should moderate their conduct and perhaps trim back the laws according to the minimal ideal of nature. But he did not identify any sort of universal basis for programmatic state action. Lipsius did. He argued the purpose of the state was to restrain the disorderly passions of individuals and impose a universal rational order upon them. In the dedication of his *Six Books of Politics,* he wrote that government existed so that the "universal multitude, unquiet, disunited, seditious" could be "brought under a certain common yoke of obedience" (P, v). He added a few pages later that government was "the only stay of human affairs": "On the other side all things run to wreck, where this settled underprop is wanting, and do soon break asunder, if they be not joined together with this glue" (P, II, 1, 16–17). In a later chapter, Lipsius listed many quotations from ancient sources to substantiate his conviction that the common people were inveterately unstable, inconstant, and irrational (P, IV, 5, 66–70). In his seminal study of Lipsius's thought, Gerhard Oestreich suggested that Lipsius's neostoical philosophy from *De Constantia* was important to his political thought only in the sense that it provided the broad intellectual foundation for the *Six Books of Politics*.[75] But a more substantial connection can be made. In the *Politics,* Lipsius portrayed the state as a divinely ordained institution responsible for imposing some modicum of universal reason upon the people (P, VI, 5, 200–1). It was a moral institution for artificially imposing divine and natural order upon the lives of individuals who would not or could not impose it upon themselves.

Lipsius's moral conception of the state is evident from the very first pages of the *Politics*. He claimed the two pillars of civil order were virtue and prudence. Virtue was the first principle of right reason and the foundation of all temporal stability and durability (I, 1, 1–2; II, 8, 25–26; IV, 14, 123). Lipsius defined virtue in a strongly religious manner. It consisted primarily of piety, or the right knowledge and worship of God, and probity, or honest and good living. Lipsius later expanded his definition to include other traditional Christian virtues such as justice, clemency, moderation, loyalty *(fides)*, liberality, and chastity (P, II, 10–17, 27–40).

Prudence was the active quality of ruling that gave effect to virtue (I, 7, 11). It applied to both divine and human things (IV, 2, 61). In divine matters, the prince was responsible for enforcing religious worship within the commonwealth. Lipsius argued that there should be "one religion" within each commonwealth because "from a confused religion there always grows dissention" (IV, 2, 62), but he added that prudence permitted the limited toleration of different religious sects within the commonwealth when necessary to preserve order (IV, 3–4, 63–66). Promoting particular religious doctrines was less important in his estimation than the overriding task of instituting a universal rational order, which was the divine political imperative.

In civil matters, prudence required virtue (as discussed above) and authority. Authority was necessary for actually imposing a rational and constant order upon human beings. It consisted of "a reverent opinion of the king and his state" fostered through three means: "the form of government, the power of the state, and the manners of the king" (P, IV, 9, 78). The form of government had to be "severe, constant, and restrained." Government had to be "severe" because any leniency in ruling over the people would breed contempt. Lipsius warned: "Do not govern [with leniency and negligence] and learn the nature of the common people" (P, IV, 9, 79). Later, he suggested that the prince should resurrect the ancient Roman office of the censor in order better to watch over and discipline the people's morals and behavior (P, IV, 11, 103–7). Government had to be "constant" in preserving the existing laws (80). Like Montaigne, Lipsius warned that change was dangerous because it opened the state to fortune and contingency. Government had to be "restrained" in the sense that all power had to be located in one central source (P, IV, 9, 81). A divided or diffuse form of government detracted from the state's authority and its ability to impose order upon the people.

The "power of the state" was the second prop of the state's authority. It consisted of all those means necessary to maintain social stability against internal and external threats including wealth, weapons, counsel, alliances, and good fortune (P, IV, 9, 82). Lipsius placed special emphasis on the importance of military power, which he discussed at length as a special form of prudence. In order to maintain peace and stability, he argued that the prince should undertake a comprehensive reform of the military system. First, he should establish a professional standing army composed of his own subjects (P, V, 11, 144). Then he should train these soldiers to use their weapons proficiently, to march in rank, to fortify a camp, and most generally, to behave with restraint and discipline (P, V, 13, 151–60). Lipsius's military reforms ultimately aimed at nothing less than the moral regeneration of the solidiery. He hoped to instill in them the basic principles of the Roman Stoa: self-control, moderation and abstinence.[76] While Lipsius's emphasis on the importance of a strong military provided a point of commonality with Machiavelli, he envisioned the military in a very different way.[77] Machiavelli saw the military as a citizen army contributing to civic liberty and glory, Lipsius as a highly disciplined professional body responsible for holding the social order constant in a hostile and turbulent world. His was a theory not of civic virtue but rather of neostoical restraint.

Lipsius identified the manners of the prince as the third main prop of his authority, serving to promote respect among the people. Piety and providence represented the two main grounds of good manners. Piety was respect for God and providence was the careful handling of political affairs. Lipsius added, in terms reminiscent of Montaigne, that because *"all mortal things are uncertain, and do suddenly perish* [a quotation from Tacitus] . . . our prince then ought to temper and moderate his understanding, yea and his actions likewise" (P, II, 15, 36–37). The activist and glory-seeking ruler was for Lipsius dangerous and unpredictable. He claimed a good prince should be a model of piety, detachment, and moderation, carrying out all plans with a keen sense of his own limitations.

For Lipsius, then, the state was supposed to extend neostoical principles to the people. He did not expect the state to transform the people into neostoical sages, although his call for military reforms did take steps in this direction. But he did call upon the state to restrain the disorderly behavior of the people and to impose a stable and rational order upon them. The role of the state was to supply an external aid in the quest for constancy. It was this positive vision of the state that underlay one of Lipsius's most controversial and (in terms of the development of state theory) most important proposals: his discussion of mixed prudence.

Lipsius stressed throughout the *Politics* that the foundation of order was virtue. No political society could exist for long without piety, probity, justice, honesty, and other traditional goods. However, he argued that because of the corruption and uncertainty of human affairs the prince would sometimes have to depart from these values to maintain constancy and order. The constancy and order of the commonwealth were for him goods that sometimes overrode the importance of abstract virtue. He rejected the ideas of "these Zenoes" who dogmatically opposed the use of all wickedness in statecraft (P, IV, 13, 112). "They seem not to know this age," he wrote, "and the men that live therein." "In this tempestuous sea of affairs of the world," where corruption and deceit were everywhere, it was sometimes "lawful and reasonable" to intermingle deceit with virtue in order to achieve a "good end" (113–14). Lipsius even announced his sympathy for the political thought of Machiavelli, "who poor soul is laid at of all hands" (114).

But Lipsius made clear that his support for Machiavellian politics was strictly limited. He distinguished between three levels of political deceit embodying different degrees of justice (P, IV, 14, 115–23). "Light deceit" consisted of distrust and dissimulation, and represented only a slight deviation from virtue. Lipsius fully approved of this form of deceit on the grounds that a perfectly trusting and honest prince would hardly be fit to rule over the corrupt world of human and temporal affairs. Yet like Montaigne, he argued that the prince ought to use dissimulation only sparingly, and even repeated Montaigne's contention that a prince who lied too often would ultimately undermine his ability to rule. The only legitimate application of light deceit was to conserve the order of the commonwealth. Richard Tuck has observed that Lipsius's position on deceit captured exactly the difference between him and Machiavelli. Lipsius believed "laws could be broken for *preservation*, but not for any other reason, such as the enhancement of a ruler's or his country's *glory*."[78] He hemmed his "Machiavellian" politics tightly within the framework of a morally based politics.

Lipsius defined "middle deceit" as offering bribes and favors to the ministers and courtiers of other princes. He was more wary of this level of deceit. He argued that it should only be "tolerated" and used against wicked princes for the good of the state. "Great deceit" consisted of outright treachery and injustice, such as when a prince broke his promises to others, banished powerful individuals from the commonwealth, or seized another's property by force. Lipsius absolutely condemned this form of deceit as contrary to all good politics but noted that in extreme necessities a prince might commission an assassination, take away certain privileges from the subjects, or seize a town or province. Again, he implied that the preservation of the rational order of the commonwealth was sufficiently important to override a strict adherence to moral values. But he warned that these sorts of actions should be undertaken with the greatest caution, since God punished wicked princes and their states: "And surely I do freely confess that whereas Europe is troubled with so many commotions, that kings and kingdoms do burn with the flame of sedition and war, peradventure the true and just cause is, that the government of the most part of them is not just and right" (P, IV, 14, 123). Lipsius believed that political order was rooted in the principles of right reason. However, he believed that rulers sometimes had to depart from these principles in order to impose a rational order upon a corrupt and disorderly temporal world. Lipsius's state theory grew out of this tension between universal justice and temporal particularity. He justified the powers of the state by arguing that they were necessary to impose a universal rational order upon a corrupt people and contingent social environment.

Pierre Charron repeated and further developed many of these themes in *De la sagesse* (1601).[79] The purpose of the *Sagesse* was to outline a theory of wisdom that would elevate human beings above the uncertainty and inconstancy of human affairs and align them with "nature." Like Montaigne, he argued that self-knowledge was the first step toward a natural morality. But whereas Montaigne had associated self-knowledge with personal introspection, Charron's study of the self focused on human nature in general.[80] Charron related no personal stories or experiences in the *Sagesse,* but instead treated the reader to a scientific inquiry into the nature of the body, soul, spirit, senses, imagination, memory, understanding, will, and passions. In fact, Charron's book may very well have served as a model for Hobbes who attempted in *Leviathan* to "read in himself, not this or that particular man, but mankind."[81] Charron saw Montaigne's personal reflections as only one piece of empirical evidence in his universal study of the essential characteristics of human nature. Self-knowledge was for Charron knowledge of the universal nature of humanity.

At the core of this self-knowledge was an awareness of the universal right reason implanted within each of us; natural morality consisted of organizing our lives around this principle. "The doctrine of all the Sages doth teach, that to live well, is to live according to nature, that the chiefest good in the world is to consent to nature, that in following nature as our guide and mistress, we can never err . . . understanding by nature that equity and universal reason which shines in us, which contains and hatches in it the seeds of all virtues, probity, justice, and is the matrix from whence all good and excellent laws do spring and arise" (II, 3, 258–59). The wise individual, according to Charron, subsumed all personal traits under the universal principles of reason:

> He then is wise, who maintaining himself truly free and noble, is directed in all things according to nature, accommodating his own proper and particular [nature] to the universal, which is God, living and carrying himself before God, with all, and in all affairs, upright, constant, cheerful, content, and assured, attending with one and the same foot, all things that may happen, and lastly, death itself. (II, preface, 222–23)

Because the stoical sage subordinated his particular opinions and beliefs to the universal law of nature, civil and political laws were unnecessary for him.[82] But very few individuals were able to achieve this level of wisdom. The "people or vulgar sort" were "inconstant and variable, without stay, like the waves of the sea," "envious and malicious," "treacherous and untrue," "mutinous, desiring nothing but novelties and changes, seditions, enemies to peace and quietness" (I, 52, 198–99).[83] Hence arose the need for the state. The purpose of the state was to discipline the people and bring them into conformity with the natural law. The following quotation speaks volumes about Charron's theory of the state:

> Even as a savage and untamed beast will not suffer himself to be taken, led and handled by man, but either flees and hides himself from him, or arms himself against him and with fury assaults him if he approaches near to him, in such sort that a man must use force mingled with art and subtlety to take and tame him; so folly will not be handled by reason or wisdom but strives and stirs against it, and adds folly to folly; and therefore it must be taken and led like a wild beast (that which a man is to a beast, a wise man is to a fool) astonished, feared, and kept short, that with the more ease it may be instructed and won. Now the proper means or help thereunto is a great authority, a thundering power and gravity which may dazzle it with the splendor of lightning. . . . Now this majesty and authority is first and properly in the person of the sovereign prince and lawmaker, where it is lively, actual and moving, afterwards in his commandments and ordinances, that is to say, in the law, which is the head of the work of the prince, and the image of a lively and original majesty. By this are fools reduced, conducted and guided. Behold then of what weight, necessity and utility authority and the law is in the world. (II, 8, 305–6)

Previous interpreters have suggested that Charron's state theory bore no integral relation to his theory of wisdom—that he saw the state as nothing more than a "necessity to keep fools in line."[84] The above quotation and other statements throughout *De la sagesse* indicate otherwise. The state played the same role for the common people that right reason played for the sage. If only in an artificial and superficial way, it brought them into conformity with the natural law. It made them live according to the right reason that they otherwise would choose to ignore. Without the civil law, Charron wrote, the majority of human beings would be altogether incapable of good living: "The sage does his duty and minds the laws not because of them but because of himself; for he is above them and does not need them. They are requisite only for the common people. And if the laws did not exist, he would do neither more nor less, and in this he differs from the common people, who cannot do well without the laws."[85]

The organizational principles of Charron's political theory were much the same as Lipsius's. In fact, he drew many of his political precepts directly out of the *Six Books of Politics*. In opening his discussion of civil prudence, he even explicitly acknowledged his debt to Lipsius: "This matter is excellently handled by Lipsius, according as he thought good: the marrow of his book is here" (III, 1, 354). He proceeded to repeat much of Lipsius's argument. He claimed that virtue and authority were the twin pillars of civil prudence, and advised the prince to maintain his authority through severity, constancy, and restraint (III, 2–3, 354–402). But Charron was no more a slavish devotee of Lipsius than he was of Montaigne. He introduced two changes into Lipsius's political theory that further contributed to the development of state theory.

Charron's first innovation was to incorporate Bodin's theory of sovereignty into his neostoical state theory. He summarized Bodin's theory thus: "Sovereignty is a perpetual and absolute power, without constraint either of time or condition. It consists in a power to give laws to all in general, and to everyone in particular, without the consent of any other, or receiving them from anyone" (I, 49, 190).[86] Lipsius explicitly rejected the principle of legislative sovereignty (P, II, 10, 28). He claimed constancy and equity demanded that the prince subject himself to the laws of the commonwealth and change them only when great profit or urgent necessity required it (P, IV, 9, 80). Charron, too, acknowledged that the prince generally ought to maintain the existing laws since "all change and alteration of laws, beliefs, customs and observances is very dangerous" (II, 8, 313). Nonetheless, he claimed the maintenance of order required a supreme legislative authority. The legislative sovereign was for him a fundamental source of command necessary for taming and disciplining the people.

Charron's other innovation came in the area of reason of state. While Charron emphasized the importance of justice, clemency, honesty, and other virtues in politics, he asserted that princes were nevertheless expected to govern by a quasi-autonomous ethic. "But you must know that the justice, virtue and probity of a sovereign goes after another manner than that of private men; it has a gate more large and more free by reason of the great weight and dangerous charge which he carries and sways" (III, 2, 358). Partially dispensing with Lipsius's graduated scale of lesser and greater evils, Charron approved of dissimulation and bribery as legitimate state practices. He drew the line only at dishonesty and treachery with friends, which he clamed was never permitted (361). He further provided a more liberal defense of various immoral actions such as the secret assassination of individuals "troublesome and dangerous to the state," the reduction of great persons, the seizure of private property, the suspension of laws and privileges, and the conquest of cities and provinces useful to the state. "Herein there is nothing violated but the form," Charron wrote. "And the prince, is he not above forms?" (362). Since the prince was the source of all social order, Charron suggested that he need not be too strict an observer of substantive moral principles. He stood to some extent above everyday morality. But Charron was still careful to distinguish his advice from that of Machiavelli. "Cursed be the doctrine of those who teach that all things are good and lawful for sovereigns" (359). A dangerous and wicked action was permissible only under three conditions: (1) "that it be for the evident and important necessity of the public weal"; (2) "that it be to defend, and not to offend, to preserve himself, and not to increase his greatness, to save and shield himself either from deceits or subtleties, or from wicked and dangerous enterprises, and not to practice them"; and (3) that it be done with "discretion, to the end that others abuse it not" (358–59). In general, then, Charron may be said to have pushed reason of state theory ever closer to an ethic of public utility. Although he maintained that the prince "must never turn his back to honesty" or depart entirely from the principles of justice, he came very close to arguing that the actions of the state were always justified insofar as they contributed to political constancy and order.

Lipsius and Charron took important steps toward developing Montaigne's ideas into a positive state theory. While they accepted his account of temporal contingency and the limits of human self-assertion, they departed from his thought in identifying a special metaphysical purpose for the state. They argued that the state existed to impose a constant and regular discipline upon the people consistent with the universal reason of God and nature. This conception of the state clearly conflicted with the individualistic elements within Montaigne's philosophy, and more precisely, with his high regard for particularity and difference. Indeed, one might almost be tempted to see in Lipsius's and Charron's state theories a partial return to the more activist politics of Machiavelli. But this would be to overlook the important differences separating Lipsius and Charron (as well as later state theorists) from Machiavelli. Machiavelli attempted to identify general rules of conduct within history; he encouraged the active manipulation and conquest of fortune and contingency. Both Lipsius and Charron advocated the reorganization of human affairs around the principles of nature; they encouraged a moderate and restrained approach to fortune and contingency. These core principles of Lipsius's and Charron's thought can be traced to the Montaignian moment. Montaigne broke from Machiavelli's historical methodology and activist humanism by portraying temporal affairs as radically contingent and nature as a basis of order. Lipsius and Charron broke from Montaigne simply by attributing a special divine and natural purpose to the state. Later state theorists were to follow this same path. In fact, the whole later history of state theory followed from these beginnings. State theorists established the legitimacy of the state by portraying the state as a metaphysically privileged institution responsible for imposing universal order and morality upon human beings within a radically contingent temporal world.

CHAPTER TWO

Jean Bodin

Prophet of the Sovereign State

*L*egislative sovereignty, which designates the state as the supreme and exclusive source of law and order within its jurisdiction, is the central principle of modern state theory. In his *Six livres de la république* (1576), Jean Bodin first defined and legitimized this principle (R, 122).[1] Admittedly, the originality of Bodin's definition has sometimes been exaggerated.[2] The Roman law declared the prince to be *legibus solutus* ("not bound by the laws") and *suprema lex* ("supreme law"). As early as the thirteenth century, canon and civil lawyers had already attributed a *plenitudo potestatis* to the pope and emperor, giving them the right to make and change the laws as necessary.[3] Sixteenth-century French theorists routinely claimed that the king possessed an "absolute" law-making power.[4] Yet despite these precedents, Bodin's theory of sovereignty was still revolutionary.

No one before Bodin had provided an unambiguous definition and defense of the principle of legislative sovereignty. Medieval jurists portrayed the *plenitudo potestatis* of the prince as an extraordinary power distinct from his *potestas ordinaria*. Although the prince was able theoretically to make or change the laws at will, he was ordinarily expected to preserve and obey the existing laws. His legislative powers were to be used only in special circumstances and when he had an explicit cause.[5] Civil lawyers similarly balanced out the more "absolutist" passages of the Roman law with other passages suggesting that the prince ought rightfully "to profess himself bound by the laws."[6] Sixteenth-century French jurists added that the king's absolute powers were only potential powers. Comparing the king's powers to God's powers, Claude de Seyssel even suggested that the customary bridles on the king's powers were the source of the monarchy's strength and longevity, because if the king's power

> were more ample and absolute, it would be worse and more imperfect, just as the power of God is not judged less but rather more perfect because He cannot sin or do ill. Because with all their great authority and power they are willing to be subject to their own laws and live according to them, kings are more laudable than if they could at their whim make use of absolute power.[7]

Before Bodin, the "absolute" law-making powers of the king were never absolute.

Bodin, by contrast, granted the sovereign authority a much wider scope of action. He claimed that in both principle and practice the prince should rightfully be able to make or change the laws at will. He transformed the king's extraordinary legislative powers into an ordinary everyday prerogative. Kenneth Pennington has maintained nevertheless that Bodin's contribution to the theory of sovereignty was "conceptual rather than substantive."[8] By his account, Bodin merely defined in a systematic way what medieval jurists had already implied. As explained in this chapter, Pennington's assessment is too conservative. But even accepting his views, Bodin's theory is still extremely important. He concretely defined and legitimized a principle that earlier theorists had skirted. His theory of sovereignty represented a conceptual breakthrough in the history of political thought that shifted the fundamental ground of legitimate order from the existing laws to the law-making prince.

In setting forth his theory of legislative sovereignty, Bodin not only broke away from medieval and Renaissance legal traditions, but also abandoned the position of his earlier writings.[9] In the *Methodus ad Facilem Historiarum Cognitionem* (1566), he still defined sovereignty in a traditional manner, arguing that the sovereign prince was rightfully subject to the existing laws. It was only in his *République* (1576) that he asserted his revolutionary theory of legislative sovereignty. From the *Methodus* to the *République*, Bodin thus traversed the distance between premodern and modern state theory. The origins of modern state theory lie hidden in the theoretical space between these two works.

Julian Franklin has provided the most influential explanation for why Bodin outlined his theory of legislative sovereignty in the *République* but not the *Methodus*. He claimed that the *République* was a response to the deteriorating political situation in France following the St. Bartholomew's Day massacre of 1572. As France spiraled downward into civil war, Bodin became increasingly convinced of the need for an absolute sovereign ruler to maintain order. But, according to Franklin, he did not very effectively define or justify this new power; he merely imposed it upon the constitutionalist framework of his *Methodus* as a "confused and strained" and "largely ill-founded" principle.[10]

There is, however, another interpretation. In this chapter it is suggested that Bodin cogently defended his theory of legislative sovereignty in the *République* by appealing to the divine and natural law. His defense rested most fundamentally upon a voluntarist theology that posited the radical dependence of all temporal order upon God's will (section 1). But it was also related to a deep skepticism about the content of divine and natural law that Bodin shared with his contemporaries. In the *Methodus*, Bodin tried to overcome this skepticism by conducting a universal comparative study of legal systems designed to identify the universal foundation of law and order (section 2). But by the time he wrote the *République*, he had lost confidence in this methodology. He had come to see human history as too variable and diverse to yield any universal law, and turned directly to nature and the Old Testament to discern the principles of law and order (section 3). In this latter work, he argued that the principle of legislative sovereignty was itself a precept of divine and natural law necessary for instituting and maintaining a universal political order in a corrupt and contingent temporal world (section 4).

This interpretation casts Bodin in the unfamiliar guise of a divine right theorist.[11] J. W. Allen once asserted that "you can eliminate from Bodin's *République* all his references to God, and to Princes as the lieutenants of God, and the whole structure will stand unaltered."[12] More recently, however, scholars have begun to recognize the deeply religious character of Bodin's political thought.[13] This chapter builds upon recent scholarship by placing Bodin's theory of sovereignty within his moral cosmology. It is argued that the *République* is best understood in light of one of Bodin's last works, the *Universae Naturae Theatrum*. In this work, Bodin expressed disillusionment with his early comparative historical studies and turned directly to the study of nature and divine law in order to discern the universal principles of human order. Bodin had already begun this turn when he wrote his *République*. The result was his theory of legislative sovereignty.

The principle of legislative sovereignty is so much a part of our modern political landscape that it is easily taken for granted. But it did not always exist. Before the late sixteenth century, political and legal theorists explicitly rejected this principle as contrary to good government. What changed? How did legislative sovereignty gain a foothold in modern political thinking? What does this principle imply about ourselves, our world, and our vision of politics? These questions are best addressed by tracing the principle of legislative sovereignty back to its origins in the political and legal theory of Jean Bodin.

THE VOLUNTARISM OF BODIN

In *Order, Empiricism and Politics*, W. H. Greenleaf suggested that early modern absolutist political thought was closely associated with "the worldview of order."[14] The worldview of order was based upon the belief that God had infused the universe with divine order. God had arranged all creatures into "a single ascending scale of things from the lowest form of material creation to the highest manifestation of the purely spiritual," or great chain of being.[15] According to Greenleaf, absolutist writers used this worldview to justify the theory of absolute monarchy by drawing analogies and making correspondences between God and the sovereign prince. Just as God was sovereign in the macrocosm, they argued that there should be an omnipotent ruler over political societies. Greenleaf identified Jean Bodin as an important exponent of this style of thought. One of Bodin's last works, the *Universae Naturae Theatrum,* is a detailed description of the vast hierarchy of beings within nature. He outlined shorter descriptions of this same worldview in his other major works. In the *République,* he used this worldview to legitimize his theory of sovereignty by calling attention to the "correspondence between God and prince, cosmos and state."[16]

In recent years, Francis Oakley has challenged Greenleaf's thesis.[17] Oakley has argued that there were actually "two different conceptions of order" in late medieval and early modern political thought. One portrayed "order as immanent, grounded in the very natures or essences of things." Advocates of this vision believed nature to be an emanation of God's being, with the implication that God himself was ordinarily subject to the natural law and sequence of cause and effect. The alternative vision of order portrayed "order as external to things, imposed, as it were, from the outside." This vision of order was based upon a voluntarist theology that depicted God as a "presently-active power" in nature. God's absolute will was directly responsible for maintaining and directing each and every affair within the universe. According to Oakley, the first of these ideas of order was "incompatible with the notion of sovereign will." It posited an already existing immanent order within nature that limited both God's and the king's powers. This idea was behind Seyssel's discussion of the limited "absolute" powers of God and the king. Only the second "voluntarist" idea of order supported an absolutist theory of politics. It freed God and the king to do what they "will."

Bodin rested his political thought upon this second vision of order.[18] In his *Methodus,* he insisted upon God's radical independence from necessity and natural law: "God is bound by no number, by no necessity, but is released from the laws of nature, not by the senate or by the people, but by Himself alone. For since He himself ordains the laws of nature and has received dominion from no other than Himself, it is fitting that He should be released from His laws, and at different times should make different decisions about the same things" (M, 236). A bit later in this same work Bodin further asserted the radical dependence of all things on God's perpetual sustaining power: "When He fails to guard a wicked man or even a good man, as is said in the case of Job, He thereby abandons him to the prince of darkness, who arranges a miserable death for a wicked and sinful man. . . . It seems that we must make the same decision about the destruction of the world and of all things. As soon as He abandons the care of these, they will collapse" (M, 316). Bodin made similar statements in his *République, Démonomanie des sorciers,* and *Colloquium Heptaplomeres* (R, 542–43, 564–65; D, 30; C, 34–35).[19]

But he most fully developed his voluntarist theology in the *Universae Naturae Theatrum*. Here he claimed that the chain of being and natural laws existed only because God was constantly operative in the world sustaining them.[20] At any moment and without warning, he could change or overturn even the most steadfast of natural laws: "He can not only bend the wills of men wherever he wants and back from wherever he wants, but also he can restrain the attacks of beasts and govern inanimate natures, and he can even keep fire from burning and can destroy and hold back the whole power of nature" (T, 27).[21] Dispensing with the traditional distinction between the ordinary and absolute powers of God, Bodin argued that God's powers were always absolute.[22] Even the physical laws of nature were perpetually enforced by God. Any assertion of the autonomous existence of natural law and necessity was to Bodin an affront to divine Providence and God's very existence, as the master Mystagogus explains to his pupil Theorus in the *Theatrum*:

> M[ystagogus]: But of course there would be no Providence if the world were governed by necessity. God would be released from the care of all things, as Epicurus and Strato of Lampsacus thought.
> T[heorus]: Why not?
> M[ystagogus]: Because Providence is seen only in two things, first that each thing is, then that it is good: but necessity excludes both of them. A necessary series of causes makes a stable and immutable order that could not be otherwise, nor the order of things changed, not even to save someone from the flames or other present or future dangers. If Providence is removed, God is removed, because he who should himself be the moderator and arbiter of nature would be coerced by a servile necessity and would not have any power to decide about the things of which he is the first and principal cause, for not even a worm is in vain. (T, 29)[23]

For Bodin, the notion of an immanent natural order implied limits on God's omnipotence. It further indicated that nature and temporal order could exist apart from God's sustaining grace. He therefore rejected this notion as contrary to true religion.

Oakley suggested that voluntarist theologies contributed to the development of absolutist political theories by providing writers with a new arsenal of correspondences and analogies.[24] If God's will were absolute over the universe, then it might plausibly be asserted that the sovereign prince's will should be absolute over the kingdom. As we shall see below, Bodin made use of this argument by correspondence in laying out his theory of sovereignty—although he was always careful to note that God's powers were incomparably greater than those of any human ruler.[25] But Bodin's philosophy reveals a much closer link between voluntarist theologies and absolutist political theories than Oakley recognized. Drawing upon his voluntarist theology, Bodin laid out a moral cosmology that broke down all distinctions between the divine and natural laws, grace and nature. In turn, he claimed that human beings were radically dependent upon divine grace for their everyday well-being. They had to align themselves actively with the divine will in order to establish peace and stability within their societies. If they failed to do so, they would fall subject to contingency and disorder. The result was a highly moralistic conception of politics—and ultimately the foundation of his theory of legislative sovereignty.

The first important implication of Bodin's voluntarist theology was the blurring of all distinctions among the religious, moral, and natural realms.[26] Since God was responsible for directing and sustaining all things in nature, no clear lines could be drawn between divine and natural events. Nature was itself a direct manifestation of God's will. Thus it was that Bodin could portray his *Universae Naturae Theatrum* as an essentially religious work.[27] Everything in nature revealed divine action and design. Even the lowliest creatures (the worm) and most mundane events (the burning of fire) pointed back toward "the infinite power of one eternal God" (T, 4). In his other writings, Bodin regularly coupled the "law of God and of nature" as if they were one and the same thing.[28] He claimed the principles of the natural law were no different from the doctrines of the Decalogue, which were themselves merely a restatement of the original principles of natural law. All came from God and taught the same moral lesson:[29]

When we read that Abraham cherished the law of the most high, what does this mean except that he followed the example of the law of nature? And indeed Philo the Hebrew said: "The commands of the two tables in no way differ from nature, and there is no need to endeavor to spend one's life according to the precepts of divine laws, since these laws contain nothing other than the law of nature and the life of our elders." However, in Moses' time the law of nature had been so defiled by the shameful crimes of men that it seemed to be completely obliterated from men's souls and antiquated, as it were, because of its duration. For this reason, God, the greatest and best, pitying the vicissitude of men, wished to renew the same law of nature and especially the prohibitions which prevent us from violating nature. Therefore, when men had become deaf to the law of nature, the divine voice was necessary so that those who had scorned nature might hear the parent of nature resounding his own words. (C, 249)[30]

For Bodin, the content of divine revelation was no different from natural law. Throughout history, God had revealed his will directly to human beings simply to remind them of the principles of the natural law.

The second important implication of Bodin's voluntarist theology was a moralistic natural philosophy. Bodin asserted that God governed the whole natural world according to his moral plan.[31] He brought forth times of plenty and famine to reward or punish human beings for their obedience to his moral dictates: "Just as the Provider of the world feeds a multitude of men by bringing forth suddenly legions of birds and fish, thus also he punishes the arrogance and pride of men when he places a limit on his liberality and withdraws fecundity from the water, earth, air, or animals because of the outrages of men" (T, 339–40).[32] Bodin, in fact, claimed that God operated a vast demonic machinery within nature to allocate rewards and punishments to human beings according to their moral deserts.[33] God sent guardian angels to warn pious individuals about impending dangers and to guide them toward divine ends. He sent demons "to damage, ruin, and corrupt by means of war, plague, and famine" when individuals strayed from the divine and natural laws (P, 12).

Bodin most directly drew out the lessons of his moral cosmology for individuals in his *De la démonomanie des sorciers* (1580). Here he asserted that even though God governed all affairs according to his omnipotent will, he had granted human beings free will to conduct their own affairs. Human beings were free to follow whatever sort of life they might choose. However, their choices were not without consequences. God rewarded individuals who chose to follow his laws by sending them order and peace and he punished individuals who rejected his laws by sending them disorder and death.

> Men have free choice to be good, or wicked, as God says in His Law. "I have," He states, "put before your eyes good and evil, life and death, choose then the good, and you will live" [Dt. 30:15]. And even more clearly elsewhere it is written, God having created man, left him his free will, and said to him, "If you wish you will keep my commandments, and they will keep you. I have given you fire and water, you have power to put your hand in one or the other. You have good and evil, life and death, and you will have whichever one you like" [Sir. 15:15–17]. (D, 56–57)

Bodin interpreted these Old Testament passages quite literally. He believed that God rewarded and punished human beings with "life and death" here and now within the temporal world. Feasts and famines, plagues and earthquakes were all meted out according to the moral deserts of human beings.

Bodin applied this same moral argument to his political philosophy. This was the third major implication of his voluntarist theology. He claimed political societies had to conform to the divine and natural laws or suffer chaos and dissension. He outlined this principle in the introduction to the original French edition of the *République*. Bodin began by lamenting the "impetuous storm" that was wracking the French state. As Franklin and others have pointed out, these statements indicate that the *République* was written in response to the religious and civil wars.[34] What has been generally overlooked, however, is Bodin's diagnosis of the cause of this disorder. France was suffering from disorder and chaos, according to Bodin, because the rulers had fallen under the influence of wicked writers who discussed public affairs without any knowledge of "laws" or even of "public right": "These men, I say, have profaned the sacred mysteries of political philosophy, a matter which has been the occasion for troubling and overturning good states" (R, iii). In particular, he singled out Machiavelli for condemnation—a writer whose ideas were assumed to be influential in the French court with Catherine de Medici and the inspiration behind the St. Bartholomew Day's Massacre.[35] Machiavelli advocated tyranny, glorified atheism, and even praised the most wicked of all princes, Cesare Borgia. And what had his advice achieved? "This man [Borgia], for all his trickery, was disgracefully cast down from the high and slippery rock of tyranny where he was perched, and in the end was exposed like a beggar to the mercy and derision of his enemies. The same has since befallen all the other princes who have followed in his tracks, and practiced those lovely rules of Machiavelli, who put for the two foundations of republics, impiety and injustice, and condemned religion as contrary to the state" (R, iii-iv). When a prince contravened "the sacred laws of nature," he invited God to wreak vengeance upon himself and his people (R, iv).[36] Indeed, Bodin asserted "there is no foundation more ruinous" to the stability of states than Machiavelli's advice. By teaching princes to practice injustice and despise the divine and natural laws, Machiavelli had taught the very opposite of what was necessary to institute peace and order. It was only by following the principles of divine and natural justice that rulers could secure harmony and order in their states.[37]

> For just as the great God of nature, very wise and just, commands over the angels, so the angels command over human beings, human beings over beasts, the soul over the body, heaven over the earth, and reason over the appetites. . . . But contrarily, if it happens that the appetites are disobedient to reason, individuals to magistrates, magistrates to princes, and princes to God, then we see that God moves to avenge his injuries and to secure the execution of the eternal law established by him. (R, iv)

God was, according to Bodin, directly involved in enforcing his divine hierarchy. Whenever individuals failed to implement his moral order, he moved directly to impose it upon them, usually with great violence. Bodin's *République* must be seen in this light. This book represented his attempt to lay out the universal principles of politics so that the French people could escape the violence and destruction that God had sent them for failing to abide by his divine and natural laws.

Bodin reiterated his moralistic political outlook later in the *République* in his discussion of pardons and punishments. While sovereign rulers could legitimately grant pardons for crimes committed against their own particular laws, Bodin asserted that they could not give a pardon "for a penalty established by the law of God" (R, 246). If the prince made a law forbidding his subjects to bear arms, for example, and someone took up arms in self-defense, the prince might rightfully forgive this offense. It was simply a civil offense. "But as for the murderer by premeditation," Bodin wrote, "'You shall drag him,' the law [of God] says, 'from my sacred altar, and you shall never have pity on him, but you shall put him to death, and then I will shed my great mercy on you.'" Despite God's clear command on this matter, Bodin observed that Christian kings were in the habit of granting pardons to premeditative murderers. They even saw their pardons as great acts of mercy. But in fact, their pardons were displeasing to God who punished their kingdoms for failing to abide by his law: "The pardons for such misdeeds draw after them plagues, famines, wars, and the ruin of republics. That is why the law of God says that in punishing people who have merited death, one removes the curse that lies upon the people." Bodin concluded that it was imperative for princes to execute premeditative murderers regardless of the circumstances. If sovereign rulers did not strictly enforce the laws of God, God would exact his punishment upon their kingdoms.

The most dramatic and terrible expression of Bodin's moralistic perspective was his *Démonomanie*.[38] The *Démonomanie* was the most widely published work on the subject of demons and witches in the late sixteenth and early seventeenth centuries and probably played some role in provoking the large-scale persecution of witches during this period.[39] In the preface, Bodin explained that he wrote his book to combat the skepticism of his contemporaries concerning the existence of witches and demons.[40] This was an important matter in his opinion because the laxness of kings and judges in punishing witches was (like their laxness in executing premeditative murderers) a major cause of disorder. Witches were self-avowed enemies of God; God punished any prince or people who tolerated them. Discussing a famous witch trial from the previous century, Bodin wrote:

> Now the impunity of witches at that time was the reason they marvelously increased in this realm, where they arrived from every direction . . . so that the witch Trois-eschelles having obtained pardon from the death sentence pronounced against him, on condition that he name his accomplices, stated that there were more than a hundred thousand in this realm—perhaps falsely and in order to lessen his impiety by having such numerous company. Whatever the case he named a very large number. But matters were arranged so well that all or most of them got off, even though they confessed such abominable wickedness that the air was contaminated. So God in His anger sent terrible persecutions, since He had threatened by His law to exterminate peoples who allowed witches to live. (D, 38)

Believing that the earlier lenient treatment of witches was directly related to public disorders, Bodin encouraged princes and magistrates to act swiftly and forcefully against all witches within their jurisdictions.

In the body of the *Démonomanie*, Bodin advised princes and judges in the science of identifying and punishing witches. First he asserted that there existed both good and evil demons throughout the universe and defined witches as those who associated with the evil demons. He then discussed the "difference between good and evil spirits . . . in order to tell the children of God from witches" (D, 63). This led to an analysis of legitimate and illegitimate types of divination, magic, and so forth. In the final book, he laid out the lawful rules for gathering evidence about and convicting witches, and reiterated the importance of punishing witches in the most severe way possible. The well-being of the commonwealth was tied directly to the persecution of witches:

> The death penalty prescribed for witches is not to make them suffer more than they are suffering by punishing them, but to bring an end to the wrath of God on the whole people; also in part to bring them repentance and to cure them, or at least if they will not change their ways, to reduce their number, surprising the wicked and preserving the elect. It is therefore, a very salutary thing for the whole body of a state diligently to search out and severely punish witches. (D, 173–74)

Bodin regarded the sanctity of the political body to be the prerequisite for peace and order within it. If the moral purity of the people were not preserved, he claimed the political society would suffer plagues, punishments, and internal chaos.

Bodin's voluntarist theology thus had important implications for his ideas about order. Not only did he believe that order was "external to things, imposed, as it were [by God], from the outside," but just as importantly he believed that human beings had to take an active part in imposing this order upon their own lives to maintain peace and stability. Ultimately, he proposed his theory of legislative sovereignty to carry out this moral purpose. But Bodin's voluntarist theology did not lead directly or necessarily to his theory of sovereignty, even if there is an analogical affinity between the two. Bodin had already developed the basic principles of his voluntarist theology in his *Methodus*. Yet this work articulates only a partial theory of legislative sovereignty. Intellectually, then, no direct line can be drawn from Bodin's voluntarism to his theory of legislative sovereignty. Other factors played a part in his decision to develop this theory in the *République*. In order to discern these other elements, it is necessary briefly to examine the argument of his *Methodus*. Only then can we fully understand the assumptions behind his theory of legislative sovereignty in the *République*.

THE *METHODUS AD FACILEM HISTORIARUM COGNITIONEM*

In the *Methodus* (1566), Bodin attempted to bring politics into line with the divine and natural law by conducting a universal comparative study of history. As he indicated at the beginning of this work, his study was provoked by a skeptical crisis in legal studies.[41] Traditionally, legal theorists had looked to Roman law to discern the universal principles of law and order. Roman law was assumed to be a written expression of right reason *(ratio scripta)* containing legal principles applicable to all times and societies.[42] Over the course of the sixteenth century, however, French legal scholars had challenged and undermined this assumption.[43] Applying the philological techniques of the Italian humanists to the study of Roman law, they had discovered that this text was actually composed of a number of distinctive laws and precepts compiled from different periods of Roman history. François Hotman provided the crowning statement of this scholarship in his *Antitribonian* (1567).[44] He concisely summarized his two central tenets in the title of the third chapter of this work: "That the State of the Roman Republic Is Very Different from That of France, and Cannot Even Be Learned from the Books of Justinian."[45] Hotman first asserted, contrary to the assumptions of civil lawyers, that laws were relative to the particular historical circumstances in which they arose. Since history was constantly changing and political communities differed according to their governments, size, military organizations, and other features, Hotman argued that the laws of one society could never be applied to others. "Consequently, the laws of one monarchy are often useless to another, just as medicines are not all suitable to all men whatsoever without consideration of their sex, their age, and their nationality."[46] It was sheer madness, by Hotman's estimation, to try to apply the Roman law to contemporary French society. The ancient Roman polity was clearly much different from the French monarchy. "Who," Hotman asked, "would not judge a man deprived of his senses who would spend his whole life and all his years curiously dissecting the duties, instructions, and rules of [Roman] officers in order to adapt them to the government of France when this nation was so different in manners and humors from our own?"[47] Hotman further questioned whether Roman law even reflected the true law of the Roman people. Drawing upon his knowledge of philology and history, he observed that Roman law contained fragments of laws collected from three distinct and even contradictory periods of Roman history. "The books of Justinian do not contain any complete description of the popular state or the true Roman empire or of Constantinople, but only an assembled mass of small pieces and diverse patches from each of these forms."[48] To make matters worse, the main editor of the *Corpus Juris,* Tribonian, had suppressed some of the best ancient laws and introduced forgeries into his collection.[49] Hotman concluded that Roman law was really just the law of the age of Justinian, which was by all accounts the nadir of Roman civilization.[50]

Bodin outlined a similar analysis of Roman law at the beginning of his *Methodus.*[51]

> The arts and disciplines, as you are well aware, are not concerned with particulars, but with universals. Nevertheless, these men [the jurists] have tried to deal with the subject of the Civil [i.e., Roman] law, that is, the legislation of one particular state. How wisely, I do not now discuss. Yet nothing can be conceived further from the dignity and value of an art. I disregard the absurdity of attempting to establish principles of universal jurisprudence from the Roman decrees, which were subject to change within a brief period. It is especially absurd, since almost all the laws of the Twelve Tables were supplanted by an

infinite multitude of edicts and statutes, and later by the Aebutian Rogation also; repeatedly the old regulations were replaced by new ones. Moreover, we see that almost all the legislation of Justinian was abrogated by following emperors. I pass over how many things are absurd in the statutes which remain—how many were declared outworn by the just decrees of almost all peoples and by long disuse. The fact remains that they have described the laws of no people except the Romans, and these, indeed, in the wrong order. (M, 2)

Many of the decrees of Roman law had been changed. Others had been overturned. The decrees that remained were in large part outworn. At best, Roman law was nothing more than the law of "one particular state." Bodin concluded that it was absurd to try to deduce a universal legal science from the study of Roman law alone. A new universal legal science was necessary.

In the *Methodus,* Bodin attempted to overcome the legal relativism and skepticism of his age by identifying a new universal foundation for the law.[52] After criticizing jurists for attempting "to establish principles of universal jurisprudence from the Roman decrees," he outlined his own methodology: "They should have read Plato, who thought there was one way to establish law and govern a state: wise men should bring together and compare the legal framework of all states, or of the more famous states, and from them compile the best kind" (M, 2). Bodin directed his *Methodus* and other early works[53] toward this end:

> To this objective I directed all my studies—all my thoughts. At the beginning I outlined in a table a form of universal law . . . , so that from the very sources we may trace the main types and divisions of types down to the lowest, yet in such a way that all members fit together. . . . Next I have established postulates, on which the entire system rests as on the firmest foundation. Then I have added definitions. Afterward I laid down as briefly as possible the precepts called "rules" according to the proposed form, as if to a norm. At one side I added, in brief notes, the interpreters of Roman law, so that from the same sources whence I have drawn, each man can take to his own satisfaction. Then from every source I collected and added the legislation of peoples who have been famous for military and civic disciplines. (M, 2–3)

The *Methodus* was the central component of this project. The study of history provided the empirical data for Bodin's universal table of law as well as a normative standard for appraising the legislation of different states. "From this subject then we have collected the widely scattered statutes of ancient peoples, so that we may include them also in this work. Indeed, in history the best part of universal law lies hidden; and what is of great weight and importance for the best appraisal of legislation—the custom of the peoples, and the beginnings, growth, conditions, changes, and decline of all states—are obtained from it" (M, 8). In a broad sense, Bodin still held to the classical humanist belief in the patterns or cycles of history. From history, he explained, "not only are present-day affairs readily interpreted but also future events are inferred, and we may acquire reliable maxims for what we should seek and avoid" (M, 9). He even repeated the classical humanist dictum that history is the "master of life" *(magistra vitae)* (M, 9).[54] He believed that the history of the major political regimes would reveal patterns and trends that would expose the universal principles of law and order.

In the first chapter of the *Methodus*, Bodin situated his historical methodology within his moral cosmology. History, he asserted, could be divided into three branches: divine, natural, and human (M, 15). The subject of divine history was God's Providence. The subject of natural history was the natural sequence of cause and effect which, he asserted in a manner consistent with his voluntarist theology, was generally "inevitable and steadfast . . . unless it is checked by divine will or for a brief moment abandoned by it" (M, 17). The subject of human history was the legislation and changes of states.[55] Divine and natural history were distinguished from human history in that they were comprised "within definite limits." Human history was variable and diverse. Bodin explained this difference in terms of human free will:

> Because human history flows mostly from the will of mankind, which ever vacillates and has no objective, we see there are born each day new laws, new customs, new institutions, and new manners, and human actions are incessantly involved in new errors unless they are guided by nature, that is, by right reason. . . . If we depart from this, we shall fall headlong into all sorts of infamy. (M, 16–17)[56]

Bodin's statement here nicely summarizes the central principles of his moral cosmology. Free will gave human beings the opportunity to invent and enact all sorts of laws, customs, and actions. But unless they were "guided by nature" and "right reason," their laws involved them in infamy and disorder, and God punished them with chaos and plagues. In order "to discern useful from useless or true from false or base from honorable," Bodin argued that human beings had to develop "prudence"; and for developing prudence, nothing was "more important or more essential than history, because episodes in human life sometimes recur as in a circle, repeating themselves" (M, 17).[57] The study of history, Bodin asserted, would enable human beings to identify the divine and natural principles of law by revealing what had succeeded and failed over the course of human existence. Whatever had succeeded could be assumed to be pleasing to God, while whatever had failed could be assumed to be contrary to nature and right reason.

Bodin's approach to law in the *Methodus* had much in common with the classical humanist tradition. Like classical humanist writers, Bodin suggested that human beings could discern the underlying principles of political order from the study of history. But he extended and transformed the tradition in several ways. While the Italian humanists focused primarily on Roman and Italian histories, Bodin broadened the scope of his investigations to include the histories of all peoples. Whereas the Italian humanists tended to study individual actions and practical political policies, Bodin further concentrated on institutions and laws.[58] He also had "more transcendent purposes" than the Italian humanists. He looked to history to discover the universal principles of divine and natural order rather than prudential rules of success.[59] Perhaps most importantly, Bodin attempted to set historical studies on a more scientific basis. He complained in the preface of his *Methodus* (much as Machiavelli complained at the beginning of his *Discourses*) that even though many writers before him had studied history, none had adequately explained "the art and the method of the subject" (M, 14). As a result, "many recklessly and incoherently confuse the accounts, and none derives any lessons therefrom." In order to draw out the universal lessons from history, it was necessary to approach historical studies in a more critical and rigorous manner. The bulk of the *Methodus* was thus dedicated to defining the rules of a scientific historical methodology. Bodin discussed the organization of historical treatises, the proper arrangement of historical materials, standards for judging the merits and accuracy of historians and histories, a framework for synchronizing different histories along one universal system of time, and other related matters. In short, Bodin aimed to perfect the humanist tradition of historical studies so that it could yield the universal principles of government and law.

Bodin devoted the central chapter in the *Methodus* to a lengthy discussion of "The Type of Government in States." Here he attempted to identify from history "what is the best kind of state" (M, 153). Bodin took some preliminary steps in this chapter toward developing his theory of sovereignty. He argued, for example, that sovereignty was necessarily located in one source: the people, aristocracy, or monarch (M, 172, 178–79). There never had been nor could there ever be a system of divided or mixed sovereignty because human societies require a system of "civil discipline and control" unified under one supreme ruler (M, 31–33). But despite this foreshadowing of his later theory, Bodin still defined the concept of sovereignty in the *Methodus* in a traditional manner. While in the *République* he designated the sovereign prince as the absolute source of law and order within society, he still associated sovereignty in the *Methodus* with a mosaic of rights:[60]

> I see the sovereignty of the state involved in five functions. One, and it is the principal one, is creating the most important magistrates and defining the office of each one; the second, proclaiming and annulling laws; the third, declaring war and peace; the fourth, receiving final appeal from all magistrates; the last, the power of life and death when the law itself leaves no room for extenuation or grace. (M, 172–73)

Bodin's definition of sovereignty here was quite similar to the definitions of many of his contemporaries.[61] Although he identified the power to make and annul laws as one of the marks of sovereignty, he did not yet consider it to be the principal power. He still listed the primary mark of sovereignty as the power to create magistrates and enforce the law. His sovereign prince was first and foremost still an executive and judicial authority.

This point is especially clear in Bodin's discussion of monarchical government. "Indeed, it is a fine sentiment," he began, "that the man who decrees law ought to be above the laws," since he may have to "repeal it, take from it, invalidate it, or add to it, or even if circumstances demand, allow it to become obsolete" (M, 202–3). "But once the measure has been passed and approved *by the common consent of everyone*," he continued, "why should not the prince be held by the law which he has made?" (M, 203; emphasis added). "Princes use sophistry against the people when they say that they themselves are released from the laws so that not only are they superior to the laws but also in no way bound by them and, what is even more base, that whatever pleases them shall have the force of law" (M, 203). Bodin observed that some kings ruled their states as "lords" acting as "masters of the laws and of all things," and this was not necessarily "contrary to nature or to the law of nations" (M, 204). But "Christian princes" invariably bound themselves to obey and preserve the existing laws by swearing a sacred oath. The French coronation oath was exemplary in this regard:

> It is significant in this respect especially, that before the priests the prince swears by immortal God that he will give rightful law and justice to all classes and so far as in him lies will judge with integrity and religious scruple. Having sworn, he cannot easily violate his faith; or if he could, yet he would be unwilling to do so, for the same justice exists for him as for any private citizen, and he is held by the same laws. *Moreover, he cannot destroy the laws peculiar to the entire kingdom or alter any of the customs of the cities or ancient ways without the consent of the three estates.* (M, 204; emphasis added)

Bodin concluded that Aristotle was wrong when he wrote that monarchs were not bound by the laws. Even more confused were the opinions of Ulpian and Pomponius, who asserted that princes were "not only freed from the laws, but even said that their will was law" (M, 205). Legitimate kings were subordinate to the laws and could change them only on special occasions and with the consent of the people.

Bodin's investigation into the cause of changes within states further confirmed this conclusion (and probably guided his decision to define sovereignty in a traditional and limited manner in the *Methodus*). He began by noting that there were two sources of change that afflicted states. The first derived from the celestial and numerological order of God (M, 223–36). God had ordained the changes of governments to correspond with certain celestial events and intervals of years. While wise rulers could make provisions to guard against these changes, they could not entirely avoid them. The other cause of change was rooted in human corruption and avarice.[62] Because "the nature of men is such that they are wont to slip downward into vices," there existed a cycle of regimes whereby monarchy changed into tyranny, aristocracy into oligarchy, and democracy into ochlocracy (M, 217). Once a good regime had decayed into a corrupt one, the subjects often rose up against their rulers or called in foreign powers to overthrow them (M, 217–18). The only way to safeguard against these changes, according to Bodin, was to place legal limits on the powers of sovereign rulers. There is "nothing more divine" than for "the kings themselves to obey their laws," he wrote, adding a bit later: "As certain things are so molded by nature that it seems they can never perish, but others cohere so badly that they can be dispersed in a single breath, so it is in the case of the state—the better it is tempered from its earliest origins, the more easily does it repel external force; indeed, only with great difficulty can it be overthrown from within" (M, 217, 220–21). Limited governments protected against disorder and change by restraining the corruption of human nature.

Bodin devoted much of the remainder of this chapter to demonstrating the superiority of limited governments throughout history. The governments of Rome, Athens, Sparta, the cities of Italy, Switzerland, Germany, the Chaldea, Greece, Arabia, Denmark, Sweden, England, Spain, and other countries all exercised unlimited powers and suffered continual changes (M, 206–10, 236–67). Only France enjoyed a durable and stable peace: "Yet from those which we have investigated it is plain that no empire has been more lasting than that of the Gauls or less given to civil wars" (M, 267). The "secret of this kingdom," Bodin declared, was "the fact that the royal power is greatly limited" (M, 256). He then added most generally:

> The more you can take from the power of the prince (and on this point one cannot be wrong), the more just will be the rule and the more stable for the future, as King Theopompus is reported to have said when power was granted to the ephors. Those who by evil arts think to increase the authority of the prince err, since they are attempting the overthrow of the kingdom and of the kings. Indeed, it is more important than empire, as the Emperor Theodosius decided, that the princely power should be subordinated to the laws. (M, 256; see also 201–5)

Bodin's sentiment here was much the same as Seyssel's and the medieval legal tradition that preceded him. He claimed that the king's true powers came from his limitations. Bodin's major innovation was simply to reground this traditional doctrine upon universal history rather than the principles of Roman or customary law.

In the last part of this chapter, Bodin discussed the relative merits of the three forms of regimes: democracy, aristocracy, and monarchy. Democracy ran counter to the natural hierarchy of "commanding and obeying, servants and lords, powerful and needy, good and wicked, strong and weak" (M, 268). It was therefore a source of instability and disorder (M, 269). Bodin raised a similar objection against aristocracy. This form of government also violated the order of nature and God, which favored the "rule of one" in all things. It, too, was therefore subject to rebellions and wars (M, 271–79). Only monarchy was consistent with the divine and natural orders. All the most durable states throughout history were monarchies, Bodin argued, and even the people of America who took nature as their guide lived under monarchical governments. He summarized his position in this way:

> Now, since the royal power is natural, that is, instituted by God, the father of nature, chosen in a remarkable decision by the Magi, praised by Homer, Xenophon, Aristotle, Plutarch, Dio, Apollonius, Jerome, and Cyprian, later established by Augustus after serious discussions with Maecenas and Agrippa, and, lastly, approved by the unanimous agreement of all peoples, or of those best known to fame, and by a lasting experience—what more must be said about the best form of state? (M, 282)

Bodin's comparative study of universal history thus demonstrated that limited monarchy was the best kind of government. It was the most stable and durable form of regime throughout history and the one most consistent with the principles of divine and natural law.

The Transition from the *Methodus* to the *République*

Bodin's arguments in the *République* contrast sharply with his conclusions from the *Methodus*. In the *République,* Bodin defined sovereignty as the "absolute and perpetual power of a republic" (R, 122).[63] It was "not limited either in power, or in function, or in length of time" (R, 124). Rather, the sovereign prince stood above all positive and customary laws and possessed the power to change the laws at will. Indeed, Bodin asserted that "the power to give law to all in general and to each in particular, and not to receive law from anyone but God" was the first and fundamental prerogative of a sovereign prince (R, 222).

Julian Franklin argued that Bodin outlined his theory of legislative sovereignty in response to the deteriorating political situation in France. No doubt political events did play an important part in stimulating the development of this theory. But contrary to Franklin's interpretation, Bodin did not merely impose this new theory upon the constitutional framework of the *Methodus*. He defined and legitimized it in terms of a new methodology. In the *République,* Bodin abandoned the core assumptions of his historical methodology from the *Methodus* and deduced the universal principles of order directly from the divine and natural laws.

Bodin's clearest statement of his methodological shift appears in his *Universae Naturae Theatrum,* written toward the end of his life (1596).[64] In the preface of this work, he reiterated his belief that "unless the science of laws . . . refers back to nature it will seem a science of injustice not of law"

(T, 2). He then noted that while scholars had been able to discover the universal principles underlying all the other arts and sciences, they had not been able to establish anything certain from the study of law. Human history had revealed itself to be nothing more than a record of fickleness, inconstancy, and variability. As a result, Bodin announced his dissatisfaction with his earlier legal and historical methodology:

> Accordingly, it is easy to understand why in all recorded ages, times, and cities, it has been impossible to establish the boundaries of this discipline [i.e., law], since it depends on human judgment and errors, so that some judge worthy of reward what others judge deserving of punishment. These considerations drew me back from making a compendium of laws, a selection of which I had gathered through long labor from almost all peoples' customs and institutions, comparing them one with another in order to establish something certain. For I realized that all edicts, decrees, and laws of people are rashly proposed according to the will and desire of human beings, unless they rely on the divine law, that is, the law of nature, to guide their blind steps like a shining thread through a labyrinth. (T, dedicatory letter, 2–3)[65]

Scholars have not paid much attention to this passage. In fact, they have only recently begun to scrutinize the *Theatrum* itself.[66] Yet this passage is extremely important for understanding Bodin's mature political thought, for here Bodin explicitly repudiated his early comparative and historical methodology. He announced that he drew back from making an arrangement of all laws and comparing them one with another once he realized that most laws were founded upon nothing more than human will and desire. In the *Methodus* Bodin had of course similarly declared that "human actions are incessantly involved in new errors unless they are guided by nature." But in that work, he still assumed that the study of human history pointed toward the universal principles of law. In the *Theatrum*, by contrast, he abandoned history and advised human beings to look directly to divine law and nature as their standard of order.[67]

> Indeed, we see innumerable testamentary laws and successionary rights introduced, repealed, substituted, superseded, or modified without reason, even though they are torn away at the root from the highest equity of divine law. But in nature nothing is uncertain. We see that fire burns among the Persians as it does among the Celts, snow is white everywhere, and the course of the celestial orbs have been fixed so that the laws that have existed from their origin always remain similar to themselves. For this reason we are warned by oracles and decrees and the voices of all the wise men to follow nature as a leader as if it were a sort of deity. (T, 3)[68]

The few scholars who have commented upon these passages have taken them as evidence that in the last years of his life Bodin became disgusted with political matters and retreated into the contemplation of nature and God.[69] But this interpretation seems mistaken for a number of reasons. In the dedication of the *Theatrum*, Bodin indicated that his book was intended to combat the disorder of the religious wars. He intended his study to point all parties beyond their factional differences toward a common understanding of the "Great God of nature."[70] In both the dedication and conclusion of this work, he further observed that his study of nature was written "when all of Gaul was aflame in a civil war," implying that the disorders of France were caused by the French people's failure to apply the laws of God and nature to political affairs.[71] In his letters and other writings of this period, Bodin likewise attributed the civil wars directly to the moral failings of the French people and their unwillingness to abide by divine and natural principles.[72] Far from representing a turn away from politics, it thus seems that the *Theatrum* signified a new approach to politics. In this work, Bodin abandoned his early humanistic studies of history and law and exhorted human beings to look directly to nature and divine law as the foundation of order.

While Bodin most clearly announced his new methodology in the *Theatrum,* there is evidence that he had developed his new approach somewhat earlier. Kenneth McRae has argued that one can detect Bodin's dissatisfaction with comparative legal and historical studies as early as 1586, with the publication of the Latin edition of his *République.*

> The young Bodin of the *Methodus* and *Distributio* appears to have expected his study of the laws and customs of all peoples to yield not only a universally valid scientific analysis of human society, but normative precepts as well, so that the study of *leges* would yield an ultimate *jus*. By the time that he wrote the Latin version of the *République* in the 1580s, there are more frequent comments on the variability of human behavior and values, as well as a recognition that the chasm between "is" and "ought" is unbridgeable.[73]

McRae supported this contention with textual evidence taken primarily from the added chapter of the Latin edition: "On the Orders and Degrees of Citizens." As in the *Theatrum,* Bodin argued here that human laws were the product of human judgment and error and revealed very little about natural right: "For the most part, we are led by the vain opinions and popular errors of men, of which both public and private laws consist."[74] He similarly noted that there were no definitions of nobility common to all peoples because honor and infamy were relative terms.[75] Significantly, he had argued in the *Methodus* that it was precisely this sort of knowledge that could be discerned from the study of history (M, 17). Bodin further observed there was no common agreement about which trades were noble or base, since "the diverse laws of people" defined them "most dissimilarly."[76] Even laws defining what was honest and dishonest, profitable and unprofitable, were not everywhere and always the same.[77] In a passage added to a later chapter, he asserted quite frankly that human laws bore no inherent relation to the principles of natural and divine law:

> Although [Seneca] was ignorant of divine laws, he was not unaware of those which we have extracted from nature herself. For if anyone should wish to open the folded tablets of his own mind, he would learn at once that a good man is he who assists whom he can, and injures no one unless provoked by injustice. These things are not included in the laws of any nation. Indeed we see many destructive and ruinous commands and prohibitions, which no more deserve the name of laws than if a madman decreed them by his own authority.[78]

In his earlier comparative studies, Bodin had assumed that the study of the laws of all people would reveal the universal principles of natural law. In his Latin *République,* by contrast, he asserted that many principles of divine and natural law were not included in the laws of any nation and that the laws of many nations were sheer madness. By 1586, some twenty years after writing the *Methodus,* Bodin had become skeptical about the existence of an underlying moral order within history.

McRae argued that Bodin's disillusionment with comparative history was a new development in the Latin edition of his *République.*[79] There is, however, evidence to suggest that Bodin reached this position even earlier than 1586. At several places in the original French edition of the *République,* Bodin made remarks indicating his more skeptical attitude toward comparative legal history. In discussing disobedience to the sovereign, for example, he declared that history was full of such a great diversity of laws that it was difficult to say what was universal and natural.

> The justice and reason that we call natural are not always so clear that they do not find detractors. Often the greatest jurisconsults find themselves stuck on this point, and hold entirely contrary opinions; and the laws of people are sometimes so repugnant to one another, that some give rewards and others punishments for the same acts. The books, laws, and histories are full of such things and recount them in great detail. (R, 416–17)

Bodin here admitted that it was difficult ever to know from the study of laws and histories what was natural and what was not, since people everywhere defined their laws in such diverse ways. He even stated in this passage the sentiment he later reiterated in the *Theatrum* when explaining his disillusionment with the methodology of his *Methodus:* "some give rewards and other punishments for the same acts."

Bodin expressed this opinion even more strongly in his discussion of slavery. In the *Methodus,* he had treated history as normative. He assumed that whatever had lasted for a long time and had been universally approved was natural and just. In discussing slavery in the French edition of the *République,* however, he explicitly rejected this assumption. Now he acknowledged that "ought" could never be derived from the study of history.

> As for that which is said about slavery, that it could not have lasted so long, if it had been against nature, this is true in natural things, which according to their [natural] property follow the immutable ordinance of God. But since God gave to human beings the choice between good and evil, it happens most often to the contrary, that they choose the worst against the law of God and nature. And this depraved opinion has so much power over human beings, that it passes as force of law, and has more authority than nature, so that there is no great impiety or wickedness that has not been esteemed and judged virtue and piety. (R, 51–52)

Bodin had clearly grown more dubious about historical studies in his *République.* Because of wickedness and free will, human beings perpetually instituted and reinstituted laws that were entirely contrary to the principles of divine and natural justice. This was true not only of slavery but of many other laws as well: "We know well that there is nothing more cruel nor more detestable than to sacrifice human beings. Nevertheless, there is hardly any people who has not done so, and all have covered this under the veil of piety for many centuries." After providing several other examples to prove this point, Bodin concluded: "This proves well that one must not measure the law of nature by the actions of human beings, even if they are inveterate; nor conclude that the servitude of slaves is of natural right." By the time he wrote the French *République,* Bodin no longer believed that "the best part of universal law lies hidden within history." Universal history, he had decided, was just as likely to reveal universal principles of human wickedness as of universal justice. Bodin had come to see the realm of human history as more completely detached from divine and natural history than he had previously believed.

There are other, less explicit indications in the French edition of the *République* of Bodin's dissatisfaction with his earlier historical methodology. In the *Methodus,* he had praised Machiavelli as the first individual to write intelligently about politics and history in "about 1,200 years" (M, 153). In the introduction to the *République,* by contrast, he condemned Machiavelli's political philosophy as contrary to all good politics. Such a radical about-face would seem to carry important implications for Bodin's methodology. For Bodin's methodology in the *Methodus* was quite similar to Machiavelli's. If, by the time he wrote the *République,* Bodin had come to conclude that Machiavelli's teachings were wicked and unjust, then what must he have concluded about his own historical methodology? History, it would seem, led one down the road to Machiavellian politics, divine wrath, and civil war.

While Bodin abandoned the strong historical claims of his *Methodus* in his *République,* it is important not to overstate the differences between these two works. In the *République,* Bodin continued to draw extensively upon his knowledge of the laws and history of different peoples. He continued, too, to employ his critical historical techniques to discern true from false reports. Where there was widespread agreement on some law, *and this law did not contradict the laws of God and nature,* Bodin further claimed that there should be a strong presumption in favor of its justice (R, 27). But the whole tenor of Bodin's later work was different. Bodin no longer regarded universal history as the normative source of right. Instead, he looked directly to the "law of God and of nature" (just as he did in the *Theatrum*) as his normative standard on all political matters. More specifically, he looked to the Old Testament and nature;[80] in the *République,* these took the place of universal history as the foundation of the universal principles of law and order.[81]

Bodin appealed to the Old Testament and nature throughout the *République,*[82] either directly or indirectly by logically deducing his arguments from them. Their central importance appears most clearly in Bodin's discussion of the fundamental principles of his political theory in the first book. Here he identified the family as the elemental unit of political societies. He claimed the proper structure and rights of the family, in turn, were dictated by nature and the Old Testament. Bodin argued, for example, that the power of the husband over the wife rested upon the authority of the Old Testament (R, 20, 27–28). So did the right of fathers to exercise the power of life and death over their children (R, 29–32). In fact, Bodin argued that governments should immediately restore the absolute power of punishment to fathers since its desuetude was at the root of much of the current social disorder: "It is necessary in a well-ordered republic to restore to fathers the power of life and death that the law of God and nature gives them . . . otherwise we must never hope to see the good mores, honor, virtue, and ancient splendor of republics restored" (R, 32). In his discussion of slavery, Bodin further designated the Old Testament as the authoritative source of right: "Since the divine laws and reason ought to take place always, and not be enclosed within the boundaries of Palestine, why should not that law so profitably and wisely made by God concerning slavery and liberty stand in force everywhere rather than that which human ingenuity has devised?"[83] Bodin here quite explicitly elevated the Old Testament above history as a normative source of universal right. He claimed the principles of the Old Testament ought to apply everywhere and always regardless of the laws that human beings had actually adopted. The central normative role of the Old Testament and nature in Bodin's theory of legislative sovereignty will be discussed in the next section.

Scholars have long recognized the shift in Bodin's views about sovereignty from the *Methodus* to the *République.*[84] Nonetheless, they have generally assumed a continuity in the methodologies of the two works. But Bodin changed both his views on sovereignty and his methology in the *République;* and the methodology of the *République* was in fact much closer to the *Theatrum* than the *Methodus.* Both the *République* and *Theatrum* identified nature and the Old Testament as the proper guides to moral behavior and good government.[85] Bodin used historical examples in his *République* primarily to elucidate his abstract definitions of natural and divine principles and to demonstrate their practical applicability to human affairs.[86] He alluded to this approach in his most explicit methodological statement in the *République*. Although all republics ought "to touch or at least to approach right government," he wrote, "nonetheless we also do not want to represent a republic as an idea without effect, such as Plato and Thomas More, the Chancellor of England, have imagined." Therefore, "we will be satisfied to follow [actual] political rules as much as possible" (R, 4). Historical data would serve to ground the principles of right government and to demonstrate their diverse applications. But the universal principles of right government would be directly deduced from divine and natural law.

From the foregoing, it may be concluded that two elements contributed to the development of the principle of legislative sovereignty: Bodin's theological voluntarism and his historical skepticism. His theological voluntarism inclined him to seek out the principles of universal right in what he regarded as a more contingent temporal universe. His historical skepticism drove him first to look to universal history and then beyond history altogether to discern these universal principles. But, then what provoked Bodin to grow more skeptical and abandon his earlier historical methodology in the *République*? The religious and civil wars certainly played some part. In the *Methodus*, Bodin identified the French constitution as an example of a best and most durable form of constitution within history (M, 259). As the French state descended into chaos, he may have lost confidence in his historical methodology. If even the best constitution within history was susceptible to corruption and chaos, then perhaps history was not such a reliable guide to order. Bodin may also have been discouraged by the difficulty of integrating all the laws of different peoples into one universal framework. He admitted in the introduction of his *Methodus* that his comparative studies were still incomplete. He had not yet had time to study and compare the laws of the people of Israel, Spain, Britain, Turkey, Italy, Germany, the Parlement of Paris, and the imperial court (M, 3–4). Once he had the opportunity to study these laws, he may have realized that history was more diverse and arbitrary than he had previously imagined. His greater knowledge of history may have increased his sensitivity to the relativity of human laws.

But probably the most important event in the development of Bodin's new methodology was a prophetic revelation he experienced sometime around 1567–68.[87] Bodin described this revelation in the opening pages of his *Démonomanie*. Although he attributed this event to an anonymous friend, his vivid and detailed description of the event as well as the similarity between his "friend's" beliefs and his own mature religious views suggest that he was actually recounting an autobiographical experience. After first observing that there were numerous examples in Scripture where God spoke to individuals through his angels, Bodin recounted his own story:

I can assure you that I have heard from a person, who still lives, that there was a spirit who was constantly near him, and he began to be familiar with him when he was about thirty-seven years old, although the person told me that he thought that his whole life the spirit had accompanied him, telling him by previous dreams and visions which he had had, to keep from vices and improper things. Nevertheless he had never noticed him in a perceptible way, as he did after he was thirty-seven years of age. This happened to him, as he said, having for one year before continued to pray to God with all his heart morning and evening, until it should please Him to send His good angel to guide him in all his actions. . . . Later he began, as he told me, to have dreams and visions full of instruction, sometimes to correct one vice, sometimes another, sometimes to keep away from a danger, sometimes to be freed from a difficulty, *then another dream not only of things divine, but human as well.* And among other things he seemed to have heard the voice of God while he slept, who said to him, "I will save your soul. It is I who have appeared to you before your eyes."[88]

If indeed this is an autobiographical description of Bodin's own revelation, it would go a long way toward explaining his shift to a methodology based upon the Old Testament and nature in the *République*. Bodin turned thirty-seven in 1566 or 1567, soon after completing the *Methodus*. Blessed with prophetic insight, he may have decided that he no longer needed history to determine the principles of divine and natural law: they were there for him to behold in the Bible and nature (and his dreams). It was his part merely to reveal them to the world. Bodin may have fancied himself quite literally to be the prophet of the modern sovereign state.[89]

THE PHILOSOPHICAL FOUNDATIONS OF LEGISLATIVE SOVEREIGNTY

In chapter 1 we saw that Montaigne initiated an intellectual break from the classical humanist tradition by emphasizing the radical contingency of human affairs and looking to nature rather than history as a foundation of order. In the *République,* Bodin similarly broke from his own humanist past. Rejecting the historical methodology of his *Methodus,* he set out a new political framework based upon nature and divine law. He argued that human history was too contingent and diverse to yield any universal principles of law and order. There were, of course, important differences between Montaigne and Bodin. Bodin defined nature in a more moralistic and religious sense than Montaigne and also demanded more fervently that human beings follow the principles of divine and natural law. These differences are most succinctly captured in these thinkers' different attitudes toward witches. Whereas Montaigne declared that all the so-called witches he had ever met seemed more insane than criminal,[90] Bodin claimed that witches not only existed but also posed a serious threat to the moral purity and stability of the political community. These differences are key to explaining why Bodin provided a fuller account (as opposed to Montaigne's only tentative one) of modern state theory. Bodin argued that the state was a divine and natural institution ordained for the purpose of establishing a universal order consistent with the will of God. He zealously believed in the power of the state to restore human beings to a universal political and moral order.

Some years back, J. W. Allen asserted that one can eliminate all references to God from the *République* "and the whole structure will stand unaltered."[91] Most scholars have tacitly endorsed this position. Yet, just the opposite is true. The whole argument of the *République* is structured around Bodin's theology. Take away all references to God and the whole structure collapses. The divine and natural orientation of Bodin's argument is evident from the very first sentence: "A republic is a right government of many families, and of that which is common to them, with a sovereign power" (R, 1). By right government, Bodin explained that he meant a state organized "according to the laws of nature" and directed toward the contemplation of God (R, 4–10). Nature, he next asserted, was organized according to a strict order of command and obedience (R, 19; see also R, iv). God ruled over the universe, reason ruled over the passions, and the soul ruled over the body. Fathers and husbands were the absolute lords of their families. A similar order of command and obedience was necessary to maintain order in political societies. The sovereign prince was the "pivot" or hinge that bound society together—"the sole union and liaison between families, corporations, colleges, and all individuals" (R, 14). The sovereign prince was at the same time the "image of God" and the "father of the people" (R, 11–12). He was the supreme will that imposed and sustained political order within the contingent realm of human affairs.

While Bodin had intimated some of these ideas in his *Methodus*, he had still looked to history to find the principles of universal law. In the *République*, by contrast, he declared that sovereignty was itself a principle of divine and natural law:

> Since there is nothing greater on earth after God than sovereign princes, and since they have been established by him as his lieutenants for commanding other men . . . whoever despises his sovereign prince also despises God, of whom he is the earthly image. That is why God, speaking to Samuel, from whom the people had demanded a different prince, said, "It is me that they have wronged." (R, 211–12)

Bodin made no statement of this sort in any of his earlier writings. In the *Methodus*, he had declared only that monarchical regimes were more consistent with the divine and natural order than democracy and aristocracy (M, 282). But in the *République*, he asserted that sovereignty was directly ordained by God:

Thus we read that the most holy people who ever were among the Hebrews, who were called the Essoi, that is, the true executors of the law of God, held that the sovereign princes, whosoever they were, ought to be inviolable to their subjects, as sacred and sent by God. One also doubts not but that the king and prophet David had the spirit of God, if ever a man did, when he had before his eyes the law of God, which says: "Thou shall not speak evil of your prince, nor detract at all from the magistrates." (R, 304–5)

Bodin's argument marked an important turning point in divine right theory. While writers had previously asserted the divine ordination of kings, they had balanced their claims with the assertion that the customs, hierarchy, and laws of society were also part of the divine and natural order. From their perspective, the monarchical office was only one node of divine order among many within society. Bodin made the sovereign office virtually the only point of divine and natural order within society. He claimed the customs, hierarchy, and laws of society were groundless in themselves and recentered all legitimate order in the institution of the state. To disobey the sovereign prince, Bodin claimed, was to disobey God himself. The sovereign prince was divinely and naturally ordained to impose a divine and natural order upon society. Should there be any confusion about the locus of sovereign power or any division of the sovereign power, the whole social hierarchy would collapse into chaos and confusion (R, 145, 267).

Since the sovereign prince was the divine and natural foundation of order within society, Bodin suggested that his powers should be modeled after those of God.[92] Just as God was the omnipotent and eternal source of order within the universe, "sovereignty is the absolute and perpetual power of a commonwealth" (R, 122). The sovereign prince played the same role in sustaining order within the commonwealth that God played in sustaining order throughout the universe. Any limitation "either in power, or function, or length of time" of the sovereign prince's powers was illogical and dangerous (R, 124). The sovereign prince was, of course, still subject to the laws of God and nature (R, 133). But in relation to other human beings and institutions, he assumed a transcendent status. "Sovereignty (that is to say, someone who is above all subjects) cannot apply to someone who has made a subject his companion. Just as the great sovereign God cannot make a God parallel to himself, because he is infinite and by logical necessity there cannot be two infinite things, so we can say that the prince whom we have posited as the image of God, cannot make a subject equal to himself without annihilating his power" (R, 215). The sovereign prince was he "who recognizes nothing, after God, that is greater than himself," and was "answerable only to God" (R, 124). He was the great god of politics located directly under the Great God of Nature and responsible for sustaining the social order.

The central prerogative of the sovereign ruler was absolute legislative authority. Bodin argued that the law-making authority was a logical deduction from the natural order of command and obedience.

> Persons who are sovereign must not be subject in any way to the commands of someone else and must be able to give the law to subjects, and to suppress or repeal disadvantageous laws and replace them with others—which cannot be done by someone who is subject to the laws or to persons having power of command over him. This is why the [Roman] law says that the prince is not subject to the law; and in fact the very word "law" in Latin implies the command of him who has the sovereignty. (R, 131)

Breaking from his earlier position, Bodin now asserted that the sovereign prince could not logically or effectively be placed beneath the laws. He even directly refuted his earlier endorsement of coronation oaths. "The prince who swears to maintain the civil laws either is not sovereign, or else becomes a perjurer if he contravenes his oath, as is necessary for the sovereign prince to do to annul or change or correct the laws according to the exigencies of the cases, times, and persons" (R, 145). In this statement, Bodin perfectly conveyed his new understanding of sovereignty. The sovereign prince was poised between the abstract and unchanging principles of divine and natural law and the diverse and changing world of human affairs. The foundation of order was the divinely ordained system of universal moral principles. But these principles had to be adapted to the contingent and changing temporal world.[93] Every society and time period required new and unique precepts. God thus ordained sovereign rulers to translate his universal moral principles into concrete laws suitable for diverse times and people. Medieval theorists such as St. Thomas Aquinas had similarly argued that one of the prince's prerogatives was to make specific applications of the principles of natural law.[94] But Aquinas had limited the prince's law-making power by acknowledging the presence of other natural points of order (for example, the great chain of being) within human society. Bodin's sovereign, by contrast, stood out as the transcendent source of divine and natural order within the corrupt and orderless world of human affairs. He was free to make or change the laws at will because there was no inherent order within human history to restrain him. Indeed, without his laws, there was no order.

From this argument Bodin further asserted that the sovereign prince had to possess all significant powers within society. Any power contrary to his own might impede his ability to impose laws upon the people and hence open the door to disorder (R, 266):

> Under this same power of making and repealing law are comprised all the other rights and prerogatives of sovereignty, so that strictly speaking we can say that there is only this one prerogative of sovereignty, inasmuch as all the other rights are comprehended in it—such as declaring war or making peace; hearing

appeals in the last instance from the judgments of any magistrate; instituting and removing the highest officers; imposing taxes and aids on subjects or exempting them; granting pardons and dispensations against the rigor of the law; determining the name, value, and measure of coinage; requiring subjects and liege vassals to swear that they will be loyal without exception to the person to whom their oath is owed. (R, 223–24)

Julian Franklin argued that Bodin was confused in asserting that sovereignty was by nature absolute and indivisible.[95] Numerous examples from premodern and modern societies demonstrate that the sovereign powers can be successfully divided and mixed. But given Bodin's cosmological premises, his conclusion appears inescapable. He argued that political order depended upon conformity to the divine and natural law. The divine and natural law mandated a clear hierarchy of command and obedience, culminating in the sovereign prince. The sovereign prince therefore had to possess absolute and indivisible power over society. Any disruption of this order was contrary to divine law and nature and bound to promote disorder and decay.

In his legislative capacity, the sovereign prince was authorized to make, change, and annul the laws for his people. Although he was still subject to the divine and natural laws, Bodin claimed that, with only a few exceptions (discussed below), the sovereign prince was free to interpret the divine and natural laws as he saw fit. When seen in this light, Bodin's theory of legislative sovereignty appears more revolutionary than Kenneth Pennington recognized. Even though Bodin continued to assert in the manner of medieval jurists that the prince was subject to the divine and natural laws, he now conflated the sovereign prince's authority with these higher laws. In most cases, he claimed the divine and natural laws did not impose any substantive limits on the sovereign prince's power, but actually justified his right to decree whatever he considered necessary and just.[96]

Bodin boldly asserted this point in explaining why sovereign rulers were not subject to their own laws. After first claiming that sovereign princes were free to change the laws at will, he raised a possible objection to his argument: "if the prince is bound to the laws of nature, and the civil laws are equitable and reasonable, it follows that princes are also bound to the civil laws" (R, 150). Bodin's point may be restated this way: If princes were subject to the natural law, and their own civil laws reflected the natural law (as they always ought to do), then why were princes not subject to their own laws? Bodin responded by explaining that the natural law consisted of various elements, including profit, honor, and justice. Since these elements could be combined in various ways, and "admit of degrees of more and less," the sovereign had considerable discretion within the bounds of the higher laws for making and annulling positive laws.[97] He could create new laws, abrogate old laws, or replace one law with another without ever departing from the natural law. In the final analysis, the sovereign's will alone gave form to the abstract principles of natural law. "The laws of a sovereign prince, although founded upon good and lively reasons, depend nevertheless only upon his mere and frank will" (R, 133).

A direct correlate of this argument was that the subjects were obliged to obey the sovereign prince's laws in nearly all cases as if they were themselves divine and natural laws. This may be considered Bodin's most direct response to the arguments of the Huguenot resistance theorists.[98] The Huguenots maintained, like Bodin, that government ought to be grounded upon the principles of divine and natural law. Based upon this premise, they further asserted that the people were justified in disobeying civil laws when they were contrary to the divine and natural laws. Bodin, too, admitted this point. But he reminded his readers that the principles of divine and natural law were not always very clear. Different societies had adopted wildly different laws throughout history. Even the most wise jurists and philosophers often disagreed about the true nature of justice: "some give rewards and others punishments for the same acts" (R, 416–17). Barring an egregious and obvious transgression of the divine and natural law (as, for example, when a prince ordered his subjects to murder all the priests in cold blood), Bodin therefore concluded that the sovereign prince's laws should be accepted as valid interpretations of the divine and natural laws. "It is a natural and divine law to obey the edicts and ordinances of him who God has given power over us, unless the edicts are directly contrary to the law of God, who is above all princes" (R, 152; see also R, 416–17). Bodin expanded upon this point in the Latin edition of the *République.*

> We often see the citizens take up arms against their prince, the laws violated, and all justice go to ruin, and why so? Because the magistrates themselves are the authors of the failure, due to their false opinion on law and justice. They say, "But the law is unfair; we cannot, we should not obey!" That is indeed an honorable speech, if you cannot. But where did you learn that you ought not? From where have you taken that doctrine? Will you force private individuals to obey your unjust commands with flogging, imprisonment, fines, and with death itself, and yet not obey the commandments of your prince? But you deny your own commands to be unjust: so does the prince deny what he commanded to be unjust. Is it you who will be the judge? Or if you will be judge, why would you think that the same should not be done with regard to your edicts for private citizens?[99]

Subjects and magistrates could rightfully appeal to the prince to try to persuade him to change his laws. However, if the prince reasserted his laws, the magistrates were obliged to enforce them and the subjects to obey them. In nearly all cases, it was a far greater violation of divine and natural law to disobey the will of the prince and disrupt the civil order than it was to obey any of the prince's more questionable decrees. The principle of legislative sovereignty was one of the few certain deductions from the divine and natural law. It therefore trumped almost all other opinions about right and wrong.

The revolutionary nature of Bodin's teaching concerning sovereignty comes out most clearly in his discussion of the *jus gentium*. Medieval jurists considered the *jus gentium,* or law of nations, to be a transcendent legal norm nearly equivalent to the divine and natural laws.[100] Bodin, too, sometimes recognized the moral authority of the law of nations. But in his most explicit statement on the subject, he asserted that the authority of the law of nations ultimately depended upon the will of the sovereign prince. Bodin laid out this opinion in his discussion of contracts. After making a number of distinctions differentiating cases where the sovereign was or was not obliged to honor his contracts, he once again raised a hypothetical objection to his views: "But, someone will say, why must we make such distinctions, since all princes are obliged to honor the law of nations, and contracts and testaments are founded on it?" (R, 161) Bodin's question here was important because it pointed to the larger question of the source of universal right among human beings. If universal right were located in the law of nations, then there would be no question about whether the prince were obliged to honor his contracts—that law decreed that princes were so obliged in nearly all cases. However, Bodin explained that in many matters the law of nations was not in clear conformity with the principles of divine and natural right. Then the sovereign prince was responsible for deciding whether or not to follow this law. By divine and natural law, he was the rightful source of moral order within the community. He wielded the final authority in interpreting the precepts of divine and natural law for his subjects:

> I say nonetheless that these distinctions are necessary because a prince is no more obliged by the law of nations than by his own edicts; and if the law of nations is unjust, the prince can depart from it in the edicts he makes for his kingdom, and forbid his subjects from using it. That is how the law of slavery was handled in this kingdom, even though it was common to all peoples. And this can also be done in other similar matters, provided that the result is not contrary to the law of God. For if justice is the end of the law, the law the work of the prince, and the prince the image of God, then it follows from this reasoning that the law of the prince should be modeled on the law of God. (R, 161)

Bodin here lucidly laid out the philosophical foundations of his theory of sovereignty. The sovereign prince was the "image of God" responsible for manifesting "the law of God" in his own state. It was his prerogative to determine what was consistent with divine law and what was not within his jurisdiction and to depart from the *jus gentium* whenever he saw fit.[101]

Bodin did recognize some limits on the powers of the sovereign authority. Above all, he insisted that the sovereign ruler was subject to the divine and natural laws. Scholars who have overlooked the theological dimension of Bodin's theory have sometimes been perplexed by this limitation.[102] If Bodin considered sovereignty to be absolute, how could he also claim it was limited by the divine and natural laws? This question reveals a fundamental misunderstanding of Bodin's theory of sovereignty. Bodin argued that legislative sovereignty was *itself* a principle of divine and natural law— its purpose was to impose a divine and natural order upon human beings. Of course, then, the sovereign prince was subject to the divine and natural laws; to disregard them would be to disregard the very source and purpose of his power. It would bring down God's wrath down upon society.

While the sovereign prince generally had wide discretion in defining the precise terms of the divine and natural laws, there were a few items that were not open to interpretation.[103] Although the law of God permitted the sovereign prince wide latitude in defining the particular punishments for most crimes, for example, he was strictly obliged to execute premeditative murderers since the law of God explicitly specified this punishment (R, 246). He was likewise bound to obey his just contracts and treaties since the divine and natural laws also explicitly decreed this principle (R, 150, 153). Most importantly, Bodin argued that the sovereign ruler could not take the private property of his subjects or impose taxes upon them without their consent. The Decalogue "expressly forbids us to steal, or even to covet another's goods" (R, 15). Moreover, sovereign rulers were "appointed by God" to render in common that which was common but to leave "to each in private that which is his" (R, 15). Since, then, sovereign rulers were subject to the laws of God and nature, and God "has pronounced loudly and clearly by his law that it is illicit to take, or even to covet, another person's goods . . . the prince can neither take nor dispose of another's property without the consent of its owner" (R, 156–57). Private property was an inalienable divine and natural right. Although Bodin's immediate successors abandoned this right, John Locke resurrected it toward the end of the next century. The twin principles of legislative sovereignty and inalienable natural rights, in turn, provided the basic premises for much of the later development of liberal state theory.

In addition to these divine and natural laws, Bodin argued that the French monarch was also subject to the two fundamental laws of France: the Salic law delineating the proper succession of the throne, and the law prohibiting alienation of the royal domain (R, 137, 160, 859–60). These limitations on the king's powers were unique in that they were not properly divine and natural laws but particular to the French monarchy. Bodin nonetheless argued that they were obligatory on the grounds that they reflected principles of divine and natural justice. By ensuring the regular succession of the royal power, the Salic law ensured the peaceful and instantaneous transfer of sovereign power from one ruler to the next. It thus preserved the order of command and obedience within the state and extended the king's perpetuity beyond the life of any individual officeholder.[104] By excluding women from the throne, the Salic law further preserved the "divine" and "natural" dominance of men over women within the French government. The law of nonalienation ensured that future kings of France would have sufficient resources to govern the kingdom. In this way, it helped to guarantee the perpetual existence of the monarchy while protecting the people against exorbitant and unlawful taxes.

The theological aims of Bodin's theory of sovereignty are most evident in the prudential advice he offered the sovereign prince in the later books of the *République*. Repeatedly he urged the sovereign prince to organize society upon the model of the divine and natural cosmos—to institute, so to speak, a miniature political universe among his people reflecting the universal order of God.[105] Just as "God the supreme artisan and parent of this universe did nothing greater or better than separating the confused and mixed parts of the rough material and putting each in its own position in a sure order," so the sovereign prince should "take pains to organize the citizens in a fitting and appropriate arrangement in the commonwealth so that the first citizens will be bound to the last, the middle citizens to both of these, and all citizens to all citizens through some connection and bond among themselves and with the commonwealth."[106] In other words, the prince was to impose his own chain of being upon the citizens. In discussing "Whether it is expedient for officers of a state to be in accord with one another," Bodin added that the sovereign prince should organize his officers into a pleasant discord (at least in a monarchy) since this was how God ruled the universe:

> Just as God maintains the contrariety of celestial movements, and of elements, sympathies, and antipathies, in a discordant accord, as of contrary voices in a very pleasant and sweet harmony, keeping the one element from oppressing the other, so the prince, who is the image of God, ought to preserve and rule the quarrels and differences of his magistrates, so that they remain somewhat contrary but their enmity redounds to the health of the republic. (R, 608)

Bodin brought these arguments to a climax in his final chapter on justice—a chapter that Michel Villey judged to be "the quintessence, the key of the entire work."[107] While there were three types of justice in the universe—arithmetic, geometric, and harmonic—Bodin claimed that God ruled the universe with harmonic justice, which consisted of a combination of the other two forms of justice. The sovereign prince ought to govern his people in a similar way. He should distribute rewards and offices not strictly according to a system of equal or proportional justice, but by finding a harmonic mean between the two: "As the great eternal King, unique, pure, simple, indivisible, and elevated above the elemental, celestial, and intelligible worlds unites the three together, making shine the splendor of his majesty and sweetness of divine harmony throughout the world, so the wise king ought to conform and govern his kingdom after the divine example" (R, 1060). Since human affairs were devoid of inherent divine and natural order, Bodin suggested that the sovereign ruler should take the place of God in ordering and sustaining them. He should impose the same harmony and moral order upon his people that God imposed upon the universe at large. It was his responsibility to institute a universal political community within a realm of human affairs that had fallen away from the order of God and nature.

One exception to Bodin's theological politics would seem to be his famous *Colloquium Heptaplomeres de Rerum Sublimium Arcanis Abditis (Colloquium of the Seven about Secrets of the Sublime)*, written toward the end of his life. In this dialogue, Bodin presented a discussion among seven men representing seven different religious and philosophical positions (Catholic, Lutheran, Calvinist, Jewish, Islamic, naturalist, and skeptic). At the end of the dialogue, the seven amicably agree to disagree about their religious and philosophical differences and vow never to discuss such matters again. Scholars have quite understandably seen this dialogue as an important early defense of religious toleration. But there is a sense in which the *Colloquium* is not really a tolerant work at all. In the course of the dialogue, all the interlocutors agree to certain fundamental religious principles such as the existence of God and the sanctity of the natural laws. Bodin saw these principles as the essence of the true religion.[108] Alternatively, the speakers agree that certain beliefs can never be tolerated within any state. One is witchcraft and the other is atheism: "However great superstition may be, it is more tolerable than atheism. For the one who is bound by some superstition is kept by this awe of the divine in a certain way within the bounds of duty and of the laws of nature. The atheist, on the other hand, who fears nothing except a witness or a judge, necessarily rushes headlong toward every crime" (C, 239). While Bodin's *Colloquium* did advocate toleration for a great number of different religions, it was thus at base not a tolerant work. Bodin still held to the theocratic ideal that the prince ought to enforce the true religion within his state. He merely defined the true religion in a more expansive or broadly encompassing sense. The persecution of witches and atheists remained an integral part of his state theory to the end.

CONCLUSION

W. H. Greenleaf argued that Bodin organized his state theory around a traditional medieval theory of order.[109] On the surface, this observation is true. Bodin defined and justified his state theory in terms of a moral conception of nature that resembled the medieval idea of the great chain of being. But Bodin's worldview was significantly different from the traditional medieval cosmology. While most medieval theorists assumed the chain of being was inherent in nature (and many even argued that God was ordinarily subject to it), Bodin argued that God imposed the chain of being upon nature and maintained each and every link of it at every moment. He further claimed that God had delegated to the sovereign authority the responsibility for imposing a divine and natural order upon human affairs. Bodin's whole vision of order thus rested upon the idea of a voluntaristic God and legislative sovereign conjointly ruling over and bringing order to a contingent and orderless temporal realm.

Bodin's contemporaries immediately recognized the importance of his theory. Within France, his ideas were quickly adopted by Jean Duret, François Grimaudet, Pierre Grégoire, Pierre de Belloy, Jacques Hurault, François Le Jay, Louis Servin, Adam Blackwood, William Barclay, Charles Loyseau, and Cardin Le Bret.[110] In England, James I and Robert Filmer incorporated his theory of sovereignty directly into their political philosophies.[111] Most scholars have assumed that Bodin's successors distorted his theory by placing it within a divine right framework.[112] Undeniably, later writers did amend certain aspects of his theory. They began to emphasize the divine attributes of the sovereign office-holder, for example, by portraying the king as a supremely wise ruler without corruption or blemish. They likewise removed the restrictions upon the sovereign ruler's taxing powers.[113] But on balance, Bodin's immediate successors understood his theory of sovereignty better than most recent scholars. Modern scholars have been far too ready to see Bodin's theory of legislative sovereignty as a new secular principle of government. His numerous appeals to divine and natural law are taken merely as evidence that he had not yet fully broken away from medieval legal discourse.[114] Yet this interpretation misses the whole dynamic force of Bodin's theory. His theory of sovereignty was so successful precisely because it provided a new universal foundation of law and order based upon the old metaphysical principles of divine and natural law. He portrayed the sovereign prince as the new source of transcendent legal norms within a contingent and diverse temporal world.

Within a few generations, Bodin's theory of sovereignty was translated into more mundane terms. Hobbes and Locke, for example, who were both strongly influenced by Bodin, identified legislative sovereignty as the key ordering principle of politics, but transferred the grounds of legislative sovereignty from divine and natural law to popular consent. The sovereign authority was now said to possess the right to make and change the laws for the people because the people had consented to establish and obey it. Yet, the theory of popular consent never provided a sound justification for legislative sovereignty. As Rousseau pointed out, it makes no logical sense to suppose that a number of free and equal individuals would ever consent to be governed by a sovereign legislator with the power to make and change laws at will.[115] Such a social contract was tantamount to voluntary slavery. It made the people subject to the will of political representatives whose interests might very well diverge from their own. Contemporary theorists have developed this critique in more detail. A. John Simmons has proclaimed that "all existing states are illegitimate"[116] on the grounds that theories of popular consent, utilitarianism, fairness, justice and gratitude all fail to justify the powers of the legislative sovereign state.[117] The theory of popular consent, in particular, cannot even justify the more limited and lawbound theories of legislative sovereignty promulgated by liberal theorists. Very few individuals have ever expressly consented to the rule of the state. Theories of tacit consent, or consent through residence, undermine the very idea of voluntary agreement. They simply assume the consent of individuals to the state based upon their existence within its jurisdiction or their receipt of benefits without offering them meaningful opportunity to dissent. In short, legislative sovereignty is incongruous with popular consent. It is an alien power that has been placed upon the matrix of popular consent, utilitarianism, and other mundane theories of obligation and legitimacy.[118]

Bodin's philosophy helps to explain the roots of these problems concerning legislative sovereignty. Bodin proposed the principle of legislative sovereignty in order to provide a new universal foundation of politics amid the social and intellectual crises of the late sixteenth century. In a temporal world lacking immanent order, he designated the sovereign will as the highest source of social morality and order. He legitimized this principle through appeal to the divine and natural law, arguing that the divine and natural law identified the sovereign authority as the sole pivot of legitimate law and order. Modern liberal theorists integrated this principle into their state theories, but it was never very compatible with their more mundane approaches to state legitimacy. Indeed, when stripped of its divine and natural foundations, legislative sovereignty is a frightfully arbitrary concept. It posits nothing less than the idea that some individual or group should possess supreme authority to define morality and law for an entire society. It further assumes that all individuals within a society share an interest in being bound together into a universal and homogeneous whole. Yet the actual interests of most individuals would seem to point to something much less—and hence to a more limited governmental principle than legislative sovereignty. The desire for peace, security, and a regularly functioning social order do not necessarily entail the need for a supreme legislative authority. Medieval societies got along just fine without one. Legislative sovereignty was invented to reestablish a self-sufficient moral community aligned with the universal moral order within a contingent temporal world. Today it stands as an exalted power without a clear source of mundane legitimacy. It is the remnant of a divine theory of politics whose origins may be traced back to the prophetic writings of Jean Bodin.

CHAPTER THREE

Cardinal Richelieu and the
Birth of Modern Executive Power

*T*he principle of executive prerogative is the most important principle of modern state theory after legislative sovereignty. Whereas legislative sovereignty establishes the right of the legislative authority of the state to make or change the laws at will, executive prerogative establishes the right of the executive authority to contravene the laws and carry out actions, even immoral ones, for the public interest. Executive prerogative complements legislative sovereignty by addressing problems that fall outside the scope of the laws. It is most often invoked in foreign affairs but may also be applied to domestic affairs during times of crisis and emergencies.[1] It is at the heart of the modern theory of executive power, which rests upon the assumption that every well-constituted state should have a permanent executive authority responsible not only for enforcing the laws but also for exercising a discretionary power in defense of the laws and public interest.[2] Like the principle of legislative sovereignty, the modern doctrine of executive power is so familiar to us that we are wont to regard it as an essential or timeless principle of political order.[3] Yet it too was invented during the early modern period.

Ancient writers were of course familiar with political realism. But political realism is different from the idea of a permanent executive office with discretionary authority to act outside the laws and morality for reasons of state.[4] Medieval thinkers more clearly located executive power in a permanent monarchical office. But they almost universally agreed that executive power should be circumscribed within the limits of morality and law.[5] While they acknowledged that the king might depart from morality and law in extraordinary situations, they assumed these situations would arise only rarely and would be self-evident to everyone. In any case, they did not make executive prerogative central to their political theories.[6] They argued that the king could best serve the public good in almost all cases by acting according to the dictates of morality and law.

Machiavelli is usually credited with inventing modern executive power.[7] He was the first modern thinker to break away from the moral and legalistic framework of medieval Christian political thought. He shocked his contemporaries by suggesting that Christian morality might not always be conducive to political success, and that the prince should be prepared to enter into evil for the sake of maintaining *lo stato*. While Machiavelli's ideas clearly contributed to the development of modern executive power, they fell short of actually defining or legitimizing this principle. Machiavelli did not, for example, assert the right of any one designated official to make use of illegal and immoral methods; he offered his advice to princes and private citizens alike. Nor did he try to justify his immoral advice by linking it to the public good. He encouraged his prince to do whatever was necessary to maintain *lo stato* in the sense of his own power and possessions.[8] Perhaps most importantly, Machiavelli did almost nothing to try to legitimize his views within the dominant Christian paradigm. He openly admitted that his teachings were immoral and wicked when judged by traditional moral standards.[9] Not surprisingly, his vision of executive power thus remained on the fringes of political thought in early modern Europe and was more often criticized than praised.

The full doctrine of executive prerogative was invented a century after Machiavelli by a group of French *raison d'état* theorists led by Cardinal de Richelieu and including Jérémie Ferrier, Guez de Balzac, Jean de Silhon, Daniel de Priézac, Gabriel Naudé, and Henri, Duke de Rohan. These theorists argued that the king alone was justified in acting outside the laws and morality for the good of society. They further claimed the king's executive prerogative was a necessary complement to the laws in maintaining a just and moral social order. In this way, they demonstrated that executive prerogative was both moral and consistent with Christian teachings. They gave the Machiavellian prince, so to speak, a permanent office within the moral order of the state. They made executive prerogative a regular and legitimate element of modern state theory.

The development of modern executive power, or reason of state, has been the focus of several important studies. Maurizio Viroli traced the development of reason of state theory up to the late sixteenth century in Italy.[10] The present study complements and extends his work by examining the legitimization of reason of state theory among French writers during the early seventeenth century. Richard Tuck demonstrated the important influence of skepticism and neostoicism in the development of reason of state theory during the early seventeenth century.[11] This study builds upon his work but focuses more narrowly on the ideological arguments of French reason of state theorists themselves. Friedrich Meinecke argued that reason of state developed in close connection with modern historical thinking and hence introduced an important new secular element into political thought.[12] By contrast, W. F. Church observed that French reason of state literature is pervaded by apparently sincere appeals to religion and justice and concluded that reason of state was originally formulated as a Christian political theory.[13] The weakness of Meinecke's and Church's interpretations is that each overemphasizes one aspect of reason of state theory to the partial exclusion of the other. Meinecke is correct to emphasize reason of state's connection with modern historical thinking; Church is correct to emphasize its sacred elements. Yet reason of state did not emerge as a wholly sacred or secular doctrine but occupied an ambiguous space between the sacred and the secular, the eternal and the temporal. As with the theory of legislative sovereignty, French thinkers set out the theory of reason of state to mediate between universal moral values and the changeable and particular world of human affairs. They argued that the prince should be endowed with executive prerogative so that he could preserve and protect the sacred political order from the turbulence and contingency of the temporal world.

In *Taming the Prince,* Harvey Mansfield examined the theoretical development of modern executive power in order to understand more clearly the nature of this concept. Modern executive power is both weak and strong, subordinate and superior to the laws, he claimed, because it emerged through an attempt to place the strong Machiavellian prince within the legal framework of the liberal state. In his preface, Mansfield wrote: "How else but amazing could one describe the acceptance of, or rather the enthusiasm for, so much one-man rule, which is what we call executive power in our modern democracies? . . . Someone has sold us on the idea so well that we are no longer aware of the marketing effort."[14] In outlining the development of executive power, however, Mansfield jumped from Machiavelli to Hobbes. He thus overlooked the intensive "marketing effort" carried out by Richelieu and his followers to make executive prerogative respectable. French *raison d'état* theorists first conceptualized modern executive power as a legitimate and necessary public office. By studying these theorists' ideas, we may come to appreciate more fully the peculiar nature of the modern executive.

RICHELIEU AND EXECUTIVE PREROGATIVE

"Machiavelli's theory was a sword which was plunged into the flank of the body politic of Western humanity causing it to shriek and rear up," Friedrich Meinecke wrote. "This was bound to happen; for not only had genuine moral feeling been seriously wounded, but death had also been threatened to the Christian views of all churches and sects."[15] Machiavelli had suggested that Christian morality was opposed to political effectiveness—that one could not be at the same time both an honest Christian and a good statesman. The good statesman had to be prepared to abandon Christian values whenever necessary for his own gain.

While Machiavelli may have struck a hard blow against Christian politics, however, he did not bring them down. Within a few years the Christians were striking back. In his *Discours contre Machiavel* (1576), Innocent Gentillet condemned Machiavelli's teachings as both immoral and ineffectual. He warned that Machiavelli's irreligious maxims were likely to draw God's wrath down upon the state and result in political failure and defeat.[16] In his *Six livres de la république,* Bodin asserted a similar view. He blamed Machiavelli for corrupting political discourse and inciting civil disorder within France. He concluded that Machiavelli's political teachings were ineffective and tyrannical.[17] Yet Machiavelli's ideas were not so easily dismissed. By the late sixteenth century, political thinkers were regularly commenting upon the contingency and variability of affairs. It was no longer clear to many writers that justice and morality alone were sufficient for maintaining order. Statesmen increasingly found themselves confronted with an apparent conflict between the demands of practical politics and Christian morality.[18]

The solution was found in the development of a "good reason of state theory."[19] Writers began to outline a political theory that would allow princes to meet the demands of political necessity while at the same time respecting the principles of Christian morality and justice. The seminal work in this tradition was Giovanni Botero's *Ragion di stato* (1589). Botero denounced the "impious" and "wicked" teachings of Machiavelli and Tacitus and declared his intention to outline a Catholic reason of state theory.[20] He proceeded to demonstrate the effectiveness of the Christian principles of liberality, piety, and justice in political affairs, while showing that immoral practices such as cruelty and impiety tended to undermine a prince's power. Yet he added that the prince ought not to be naive about the need for fear, dissimulation, distrust, and other vices in politics. "Since in this world nothing can come into being without corruption," he wrote, "so every good act carries some evil with it."[21] Botero thus recognized that some evil was necessary in politics. But how much? And when? In the end, Botero never very clearly answered these questions. His book contained a mixture of moral arguments and concessions to immorality without drawing any clear line between them. Critics concluded that Botero himself had become tainted with Machiavellianism in the process of trying to refute it.[22]

More cogent theoretically were the theories of writers such as Justus Lipsius, Girolamo Frachetta, Pedro de Ribadeneyra and Tommaso Campanella.[23] While all of these writers acknowledged that a prince might make use of some lesser forms of evil for the preservation of the social order, they maintained that he was obliged to restrain his actions within the limits of certain moral and religious principles. In his *Six Books of Politics* (1589), for example, Lipsius argued that the prince might legitimately engage in light and medium forms of deceit such as practicing dissimulation or bribing the courtiers of foreign courts.[24] But he claimed that moral law strictly forbade princes from practicing great deceits that involved outright treachery.[25] Frachetta similarly argued that although princes might make use of some expedients for the public good, they were always obliged to bow before the limits of justice and religion: "Princes should use reason of state in such manner that it conforms to divine and human laws, that is, [is] subordinate to justice and religion, and not otherwise."[26] In Spain, Ribadeneyra wrote that although a prince might exercise some moral flexibility in governing the state, he was obliged to "risk all the states, kingdoms, lordships, and possessions he had in this world" rather than to overstep God's law.[27] A variant of these ideas was developed by Tommaso Campanella. He tied good reason of state to the ends of Catholic universalism. Specifically, he argued that the prince was free from the normal strictures of law and morality insofar as his actions contributed to the end of establishing a universal Catholic monarchy.[28] By the early seventeenth century, Christian thinkers had thus gone a good way toward legitimizing certain forms of political immorality. But they still circumscribed legitimate executive action within the limits of substantive moral precepts and harnessed it to the interests of Catholic universalism. No one had yet dared to assert the morality of unrestrained executive action performed in service of national politics.

This project was taken up by Armand Jean du Plessis, the Cardinal de Richelieu (1585–1642).[29] When Richelieu assumed the position of chief minister of France in 1624, the French court was dominated by the *dévots* party. The *dévots* advocated an approach to statecraft similar to that of the counter-Reformation theorists such as Lipsius, Frachetta, Ribadeneyra and Campanella.[30] While they acknowledged that the king might exercise some moral latitude in statecraft, they maintained that he was nonetheless constrained to act within the substantive limits of divine law and to promote the Catholic cause at home and abroad. Richelieu, by contrast, supported a dramatically different set of policies. He favored war against the Catholic Hapsburgs, alliances with Protestant powers, and a free hand for the king in all matters relating to the "interests of state." The *dévots* took these policies as proof that Richelieu was a "Machiavellian" statesman unconcerned with morality and justice—a label that has clung to the cardinal into contemporary times. But Richelieu and his supporters portrayed these policies in a very different light.[31] Indeed, Richelieu orchestrated a vast propaganda campaign to explain and justify royal policies to the reading public.[32] In the various pamphlets and books written under his supervision, he aimed at nothing less than a radical reformulation of the legitimate scope of executive power. He and his supporters argued that the king's apparently wicked and irreligious actions were actually a manifestation of a higher form of morality necessary for the preservation of the political community. They organized their arguments around three important points: (1) that the king's discretionary powers were mandated and directly inspired by God; (2) that the political community was a moral entity whose existence was to be preserved at almost any cost; and (3) that human and temporal affairs were disorderly and corrupt and posed a constant threat to the integrity of the political community. Through these arguments, Richelieu and his propagandists established the moral legitimacy of the prudential executive ruler. They transferred the grounds of political morality from a set of substantive moral values and universal ends to the action of the state itself.

One of the first attempts to articulate this new reason of state theory was the *Catholique d'estat* (1625). The main author of this work was the converted Protestant minister Jérémie Ferrier. But a number of other individuals probably had a hand in its composition, including Father Joseph, Pierre de Bérulle, and perhaps Richelieu himself.[33] The occasion of this work was the French invasion of the Valtelline valley in 1624. The Valtelline valley, located in southeast Switzerland, was a vital communication link between the Spanish and Austrian Hapsburgs. In late 1623, the Spanish Hapsburgs took control of this valley from the Protestant Grisons, who were allied with the French. When Louis XIII objected to the Hapsburg invasion, the Hapsburgs ceded control of the valley to papal troops and asked the pope to mediate their dispute with France. Then, shortly after becoming first minister in 1624, Richelieu convinced the king to invade the valley. The French invasion created a great stir throughout Catholic Europe. The "Most Christian King" had attacked papal troops and provoked war with the Catholic Hapsburgs for the sake of aiding a Protestant people and promoting his own state interests. A number of polemics quickly appeared condemning the action.[34] The anonymous author of the *Admonitio ad regem* accused Louis XIII of impiety and warned that divine punishments would imminently befall France. He added that the king's actions absolved the French people of their obedience to him and even authorized them to take up open resistance.

The *Catholique d'estat* provided an ideological defense of the French monarchy's actions.[35] At its center was the theory of the *direct* divine right of kings. This theory was first developed in France during the early sixteenth century, but had become especially prominent after the publication of Bodin's *République*.[36] According to this theory, the king derived his authority not from the pope, emperor, customary laws, or people, but directly from God. Ferrier and his contemporaries expanded upon this theory, claiming that the king was not only directly ordained by God, but also was directly inspired by him. The king's actions were a direct expression of divine will. When God wanted to bring about war or peace or bestow prosperity or destitution upon a people, he most usually moved kings to do his bidding. The king's actions were hardly distinguishable from those of God himself:

> It is because of God's will and on his authority that kings reign. And whenever Your Majesty performs royal acts as you ordinarily do you have the honor of lending your hand to God and serving as his associate in ordering the universe. You have the honor of having at your side God who urges you forward,

> causes you to act, and cooperates with you in such manner that you are never without God who is more present in the actions of kings than other men because he guides all others through them. It is a glory above the thoughts and speech of mortals that kings are the most glorious instruments of divine Providence in the government of the world. (CE, introduction)

The king was an instrument in God's hands, divinely guided and directed in all his actions.

Given the divine nature of the king's power, Ferrier asserted that theologians and moralists were wrong to try to bind the king's actions by substantive principles of justice. Kings governed according to an inscrutable divine wisdom. When moralists tried to prescribe limits to the king's actions, it was as though they were attempting to place limits on the divine will itself:

> The ancients, who were not at all flatterers, called you "corporeal and living gods," and God himself has taught men to use the same language and he desires that you be called gods. And since he calls you this, he wishes that you would be gods, and undoubtedly detests all who would tie your hands, diminish your rights, decry your actions that ought to be venerated, and want to be judges and censors of your majesty in the things where you have only God as a judge. (CE, introduction)

"The laws of the state," Ferrier wrote in a related passage, were different from the "maxims of the schoolmen" (CE, 19). Kings and their ministers possessed a "secret" and "mysterious" reason that was beyond the comprehension of private individuals. When theologians or other persons attempted to judge or restrain their actions, they effectively asserted their own superiority over divine foresight. The result was chaos and misery: "all order in the universe is broken, states are destroyed, religion is despised, and because of imaginary ills that frighten the people they are sent headlong toward inevitable ruin" (CE, 19–20).

In the above passages, Ferrier touched upon one of the central themes of the French reason of state literature: the idea of *arcana imperii,* or mysteries of state.[37] The idea of mysteries of state can be traced back to the twelfth and thirteenth centuries, when Roman jurists attempted to establish a sacred status for the emperor equivalent to that of the pope. But it took on particular importance during the sixteenth and seventeenth centuries, when French and English theorists came to associate mysteries of state not simply with the sacredness of royal power but more personally with the special divine wisdom of the king. The king was portrayed as a morally perfect and supremely rational individual whose policies, even when apparently wicked, were actually in some providential or mysterious sense good. An important consequence of this doctrine was to grant state rulers a monopoly over morally questionable actions. Not just anyone could claim to do evil for good. By their very nature, mysteries of state were institutionalized in the office of the king.

Ferrier applied this principle to demonstrate that kings were justified in carrying out whatever policies they deemed necessary for the good of their people. He assured his readers that this was not a Machiavellian teaching, but one consistent with the highest principles of faith.[38] In carrying out seemingly immoral or irreligious actions, the king was not engaging in impiety but only exercising his divine wisdom to execute a higher "mysterious" justice consistent with God's providential plan. The true "Catholic of state," or good Christian, did not question the king's actions: he accepted them as a direct expression of divine wisdom. Anyone who thought otherwise was a "hypocrite," "an enemy of God," "impious and an atheist" (CE, 5, 24).

> The true Catholic of state and *politique,* that is, a good and God-fearing man who is not at all a factious Catholic and a traitor to his country, obeys the law of God without examining the actions of kings. He knows the power of states is from Heaven. If wars occur to punish the universe, it is true that he does not desire them and ardently prays to God for peace among Christian princes; it is true that he is afflicted in his soul and expresses his grief before the altar at mass, beseeching God through prayers to lessen his ire against Christendom. But for all that he does not cease to obey God by praying for his king and the success of his armies. In these uncertainties of public misfortune, and according to his duty, he lowers his head, fills the air with lamentations, and leaves the outcome to God. For he alone protects states and gives them peace or war as he pleases. Subjects may neither censure nor judge the justice or injustice of the arms of their kings; their role is merely obedience and fidelity. (CE, 17–19)

While still holding to the traditional belief that earthly peace depended upon conformity to divine justice, Ferrier radically redefined the meaning of this belief. He argued that divine justice was manifested not through objective moral values but through the prudential actions of the king himself. The good subject and loyal Christian obeyed the prince no matter how impious his actions might seem to be. If he had a complaint with the king's actions, Ferrier directed him to take it up with God through prayers and lamentations.

Significantly, Ferrier applied his arguments not just to Louis XIII and Richelieu, but also to other Catholic rulers. He pointed out that Louis XIII and Richelieu were not the only rulers to have ever allied with non-Catholic powers. The Hapsburgs had long ago forged alliances with Protestant and non-Christian powers. Charles V had even granted legal recognition to Protestantism within the empire and admitted Protestant soldiers into his armies (CE, 74–89). Ferrier cited these facts, he insisted, not to impugn the Hapsburgs' integrity, but only to demonstrate the absurdity of criticizing French foreign policy in terms of conventional moral standards.[39] In criticizing Louis XIII and Richelieu, foreign authors had inadvertently condemned their own princes and the true principles of Christian political morality. Christian piety did not require state rulers to behave according to fixed moral maxims. Rather it mandated only that they try their best to advance the interests of their states, the Church, and Christendom with a clear conscience.

> These doctors are so blinded by their desire to injure us that they do not see that in order to defame us in one affair, they betray their own princes and convict them in a hundred similar affairs. While they injure them, I honor them for their exalted quality and their most commendable conduct. For they have been able to gain such advantage on certain occasions that the good of Christendom followed from it, or at least was not noticeably concerned. . . . I shall speak frankly, but I beg these good doctors and theologians to do us the kindness and courtesy to believe that our rulers are as good of Christians and as intelligent as those of the House of Austria when it comes to using similarly questionable means toward the same ends and advantages, and with the same conscience. I mean with a conscience sufficiently clear and strong to guide these unseemly events and turn them to the benefit of the state, the Church, and Christendom. (CE, 88–89)

With this statement, Ferrier's new description of political morality was complete. He had transferred the morality of political action away from objective values and the ends of Catholic universalism to the conscience of statesmen. As long as state rulers pursued the interests of their states, the Church, and Christendom, it did not matter what methods they used. They were doing God's work and hence were above the law and morality. Interestingly, Ferrier did not consider the possibility that the ends of the state, Church, and Christendom might come into conflict. God did not work at cross-purposes. He assumed that the interests of the state were so closely bound up with the interests of the Church and Christendom that one could hardly pursue the true interests of the former without at the same time promoting the interests of the latter.

In the years following the Valtelline controversy, Richelieu encouraged French thinkers to develop a more abstract and theoretical defense of reason of state theory. One important work to come out of this effort was Jean-Louis Guez de Balzac's *Le prince* (1631).[40] Balzac devoted much of his work to an exalted description of the king. Louis XIII's virtue was so perfect that he seemed to "share in the morality of Jesus Christ" (P, 80–81). The king was so utterly devoid of sin that he could not even accuse himself in the confessional without slandering himself (P, 117). His reason was not that of ordinary individuals but directly inspired by God:

> If we may believe those who have the honor of approaching the king and observing his inner life and the motivation of his acts, he is so fortunate in what he conceives and he judges so accurately the most mysterious things that it seems certain that he does not view them in our manner but is guided

by a purer light than that of ordinary reason. Most of his great decisions have been sent to him by Heaven. Most of his resolutions stem from a superior prudence and are inspired immediately by God rather than propositions made by men. (P, 274–75)

Balzac took his description of the king to dizzying heights. He even acknowledged that some of his readers might have difficulty accepting some of his claims. But he retorted that anyone who doubted what he said was a poor and misinformed subject. The king was no ordinary mortal but a morally pure and rationally inspired demigod.

Beyond providing one of the most exalted descriptions of the king ever penned, Balzac took important steps in his *Prince* toward further developing the theory of reason of state. In particular, he explained why it was sometimes necessary for the morally pure sovereign ruler to perform morally questionable actions. His explanation centered upon the corruption of human beings and disorder of the world. Like so many other seventeenth-century authors, Balzac asserted that the moral order of the universe had collapsed. Human beings now lived amid chaos, corruption, contingency, and decay. Rulers had to adapt to these conditions if they were to be effective. They could not hope to govern strictly according to Christian virtues, but had to enter into the evil of the world in order to combat it. He laid out this view most concisely in his *Aristippe:* "The world lost its innocence long ago. We live in the corruption of centuries and the decrepitude of nature. All is deficient; all is diseased in the assemblies of men. If therefore you wish to govern effectively, if you seek to work successfully for the good of the state, accommodate yourself to the defect and imperfection of your material. Rid yourself of that importunate virtue of which your age is incapable."[41] While the king was perfectly virtuous, the world was not. If the king were to govern effectively in the world, it was necessary that he sacrifice some of his perfection and enter into the wickedness of affairs.

In *Taming the Prince,* Mansfield argued that Machiavelli's understanding of "nature" as dangerous and disorderly played an important role in the development of modern executive power.[42] Once it was discovered that nature could not be relied upon to execute the laws or enforce order among human beings, then writers began to expand the powers of the human executive to fulfill this task. Balzac's thought followed this general pattern. He, too, asserted the need for a more unbridled executive because of the decrepitude of nature. But Balzac departed from Machiavelli in several important respects. Balzac showed none of Machiavelli's confidence in the ability of human beings to discern general lessons from the study of history. Nor did he share Machiavelli's belief that human beings in general could take control of the times. Like Montaigne, he claimed temporal affairs were highly unpredictable and mutable. It was only the king who, by virtue of his divine wisdom and inspiration, could predict and direct affairs. But even his powers were limited. Absent from Balzac's theory was the idea of the glorious prince bending fortune to his will. His whole approach to temporal affairs was, in comparison to Machiavelli's philosophy, defensive and edgy (if not downright paranoid). He wrote that princes "do not make occasions, but receive them; they do not command the times; they possess only a small part of them, that is, the present, which is an almost imperceptible point in comparison to the vast extent of the future, which has no bounds. To arrive at their end, it is necessary that they go quickly and leave early. They must make haste among sudden and transitory things" (P, 193). Drawing on Psalms 101, he added that the "wise prince" who was "enlightened by God" killed the wicked in the morning "because, in my opinion, he was not assured of the afternoon, and did not know if his good fortune would last until then" (P, 193–94). For Balzac, even the divinely inspired prince had at best only a tenuous grip on the highly contingent temporal world.

Applying these lessons to contemporary affairs, Balzac argued that the prince was justified in taking whatever precautions were necessary upon "any sign of change of the times and the least presage of a storm" (P, 195). In particular, he defended the king's right to make use of preventive arrests and summary executions for the public welfare. Although these actions might violate the form of justice, they were not unjust in themselves, for they represented a higher form of justice that supplemented the law. The following passage, worth quoting at length, aptly summarizes Balzac's theory of executive prerogative:

> To tell the truth, it seems to me entirely reasonable to anticipate certain crimes that cannot be punished after they are committed and not to wait to correct the evil until the criminals have become masters of their judges. . . . If the authors of our rebellions had been quickly seized, not only would they have been saved but an infinite number of other lives would have been spared, as well as all the blood that was spilled during the civil wars. If the evil winds had been contained, the sea would not have become agitated; if kings had enough prudence, they would have little need of justice. I mean that punctilious and scrupulous justice, which will not remedy the crimes that are forming, because they are not yet formed; which wants to wait until the rebels have ruined the state, so that it may proceed against them legitimately; which in order to observe the terms of a law, lets perish all the laws. This sovereign right is a sovereign injustice, and it would be a sin against reason not to sin in these cases against the forms. If the virtues did not lend aid to and succor one another, they would be imperfect and defective. Prudence must relieve justice in many things. It should prevail when justice moves too slowly and would never arrive. It must prevent crimes whose punishment would be either impossible or dangerous. Justice is rendered only according to the actions of men, but prudence has jurisdiction over their thoughts and secrets. It extends even into the future; it concerns the general welfare; it provides for the good of posterity. And to this end it is con-

strained here and there to employ means that the laws do not ordain, but necessity justifies, and that would not be entirely good if they were not for a good end. (P, 199–203)

Balzac here outlined an exemplary definition and justification of executive prerogative. Because human affairs were corrupt and contingent, law and justice were often too slow and scrupulous in addressing crimes and injustices, requiring the prince's executive prerogative to complement them. Executive prerogative addressed those areas and circumstances of political life where the laws were weakest: the "thoughts and secrets" of individuals, "the future," "the general welfare," and "the good of posterity." In exercising executive prerogative, the prince overstepped the laws to protect them and broke the form of justice to preserve its spirit. His actions were not evil but extraordinarily good. Executive prerogative provided the just and necessary response to a temporal world that could not be tamed by formal justice and laws alone.

Balzac's contemporaries were understandably disturbed by his arguments. The most penetrating criticisms of his work came from one of Richelieu's staunchest opponents, Mathieu de Morgues.[43] Surely, Morgues argued, the king might occasionally bend the laws or morality to address some emergency. But "upon a minor misgiving. . . . For a fancy? For a dream?"[44] As Morgues correctly noted, Balzac's theory of executive prerogative depended heavily upon the assumption that the king was morally pure and infallible. But, he queried, "What if that 'prudence which penetrates the thoughts and secrets of men' but is neither divine nor infallible is mistaken, who will recall to life the men unjustly killed?"[45] Balzac responded to these criticisms with outrage. He was appalled at the suggestion that Louis XIII was anything less than perfect. He defended his work by asserting that Morgues's criticism ignored the special knowledge and miraculous powers of the king. He further noted (in response to another critic) that anyone who regarded "the public as something holy" and "the head as its most sacred part" must assent to his conclusions.[46] Executive prerogative was absolutely necessary to protect justice and public order in a corrupt and contingent temporal world.

The same year in which Balzac first published *Le prince* there appeared another important work of reason of state theory: Jean de Silhon's *Le ministre d'estat* (1631).[47] Silhon was a central figure in the intellectual world of seventeenth-century France. He was a close adviser of Richelieu and later of Mazarin, the friend and disciple of Descartes, and a member of the French Academy.[48] His first major work, *Les deux veritez* (1626), aimed to defend the truth of Catholic doctrine against skepticism and atheism.[49] In his *Ministre d'estat,* he turned to politics outlining the principles of a Catholic political theory. Silhon began this work in a traditional manner by asserting that divine Providence governed the entire course of affairs and that fortune was nothing more than a "fancy" of our brains (ME, 1–2). Nonetheless, he acknowledged that the idea of fortune was a useful metaphor since the outcome of affairs was largely beyond human control: "Hannibal acted the full duty of a brave captain, and yet was overcome by Scipio. Cicero forgets nothing of the charge of an excellent orator, and yet Milo was condemned." Silhon explained that God left the working of nature for the most part to "secondary causes," so that virtue and goodness did not always prevail. As a result, human beings effectively lived in an unpredictable and disorderly world where they were responsible for governing their own affairs.

The political conclusion that Silhon drew from this analysis was that "prudence" was absolutely necessary in civil life. "Because all laws are not good at all times and cannot provide against all occurrences and the accidents of life," he wrote, it was necessary to appoint "some wise person whose prudence may supply the defects of the law and give them such a just temper and salutary proportion so that they may fit the times, men, and affairs" (ME, 8). Like Balzac and other French reason of state thinkers, he asserted that prudence could not be expressed through fixed rules, scientific maxims, or historical examples.[50] In a statement reminiscent of Montaigne's *Essays,* he wrote that "the way also of examples is so deceitful, and the past makes such a poor judge of the future, that one cannot conclude anything from it. And as one hardly ever sees two faces equally beautiful, nor two days that resemble each other perfectly, so the condition of affairs is also always diverse, where the virtue and the fortune of those who manage them are not equal" (ME, 10).[51] Prudence was a rare knowledge possessed by only a few individuals who were blessed with superior reason and morality. These individuals alone were equipped to take the reins of the state and supply the "defects of the law." Silhon pointed to the Aristotelian king as his model ruler.[52] Aristotle had argued that "one best man" might be given prerogative powers over the laws insofar as his virtue exceeded that of all other individuals.[53] But he, of course, doubted the possibility of perfect kingship. The king would have to be "like a god among men" to possess such preeminent virtue.[54] Silhon and other French reason of state theorists ignored these doubts and embraced the Aristotelian theory of kingship. They insisted that the king was in fact a perfectly just individual blessed with extraordinary virtue. Indeed, in one of the more ironic twists in intellectual history, Aristotle came be known alongside figures such as Tacitus and Machiavelli in seventeenth-century France as one of the founders of reason of state doctrine.[55]

For Silhon, then, the perfect prince was a superior individual who supplied the defect of the laws and provided against the accidents of life. He wrote: "It does not suffice for a prince to have ordinary intelligence or a common share of morality. But to satisfy his duty and fill up worthily his charge, it seems that he ought to have a more illuminated reason and a more perfect disposition of will than his subjects" (ME, 20). Having made this claim, Silhon immediately began to backpedal. Sensing that his argument might be used to challenge the legitimacy of kings, he explained that he did not mean to say that mediocre kings were unfit to govern. Kings "must be taken as God sends them." Even "stupid and depraved" kings, he wrote (in apparent contradiction to his previous claims), had to be obeyed. In any case, the French did not have to worry about such problems. God had endowed Louis XIII with all the qualities of a model ruler and supplied him with a first minister, Richelieu, who possessed "the pure use of reason" and "perfect virtue" (ME, 24–25). The French state was ruled by a god among men. Its sovereign ruler was reason incarnate.[56]

From these general remarks about prudence and kingship, Silhon proceeded to delineate his theory of reason of state. Kings were ordained by both God and the people to protect the public order and promote the public good. This was their highest duty. They were therefore morally obliged to do whatever was necessary to preserve this "sacred trust." Silhon even went so far as to suggest that injustice occurred not when the king stepped beyond traditional moral limits, but when he sacrificed the interests of the state to some fixed moral ideal:

> Individuals may relinquish their rights in many things and voluntarily suffer losses in order to perform generous actions. In this they risk only what pertains to them, they lose only that of which they are masters and proprietors, and the injury they suffer is sufficiently compensated by the glory of the good that they do. But princes (and this touches ministers even more), instead of being generous when they abandon the interests of their states, become imprudent. They are unjust if they sacrifice that which is not theirs and has been placed in their hands as a sacred trust by the people who surrendered it. And since the first obligation they have is to prevent those who have given them their liberty and put themselves under their domination from becoming miserable, it is certain that princes injure their dignity and sin against their being, if they permit the loss of some right of their state, or the diminution of some part, and that their subjects may justly oppose this and refuse to consent to it. (ME, 63–64)

Silhon here inverted the traditional justification for disobedience to the king. Subjects were justified in resisting the king not when he contravened Christian morality but rather when he failed to do so, and society suffered as a result. It was not the king's part to play the scrupulous moralist, or to place his own soul above the good of the community. His morality was dictated by "interests of state."

Silhon's argument marked an important milestone in the development of reason of state theory. Building upon the arguments of Ferrier, he asserted that political communities were autonomous moral entities standing apart from international society and substantive values. No longer was the king expected to place the interests of universal Catholicism or even the dictates of divine law above the public good. On the contrary, Silhon now claimed that God wanted the king to do whatever was necessary to fulfill his "sacred trust" of protecting society against contingency and disorder.

This theme was taken up and further developed a few years later by Daniel de Priézac. Priézac was a provincial lawyer who first made a name for himself by defending Richelieu's foreign policies against the criticisms of the famous Catholic theologian Cornelius Jansenius. In his *Mars Gallicus* (1635), Jansenius cogently asserted the traditional religious case against Richelieu's foreign policies. Sweeping aside all theological subtleties, Jansenius asked simply: "Do they believe that a secular, perishable state should outweigh religion and the Church?"[57] In his *Vindiciae Gallicae* (1638), Priézac responded by claiming that Jansenius had posed a false dilemma in juxtaposing the Church and state interests.[58] French foreign policy was indistinguishable from the interests of Christendom, he argued, because the king's actions taken on behalf of the French state invariably redounded to the benefit of Christendom. Priézac supported this claim by reciting a long list of services that French kings had performed on behalf of the Church. As for Louis XIII's alliances with heretic powers, Priézac asserted that these were undertaken simply in fulfillment of his divine duty to protect the French state against aggressors. "What evil has he done by having ties and counsel with Protestants and promising to aid them under certain conditions? Surely, since he did this for the defense and security of his state, in this case justice and good faith are inviolate."[59] Echoing Ferrier's arguments, Priézac asserted that as long as the sovereign ruler acted with a clear conscience, there could be no conflict between state interests and the interests of Christendom.

In the *Discours politiques* (1652), Priézac expanded upon these themes. The Church and state, he argued, were coequal partners in carrying out God's designs. They were both divine institutions whose purposes and powers were deeply intertwined:

> Although the priesthood and royalty are two different likenesses of the grandeur and glory of God, he bound them together with such exquisite and admirable means that they may not be separated without corrupting and violating his most perfect and vivid images. . . . Indeed, if religion is the basis, the foundation, and the guardian power of the state and the eternal flame that watches over its safety, the state is also the buttress, support, protection, and the defense of religion. The one and the other need to lend each other their strength and to cooperate in order to establish the realm of heaven on earth.[60] (D, 159–60)

Religion was the foundation of the state. It was proper for "the state to serve religion and not religion the state" (D, 163). But the state was ultimately responsible for defending and manifesting religious principles (D, 163–64). The state was the institution that most directly established the "realm of heaven on earth."

This religious perspective fundamentally informed Priézac's account of reason of state. Inasmuch as states were responsible for instituting a "heaven on earth," he claimed they ought to be organized after the model of divine government. This meant they necessarily had to have a godlike power, standing above the laws and capable of overturning them for the good of the whole: "Surely, if the civil government should be a miniature image of the great polity of the universe, and if it follows as is necessary to give the latter a superior virtue that is not constrained by any ordinary rules, it is also necessary that there be in the republic a universal reason that is freed from all ties of civil law and retains supreme authority over it" (D, 205).

Priézac here made use of the medieval distinction between the ordinary and extraordinary powers of God.[61] The ordinary powers of God were generally associated with the natural laws that governed the universe. His extraordinary powers referred to his ability to overturn these laws and perform miracles for the greater good. Priézac associated the ordinary powers of God with the legislative capacities of the state, which functioned to establish universal laws for society. He associated the extraordinary powers of God with the executive power, which perfected human society by raising it above nature. It was like the divine law in relation to nature: "For in order to elevate human beings above the forces of nature, there is need of the divine law, which alone can give them their perfection; so also it is necessary in political government that there be a superior and master reason over all the others, so that by its guidance the people are conducted to a more perfect and happy end" (D, 206). Priézac's argument was quite revealing of the logic of executive prerogative. If society were governed simply by the universal laws of the sovereign legislator, he warned that it would soon be overrun by nature. Executive prerogative perfected society by elevating it above the contingencies of nature. It was this purpose that justified the horrible and unjust means that the prince sometimes employed in his pursuit of state interests. These means were never just in themselves, but they were justified by the good they brought to society (D, 211). They were necessary to maintain the religious-political order amid the corruption and contingency of the temporal world.

Cardinal Richelieu laid out his own reason of state theory in his *Testament politique*.[62] Although he reiterated many of the same themes outlined by Ferrier, Balzac, Silhon, and Priézac, Richelieu brought a fresh approach to reason of state theory. Conspicuously absent from his work were the long laudatory passages about the king. While he still advocated the theory of divine right of kings, he made no mention of the mystical wisdom of Louis XIII. Richelieu knew firsthand the many human failings of his king and even rather boldly pointed some of them out in his book. He premised his reason of state theory primarily upon the twin foundations of the sanctity of the political order and the corrupt nature of temporal affairs.

Richelieu defined the "state" in a traditional manner as the whole body of society including the three orders of Church, nobility, and people (TP, 256). Within the state, he claimed that each individual was assigned a fixed position and function "by nature." The purpose of the government was to maintain the social order apart from the corruption and change of the temporal world. In particular, he advised the king to check the movements of individuals from one estate to another, since otherwise "France will no longer be what it has been and what it ought to be, but only a monstrous body which, as such, will have neither subsistence nor duration" (TP, 256–57). He further argued in a traditional manner that religious principles were the foundation of social order. "The rule of God is the foundation of the government of states, and, in effect, it is a thing so absolutely necessary that, without this foundation, no prince could ever rule well nor any state be happy or self-sufficient" (TP, 321). The sovereign ruler was obliged not only to govern according to the principles of divine law, but also "to establish God's true church" within the state (TP, 321–23). If the king did not submit to the laws of God, Richelieu warned, he should not expect the subjects to obey his own laws (TP, 264–66).

Yet, Richelieu continued, Louis XIII hardly needed to be reminded of the sacred nature of his power and obligations. The king's piety was so strong that he never even considered deviating from Christian morality. More important in the king's case was to remember that Christian piety did not necessarily translate into a strict duty to follow the letter of the moral law. Much like Silhon, Richelieu argued that sovereign rulers were permitted and even required by moral law to employ morally dubious means for the good of their states. "Although devotion is necessary to kings, it ought to be devoid of over-scrupulousness. I say this, Sire, because the delicacy of Your Majesty's conscience makes you often fear to offend God in doing certain things that surely you cannot abstain from doing without sin" (TP, 264–65). Richelieu maintained that God expected kings to transgress the moral law on some occasions for the good of the state. It would be a "sin" for a king not to perform any action necessary for the public good on account of moral reservations. Indeed, it reflected a fundamental misunderstanding of the nature of the state rule. The divine foundations of the state did not place substantive limits on the king's actions, but instead freed him from conventional moral constraints. Whatever the king did for the good of the state was by definition good. Richelieu summed up his advice in the following way: "That which is done for the state is done for God, who is the basis and foundation of it" (TP, 201).

Repeating the views of other reason of state theorists, Richelieu explained that it was necessary to carry out seemingly immoral or excessive actions at times because the world was a wicked and uncertain place. He cited the following doctrine as a "certain maxim":

> That it is necessary on certain occasions, in which the welfare of the state is concerned, to assume a male virtue that sometimes goes beyond the rules of ordinary prudence; and that it is sometimes impossible to avoid certain evils, unless something be given to fortune, or rather to divine providence, which seldom refuses its assistance when our exhausted wisdom can no longer furnish us with any. (TP, 128)

Richelieu's point here echoed Balzac's earlier defense of executive action.

Since neither God nor fortune could be counted upon to maintain the welfare of the state, it was necessary for the king sometimes to exceed the bounds of common morality in order to fulfill this task. It was only after the king had exhausted all his efforts that he might hope for some assistance from divine providence. But he should not expect God to execute the law for him. God had ordained the king to maintain justice and order for him. It was the king's job—not God's—to preserve the state.

Richelieu applied this dictate to a variety of morally questionable policies. In the opening pages of his *Testament,* he defended the morality of French alliances with Protestant countries by claiming that nothing done for the preservation of the state could ever be considered unjust: "There is no theology in the world but will grant, without going against the principles of natural reason, that as necessity obliges those whose life is threatened to make use of all means to preserve it; so a prince has the same right to avoid the loss of his state" (TP, 109). What was done for the preservation of the state was, according to Richelieu, always consistent with natural right. He later applied this same argument to his discussion of preventive arrests.

> Although in the course of ordinary affairs justice requires an authentic proof, it is not the same in those cases that concern the state, because in such cases what appears only as dangerous conjectures should sometimes be held to be sufficiently clear, inasmuch as the factions and conspiracies that are formed against the public welfare are ordinarily handled with such cunning and secrecy that one never has clear proof of them except after they happen, at which time they are beyond remedy. It is necessary on such occasions to begin sometimes with the execution. (TP, 343–44)

Remarkable in this passage is Richelieu's total identification of extraordinary justice with cases involving the state. Because such cases involved something far more important than private rights, the king was justified in exercising extraordinary means in prosecuting them—a practice both Louis XIII and Richelieu made ready use of throughout the 1620s and 1630s.[63] Richelieu even claimed it was a divine duty for kings to preemptively arrest and punish individuals who represented a threat to the social order. The king would have to answer before God if he allowed some group to threaten the public peace rather than taking preemptive action against them. "I repeat again that it is more important than it seems not only to extinguish the first sparks of such divisions as soon as they appear, but also to prevent them by banishing those who have no other care than to ignite them. The peace of the state is a thing too important to allow one to neglect this remedy, without being accountable before God" (TP, 369).

If, on the one hand, Richelieu claimed the corruption and contingency of human affairs justified the king's use of extraordinary prudence, on the other hand, he also claimed it justified his toleration of certain injustices within the state. Most importantly, he advocated a limited tolerance for the

Huguenots on these grounds. Although the king was obliged by religion to establish the "true worship of God" within the state, he was under no compulsion to sacrifice peace and order to ensure this end. His first duty was the preservation of the state. Richelieu acknowledged that the state would be more stable and just if it were founded upon the true religion. But without the state there would be no stability, justice, or religion; therefore the king was fully within his rights in tolerating the existence of the Huguenots.[64] Ever the practical statesman, Richelieu insisted that the existing moral order of the state should never be sacrificed for abstract moral principles.

> All the sovereigns of the world are obliged by that principle to promote the conversion of those who living under their reign have strayed from the road to heaven. But just as man is reasonable, princes perform their duty in utilizing all reasonable means to arrive at a good end; and prudence does not permit them to attempt anything so hazardous as to risk uprooting the good grain while attempting to pull out the tares, since it would be difficult to purge the state in any but a gentle way, without a shock capable of destroying it, or at least of causing it a great harm. (TP, 323)

As this statement indicates, Richelieu was not simply a Machiavellian statesman who disregarded all higher morality in favor of power politics. He never lost sight of the higher ends that government was supposed to serve. But the first duty of government was the preservation of the political order and the good that already existed within it. The king's executive prerogative was a necessary and legitimate power for preserving this moral community against contingency and disorder.

Gabriel Naudé and Coups d'État

Many other French thinkers offered similar accounts of reason of state theory, including Charles de Noailles, Pierre Blanchot, Jean Sirmond, Louis Machon, and François de La Mothe le Vayer. But the writer who most carefully analyzed French reason of state theory during Richelieu's reign was the cardinal's librarian, Gabriel Naudé. In his *Considérations politiques sur les coups d'état* (1639), Naudé provided a detailed philosophical analysis of the principle of executive prerogative.[65] His work is generally considered the most sophisticated (if not necessarily the most representative) expression of French *raison d'état* theory.[66] Indeed, the *Coups d'état* is sometimes treated in isolation from the mainstream of French *raison d'état* theory because Naudé made no use of direct divine right theory.[67] He has sometimes even been seen as an advocate of a wholly secular "Machiavellian" theory of politics.[68] This interpretation is misleading for two reasons. First, Naudé premised his theory not upon a Machiavellian worldview but rather upon the ideas of Montaigne, Lipsius, and especially Charron.[69] The result was a very different approach to statecraft from the one set forth by Machiavelli. Second, although

Naudé did not make use of divine right theory, he situated his *raison d'état* theory within a moral political framework. He associated political order with the universal principles of justice and natural law and argued that coups d'état were morally justified as a means of preserving this order. His theory was important because it paved the way for the moral legitimization of executive prerogative quite apart from appeals to direct divine right theory.

Naudé began his discussion of reason of state theory by criticizing Lipsius's division of prudence into the normative categories of acceptable, tolerable, and unacceptable. Prudence was a discretionary quality that was best defined in terms of two nonproscriptive categories: ordinary and extraordinary. Ordinary prudence consisted of those actions that rulers took every day for the public interest; extraordinary prudence meant those actions undertaken in special circumstances and according to the rulers' own secret wisdom for the public interest (CP, 88–91).

Naudé went on to develop his own tripartite division of statecraft. The highest level consisted of "the general science of the establishment and conservation of states and empires" as contained in the books of the ancient philosophers and the divine and natural law (CP, 98). This science included "universal rules," such as "that things do not happen fortuitously or necessarily; that there is one God who is the first author of things, who has care of them, and who has established the reward of paradise for the good, and the punishments of hell for the wicked." Like other French reason of state theorists, Naudé argued that these universal principles formed the necessary foundation of political order.

Below these universal principles were the more particular "maxims of state," consisting of actions that transgressed the moral and natural laws but were "legitimized" by the "public good or utility" that they self-evidently brought the state. Examples of these maxims included the decision by the Roman emperors to contravene the marriage laws for the sake of preserving the peace of the empire, the practice of governing foreign affairs by rules of expediency, the execution of prisoners of war when their number had become too great, the Chinese law mandating death to all strangers who entered their country, and "other like laws and fashions practiced particularly by each nation, which have nothing other for a foundation than the right of the state, but are nonetheless very religiously observed, as being entirely necessary to the operation and conservation of the states that provide them" (CP, 98–101).

The third branch of statecraft consisted of "coups d'état": those "bold and extraordinary actions that princes are constrained to execute in difficult and desperate affairs, against common law, without maintaining any of the procedures or forms of justice, and hazarding particular interests for the public good" (CP, 101). In contrast to maxims of state, coups d'état were not written into the particular laws of any country and did not follow any generally recognizable rules of utility. They were entirely prudential actions springing solely from the king's mind. Naudé described them as "mysteries of state," "secrets of state," and "arcana imperii" (CP, 84, 89).[70] He even criticized Machiavelli and other writers for trying to treat this branch of statecraft through general maxims and precepts. "These writers have corrupted the words," he explained, who associate "secrets of state" with the

> general precepts and universal maxims founded on the justice and right of sovereignty, and consequently permitted and practiced everyday and seen by everyone. Nor do they apprehend that there is a great difference between these [general precepts] and those [secrets] we speak of, since anyone can know the first through only a little study of the authors who have treated them, whereas the latter, which are now in question, are born in the most retired cabinets of princes, and are neither discussed nor deliberated in the full senate, nor in the middle of the parlement, but between two or three of the most discreet and trusted ministers that a prince has. (CP, 91)

Coups d'état were entirely circumstantial and unpredictable. They included any action the prince might take for the public good.

In contemporary usage, coups d'état have come to be associated with the violent overthrow of the government, usually by some group purportedly acting for the public good. Naudé certainly did not mean to define coups d'état so broadly. Central to his whole theory was the idea that coups d'état were only to be practiced by the prince and his closest advisers. Nonetheless, the origins of the contemporary usage are discernible in Naudé's work. It is but a small step from Naudé's defense of coups d'état exercised by the prince for the public good to a defense of coups d'état exercised by some group against the prince for the public good. The essential point was that they were extraordinary actions taken for the public welfare.

While coups d'état appeared on the surface to be immoral, Naudé argued that they were not wicked in themselves. Just as a sword could be used for good or evil, so a prince might wield coups d'état in a moral or immoral fashion (CP, 76, 107). In the third chapter, Naudé therefore outlined "With What Precautions and on What Occasions One Ought to Practice Coups d'Etat" (CP, 107). He did not identify any substantive moral limitations on the actions of the king. Borrowing from Charron (but ignoring his prohibition on outright treachery), he merely specified the manner in which coups d'état ought to be practiced. Above all, he argued that rulers should always employ coups d'état "defensively and not offensively, for conservation rather than aggrandizement, to protect oneself from tricks, wickedness, and harmful enterprises and surprises rather than to commit them" (CP, 107). By the same token, coups d'état were to be used strictly for the good of the people, "not as it may seem good to them [princes], but according to reason and the public good" (CP, 108). Princes were also to rely on coups d'état as little as possible and to adopt the most gentle means available in executing them (CP, 108–9). Finally, princes were advised to perform coups d'état with regret, "like a father who suffers to have the limb of his child cut off to save his life" (CP, 109). When these conditions were met, Naudé contended that coups d'état were no less moral than maxims of state, and were distinguished only by their wholly prudential quality:[71] "They have nevertheless the same justice and equity that we said was in the maxims and reasons of state; but in those maxims it is permitted to publish them before the coup, but the principal rule of these is to remain hidden up to the end" (CP, 101).

Naudé's fourth chapter, entitled "What Opinions It Is Necessary to Hold in Order to Undertake Coups d'Etat," identified the underlying assumptions of his reason of state theory. Here he explained why he considered it both just and necessary for rulers to perform morally dangerous coups d'état (CP, 133). Like other French reason of state thinkers, he pointed to the variability and contingency of human and temporal affairs. He specifically listed three opinions that explained the need for coups d'état. The first was found in Boethius's *De Consolatione:* "It is an axiom founded on the eternal law, that there is nothing born in the world that is not subject to some change" (CP, 133).[72] Peter Donaldson saw in this statement an important parallel between Naudé and Machiavelli. He argued that Naudé ascribed to a "principle of inevitable, periodic alteration that . . . is very similar to the Polybian concept of anacyclosis as used by Machiavelli."[73] In fact, though, Naudé's view of temporal change owes more to Montaigne than Machiavelli. Machiavelli used the idea of anacyclosis or periodic alteration to indicate that there was an order *within* history so that past events could be used to manipulate and predict present and future affairs. Naudé had no such faith in historical cycles. Although he did refer to "this great circle of the universe," he did so only to highlight the mutability of all temporal things (CP, 133–34). In what might be considered a direct criticism of Machiavelli, Naudé even charged that only "weak spirits" believed there were general rules for governing human affairs (CE, 134). The true statesman recognized the utter orderlessness of time and relied solely upon his own prudence to maintain order.

While Naudé's first opinion in support of coups d'état related to the mutability of all things, his second opinion addressed the extreme contingency of affairs. The world itself, he claimed, was created from nothing and was "composed only of a concourse of diverse atoms." Consequently, the greatest changes "very often happen without thinking about them, or at least without making great preparations for them" (CP, 136). Sometimes even the most seemingly insignificant political events erupted into full-scale revolutions. "Who would have ever believed," he asked, "that the abduction of Helen, the rape of Lucretius by Tarquin, and that of the daughter of Count Julian by the king Roderic, could have produced such notable effects in Greece, Italy, and Spain?" (CP, 136). The lesson for princes was "to consider all the least circumstances they encounter in serious and difficult affairs" and, alternatively, to remember that "it is not necessary to overturn the whole world in order to occasion changes of the greatest empires" (CP, 136–37). Because of the contingency of affairs, a coup d'état was often sufficient to save a political society in dire straits or to bring down the greatest of powers.

Naudé's third opinion pertained to the great mutability of human beings themselves. Here again his thought departed from Machiavelli's. Whereas Machiavelli argued that the people provided the firmest foundation for stability and order,[74] Naudé countered that "the people" only magnified the change and flux of the temporal world. The people were comparable "to a sea subject to all sorts of winds and tempests, a chameleon that can take on all sorts of colors except white, and a drain and cesspool into which flows all the waste from the house. Their most noble quality is to be inconstant and variable, to approve and disapprove something at the same time, to run always from one extreme to the other, believing lightly, mutinying promptly, and always grumbling and mumbling" (CP, 139). Naudé's sentiment here was not unique. Lipsius and Charron had outlined similar views of the people. Richelieu likewise described the people as wildly inconstant and fickle (TP, 253–56, 385). All these writers agreed that because of the people's great instability, the king should be prepared to use violent or deceptive measures to maintain justice and peace among them.

Toward the end of his final chapter, Naudé drew together the various strands of his *Coups d'état.* He began by reiterating that universal justice was the foundation of states. The prince ought to rule "according to the laws of God and nature, nobly, philosophically, with integrity and without pretension, having virtue without art, religion without fear or scruples, and a firm resolution to do good, without any other respect or consideration than to live so, so that he may live as a good and honorable man" (CP, 163–64). But since temporal affairs were so corrupt and changing, the prince also had to recognize that "this natural, universal, noble, and philosophical justice is sometimes out of use and incommodious in the practice of the world." In governing society, it was necessary "very often to use the artificial, particular, political [justice], made and adjusted to the needs and the necessity of policies and states, since it is loose and soft enough to be accommodated, like the Lesbian rule, to human and popular feebleness, and to the diverse times, peoples, affairs, and accidents" (CP, 163–64).[75] In other words, rulers had to be prepared to transgress the universal principles of justice in order to combat corruption and preserve order and justice. Although their actions might appear to be violations of justice, they were actually higher manifestations of it. In performing coups d'état, the prince saved the spirit of justice by sacrificing its form. Naudé even went so far as to compare the actions of the prince to the miracles that God sometimes performed outside the laws of nature to preserve his perfect natural order.[76]

Naudé elaborated on this point in a complex passage comparing the king's coups d'état to God's decision to sacrifice Christ for the salvation of humanity:

> Princes are masters of the laws to lengthen or shorten, confirm or abolish, not as it may seem good to them, but according to reason and the public good: the honor of the prince, the love of the country, the health of the people eas-

ily outweigh some small faults and injustices; and we shall apply the saying of the prophet, if we can do so without blasphemy: "It is necessary that a man die for the people, so that the whole nation will not perish." (CP, 108)

The prophet here is Caiaphas, and the man is Jesus. Hence Naudé's concern about the blasphemy of his argument. In the passage cited from John (11:50), Caiaphas advised the council of priests to sentence Jesus to death for the good of the nation. Authors before Naudé had generally pointed to this passage as proof that reason of state was inherently evil.[77] Naudé, however, interpreted this passage in just the opposite manner—as proof of the supreme justice of coups d'état. He focused on the ensuing passage in John where Caiaphas was described not as a narrow-minded statesman but as a "prophet": "He did not say this of his own accord, but being high priest that year he prophesied that Jesus should die for the nation, and not for the nation only, but to gather into one the children of God who are scattered abroad" (John 11:51–52). When seen in this light, Caiaphas's advice appears not as an act of political expediency but as an expression of God's higher justice. Caiaphas was acting for the salvation of all of humanity when he ordered Jesus' death. His apparently wicked action resulted in the greatest of goods. Princes were encouraged to follow suit. In sacrificing an individual or two for the salvation of their people, they were imitating no less an authority than God himself.

Medieval thinkers had often compared kings to God. But they had always remained keenly aware of the great distance separating human nature from the divine nature. Because of the sinfulness of human beings, they asserted that kings should be subject to the limitations of law and morality. Only God could rule above law and morality. Naudé and other French reason of state thinkers blurred this distinction.[78] Because of the corruption and contingency of temporal affairs, they asserted that kings had to act above law and morality to maintain law and morality. They looked to the executive ruler to take the place of God in enforcing justice and order within the tumultuous temporal world. His actions were not immoral or unjust, they claimed, but manifested a higher and mysterious form of morality and justice comparable to God's miracles.

THE RATIONALIZATION OF STATECRAFT

French *raison d'état* theorists were fully aware of the extraordinary powers they were attributing to their king. Their frequent appeals to the king's divine inspiration must be understood in this light. If the king were to exercise godlike powers, they recognized that he would have to behave like a god. Otherwise executive prerogative would be little different from tyranny. His extraordinary actions had to be performed not for his own interests or the interests of his clients but for the public interest. For many writers, it was sufficient simply to assert the king's divine inspiration and moral integrity, but a number of writers outlined a new governmental ethic to accompany their theory of executive power. These writers described the behavior that the king would have to exhibit in order to fulfill his executive duty successfully. They specifically claimed that the king would have to separate himself from all private attachments and personal feelings and govern strictly for the objective interests of the state. In this way, they took an important step in developing the "dehumanized" and "instrumental" governmental ethic that Max Weber associated with modern state theory.[79]

One of the clearest statements of this new rationalistic approach to statecraft was Duke Henri de Rohan's *De l'intérêt des princes et des états de la chrétienté* (1638). Rohan had been a leader of the rebel Huguenot forces until the fall of La Rochelle in 1629. Afterwards, he became a staunch supporter of Richelieu, largely because of the cardinal's anti-Hapsburg foreign policy. In the opening lines of his *Intérêt*, Rohan announced his intention to move beyond humanistic maxims and lay out a new ethic of statecraft.[80] Echoing the sentiments of Richelieu and other French reason of state thinkers, he asserted that the great variability and contingency of human and temporal affairs rendered historical examples useless in the practice of politics.

> There is nothing so difficult as the art of ruling *(savoir régner)*, and those who have been the most skillful in this profession have confessed at their death that they were novices. The reason for this is that one cannot lay down immutable rules for the government of states. That which causes the revolution of the affairs of the world, also causes the fundamental maxims of good government to change. This is why those who are guided more by past examples in these matters than by present reasons necessarily make considerable mistakes. Moreover, [past examples] are not at all suitable for judging the true interest of a state and knowing how to follow it. It requires a supernatural knowledge to observe the mutations of so difficult a thing to comprehend.[81]

Rohan's statement was fully consistent with the ideas of other French reason of state thinkers as well as the earlier ideas of Montaigne. He claimed fixed maxims and historical examples were for the most part useless in politics. The revolutions and mutations of temporal affairs rendered all political actions particular and circumstantial.

Rohan proposed to replace historical maxims with "interests of state." These, he claimed, were the cornerstone of the state's stability and success.

> Princes rule people and interest rules princes. The knowledge of this interest is raised as much above the actions of princes as they themselves are over peoples. The prince may be deceived, his council may be corrupt, but interest alone never fails. According to whether it is well or badly understood, it preserves or ruins states. (IP, 161)

Rohan defined the interests of states as whatever served to conserve and augment state power. Consequently, these interests varied with the times and, as Rohan noted above, required a "supernatural knowledge" to comprehend. But at any given time, the interest of a particular state could be objectively defined by analyzing its geopolitical situation, military strength, religious character, and relation to other states. In seventeenth-century Europe, for example, there were two principal powers: Spain and France. The interest of each country was to gain an advantage over the other. The best means for Spain to secure itself against France was to proclaim itself the leader of the international Catholic cause and to try to forge alliances with other Catholic states. It was likewise in Spain's interest to lend covert aid to the Huguenots; to make peace with England; to incite the Swiss Catholics to war against the Swiss Protestants; and to promote peace in the Low Countries (IP, 163–69). The interest of France was to oppose Spanish policies at every turn. Rohan called upon the French king to grant tolerance to the Huguenots at home and to offer aid to Spain's Protestant enemies abroad (IP, 170–73). France also had an interest in driving a wedge between the pope and the Spanish throne. Rohan discussed the interests of the other countries of Europe in a similar fashion, paying particular attention to their interests in relation to the two great powers.

After outlining the true interests of the different states of Europe in the first half of his work, Rohan proceeded in the second half to demonstrate the importance of these interests to the well-being of states. He argued that sovereign rulers were obliged to pursue their state interests regardless of personal preferences. When rulers placed their own subjective inclinations above objective state interests, they brought harm to themselves and disorder to their people.

> After having established the true interest of each prince and state, it ought to be made evident by recounting the principal affairs that have agitated Christendom for the past fifty years, that the ill successes that have happened there have proceeded not from any other cause than the neglect of this interest; so that it is easy to learn that in matters of state one ought not to suffer himself to be led by inordinate desires, which carry us often to undertake things beyond our strength, nor by violent passions, which agitate us diversely when we are possessed by them, nor by superstitious opinions, which give us ill-conceived scruples, but rather by our proper interest guided by reason alone. (IP, 187)

Rohan criticized Henry IV for indulging his personal inclination for repose rather than pressing ahead with the war of Savoy when this war was clearly in France's interest (IP, 198–99). He condemned James I's statecraft on similar grounds (IP, 210–11). According to Rohan, princes had to dedicate themselves wholeheartedly to the interests of state. They had to divest themselves of all personal desires, passions, and superstitions in order to govern in a wholly impersonal and instrumental manner. The interests of the state became the guiding logic and moral imperative of statecraft once it was unhinged from universal moral principles. Not only did Rohan and others claim that nothing done for state interests was immoral; they also began to argue that the prince was morally obliged to orient all his actions around state interests. The prince, too, was subject to the logic of reason of state.

In his *Coups d'état*, Naudé similarly outlined a depersonalized ethic of statecraft. He articulated his theory, however, in terms of neostoical values rather than state interests. The essential quality of a good ruler, he claimed, was a "strong spirit." A strong spirit was not a bold or glory-seeking individual but one who was able to raise himself above the confusion and corruption of human affairs and to rule over them unperturbed, like a god:

> One of the first and most necessary parts [of a strong spirit] is to think often of that saying of Seneca: "what a contemptible thing is man, unless he elevates himself above human things." That is, unless he contemplates all the world with a firm and steady eye, almost as if he were at the top of a high tower, viewing it like a theater, rather badly ordered and full of much confusion, where some play comedies and others tragedies, and where he is permitted to intervene like some deus ex machina, whenever he wishes to do so, or whenever diverse circumstances persuade him to do so. (CP, 80–81)

Naudé's description of the perfect ruler closely resembled Charron's description of the stoical sage—never mind that Charron believed very few individuals would ever be able to attain the wisdom of the stoical sage. Naudé argued that anyone entrusted to execute "coups d'état" would have to be an extraordinary person. He would have to elevate himself above the turbulent temporal world so that he could intervene in the course of affairs at the proper moment like "some deus ex machina."

In the final chapter of his *Coups d'état*, Naudé further discussed this depersonalized ethic while describing the characteristics of the ideal minister of state. He identified the three most important virtues of state ministers as fortitude, justice, and prudence. While these qualities were standard classical and Christian virtues, Naudé defined them in a peculiarly "neostoical" way. He defined "fortitude," for example, in terms closely resembling the stoical ideal of detachment, or *apatheia*. "By fortitude, I understand a certain temper and disposition of spirit always equal in itself, firm, stable, heroic, capable of seeing, hearing, and doing all things without troubling oneself, losing oneself, or amazing oneself" (CP, 159). The ideal minister did not look outside of himself for reassurance or direction. He scorned all "credulity and superstition." He accepted the world for the chaotic place that it was, reflecting constantly "on the condition of our nature, which is feeble, frail, and subject to all sorts of maladies and infirmities; on the vanity of the pomp and honors of this world; on the feebleness and weakness of our spirit; on the changes and revolutions of affairs" (CP, 159–60). Recognizing that all earthly things were vain and fleeting, he was totally self-possessed and detached. He lived "in the world as if he were outside of it, [and] under the heavens as if he were above them" (CP, 160).

Naudé defined "justice" in much the same way. As indicated above, he associated justice with obedience to the divine and natural laws. But because of the corruption and variability of temporal affairs, he claimed rulers sometimes had to act outside of these laws for the public good. In choosing ministers, Naudé thus suggested that rulers should pick those individuals who were "just" not in the sense of being committed to any fixed standard of good, but instead detached from all fixed standards of justice. The most "just" ministers were those who were "most pliable" and best able "to accommodate themselves to diverse circumstances" and "to take on all sorts of forms" (CP, 164). They were those individuals who were willing to forsake private moral beliefs in order to execute the justice of the state. They were "strong spirits" capable of following the ethical standards set by the prince.

Naudé identified the third characteristic of a good counselor as "prudence." In the sovereign ruler, prudence consisted of the ability to undertake morally dangerous actions for the good of the state. In the counselor of state, it consisted of "modesty, experience, conduct, restraint, discretion, and particularly that which the Italians call by a term proper to themselves secrecy" (CP, 164). This notion of secrecy was especially prevalent among French reason of state thinkers. Given the morally perilous and extraordinary nature of executive actions, Naudé and others insisted that state business had to be kept secret. If the king's plans were exposed in advance, he would not be able to surprise his enemies with his sudden coups d'état. Just as importantly, Naudé noted that the people might not always understand the need for immoral executive actions. It was therefore best not to tell them until after the fact, when the good effects were evident to all. In short, then, the minister had to be discreet and restrained. When these qualities were coupled with Naudé's definitions of fortitude and justice, they amounted to a highly impersonal and dehumanized approach to statecraft. State rulers were supposed to raise themselves above all passions and contingencies so that they could do the same, in turn, for their people.

Among French reason of state thinkers, Richelieu provided the most detailed account of this new rationalistic state ethic. While he wrote his *Testament* primarily to convince Louis XIII to govern according to reason of state, he also wrote it to encourage his king to adopt a more impersonal and calculating approach to ruling. The two aims were interlinked, for Richelieu argued that executive prerogative could only be effectively exercised by an impartial and rational ruler. In some of the most personal passages in this work, he rebuked the king for being "restless" and "impatient" and prone to "great emotional outbursts" (TP, 268–69). "It is difficult for you not to act impulsively," he wrote, "and sudden waves of emotion occasionally overtake you when you least expect them" (TP, 273). This was unacceptable if the king were to fulfill his duties. Although the king was not bound by any substantive moral constraints, Richelieu argued that he was bound by certain procedural standards. As the divinely ordained executive of the state, he was obliged to detach himself from his passions and interests and govern strictly for the permanent public interests.

The most important quality of a good ruler, according to Richelieu, was piety. Piety consisted primarily of devotion to God and religion, but also of devotion to the public interest. God had ordained kings to rule not according to their private whims but according to the permanent interests of the state (TP, 330–33). Probably drawing upon Rohan, Richelieu argued that Spain's long prosperity was due to the single-minded devotion with which her ministers pursued the public good (TP, 331). France's misfortunes, by contrast, could be traced to ministers who pursued "their private interest to the prejudice of the state." Richelieu asserted:

> The public interest ought to be the sole objective of the prince and his counselors, or at least both are obliged to have it foremost in their minds and prefer it to all particular interests. It is impossible to conceive of the good that a prince and those serving him in his affairs can do if they religiously follow this principle, and one can hardly imagine the evils that befall a state when private interests are preferred to the public, and the public is ruled by the private. (TP, 330)

The pursuit of the public interest was, for Richelieu, a religious duty. What distinguished his appeal to the public interest from the views of medieval and Renaissance theorists was the fact that he detached it from substantive moral virtues. By his account, the moral statesman was not obliged to conform his actions to the traditional moral law, but he was obliged to carry out his prudential actions with a single-minded devotion to the public interest. This connection between divine right theory and rationalization has previously gone unnoticed, and yet it stands at the origin of the impersonal modern ethic of government.

Closely related to Richelieu's notion of state interests was the idea of reason. It was through reason that the good prince executed the public interest. Richelieu associated reason, in turn, with the neostoical virtues of detachment, firmness, and patience.[82] He wrote that there was "nothing in nature less compatible with reason than emotion" (TP, 326). The rational prince was immune to all "distracting interests, pity and compassion, favoritism, and importunities of all kinds" (TP, 333). He likewise displayed a "firm will" (TP, 326–27). Once he had decided upon some course of action, he carried it out vigorously and decisively. But he also had to possess the patience to choose the right time to implement his plans. "If, at one time, it is inappropriate to execute a good plan, one should wait for another and turn to another plan, and if difficulties oblige one to suspend this plan as well, reason indicates that one take up the first project again as soon as the times and occasion are favorable" (TP, 328). Summarizing his position, Richelieu wrote that reason required a fine balance between firmness and patience in the pursuit of the public good. "In a word, nothing ought to turn us away from a good enterprise unless some accident renders it completely impossible, and we must never fail to bring about the execution of that which we have resolved to accomplish with reason."

Richelieu reprised the central themes of his new governmental ethic in the chapter, "The Uses of Punishments and Rewards," wherein he asserted his belief that a different standard of justice applied to rulers than to private individuals. Although "Christians ought to forget all their personal injuries," he wrote, "magistrates are obliged to forget nothing involving the public interest" (TP 342–43). When kings or magistrates allowed crimes to go unpunished, their subjects became unruly and disobeyed the laws. Then the state was overrun with disorder and injustice. The public interest therefore required kings to forgo Christian charity and carry out justice in a wholly impartial manner:

> While conscience might allow a serviceable action to go unrewarded and a notable crime to go unpunished, reason of state would not permit it. Punishments and rewards concern the future more than the past. A prince must be severe of necessity to prevent the evils that might be committed in the hope of a pardon, if he were known to be too indulgent; and he must be very kind to those who are useful to the public, to encourage them to continue to do good and everybody else to imitate them and follow their example. It would be a pleasure to pardon a crime if such impunity did not leave one to fear evil consequences, and the necessity of state might sometimes legitimately dispense one from recompensing a service if in depriving those of their reward one did not also deprive them of the hope of future rewards. (TP, 345)

Since actions involving the state involved far more than the king's person, it was not his place to forgive or reward them as he saw fit. He was morally obliged to promote the permanent interests of the state. Richelieu even noted the great sadness he felt in putting to death several members of the nobility over the protestations of their friends and families (TP, 102–3). But what could he do? Personal sentiments were of no account in his approach to statecraft. God, reason, and the interests of state all dictated an objective enforcement of penalties.

TAMING THE PRINCE

In *Taming the Prince*, Mansfield argued that classical liberal authors such as Locke and Montesquieu developed their theories of executive power by placing the Machiavellian prince within a constitutional framework.[83] This is, however an imprecise account of the development of the liberal executive. When Locke and Montesquieu laid out their liberal state theories, they borrowed their ideas about executive power not from Machiavelli but rather from Richelieu and his cohorts, who demonstrated the legitimacy and utility of executive prerogative within the state. Richelieu and other

French thinkers located executive prerogative in the public office of the prince and showed that this power was not necessarily tyrannical or immoral but could actually serve the laws and justice. They claimed executive prerogative addressed problems that the laws and ordinary justice were too slow or clumsy to handle. In the *Second Treatise,* Locke took for granted the legitimacy of this power. He even had a copy of Naudé's *Coups d'état* at his side while composing his *Second Treatise* and incorporated some of Naudé's ideas about executive prerogative directly into his state theory.[84] He asserted that the executive officer should possess the "power to act according to discretion, for the publick good, without the prescription of the Law, and sometimes even against it . . . which is called Prerogative." He further defended executive prerogative in terms that would not have been unfamiliar to any of the French reason of state theorists:

> For since in some governments the law-making power is not always in being, and is usually too numerous, and too slow, for the dispatch requisite to execution: and because also it is impossible to foresee, and so by laws to provide for, all accidents and necessities, that may concern the publick; or to make such laws, as will do no harm if they are executed with an inflexible rigour, on all occasions, and upon all persons, that may come in their way, therefore there is a latitude left to the executive power, to do many things of choice, which the laws do not prescribe.[85]

Like French reason of state theorists, Locke argued that executive prerogative was a necessary supplement to the laws for preserving the public order from accidents, necessities, and unforeseen contingencies.

Locke's main contribution to the theory of executive power was to separate it from the legislative authority of the state. He further gave the legislative body the authority to remove the executive officer if he should misuse his prerogative powers.[86] While these reforms were significant, they actually represented an extension of the rationalizing tendencies of French reason of state theory. French reason of state thinkers agreed that the executive authority should be above all passions and bias. Locke portrayed the separation of powers as a means for institutionalizing this ethic. "And because it may be too great a temptation to humane frailty apt to grasp at Power, for the same Persons who have the Power of making Laws, to have also in their hands the power to execute them," Locke asserted that in well-constituted states "the Legislative and Executive Power come often to be separated."[87]

Montesquieu argued in a similar vein in his *Spirit of the Laws.* Early in this work he targeted French reason of state theorists for criticism:

> Cardinal Richelieu, thinking perhaps that he had degraded the orders of the state too much, has recourse to the virtues of the prince and his ministers to sustain it, and he requires so many things of them that, in truth, only an an-

gel could have so much care, so much enlightenment, so much firmness, and so much knowledge; one can scarcely flatter oneself that, between now and the dissolution of monarchies, there could ever be such a prince and such ministers.[88]

Montesquieu aimed to lay out a political theory suitable for mere mortals. Like Locke, he placed his faith in institutional arrangements rather than the virtues of princes and ministers. In the first place, he argued that the legislative and executive powers should be separated, adding that the judicial power should also be separated from these other two.[89] He also dismissed the right of the executive authority to carry out arbitrary arrests and imprisonments.[90] He thus limited the scope of executive prerogative primarily to matters relating to war, peace, and national security. But within this limited field of action, he still favored a strong and discretionary executive. He claimed that "the executive power should be in the hands of a monarch, because the part of the government that almost always needs immediate action is better administered by one," and noted that the legislative power should not have the right to check executive actions: "for, as execution has the limits of its own nature, it is useless to restrict it."[91]

In sum, Richelieu and his propagandists carved out a legitimate role for the executive authority to exercise a discretionary power for the public interest. Later writers whittled down the scope of this authority, but maintained its role within the state. Today the ideas of Richelieu and his supporters still continue to inform our understanding of executive authority.[92] Somewhat surprisingly, then, this power has only infrequently been the topic of deep critical and historical reflection. In his own study of the development of executive power, Mansfield concluded that the history of modern executive power pointed to a fundamental ambivalence: the modern executive authority is both subordinate and superior to the laws, lawful and tyrannical. The present study points to an outright incoherence. The legitimacy of modern executive prerogative was originally founded upon divine right theory. This was no accident. French reason of state theorists understood that the only way to justify the enormous powers they were claiming for their king was to assert his divine ordination and inspiration. Even writers who made much less of the king's divine inspiration, such as Richelieu, Naudé, and Rohan, asserted no less unrealistic expectations for the king's character. The king was supposed to be a perfect stoical sage standing above the times, removed from all partisan and class interests and detached from his own passions and dispositions. He was supposed to be the perfect universal representative of the public interest. When writers such as Locke and Montesquieu incorporated the theory of executive prerogative into their political philosophies, they limited the powers of the executive officer. But they did not eliminate the need for pure virtue within the scope of his authority. Mansfield noted this point in *Taming the Prince*. He asserted that liberal theorists have relied far too much upon institutions and offices to create good government and given too little thought to "the need for virtue."[93] This is no doubt true. Yet Mansfield himself failed to acknowledge the more-than-human virtue required of the modern executive officer. Aristotle questioned whether any individual would ever be sufficiently virtuous to exercise the sort of prerogative powers associated with the modern executive. We must wonder with him whether our modern theory of executive power is not a standing invitation for abuse.

The ideas of French reason of state theorists highlight still other problems with the modern doctrine of executive power. Richelieu and his supporters premised their theory of executive prerogative upon several dubious assumptions. They claimed that: (1) the political community was a distinct and quasi-sacred entity; (2) the political community possessed clearly identifiable and objective interests that state rulers were uniquely able to discern and implement; and (3) the temporal world, and especially the "outside" world of foreign affairs, was dominated by corruption, chaos, and contingency and thus posed a continual threat to the integrity and peace of the political community. While these assumptions are still embraced by members of the "neorealist" school of international relations, they are increasingly out of step with contemporary affairs.[94] By most accounts, the boundaries between states are breaking down; global interdependence is on the rise; the interests of "the people" under national governments are becoming increasingly diverse. Studying the historical and theoretical development of the principle of executive prerogative reminds us of the peculiarity of this principle. It has not always existed but was invented in particular circumstances for particular reasons. It makes us question whether this principle, forged by Richelieu and his propagandists, is still relevant to our political affairs today.

CHAPTER FOUR

Louis XIV and the Ideology
of the Regulatory State

*I*n 1666, Louis XIV struck a medal to commemorate his first military review. The left side of the medal shows several rows of soldiers standing in rigid formation with their rifles raised in unison. On the right side the king stands commanding the soldiers with a baton in hand. The inscription on the medal reads, *Disciplina militaris restitua.* For Michel Foucault, this medal provided "evidence of the moment" when the new technology of disciplinary power began to emerge in the West. "Paradoxically but significantly, the most brilliant figure of sovereign power is joined to the emergence of the rituals proper to disciplinary power."[1] According to Foucault, Louis XIV's disciplinary techniques soon passed from the hands of the king to a variety of social institutions including prisons, schools, hospitals, and workshops.[2] Nonetheless, the detailed regulation and surveillance of society remained a core component of modern state power. In fact, it became one of the distinguishing features of the modern state. While medieval and Renaissance monarchies concerned themselves only with general matters relating to the whole order of the kingdom, Alexis de Tocqueville observed, the modern state "takes control of the humblest citizen and directs his behavior even in trivial matters."

> It provides for their security, foresees and supplies their necessities, facilitates their pleasures, manages their principal concerns, directs their industry, makes rules for their testaments, and divides their inheritance. . . . It covers the whole of social life with a network of petty, complicated rules that are both minute and uniform, through which even men of the greatest originality and the most vigorous temperament cannot force their heads above the crowd.[3]

The French anarchist Pierre-Joseph Proudhon described the functioning of the modern state in even more vivid terms: "To be governed is to be at every operation, at every transaction, noted, registered, enrolled, taxed, stamped, measured, numbered, assessed, licensed, authorized, admonished, forbidden, reformed, corrected, punished."[4]

Louis XIV never came close to imposing this sort of regulatory power upon his people. He was limited by technological, financial, and cultural constraints. In fact revisionist historians have shown in recent years that Louis XIV's power was far from "absolute." He governed France by means of clientage networks, patronage, persuasion, and other arrangements that made his power largely dependent upon the cooperation of local nobles and elites.[5] Nonetheless, the king and his ministers did succeed in extending royal power over the daily lives of people much farther than previous governments had done. They greatly expanded the powers of the provincial intendants. They passed detailed regulations concerning the forests, waterways, civil and criminal laws, foreign and domestic trade, manufacturing, and other activities. They collected extensive information about the population and established a new records bureau. They reorganized the military and tax systems. And they created a public police force to monitor and discipline the population of Paris and eventually all the other important urban centers of France.[6]

Perhaps most importantly—and quite apart from the success or failure of their policies—Louis XIV and his supporters articulated a new regulatory vision of state power. Bodin outlined the ideal of a centralized law-making sovereign. Richelieu and his supporters defended the notion of discretionary executive power. Louis XIV and his advocates now added the vision of a regulatory state responsible for disciplining, monitoring, classifying, and ordering all affairs within society. Whereas *raison d'état* theorists had justified only the king's extraordinary and periodic interventions into society (that is, his coups d'état), Louis XIV and his ministers legitimized the king's permanent and all-pervasive presence throughout society. The regulatory theory of Louis XIV thus represented a significant and new principle of modern state power.[7]

Why did Louis XIV and his supporters think it was necessary to extend the state's powers throughout society? How did they explain and legitimize their regulatory vision of the state? Jay Smith has studied these questions with reference to the early modern "culture of merit."[8] During the seventeenth century, French political culture was still organized around a personal modality of service. The nobility measured their dignity in terms of service to and recognition by the king. Much of the nobility's hostility toward Richelieu stemmed from his efforts to mold Louis XIII into a more rationalistic and impersonal ruler removed from personal ties with his people. In the years leading up to the Fronde, the nobility complained that Louis XIII and Richelieu had "raised royal authority too high" and the king had become out of "touch" with his people.[9] Louis XIV was able to reassert and expand royal power by playing upon this traditional idiom of personal power. He invited the nobility back into his court and personal service. He made himself accessible to his subjects. He regularly applied his healing touch to the scrofulous. Above all, he portrayed the extension of his royal powers as an extension of his royal gaze and touch throughout society. By framing his new regulatory ambitions in terms of the traditional idiom of personal service, Louis XIV was able, Smith argued, to recruit the nobility into his state-building activities and ease the transition to state centralization.

It is suggested here that Louis XIV and his proponents legitimized the expansion of royal powers not only by playing upon an ethic of personal service, but also by appealing to the general statist ideology already developed by writers such as Montaigne, Bodin, and Richelieu. Louis XIV, Colbert, Bossuet, and others argued that human society was mired in personal interests and passions resulting in uncertainty and discord among the people. The king, by contrast, was divinely ordained and blessed with superior reasoning and moral capacities. He alone was capable of instituting a harmonious and sanctified political community amid the contingency and particularity of human affairs. But he could not fulfill this duty by means of legislative and executive power alone; to establish a harmonious and moral order, the king had to exercise a permanent and pervasive regulation and surveillance over all social affairs. The regulatory powers of the state thus grew out of the same nexus of ideas that gave birth to legislative sovereignty and executive prerogative. They were the last important element of modern state theory.

Smith concluded his study by pointing to a contradiction in Louis XIV's ideology. Louis XIV forged an uneasy synthesis between a personal modality of service and a public modality of the state.[10] The contradiction between the personal and impersonal, the traditional and modern, in the French administrative system was resolved only during the French Revolution, when the personal modality of service was finally jettisoned in favor of bureaucratic rationality. Situating Louis XIV's thought within the more general statist ideology, it can be seen that his philosophy points to even deeper problems at the heart of modern regulatory power. Louis XIV recognized that it would take a superhuman capacity to regulate all social affairs in a rational and universal manner. When this capacity proved to be beyond the abilities of any one individual, later writers transferred regulatory powers from the king to the abstract bureaucratic state. Nevertheless, the bureaucratic state continued to rest its legitimacy upon the myth of its super-rational and impartial authority, and continued to pursue the goal of forging a rational and unified social order. The ideology of the Sun King thus remained embedded within the regulatory state even after the absolute monarch was removed from the throne. The exalted ideals of this ideology explain much of the disrepute of state regulatory powers in modern times. On the one hand, the inability of state officials to achieve a superlative degree of reason and impartiality stands as a constant rebuke to the legitimacy of state regulatory powers; on the other hand, the state's goal of creating a universal rational society sets it at odds with the diversity of contemporary societies.

LOUIS XIV (1638–1715)

Louis XIV explained his political theory in his letters, in a few short writings, and most fully in *Mémoires pour l'instruction du dauphin*.[11] The king composed the *Mémoires* between 1661 and 1672 in collaboration with his royal secretaries Jean-Baptiste Colbert, Octave de Périgny, and Paul Pellison.[12] Although the secretaries did much of the actual writing and compiling of the *Mémoires,* Louis XIV provided the substance of the work and reviewed and corrected successive texts. He wrote this book to instruct his son in the art of ruling and to provide "a public accounting" of his actions. He explained that since it was impossible to explain many of his governmental actions when he carried them out, he also hoped his *Mémoires* would provide a means "to correct history if it should go astray and misunderstand from not having fully penetrated into my plans and into my motives" (M, 22).[13]

The *Mémoires* revolve around the idea of providential order.[14] Louis XIV never tired of reminding his son that all human and temporal affairs were ultimately in the hands of "a rational mind, infinitely greater and higher than ours" (M, 59). At the same time, though, he argued that this order was at least partially accessible through reason. He warned his son against the "dangerous error" of "imagining that the world is governed by certain fortuitous and natural changes that were impossible to predict or avoid" (M, 99). This was "a notion that ordinary minds easily accept because it appeals to their limited insights and to their laziness and permits them to call their errors misfortune and the industry of others good fortune." In fact, what ordinary minds called "the caprice of fate" was actually the plan of "wise Providence" (M, 225). Louis XIV assured his son that an enlightened king could usually gain some insight into the workings of this power.

> As much, my son, as you must acknowledge your submission to a Superior Power capable of upsetting your best-laid plans whenever It pleases, always rest assured, on the other hand, that having Itself established the natural order of things, It will not easily or constantly violate it, either in your favor or to your prejudice. It can assure us in time of peril, strengthen us in our labors, enlighten us in our doubts, but It hardly does our work without us, and when It wants to make a king fortunate, powerful, supported, and respected, Its most normal course is to make him wise, clear-sighted, fair, vigilant, and industrious. (M, 99)

Andrew Lossky has argued that Louis XIV significantly changed his opinion about Providence later in life.[15] Especially in the last two decades of his reign, when he suffered a succession of military defeats and personal losses, Louis XIV abandoned his early rationalism and came to believe that Providence exercised a decisive and arbitrary influence over human affairs. Without doubt, Louis XIV did become obsessed with the workings of Providence in his later years. Specifically, he came to believe that God was punishing him for his excessive pride.[16] But it seems an overstatement to say that he changed his worldview in any significant sense. Louis XIV's early "rationalism" was hardly "classicist," as Lossky claims. Even in his early writings (as, for example, in the above passage), Louis XIV indicated that it was God who ultimately supplied the wisdom necessary to penetrate into affairs. In another passage, he expressed confidence in his plans because Providence seemed to be "directing all things toward the same purpose It inspired in me" (M, 26). Louis XIV further acknowledged in the *Mémoires* his belief in the utter dependency of human beings upon Providence. At any moment, he noted, Providence might arbitrarily abandon or punish an individual in order to remind him of his dependence upon God.

> The caprice of fate, or rather that wise Providence that rules supreme over our interests for purposes beyond our comprehension, chooses sometimes to deflate the pomp of the loftiest men in order to oblige them, in the midst of their greatest advantages, to recognize the source of all their blessings and to merit through a continual avowal of their dependence, the assistance necessary for the success of their plans. (M, 225)

Any change that may have occurred in Louis XIV's ideas about Providence from the beginning to the end of his reign would thus seem to have been more a change of emphasis than substance. The king did not shift from a Cartesian worldview to a providentialist one. Rather, he appears only to have come to believe in his later years that God had abandoned him, with the result that he was no longer capable of penetrating into the true nature of affairs.

In the *Machiavellian Moment*, J. G. A. Pocock contrasted the medieval providentialist approach to history with the humanist discourse of virtue and fortune.[17] The humanists asserted an element of contingency within human affairs and a place for human self-assertion quite out of line with providential history. Louis XIV combined these two frameworks. He argued that conforming oneself to the providential order entailed adapting oneself to changing times and circumstances.[18] He even borrowed freely from the humanist discourse of fortune and virtue to explain his providentialist views. He wrote that "the entire art of politics consists of playing on circumstances" and that "virtue" consists "of acting rationally, that is, as time and circumstances require" (M, 96, 99). He added more generally a bit later: "Wisdom lies in choosing the proper policy at the proper time, and nothing renders the fortunes of a prince more stable and less changing, perhaps, than his ability to change his tone, his expression, his bearing, and his direction when necessary" (M, 169). Louis XIV thus overlaid the humanist theory of fortune with a providential theory of history. Anyone who could adapt to the times could not just conquer fortune but actually enter into providential history.

Louis XIV argued that few individuals, however, possessed the virtue or reason necessary to discern the true nature of times and circumstances. The problem lay with their passions and interests. Like so many other writers of his generation, Louis XIV claimed that the passions and interests of human beings tended to corrupt their reasoning capacities.[19] Specifically, they distorted individuals' perceptions of the world by inclining them to view objective external events in terms of their wants and desires:

> The fire of the most noble passions, as well as that of the most common, always produces enough smoke to obscure our reason. One often wonders how, out of many who see and hear the same thing, hardly two reports are ever the same; and yet this variety comes only from the different interests and passions of men, who unconsciously reconcile everything they see around them to their state of mind. (M, 228)

The *Mémoires* are filled with reflections upon the distorting effects of the passions and the interests. The king constantly found himself bombarded by advice that reflected the particular interests of his ministers and officers (M, 75, 158, 242). No matter how hard they tried, most individuals could not help but to distort their account of affairs according to their own bias and interests. In an interesting appropriation of Machiavelli's thought, Louis XIV applied this insight to explain why most individuals were afflicted with inveterate disorder in their lives.[20]

> Since most men are accustomed to act emotionally rather than rationally and since they are most often guided by their disposition and by their passions, their disposition, which remains the same, almost always maintains them on the same course. Whatever disorder they may see in their affairs, whatever misfortune may befall them, they don't have enough good sense to seek its cause in their conduct. They attribute the entire thing solely to the caprice of fortune and do not consider that if, on feeling its first blows, they would have devised a new way of dealing with it, they would assuredly have guarded against the worst cruelty, for it is certain that one of the best remedies against these changes is to change with them. (M, 169)

While this passage was clearly inspired by Machiavelli, Louis XIV gave it a wholly new meaning.[21] He presented the problem of fortune as a problem of cognition and morality. Human beings were subject to fortune and disorder primarily because their passions and emotions distorted their reason, making them incapable of perceiving the true order of things. If human beings could only suppress their passions and exercise their reason, Louis XIV claimed they could elevate themselves entirely above the realm of fortune and contingency and bring divine order and stability to their lives.

Although private individuals would always struggle to adapt their affairs to the providential order, Louis XIV contended that "the able monarch, like the wise pilot, can sail with every wind," always "choosing the proper policy at the proper time," bringing "glory" and "greatness" to the "state" (M, 169–70). Louis XIV explained the special virtue of kings in a variety of ways.[22] First and foremost was his theory of the divine right of kings.[23] During the seventeenth century, French state theorists argued not only that the king was directly ordained by God but also that he shared in some modicum of divine wisdom. Louis XIV wholeheartedly embraced this exalted vision of rule.[24] He claimed that God had directly ordained kings to rule as "His lieutenants" and forbade all forms of disobedience, "reserving to Himself alone the right to examine their conduct" (M, 244–45). God further endowed kings with a special light for governing human affairs. "There are undoubtedly some [functions]," Louis XIV wrote, "where taking, so to speak, the place of God, we seem to participate in His knowledge as well as in His authority, as for example in regard to discerning character, distributing positions, and dispensing graces, things that we can decide better ourselves than our councilors can, because in our higher sphere we are further removed from the petty interests that might lead us to be unjust" (M, 227–28). In other matters, when reason failed, Louis XIV claimed that the king's instincts were still superior to those of private individuals. "Wisdom demands that in certain instances much be left to chance. Reason itself then suggests compliance with certain blind movements or instincts beyond reason, seemingly inspired by Heaven, known to all men, and more worthy of consideration in those whom It has Itself placed in the first ranks" (M, 38–39). With the full confidence of one who believed in his own divine inspiration, Louis XIV wrote that "the function of kings consists primarily of using good sense, which always comes naturally and easily" (M, 30).

While Louis XIV is probably best known for his divine right theory, he also justified monarchical rule through a number of other arguments. He claimed birth and upbringing, for example, bestowed special advantages upon monarchs. Because kings were born into their high status and were trained from an early age to rule, they developed a sense of internal dignity that allowed them to distance themselves from external changes of fortune. By contrast, because the bourgeoisie measured their status in terms of external accomplishments and goods, they were much more susceptible to changes of fortune. Comparing monarchical government with the rule of the "low-born," the king wrote:

> It is a rather usual fault of those who are not born to greatness to be stunned by it when they attain it and to be able to sustain neither the brilliance that adorns it nor the storms that can threaten it. . . . Lacking both naturalness and breeding in all their actions, they always advance or retreat at the wrong time.

They never fail to do too much or too little, and the most uniform and constant thing about their vacillating behavior is that they always become excessively proud in the midst of good fortune and fall into extreme despair the moment it turns against them. But princes must assuredly be completely free from this failing, because deriving their principal greatness from their merit or from their birth, the ups and downs of fortune should affect neither their bearing nor their feelings. (M, 212)

Louis XIV believed that kings were, so to speak, natural born stoics. Their status raised them above the petty interests of private individuals and allowed them to take a more disinterested and rational approach toward human and temporal affairs.

Louis XIV argued that the public nature of the king's duties further contributed to his special reasoning capacities. Whereas private individuals always experienced a conflict between their own personal interests and the public good, the king's private interests were always identical with the public good (M, 42, 67–68).[25] The king profited only to the extent that his people prospered. His glory was tied to the glory of the state.[26] When it came to making decisions about state matters, he was therefore largely immune from private passions. He could rule with an objectivity that usually escaped private individuals. In explaining why, for example, he was able "to penetrate in so short a time" into the "terrible confusion" and "obscurity" of the royal finances "that so many able superintendents had never yet clarified," Louis XIV pointed to "the natural difference between the interest of the prince and that of the superintendent" (M, 64–65). While the superintendent and other private individuals always approached "their position with no greater care than to preserve their own liberty to dispose of everything as they see fit," the king approached state matters with no other interest than to promote the public good. He was able to exercise his reason free from the distractions of private interests. Louis XIV concluded: "The prince alone should have sovereign direction over [the finances] because he alone has no fortune to establish but that of the state, no acquisition to make except for the monarchy, no authority to strengthen other than that of the laws, no debts to pay besides the public ones, no friends to enrich save his people" (M, 64).

Louis XIV summarized his case for monarchy in the following terms: "a sovereign may be sure of this about himself: that since his rank is above other men, he can also see things more clearly than they" (M, 227). By divine right, birth, breeding, and public office, he was raised above private interests and blessed with an impartial reasoning capacity. He could penetrate into the true nature of the times and circumstances to a degree impossible to private individuals. Louis XIV argued that it was his duty, therefore, to use his reason to institute "a natural and legitimate order" among human beings (M, 43). In the tradition of neostoical thought, he claimed it was the special responsibility of the state to bring human beings into line with the divine reason.

Consistent with these beliefs, Louis XIV argued that the king should possess absolute and undivided control over legislation and jurisdiction because the parliaments and courts tended to use these powers for their private interests (M, 40–44, 196–97).[27] He further asserted that his special reasoning and moral capacities entitled him to dispose of the lives and goods of his subjects, contravene the laws and morality, and perform all other sorts of extraordinary actions as he saw fit. "What they [kings] seem to do sometimes against the common law is based on reason of state, which is the first of all laws by common consent, yet the most unknown and the most obscure to all those who do not rule" (M, 43–44). But Louis XIV devoted the main part of his *Mémoires* to legitimizing the regulatory and disciplinary powers of the state. In order to impose a rational and universal order upon society, Louis XIV claimed he had to know, touch, and regulate all affairs. His reason and power had to extend down to the minutest of social affairs. On this point Louis XIV's statist ideology joined seamlessly with his attention to personal merit and service. As Smith demonstrated, Louis XIV portrayed his regulatory powers as an extension of his personal gaze and touch. Yet the king's appeal to the rhetoric of personal power was not just a smokescreen to cover his state-building aspirations. Louis XIV appears to have sincerely believed that political order depended upon his direct and personal control of all affairs.

Louis XIV best expressed this conception of royal power in his discussion of the Fronde. The Fronde, he wrote, was not really the fault of the "nobility, clergy, or third estate" who had all fallen into "terrible lapses" in the past and were prone by their very nature to selfish and disorderly conduct (M, 42). No, the real fault lay with king himself, who had allowed the "laxity of the monarchy" to get "out of hand during my minority" (M, 102). Without the severe hand of the king to guide affairs, the French people naturally reverted to their private interests and pursued selfish goals at the expense of public order.

> For as soon as a young king relents on his commands, authority flees and tranquility accompanies it. Those who are closest to the prince, being the first to know his weakness, are also the first to abuse it; then come those of the second rank, and so on down the line for those in any position of power. Everything falls upon the lowest classes, oppressed thereby by thousands of tyrants in the place of a legitimate king, whose indulgence alone creates all this disorder. (M, 45)

Louis XIV claimed to harbor no grudges against the Frondeurs (M, 42). They could hardly help themselves. The Fronde simply revealed the true nature of humanity in the absence of the disciplinary power of the king. It was for Louis XIV the equivalent of the state of nature. Without the heavy disciplinary hand of the king over society, individuals naturally reverted to a state of civil war.

Louis XIV claimed the only remedy for this disorder was to assert his own personal and direct control over all social and political affairs. This required two related reforms. In the first place, he had to concentrate all authority in his own hands. On March 10, 1661, only one day after Mazarin's death, he summoned his ministers to court and informed them that he would govern alone without the aid of a first minister. He then proceeded to instruct his ministers that they were "not to sign anything at all any longer without discussing it with me"—"not even a passport"[28]—and "announced that all requests for graces of any type had to be made directly to me" (M, 30–31). The second step toward establishing order was to extend his regulatory powers throughout the kingdom. Louis XIV made himself directly accessible to all his subjects so that they might inform him of the disorders throughout the kingdom (M, 31). He endeavored to cast "an eye on the whole earth," to learn "the news of all the provinces and of all nations," and to become aware "of an infinite number of things that we are presumed to ignore" so that he might begin to address the particular problems of the provinces (M, 30). In short, he aspired to know and regulate all affairs "if it were possible for a single man to know everything and to do everything" (M, 32). Louis XIV aimed to engulf all of France in his person: "L'état, c'est moi." While the king probably never actually uttered this phrase, the sentiment aptly conveys his aspirations.[29] He believed that the stability and happiness of the French society—nay, its very existence—depended upon his regulation and surveillance of each and every part of it.

Louis XIV provided numerous examples in his *Mémoires* to demonstrate the benefits of a more expansive regulatory authority. In 1662, for example, he noted that France confronted a grave food shortage. Predictably enough, in the king's eyes, his subjects reacted in wholly particular and self-interested ways: there were "artisans who raised the prices of their products in proportion to the cost of living, the poor making their complaints and their murmurs heard everywhere, middling families who held back their usual charities from fear of an impending need, the most wealthy burdened with their servants and unable to do everything" (M, 83). It was not possible to rely on "the remedies at hand" to resolve this crisis because even the existing magistrates were "all too often weak and incompetent, lacking in zeal, or even corrupt." The only solution was for the king to stake out a new course by taking matters directly into his own hands.

> I became intimately acquainted with the needs of the people and with conditions. I obliged the more affluent provinces to aid the others, private individuals to open their stores and to put up their commodities at a fair price. I hastily sent orders everywhere to bring in as much wheat as I possibly could by sea from Danzig and from other foreign countries. I had my treasury purchase it. I distributed most of it free to the lower classes of the biggest cities, such as Paris, Rouen, Tours, and others. I had the rest sold at a very modest price. (M, 83–84)

Louis XIV took it upon himself to do what his subjects, because of their narrow self-interests, could not do by themselves. He reordered and regulated their social relations so that each could attain basic needs. So successful was his venture that the king announced his intention to establish a permanent regulatory system to distribute welfare "if God gives me the grace to execute everything that I have in mind." "I mean [there should be] no one, however impoverished he may be, who is not assured of his sustenance either through his work or through normal and regulated aid" (M, 84). Henceforth the king would be responsible for providing sufficient work and food for the people. Since human beings were incapable by themselves of ensuring that everyone would attain their natural necessities, Louis XIV indicated that he would enforce the "natural order of things." Using the case of the famine to reflect generally upon his duties, he wrote:

> We hardly note the admirable order of the world and the regular and useful course of the sun until some disturbance in the seasons or some apparent disorder in the machine makes us give it a little more reflection. As long as everything in a state is prosperous, it is easy to forget the infinite blessings that royalty provides and merely envy those that it possesses. Man, naturally ambitious and proud, can never understand why another should command him until he feels the need for it. (M, 84–85)

Louis XIV suggested here that the apparently natural order of society actually depended upon his constant vigilance. People tended to forget that the social order was neither inevitable nor self-sustaining until some catastrophe struck. Then the king was called upon to set things right. But Louis XIV's deeper point was that his extraordinary interventions into society were really only the most overt expression of the sort of power he always exercised over it. The apparently natural order of society actually derived from the perpetual and minute regulations of the king.

Louis XIV further trumpeted the benefits of his regulatory powers in discussing military affairs. At the beginning of his personal reign, the king claimed that his military, like most other areas of French society, was rife with disorder. Discipline was nonexistent; ranks were confused; officers used their positions for personal gain. Louis XIV responded by asserting (or at least attempting to assert) direct and pervasive control over all military matters.[30] He set about "carefully reviewing" all of his troops (M, 150). He regulated ranks. He "went to the trouble of distributing even the most minor offices in the infantry as well as in the cavalry myself, something that my predecessors had never done, having always relied on the superior officers for this" (M, 151). He further "assigned quarters to the troops," "settled differences between units and between mere officers," set out a new set of regulations for "order and discipline among the troops in their quarters," and generally "believed that I had to make sure of everything myself" (M, 151, 153). The result was a more orderly and disciplined body of officers and soldiers. "So must you be entirely convinced," Louis XIV wrote his son, "that our dedication to the public welfare or to the good of our service is the only means of satisfactorily achieving them." Once a king relented on any detail of affairs, it fell prey to the particular interests of private individuals. In a passage that nicely summarizes the core assumptions of Louis XIV's conception of kingship, he wrote:

> When private individuals discover that the prince lacks dedication, that whatever good and evil they may do go equally unnoticed, that in either case they will be equally treated, and that he who has so many people working for him at once will not go to a moment's trouble to see how he is being served, they gradually develop a cowardly indifference that makes their courage fail, their vigor slacken, their mind soften, and even their body grow heavy. . . . But when, on the contrary, a prince is always seeking what is best for his service, when it is realized that nothing escapes his attention, that he discerns everything, that he weights everything, and that sooner or later he punishes and rewards everything, this cannot help but make him both better obeyed and more highly esteemed. His dedication seems to descend from rank to rank down to the lowliest officer of his troops; each one who is at fault fears, each one who has served well hopes, and all constantly strive to do their duty as the only means of making their fortune. (M, 152)

Louis XIV believed his attention to details was the lifeblood of society. It was his gaze and touch that motivated individuals to vigorous and public action.[31] If the king limited his attention only to general concerns, or left matters to the whims of private individuals, dissension and misfortune would ensue. As the sole source of universal reason within society, the king had to extend his powers down to the least details of the people's daily lives in order to promote order and prosperity among them.

Louis XIV most vividly depicted his regulatory aspirations through the symbol of the sun. In explaining why he chose this symbol to represent his reign, he wrote that it was because nothing else

> makes a most vivid and a most beautiful image for a great monarch . . . by virtue of its uniqueness, by the brilliance that surrounds it, by the light that it imparts to the other heavenly bodies that seem to pay it court, by its equal and just distribution of this same light to all the various parts of the world, by the good that it does everywhere, constantly producing life, joy, and activity everywhere, by its perpetual yet always imperceptible movement, by never departing or deviating from its steady and invariable course. (M, 103–4)

Louis XIV saw himself and wished others to see him as the Sun King: a public and rational ruler imparting order and morality to all corners of society and to each of his subjects' lives. His power was the light of the sun, the earthly manifestation of divine reason. He feared that whatever he did not touch or see would become part of the dark shadow world of the passions and the interests.

In the *Mémoires*, Louis XIV not only outlined a new regulatory vision of the state, but also identified a number of new governmental techniques for fulfilling his regulatory aspirations. The main tenets of this new style of rule were information-gathering, surveillance, and impartiality. Taken together, these techniques represent a significant extension of the rationalistic theory of rule proposed by Montaigne, Lipsius, Naudé, and Richelieu. Louis XIV outlined the basic principles of a new impersonal and disciplinary statecraft that aimed to bring all of society under the rationalizing gaze of the sovereign.

If the king were to regulate everything, he had to know everything. It was only by knowing the exact circumstances of each event that the king could apply the proper remedy to it. Hence Louis XIV asserted that information-gathering was essential to his regulatory authority:

> Nothing is so necessary for those who work on important affairs than to know what is really happening to their interests. Neither our ministers nor ourselves can deliberate with any assurance unless we have very exact knowledge of what goes on around us; and since reason itself, which governs all the other human faculties, cannot operate without the evidence of the senses, sovereigns cannot act in their counsels without a constant flow of news from their agents. (M, 215)

Earlier thinkers had made similar calls for information-gathering. Jean Bodin and Antoine de Montchrétien had suggested that the king should commission a census to inform himself about his subjects and kingdom.[32] But what was new with Louis XIV was his emphasis on the need for continual, detailed, and exact information about all social affairs. He saw detailed information as a prerequisite to the king's virtue. If Machiavelli had proclaimed that historical maxims could aid a prince in his struggle against fortune, Louis XIV—the "roi-bureaucrate"—now asserted that detailed information was the key to success:[33]

> Don't be astonished if I so often exhort you to work, to see everything, to listen to everything, to know everything. I have already told you: there is a vast difference between general insights that are usually useful only for discussions and particular ones that must almost always be followed in practice. Maxims are most often misleading to vulgar minds. Things are rarely as they should be. Laziness stops at common notions in order to avoid thinking and acting. The effort lies in evoking particular circumstances in order to profit from them, and one never accomplishes anything extraordinary, great, and wonderful without thinking about it more and more often than others. (M, 95)

In order to govern rationally—that is, according to the order of Providence—Louis XIV claimed he had to have a very precise knowledge of "times and circumstances" (M, 96). Ignorance of the least detail could lead the king to make a wrong decision, causing him to fall out of line with the providential order and inviting misfortune into public affairs.

Louis XIV further argued that the success of his regulatory aspirations depended upon the implementation of new surveillance and disciplinary practices. Ideally, of course, the king would personally regulate everything within the kingdom. But he recognized that this was practically impossible. He was constrained by the limitations of his own physical body. To extend his presence throughout the kingdom, Louis XIV therefore devised a number of strategies and procedures to ensure that his will would be done even when he could not be present personally to enforce it.

Most importantly, Louis XIV asserted that the king had to make a careful selection and placement of officers. "We obviously cannot do everything," he wrote, "but we must provide for everything to be done well, and this depends primarily on whom we choose. In a great state, there is always someone proper to every task, and the only question is to know who they are and to put them where they belong" (M, 255). Making only the slightest concession to his physical limitations, Louis XIV observed that since he could not actually do everything himself, he would at least endeavor to know all the potential public functionaries within his kingdom and place each one personally in the position most suited to the public good. Yet even assuming he were successful at this first Herculean task, Louis XIV noted that his work would still be incomplete. His administrative appointees would inevitably succumb to their personal passions and interests. Even the most well-intentioned officials invariably confused their own interests with the public good.[34] "Were their heart merely of a different mold than ours, and it always is, were their ideas and their inclinations different from ours, which never fails to happen, they would mislead us out of affection. They would then secretly oppose our wishes for the good of the state as they see it, and their good intentions would render us just as incapable of doing anything as their disloyalty" (M, 82). The king had to do more, therefore, than merely appoint each of his officials. He also had to subject them to a continual and pervasive surveillance. In the *Mémoires,* Louis XIV described several surveillance techniques. "The first is that you know your affairs thoroughly, because a king who does not know them is always dependent on his servants and most often cannot avoid consenting to their wishes" (M, 238). Detailed information was necessary not only for making decisions, but also for keeping tabs on administrative officials. A king who did not keep abreast of all affairs left them subject to the "caprice" of his ministers (M, 82). Louis XIV further suggested that a king should conduct periodic spot checks of his officers. He recounted how he would approach each of his ministers "when he would least expect it" to discuss the details of some matter "so that he would realize that I might do the same on other subjects and at any time" (M, 32). He likewise sent out special agents (that is, intendants) to conduct spot checks of his military officers and troops. His explanation of this procedure is quite revealing:

> I knew how easily captains and commanders who believed themselves out of my sight could relent on their duties and how their own interest could lead them to conspire against my service. That is why I sent special agents everywhere, with orders to catch the troops by surprise initially in order to check innocently on their condition, warning the commanders to put things in better order promptly and making it clear that they would return as often as they deemed it necessary. (M, 151)

The purpose of Louis XIV's spot checks was to make his officers believe that they were under the king's "constant surveillance" and "continual observation" (M, 148, 151, 179). In this way he hoped his officers would internalize his commands and begin to act on his behalf even when he was not there personally to oversee them.

Louis XIV further attempted to control his royal officers by manipulating their passions and interests. He suggested that a king should "divide your confidence among many, so that each who shares in it being naturally opposed to the advancement of his rivals, the jealousy of one often serves as a brake to the ambition of others" (M, 239). By setting each of his ministers in competition with the others, a king could use their passions and interests to check one another's ambitions. Alternatively, Louis XIV suggested that the king should also endeavor to link his officers' private interests directly to the public good. Since "it can be established as a general principle of human conduct that there is hardly anyone who does not have some natural and secret inclination toward his personal advantage," he wrote, the wise monarch needed to learn "how to play on these great springs" so that "even the most unscrupulous do not dare to depart ever so slightly from the right path" (M, 162). He should arrange affairs so that his officers were able to fulfill their private desires only "in honest practices, in meritorious actions, and in observing the rules of their profession" (M, 152). Here, then, we find a classic statement of what Albert Hirschman called "harnessing the passions."[35] The king aspired to manipulate the social reward structure so that his officers would be drawn to fulfill their private desires only in actions that contributed to the public good.

The final important element in Louis XIV's theory of statecraft was the principle of impersonal rule. Before the king could align his officers and people with universal reason, he first had to detach himself from all private passions and interests and make himself the perfect embodiment of the public will. Montaigne and Lipsius had first suggested this ethic of impersonal rule, and Richelieu and Naudé had further developed it. Louis XIV, however, was in the unenviable position of trying to live it. He explained to his son that despite the advantages of divine wisdom, birth, and public office, kings were not entirely immune to the passions and interests. "It must be confessed in good faith that there are also other instances when leaving, so it seems, the independent role of sovereigns, we become as biased as, if not more than the lowliest private individual" (M, 228). The independent and rational role of the king was only a potential capacity that the actual king had to strive to realize. The king thus had to work actively to make himself the embodiment of universal reason by suppressing all personal feelings, passions, and what we might call "personality." He had to "dehumanize" himself in the interests of the state (M, 28–29, 54–61, 111, 124, 132, 144–45, 236).[36] The king, Louis XIV wrote, should be a "perfect model of virtue . . . completely immune to the failings of the rest of mankind" (M, 246). When this proved impossible, Louis XIV indicated that the king at least had to try to hide his failings: "Exercising a divine function here below, we must try to appear incapable of the agitations that could belittle it, or if our heart not being able to belie the weakness of its nature feels the rise of these vulgar emotions in spite of itself, our reason must be extremely careful to hide them if they are harmful to the good of the state, for which alone we are born" (M, 133). The king's advice here was not mere vanity. It reflected his understanding of the nature of his legitimacy, which he tied directly to his superior reasoning and moral capacities. If the king revealed himself to be a common mortal susceptible to private passions and interests, the legitimacy of his rule might be questioned. The rule of a passionate and self-interested king was hardly different from tyranny. The king's regulatory ideology only made sense given the assumption that the king was the embodiment of pure reason and morality.

In *Discipline and Punish,* Foucault described Napoleon Bonaparte as a model of the "panoptic" prince. "He wished to arrange around him a mechanism of power that would enable him to see the smallest event that occurred in the state he governed; he intended, by means of the rigorous discipline that he imposed 'to embrace the whole of this vast machine without the slightest detail escaping his attention.'"[37] More than a century before Napoleon, Louis XIV had already outlined the ideal of and provided the justification for the "panoptic" prince. He claimed the only way individuals could be made to act for the public good was by extending the king's surveillance and regulations over all aspects of their lives. The total regulation of society was necessary to establish a public and rational state reflecting the universal divine and natural order. An important part of this regulatory ideal was the creation of a new administrative apparatus wholly dependent upon and reflecting the public will of the king. State officials had to be made to work for the public good even if only by subjecting them to a system of private incentives and rewards. Louis XIV, of course, never rationalized his administration to the extent he proposed. Nor was he ever able to regulate society as thoroughly as he wished. But regardless of the success of his reforms, Louis XIV's thought marked an important new vision of the nature and purpose of the state. He invented the regulatory theory of the state.

THE PUBLIC IMAGE OF LOUIS XIV

The regulatory ideology of the *Mémoires* received ample and varied public expression during Louis XIV's reign. There appeared innumerable books, poems, paintings, statues, plays, and panegyrics lauding the divine inspiration and godlike qualities of the king.[38] Louis XIV was described as "the god-given," "a living god," "a visible divinity," "august," "wise," "immortal," "glorious," and "invincible."[39] He was portrayed as Apollo and Mars, Jupiter and Hercules, Alexander the Great and Caesar. Many of these works served the broad purpose of exalting the king's person. Others praised his military accomplishments or defended his military policies. But a number of works served more specifically to publicize and justify the king's regulatory ambitions.

The king's letters to his provincial officers were one important avenue for publicizing his regulatory ideology. While less public than a book or pamphlet, these letters served to inform royal officials of the king's wishes and desires. One of the pervasive themes of these letters was the king's desire to receive detailed information about all affairs in even the most remote corners of the provinces, which he considered essential for making precise decisions about all matters. A letter to his minister of war Louvois in 1676 clearly conveys this sentiment: "Continue to send me and send me from all sides, as you have done, the copies of letters [between yourself and your subordinates] in order that I may be very well informed of everything, so that I do not give orders that can leave those to whom they are addressed uncertain."[40] Statements like these appear throughout the king's letters.[41] John Wolf has written that Louis XIV's letters "fairly bulge with demands for information; he wanted to know everything that could be known about his kingdom and about the affairs of neighboring states."[42] He repeatedly demanded of his officers, "You will report exactly what you hear," "I desire exact and complete information," "I expect you to give me information of the place where you are." The king most broadly set out his regulatory ambitions in his *Instruction pour les maîtres des requêtes* of 1663. The purpose of the *Instruction* was declared in the preamble:

> The King wanting to be clearly informed of the state of the provinces within his kingdom, His Majesty has willed that this memoir be sent in his name to the *maîtres des requêtes,* so that they can work each in the expanse of their jurisdictions to inform themselves carefully and exactly about the matters specified by all the articles contained herein.[43]

The "articles contained herein" charged the *maîtres* with gathering detailed information about all aspects of their provinces and reporting it to the king so that he would be able more easily to order all affairs. The *maîtres* were given the task of collecting and correcting all maps of their areas. They were supposed to compile detailed information about all the ecclesiastical, military, judicial, and financial officials. Louis XIV directed them to investigate the family alliances, property, and habits of the nobility. The *maîtres* were further called upon to provide a detailed account of the character of the people in each province and city, including the sorts of goods they produced, their commerce, and manufacturing. They were also expected to look into the financial and judicial systems and to report any abuses they might find, as well as provide recommendations for improving manufacturing, canals, roads, bridges, and waterways. The list of demands went on for pages and was punctuated in the final paragraphs by the assertion that the *maîtres* should take these instructions only as a starting point for their investigations. Louis XIV was sure his officers would find "an infinity of things" to add to their reports. The response of the *maîtres* was less than enthusiastic. Twenty years later Colbert was still trying to obtain most of the information requested in the *Instruction*. Yet even if the king's ambitions were never realized, his correspondence at least made his ambitions clear to all. No official in the royal administration under Louis XIV could have remained unaware that the king and his ministers were aspiring to a new ideal of state power. He was striving for the detailed surveillance and minute regulation of all social affairs throughout France.

The letters of Colbert gave expression to another important area of French regulatory policy: mercantilism.[44] Colbert's mercantilist policies involved not only the extensive regulation of imports and exports, but also the detailed regulation of domestic manufacturing. Colbert dictated what could be manufactured, by whom, when, where, and how. In the fields of textile manufacturing and dyeing, especially, he drew up very precise regulations specifying the qualifications of workers, the legal means of production, and the required width, length, and thickness of different types of cloth. A few clauses from his regulations for Beauvais may serve as an example:

> 21. Wide ratines to have a fixed number of threads in the warp. To be 30 to 34 ells long and $1\frac{1}{4}$ to $1\frac{1}{3}$ ells wide when finished.
> 22. Spanish-style serges to have a fixed number of threads in the warp. White ones to be 28 to 31 ells long and 1 ell wide when finished. Grays ones to be 24 to 27 ells long and $1\frac{1}{4}$ ells wide when finished. . . .
> 30. If a weaver makes a poor selvage, 5 sous fine.
> 31. If a weaver leaves a piece of cloth dirty and mussy, 2 sous fine.[45]

Colbert justified his detailed regulation of manufacturing in two ways. First, he asserted that his policies were based upon "the universal and fundamental law" of commerce and industry.[46] He constantly asserted that his policies would redound to the good of society, the state, and the merchants involved.[47] His detailed regulation of the textile industry, for example, was based on what he took to be the objective truth of commerce: that only high-quality goods could win over foreign and domestic markets.[48] Second, Colbert asserted that state regulation was necessary to ensure high-quality goods because the typical French merchant and manufacturer were greedy, passionate, self-interested, and irrational.[49] They placed short-term gains before long-term interests, their own selfish desires ahead of the general advancement of French manufacturing and commerce. Colbert thus believed that the state had an obligation to intervene in commerce and manufacturing for the merchants' and manufacturers' own good as well as the good of society as a whole. Like Louis XIV, he claimed that only the king and his ministers were sufficiently removed from the petty interests of private individuals to recognize the true interests of the people. Any matter that escaped their regulation was apt to be corrupted by private interest and ambition. Two quotes nicely capture Colbert's sentiments about these matters.[50] He wrote in a letter to the intendant at Toulouse:

> All merchants in general want to have complete liberty in everything that concerns their trade, and particularly in manufacturing where they always want to change and reduce the lengths, widths, and workmanship in pursuit of some petty gain that they make and that tends to the entire ruin of manufacturing, of which the principle consists, in a state as flourishing and great as this, in making them always equal in goodness, length, and width.
>
> To attain this point of fidelity, which is the principle of every sort of commerce, it is necessary to go far beyond the reasons of petty individual interests that do not merit to enter into the general reasons of the good of the state.[51]

And then again in another letter he wrote:

> In the kingdom, I have always found manufacturers obstinate in continuing in the errors and abuses that they commit in their manufacturing. But when one has used authority in order to make them execute the new regulations, as much for length and width as for good workmanship and dyeing, they have sensibly witnessed the augmentation of their manufacturing, and foreigners come to buy their products in the kingdom with a lot more abundance than before; so that it is necessary to be ready to employ firmness and authority in order to vanquish the obstinacy of the manufacturers.[52]

Colbert applied similar arguments to justify the regulation of foreign trade.[53] In terms closely resembling the arguments of Louis XIV's *Mémoires*, he portrayed merchants and manufacturers as petulant children in need of a wise king to guide their activities toward their own and society's good.

Louis XIV's regulatory ideology received a more public defense in Pierre Le Moyne's *De l'art de regner* (1665). In the dedication of this work, Le Moyne declared his intention to paint a portrait of the king to serve as an example of the perfect ruler. The symbol that Le Moyne chose to represent the king's rule was, not surprisingly, the sun. He chose this symbol "because I did not believe I could find any figure more illustrious to represent Your Majesty nor any model more complete to instruct other princes."[54] In the opening pages of the work, Le Moyne outlined the Sun King's virtues in verse:

I cast my eye over everything, but an enlightened eye
That never mistakes appearances for the truth.
With my gaze I create the light
That pierces the fog of the darkest matters:
Equally present whether I am far or near
I cut through trouble, I penetrate secrets:
And the obscurity that affairs blacken
Is never too black for my eye to enlighten.

Le Moyne's verse painted the perfect picture of the all-seeing and all-doing prince. Jean-Marie Apostolidès dubbed his description of governmental power "ocular imperialism."[55] The king's gaze brought light to everything. Yet Le Moyne considered his description as yet incomplete, for the Sun King surpassed the sun in one respect. "It is an error," he hastened to add, "to think that each night I sleep in the sea, far from the world and noise." After the sun set, the king continued to work. He was ever-present and ever-vigilant: "There without relaxation, and without diversion, both night and day I am in action" (AR, epistle).

The first part of Le Moyne's treatise developed these themes in a more substantive manner. The prince was the "image and lieutenant of God in his state" (AR, 26). It was his duty to "regulate" and "align" all those actions within the world "that Nature has not regulated" (AR, 6). In Le Moyne's estimation, this comprised the whole of society, which was naturally disorderly. The prince alone gave society "its being and form, its consistency and status" (AR, 8). Without his authority society would be like a ship without a rudder or compass, "exposed to all the abuses of the winds, and all the caprices of fortune." The king's duty was to impose a harmonious order upon society in imitation of the divine and natural order of the universe (AR, 21, 26–27).

To impose this order, Le Moyne claimed the king would have to assert a total and precise control over everything within society. "It is necessary that they [princes] apply themselves entirely and continually; that their spirit, their eyes, and even their hands touch everything; that they move precisely all the springs [of society], and make all the pieces move in harmony" (AR, 11). In fact, Le Moyne noted that the prince's *métier* was the only one without limits. The laborer had his field of activity, and the scientist had his. "It is only the art of reigning that enters into every function of civil life, that takes upon itself all jobs and bears all charges" (AR, 12). Aristotle had made a similar point about politics in his *Ethics*, dubbing it the "architectonic" science, and Le Moyne did not fail to draw upon the philosopher's authority.[56] But whereas Aristotle had indicated that political rulers were responsible only for integrating the different parts of the city into a whole and directing them toward the good, Le Moyne declared that the prince was responsible for the detailed regulation of each and every activity within his kingdom (AR, 13–14).

Adding to the prince's already heavy burdens, Le Moyne observed that the people were by nature disobedient and stubborn. Far from recognizing the benefits of the prince's regulations, they habitually subverted his decrees and upset his designs. The people were like a sick man, Le Moyne wrote, "who preferred his sickness to the remedies," "who cried out at the sole proposition of one day of diet" (AR, 15). The king was therefore faced with a thankless task. He had to impose and enforce rules upon subjects who opposed him at every turn. It was usually only too late, Le Moyne wrote in a manner reminiscent of the *Mémoires,* that the people came to understand the infinite benefits they received from their king: "And when a province detaches itself and breaks union from the monarchy, when revolt puts trouble and disorder in a people, what pains for a prince who wants to make the effort to reestablish his affairs and what confusion for those who abandoned him" (AR, 12). Like Louis XIV, Le Moyne asserted that the order of the kingdom depended upon the king's detailed regulation of each part of it, regardless of the people's apparent desires.

The king's regulatory ideology received dramatic expression in Molière's *Tartuffe* (1664).[57] The play opens with a scene of disorder and moral corruption. The protagonist of the play, Orgon, has become enamored with the religious hypocrite Tartuffe. Orgon's children and servants recognize Tartuffe's hypocrisy, but are powerless against him. As a result, the family is in disarray: an imposter has usurped the master's place and the children and servants are in rebellion. The family is, remarks the grandmother, "like a court in which misrule is king."[58] Early in the play, Orgon decides to break off his daughter Marianne's engagement with a young gentleman in order to marry her to Tartuffe. As the play unfolds, Orgon is slowly enlightened to Tartuffe's villainy. But each revelation only thrusts the family into deeper chaos and despair. When Orgon's family initially confronts him with Tartuffe's dishonesty, Orgon concludes that they are merely trying to defame his pious friend and redoubles his efforts to marry him to Marianne. By the time Orgon finally learns the truth about Tartuffe, he has already signed over his estate to him and given him a strongbox containing incriminating evidence about a friend. As the final act opens, all appears to be lost. Tartuffe has enlisted the aid of a local bailiff to evict the family from their home and has summoned one of the king's officers to arrest Orgon for complicity in his friend's crime. The bailiff arrives and serves a writ of eviction. Then, at the last moment, everything is set aright by a "rex ex machina."[59] The king's officer arrives, unexpectedly arrests Tartuffe, and restores the family estate to Orgon. The play concludes with an encomium to the king:

> Sir, your escape was narrow, but complete.
> We live under a king who hates deceit,
> A king whose eyes see into every heart
> And can't be fooled by an impostor's art.
> The keen discernment that his greatness brings

Gives him a piercing insight into things;
Nothing can disconcert his readiness,
And his firm reason always shuns excess.[60]

Louis XIV could hardly have asked for a more apt dramatic representation of his regulatory ideology. In the play, the decent but gullible Orgon is wholly taken in by Tartuffe's boldfaced lies. Although the children and servants recognize Tartuffe's hypocrisy, they are impotent to stop him. Even the local magistrate is deceived by Tartuffe's lies. It is only the intervention of the omniscient and omnipotent king that is finally able to restore order and morality to this desperate world. The king sees through Tartuffe's deceit. He oversteps the incompetence or corruption of local officials. He penetrates the true nature of individuals and restores justice and harmony to even the most private affairs of the kingdom, the family life of his subjects.

The king's regulatory ideology found various other avenues of expression. The many panegyrics to the king emphasized his direct role in bringing order to all affairs within the kingdom.[61] In his "Panégyrique du roy" of 1671, for example, Paul Pellison, who aided in the composition of the *Mémoires,* catalogued a long list of favorable developments in France in recent years—calm in the provinces, abundance and security in Paris, the increase of manufacturing, the flourishing of the arts and sciences, the newfound discipline of the army. He attributed all these developments to Louis XIV's diligent efforts "night and day" to regulate all aspects of social affairs: "there is nothing either inside or outside the kingdom, very small or very great, that does not pass and repass before his eyes."[62] The Académie royale des médailles et des inscriptions struck numerous medals to commemorate the king's regulatory reforms. A medal from 1661 shows the king "taking over the government" and announces the resulting "order and happiness." On this medal, the king is shown as Apollo holding in his right hand a rudder, which, according to the official history of medals, demonstrates "that he governs everything by himself."[63] In the other hand he holds a lyre, "symbol of the perfect harmony of all the parts of the kingdom." The next medal commemorates "the king accessible to all this subjects."[64] It depicts a poor woman and her child humbly presenting a petition to the king. The official history explains: "Since the prince took control of the government of the State, he applied himself not only to make himself feared to his enemies, but also to procure a perfect felicity for his people. To be in a better state to provide for all of their needs, he took care to be instructed of them himself and desired that the doors be thrown open to all." Another medal from 1661 shows the sun in a chariot spreading light over the earth and bears the inscription: "The assiduity of the king in his counsels."[65] Still other medals from the early years of the king's reign depict "the duel abolished," "the liberality of the king during the famine," "the establishment of manufactures," and of course the "military review" of 1666.[66]

The most awesome display of the king's powers was his court at Versailles. The Palace of Versailles was itself a tribute to the king's ordering powers over nature. Chandra Mukerji has argued that the gardens in particular were designed to convey a vision of the king triumphing over the forces of natural disarray. The geometric design of the gardens, the manicured lawns, clipped trees, flower beds, terraces, and elaborate water system all represented the king's ability to control nature in ways synonymous with God's order over the natural world. At the center of it all was the Apollo fountain with its image of the Roi-soleil. "The garden was a creation built in Creation," Mukerji has written, with Louis XIV playing the part of God.[67]

The same order was apparent in the king's court life. The king presented himself to his court as the very embodiment of reason. He wrote in his *Mémoires* that he tried to repress all display of emotions and feeling before his courtiers (M, 133). He further subjected himself to a rigorous and precise daily schedule. Nearly every aspect of the king's daily life, from waking up in the morning to going to bed at night, was ritualized. The king involved the nobility in these rituals according to a strict hierarchy of rank. Rank determined who could dine with the king, who could serve him his plate, who could enter his bedchamber, who could hand him his shirt in the morning and pass him his candle at bedtime. There were formal rules about who could sit on a chair or a stool in the king's presence and who had to remain standing. In *The Court Society,* Norbert Elias argued that Louis XIV's careful manipulation of court ceremony provided an important means of controlling the status hierarchy of the nobility and hence of asserting his power over society.[68] Just as importantly, Louis XIV made his court life a symbol and expression of his regulatory ambitions. The court society of Versailles represented in small the king's aspirations for the regulation of French society at large. It was a precise order where every detail of social life revolved exclusively around Louis XIV.

THE APOGEE OF THE REGULATORY IDEOLOGY: JACQUES-BÉNIGNE BOSSUET

While Louis XIV's regulatory ideology dominated the intellectual and cultural landscape during his reign, it was not uncontested. From the beginning of Louis XIV's reign, some members of the nobility challenged his ideology with neo-Thomistic notions of nature and society.[69] Cartesian philosophers outlined a mechanical theory of nature that at least implicitly undermined the absolutist idea of a contingent temporal world. Jansenist theorists struck a subtle blow at Louis XIV's regulatory ideology by showing how the selfish interests of individuals could naturally generate cooperation and order.[70] French social contract theorists argued that the sovereign power was based upon an original grant by the people and consequently subject to limitations. The author who more than anyone else took it upon himself to answer these challenges and reassert the absolutist worldview was Jacques-Bénigne Bossuet (1627–1704). Bossuet was a famous preacher, bishop of

Meaux, tutor to the dauphin from 1670 to 1680, spiritual counselor to Louis XIV, and the quasi-official political theorist of Louis XIV's court. His sermons and books touched upon almost all of the significant events and intellectual issues of his day.[71] In his vast body of works, he laid out a comprehensive defense of the statist ideology and the most complete statement of regulatory state theory written during Louis XIV's reign. Yet if Bossuet's writings represent the supreme statement of the regulatory ideology, they also mark the point at which the weight of this ideology became too much for any one individual to bear. Bossuet painted the state in such magnificent brush strokes that the realities of Louis XIV's rule came to pale in comparison. By the end of Louis XIV's reign, even Bossuet was questioning the king's aptitude to know and regulate all things within society.

Like Louis XIV, Bossuet placed Providence at the center of his thought. But he developed his providential theory in much more detail than Louis XIV. Following Bodin and other state theorists, he ascribed to a voluntarist theology, arguing that God ordered temporal affairs not immanently through general laws but externally moment to moment through his free will. He presented his theory of Providence most concisely in two sermons delivered early in his career[72] and then, more fully, a few years later in a heated debate with the Cartesian philosopher Nicolas Malebranche (1638–1715).[73] In his *Traité de la nature et la grâce* (1680), Malebranche asserted that "God acts by general wills [*volontés générales*]" and "general laws which he has established."[74] Indeed, "what is called nature," Malebranche wrote, "is nothing other than the general laws which God has established to construct or to preserve his work by very simple means."[75] While God could descend to conduct particular affairs or even act outside of his established laws if he so desired, he almost never did. For to act particularly and directly was, according to Malebranche, a sign of weakness and imperfection. "Certainly it requires a greater breadth of mind to create a watch which, according to the laws of mechanism, goes by itself and regularly . . . than to make one which cannot run correctly if he who has made it does not change something in it at every moment." The same was true of the world at large:

> Thus to establish general laws, and to choose the simplest ones, which are at the same time the most fruitful, is a way of acting worthy of him whose wisdom has no bounds; and by contrast to act by particular wills [*volontés particuliéres*] indicates a limited intelligence which cannot compare the consequences or the effects of the last fruitful causes.[76]

When Bossuet first read Malbranche's *Nature et grâce,* he is reported to have scrawled "pulchra, nova, falsa" across the manuscript.[77] A few years later, in his "Orasion funèbre de Marie-Thérèse d'Autriche" (1683), he responded to Malebranche's thesis in a more public and formal (but no less vitriolic) manner:

> What contempt I have for those philosophers who, measuring the counsels of
> God by their own thoughts, make him the author only of a certain general or-
> der from which the rest develops as it will! As if he had, in our manner, only
> general and confused views, as if the sovereign intelligence could not compre-
> hend in his designs particular things, which alone truly exist![78]

God "does not content himself with willing that things should be in general," Bossuet added in his "Traité du libre arbitre." He goes "always to the
final precision of things . . . he descends to that which is called such-and-
such, that is to say, to that which is most particular."[79] Summarizing his differences with Malebranche in a letter to one of Malebranche's disciples, the
Marquis d'Allemans, Bossuet wrote:

> It is easy for me to show you that the principles upon which I reason are di-
> rectly opposed to those of your system. . . . There is a great difference in say-
> ing, as I do, that God conducts each thing to the end which he proposes for it
> by some precise means, and in saying that he contents himself in giving some
> general laws, from which it follows that a lot of things enter only indirectly
> into his designs. And since I am very attached to finding every link in the
> work of God, you see that I distance myself from your ideas of general laws.[80]

In arguing so vehemently for a *providence particulière,* Bossuet defended in
his own terms an important tenet of early modern state theory. He claimed
that God ordered human and temporal affairs not through an immanent
set of natural laws but externally through his arbitrary will.

Bossuet proceeded from his theory of Providence to develop his theory of
temporal order. Eschewing all rational or natural theories of order, he asserted the radical dependency of human beings upon God. He claimed the
only grounds of stability and order for human beings were the two institutions that God had chosen *en particulière* to carry out his designs: the
"Church" and the "State." He wrote his *Discours sur l'histoire universelle* to
demonstrate just this point (D, 4, 6).[81] After outlining the various ages and
epochs of the world in the first part of this work, he turned in the second
part to demonstrate the special grace that God had bestowed upon the
Judeo-Christian religion. While human history was comprised of endless
changes and fluctuations, he asserted that the Judeo-Christian religion has
"always been uniform or, rather, always the same since the Creation of the
world. The same God has always been acknowledged as the Creator, and the
same Christ as the Savior, of mankind" (D, 114). This "continued existence"
of the Judeo-Christian religion "without interruption and without alteration during so many ages, in spite of so many intervening obstacles, shows
clearly God's sustaining hand." For what other religion had endured so
long? The very fact that this religion persevered while so many others had
faded away was proof enough of its divine ordination (D, 114–15).

God first announced the precepts of his religion to Adam and Eve. He reestablished his religion through Abraham and the people of Israel once idolatry had spread among humankind. When ignorance and blindness overcame the Jewish people, he resolved to have his law written down and promulgated by Moses. And so Bossuet's account of the true religion continued down to the coming of Jesus Christ, who was sent to establish a new order of things. Christ founded his new order in the institution of the Catholic Church which, Bossuet concluded, has persevered unchanged to the present times by virtue of God's grace:

> This Church, constantly attacked and never vanquished, is a perpetual miracle and a shining testimony to the immutability of God's counsels. Amid the agitation of human affairs, it stands steadfast, with an invincible power, so that, by an uninterrupted continuity of more than 1,700 years, we trace it back to Jesus Christ, in whom it takes up the succession of the ancient people and finds itself united to the prophets and patriarchs. (D, 263)

While Bossuet's central teaching in the second part of the *Discours* was that God's grace directly sustained the Catholic religion, an important ancillary lesson was that there was only change, chaos, and confusion outside the Church. After Christ had founded the Catholic Church, Bossuet argued that the Jewish people had fallen subject to all the vicissitudes and decay of temporal affairs. "Henceforth Judah means nothing to God or to religion, any more than do the Jews; and it is just that, in punishment of their hardness of heart, their remnants be dispersed over the whole world" (D, 206).[82] Bossuet took up this theme with even more vigor in his *Histoire des variations des églises protestantes* (1688). The central purpose of this work was to chronicle the infinite "variations" the Protestant religion had suffered during its short history and to try to explain their cause. After spending the better part of this work analyzing the growth and diffusion of Protestant sects and beliefs since the Reformation, Bossuet turned to explain why this was so. He concisely summarized his argument in the following statement:

> The cause of these variations [of the Protestant churches] is their not having known the authority of the Church, the promises that it received from heaven, nor, in a word, so much as what the Church is. For it was the fixed point around upon which it was necessary to base all the steps they were to take; and for lack of being checked there, the heretics, either curious or ignorant, have been set free to their human reasoning, their grief, and their particular passions.[83]

Nowhere was Bossuet's mistrust of human reason more evident than in this passage. Once human beings abandoned the authority of God's ordained institutions and doctrines, whether by turning to the Protestant religion or Cartesian reason, there was no end to their confusion and disorder. "Everyone thinks he has a right to change and model what he has received according to his own fancy," he wrote, and "each is given the liberty to say 'I understand this, and I don't understand that,' and on this foundation alone to approve or reject whatever they want."[84] Individual faith and reason were for Bossuet both corrupt and lame instruments. Once human beings broke free from the divine guidance of the Church, they would never cease to involve themselves in new errors.

Bossuet began the third part of his *Discours* by observing that there was simply "nothing comparable" to the continuity of the "true Church" in political affairs (D, 299). In fact, in the *Discours,* he argued that the primary purpose of "empires" throughout history was simply to protect or punish God's chosen people. "God used the Assyrians and the Babylonians to chastise his people; he used the Persians to restore it, Alexander and his first successors to protect it, Antiochus the Illustrious and his successors to test it, and the Romans to protect its liberty from the kings of Syria, whose only thought was to destroy it" (D, 299). It was only in his *Politique tirée des propres paroles de l'écriture sainte* that Bossuet developed his positive account of the state.[85] In contrast to his *Discours,* where he argued that "empires" served only to protect or punish God's people, he claimed in his *Politique* that "States" played an independent and positive role in carrying out God's plans.[86] As the title of this work indicates, he based his argument upon the "very words of Holy Scripture."[87] The holy Scripture revealed the direct words of God and hence provided a certain source of truth in an otherwise uncertain world. Bossuet especially relied upon the books of the Old Testament, where the "political" principles that God had used in governing his chosen people were most evident (P, 1).[88]

In the first book of his *Politique,* Bossuet outlined the positive role states were to play in God's providential plan. "Man is made to live in society," he began. God originally commanded all human beings to love one another as brothers and even gave them different talents so that their natural interests would draw them together into society (P, 3–8). In beginning his argument this way, Bossuet adopted the basic premises of St. Thomas Aquinas's political philosophy. Mutual dependency and self-interest naturally inclined human beings to live together in society. More specifically, he claimed God originally intended human beings to live together in "nations." Although human beings were first divided by original sin, some sort of division would have been inevitable even without sin. This was because "the multiplication of the human race" would have forced human beings to move to distant countries and to establish distinct societies (P, 10–11). God himself had given the Israelites "a land which they should inhabit in common" and promised to make them "a great nation" (P, 11).[89] The development of different languages, too, played a role in dividing people into distinctive nations. Bossuet concluded that the "love of one's country" was a wholly "natural" and good sentiment (P, 12). It was part of God's providential plan for human beings live together in national communities.

Bossuet counterposed this Thomistic teaching about human sociability with an Augustinian doctrine of original sin. Whereas Aquinas claimed that human beings retained a degree of natural reason and morality even after original sin, Bossuet claimed that original sin burst asunder all fellowship and morality. "God was the bond of human society. The first man having separated himself from God, by a just punishment division was cast in his family, and Cain killed his brother Abel" (P, 8). Afterwards, "the whole of the human race was divided." Individuals came to be governed by their selfish passions and thought "only of satisfying them without considering others" (P, 9). Jealousy and hatred became prevalent and provoked widespread treason and murder. Bossuet concluded aptly enough with a quotation from St. Augustine: "Thus human society, established by so many sacred bonds, is violated by the passions, and as St. Augustine says: 'There is nothing more sociable than man by nature, or more unsocial than man by corruption'" (P, 10).

The divine purpose of states, then, was to restrain the corruption and sinfulness of human beings in order "to form nations and unite the people" (P, 14). For "it was not enough that men inhabited the same country, or spoke the same language." Even within their diverse nations, individuals were still "untractable by the violence of their passions, and incompatible by their different humors." God established states to put "a bridle on the passions, and to the violence become natural to men," and to ensure "that union is established among men." "Behold, such is the unity of a people, when each one renouncing his own will, transfers and reunites it to that of the prince and the magistrate. Otherwise there is no union; the people become wanderers, like a flock dispersed" (P, 15). While Aquinas had looked to government only to consolidate the already existing natural society among human beings, Bossuet claimed the state was necessary to mold a number of corrupt and intractable individuals into a divinely ordained "nation-state." He accorded to the state the same role in worldly affairs that he attributed to the church in religious ones. Outside these institutions there was only disorder.

In the last article of the first book of his *Politique,* Bossuet reiterated in the strongest terms possible his sacred vision of the "nation-state." Here he set forth the bold proposition that Christian love found its fullest expression in the love of one's *patrie,* or what he elsewhere called one's "State."[90] "If we are obliged to love all men," he began, "and as it is true to say that to a Christian there is no such thing as a stranger, it is more reasonable that we should love our fellow citizens. All the love we have for ourselves, for our family, and for our friends is reunited in the love we have for our country, where our happiness, and that of our family and of our friends is included" (P, 27–28). It was only in the "state" that human beings were reunited into the harmonious and moral relations that God intended for them. Everything outside was mired in chaos, passion, and deceit. Turning in the next proposition to analyze Christ's attitude toward his own nation, he noted that Christ was always a "good citizen, and served as a strong recommendation around himself to love the Jewish nation" (P, 31). Like Naudé, he made innovative use of Caiaphas's pronouncement that "it is necessary Jesus should die, 'that the whole nation might not perish,'" concluding that nations played an important role in the salvation of humanity: "Thus he shed his blood with a particular regard for his nation; and in offering up the great sacrifice, which was to effect the expiation of all the universe, he willed that the love of the country should find a place in it" (P, 33).[91] As this statement makes evident, Bossuet did not see the "nation" as simply a secular union of individuals. It was an ethical community embodying the highest natural ends of human existence. In forming individuals into nations, state rulers did far more than just establish a secular peace. They acted as coequal partners with the Church in manifesting and carrying out God's providential plan.[92]

The central books of the *Politique* are devoted to an explication of state powers. In these books, Bossuet identified the powers that God intended states to possess in order to carry out their divine function. He argued that all legitimate states shared four essential characteristics: they were sacred, paternal, absolute, and subject to reason. In discussing these characteristics, Bossuet emphasized in particular the important regulatory functions of the state.

Bossuet claimed state authority was sacred in a twofold sense. Most generally, the institution of the state, or sovereign office, was divinely ordained apart from individual rulers. Employing the traditional imagery of the king's two bodies, Bossuet wrote that "the prince dies, but authority is immortal, and the state subsists forever," adding later that "the royal throne is not the throne of a man, but the throne of God himself" (P, 18, 58). More particularly, though, he contended that God also ordained individual persons to govern. "The person of kings is sacred" (P, 58). Like most other seventeenth-century French divine right theorists, Bossuet maintained that God had put "something divine into kings"—"a degree of penetration akin to the power of divination" (P, 60, 161–62). The main implication of these assertions was that the prince had to order all affairs for his subjects, and the subjects had to obey all their prince's commands. The prince was the source of all order within society. He was the "state": "One owes the prince the same service one owes to his country. No one can have any doubts about this, since we have seen that the whole state is in the person of the prince. In him [is found] the will of the whole people. It is for him to make everything converge in the public good" (P, 167). Like Louis XIV, Bossuet claimed that the king was coterminous with the state (here understood as the whole assemblage of people) because the state would not exist without him. The prince forged the mass of particular and disorderly individuals into a national union. He had to encompass all things and be obeyed in all things to maintain the peace. His policies were equivalent in political affairs to the inscrutable wisdom of Providence in nature. "The prince knows the whole secret and the whole outcome of affairs. To fail to observe his orders for a moment is to expose everything to chance" (P, 168).[93] The one exception to this rule was when the king's commands contradicted God's laws (P, 174). As God's representatives, sovereign rulers were subject to his divine and natural laws (P, 61–62). Princes could not legitimately enslave their people, dispose of their lives or property without good cause, or contravene the fundamental laws of the kingdom (P, 263). If the king performed any of these actions, the subjects might legitimately disobey him. But Bossuet argued that the only acceptable forms of disobedience were respectful remonstrances and prayers (P, 179–84).

Bossuet more emphatically stressed the importance of regulatory powers in his discussion of "paternal" power. From ancient times writers had appealed to the notion of paternal powers to describe the powers and duties of the king.[94] During the seventeenth century in England, Robert Filmer applied this notion more literally to describe the origins and nature of political power.[95] Bossuet still held to the more traditional metaphorical understanding of paternal power. Nonetheless, he extended this metaphor to legitimize more extensive regulatory powers for the king.[96] He argued that God expected kings to exercise a paternal care over each of their subjects. They were to ensure that "the earth is well cultivated . . . the seas are free . . . commerce is rich and true . . . [and] each lives in his house peacefully and safely."[97] A good king extended his virtue and munificence "like a sun . . . into the most remote provinces," granting "some their honors and offices, others their fortune and life, all the public safety and peace, so that there is no one who does not cherish him like a father."[98] Bossuet especially stressed the direct protection and care state rulers owed to the weak and poor.[99] "In a regulated government, widows, orphans, wards, even infants in the cradle are strong. Their property is preserved for them; the public takes care of their education; their rights are defended, and their cause is the cause of the magistrate" (P, 17). He even went so far as to declare that the king ought to have a monopoly over the care of the people. "It is a royal right [*droit*] to provide for the needs of the people. Whoever undertakes it to the prejudice of the prince, undertakes against royalty. It is for this that royalty is established, and the obligation to take care of the people is the basis of all the rights that sovereigns have over their subjects" (P, 65). Bossuet here extended Louis XIV's regulatory ideology in significant ways. Only twenty years earlier, Louis XIV had bragged about his intervention into the food shortage in France and suggested that maybe one day he would be able to ensure that all of his people had sufficient food and work. Bossuet now asserted that if anyone in French society was wanting, it was the king's responsibility to aid them (P, 66). He transformed state regulation from an act of beneficence to a duty of the king.

The third essential element of the state was "absolute" power. Bossuet again highlighted here the need for the sovereign's powers to pervade society. Building upon Bodin's doctrine of sovereignty, Bossuet asserted that the king was the sole legitimate source of justice and order within society. Citing a number of Old Testament passages, Bossuet declared: "The judgments of sovereigns are attributed to God himself. . . . One must, then, obey princes as if they were justice itself, without which there is neither order nor justice in affairs" (P, 82). In order to enforce his decisions, Bossuet added that the prince had to possess a monopoly over the means of violence (P, 83). While Bodin had made a similar point, Bossuet emphasized much more strongly the need for the prince to make his coercive authority penetrate to all corners of society. He legitimized this extension by reminding his readers about the natural character of human beings. "Fear is a bridle necessary to men because of their pride and their natural indocility," he wrote. The king therefore "must make himself feared by great and small alike." "If there is in the state an authority capable of stopping the course of public power, or of hampering its exercise, no one is safe" (P, 87–89). Whatever the king did not touch was liable to fall into chaos and anarchy. He had to extend his coercive powers to all parts of society and directly take responsibility for the protection of each subject: "The prince is then by his charge to each individual 'a shelter and cover from the wind and storm, and a jutting rock under which one finds shade in a desert land' [Isa. 32:2]" (P, 17).[100]

In describing the fourth and final characteristic of state authority, Bossuet once again echoed Louis XIV's state theory. He claimed the rule of the prince was rightfully "subject to reason." This quality had two main components. In the first place, state rulers were obliged to govern impartially and objectively (P, 103–10). This duty followed directly from the sacred nature of sovereign authority. In discussing the "sacred" quality of kings, Bossuet asserted that the sovereign power should never be considered a private possession of the king. "Their power coming from on high, as has been said, they must not believe that they are the owners of it, to use it as they please" (P, 61). He added that God had prepared kings to serve as the impartial "fathers" of their people by elevating them above the petty passions and interests of private individuals. "He places an image of his greatness in kings, in order to oblige them to imitate his goodness. He raises them to a condition in which they have nothing more to desire for themselves" (P, 63). Like Louis XIV (and Richelieu before him), Bossuet claimed that the king was morally obliged to detach himself from all personal passions and commit himself to an impersonal public ideal: "The prince is not born for himself, but for the public. . . . [God] gave him his people to lead, and at the same time made him forget himself" (P, 64).

The other dimension of rational rule was related to information-gathering. Bossuet argued that kings had to know everything within their realm in order to govern in a rational way. They had to study the details of the law and public affairs (P, 114–17). They needed to know "occasions and times" (P, 117–18). They further had to possess a detailed knowledge of the people. "Above all other things it is necessary that he know the disposition of his people; and this is what the wise man recommends to him in the image of the shepherd: 'Be diligent to know the countenance of thy cattle, and consider thy own flocks' [Prov. 27:23]" (P, 118). Bossuet concluded that the king had to subject his whole kingdom to a constant and pervasive surveillance. If he made his presence felt everywhere, no one would resist his commands:

> Under an able and well-informed prince, no one dares to do evil. One believes him always present, and even the diviner of thoughts. "Detract not the king, no not in thy thought; do not speak against him in thy private chamber; because even the birds of the air . . . will tell what thou hast said" [Eccles. 10:20]. News flies to him from every quarter: he knows how to discriminate between these items, and nothing escapes his knowledge. (P, 123–24)

Like Louis XIV, Bossuet portrayed the panoptic prince as his new ideal ruler. He wanted the prince to embrace the whole of society under his rationalizing gaze in order to bring harmony and order to all parts of it.

At the end of the fifth book of his *Politique,* Bossuet eloquently summarized his regulatory theory of the state. Drawing together his reflections on the sacred, paternal, absolute, and rational components of the sovereign's power, he claimed the king was comparable in the state to God in the universe: just as God exercised a *providence particulière* over the universe, so the king did the same in his kingdom. Should either of these powers lapse even for a moment, all would be lost to chaos and anarchy:

> The power of God can be felt in a moment from one end of the world to the other: the royal power acts simultaneously throughout the kingdom. It holds the whole kingdom in position just as God holds the whole world.
>
> If God were to withdraw his hand, the entire world would return to nothing: if authority ceases in the kingdom, all lapses into confusion.
>
> Consider the prince in his cabinet. From thence flow the commands which coordinate the efforts of the magistrates and captains, of citizens and soldiers, of provinces and armies, by land and by sea. It is the image of God, who directs all nature from his throne in the highest heaven. (P, 160)

Perhaps no passage more succinctly captures the regulatory ideology of Louis XIV. Bossuet modeled his notion of sovereign authority directly around his theory of *providence particulière.* He portrayed the sovereign prince as the crucial link between God and humanity. God chose the sovereign ruler *en particulière* to impose a universal order upon political affairs. In turn, the prince had to exercise his *providence particulière* over the least social affairs of his people in order to bind them together into a rational and harmonious nation-state. Without the detailed regulation of God's particular chosen representative, Bossuet argued that society would collapse into chaos and confusion.

The Fading Myth of the Regulatory State

Bossuet set aside his *Politique* in 1679 after having completed only the first six books. When he resumed work on this text some two decades later, his arguments took on a different tenor.[101] Whereas the first six books outlined broad justifications for the king's powers, the last four books focused upon the limitations on his powers as well as the "disadvantages and temptations which accompany royalty" (P, 394). Bossuet even devoted a whole book to a discussion of just and unjust wars, wherein he implied that Louis XIV's incessant military campaigns were neither beneficial to France nor pleasing to God.[102] Bossuet's arguments in the second half of the *Politique* clearly reflect his disenchantment with Louis XIV's policy and personal choices during the later part of his reign. But Bossuet's disenchantment was to some degree inevitable. He raised up the royal power so high that it is hard to imagine anyone meeting his ideal. Bossuet envisioned a perfectly rational and just king imposing a perfectly regular and moral order on all corners of the kingdom. When Louis XIV proved to be merely a man, Bossuet found it necessary to reassert limits and restraints on the very powers he had helped to unleash.

Bossuet was by no means alone in these sentiments. From the 1680s onward, criticisms of the king's rule became increasingly prevalent.[103] Jean de La Bruyère outlined one important line of criticism in his highly popular *Les caractères* (1688).[104] La Bruyère made clear in this work that he was not at all opposed to the king's regulatory ideology. He fully endorsed the principle that the king should exercise a perpetual and detailed regulation over all social affairs. His concern was simply that Louis XIV was diverting too much of his energy to the pursuit of military glory and neglecting his regulatory functions:

> The science of details, or a diligent attention to the least needs of the republic, is an essential part of good government, too much neglected, to tell the truth, by kings and ministers lately. . . . What use is it to me, in a word, or to any other of the people, if the prince is happy and covered with glory for himself and his family, my country powerful and formidable, if, sad and anxious, I live there in oppression or in indigence; if, protected from the enemy, I am nonetheless exposed in the streets of the city to the assassin's dagger and fear less being pillaged or massacred at night in the deep forests than in the crossroads; if security, order, and property do not make life in towns delightful, and have not brought, along with abundance, sweetness in society.[105]

Only a century before, the king had been expected to do little more than maintain the rights and dignities of the different estates of society. La Bruyère now portrayed the king's detailed regulation of society to be a duty. He blamed the king personally for all that he found wrong around him and reprimanded him for not regulating society thoroughly enough!

La Bruyère added an even more incisive criticism a few pages later, questioning whether it was possible for Louis XIV or any other individual ever to attain all the virtues necessary to fulfill the regulatory functions of the king. He began the last article of his chapter "On the Sovereign or the Republic": "What gifts from heaven are necessary to rule well!"[106] La Bruyère then proceeded to fill two pages with a long list of all the qualities "contained in the idea of the sovereign." The sovereign ruler had to have a perfect temper and an open heart. He had to know who was deserving of favors, how to discern intelligence and talent, and how to select his generals and ministers. He had to have "vast abilities extending not only to external affairs, commerce, maxims of state . . . but also to know how to encompass internal affairs and the details of the whole kingdom." He needed to be a military genius, to be totally dedicated to the public good, and have such extensive knowledge that he "sees everything with his own eyes, that he acts immediately and by himself, that his generals are, no matter how far away, only his lieutenants, and his ministers only his ministers." "True," La Bruyère concluded, "it is rare to see all these virtues united in a single individual." But if anyone ever did unite all these qualities in one person, he would "well deserve the name Grand." This final reference was an allusion to Louis XIV, who since 1671 had been officially known as "Louis le Grand." La Bruyère left ambiguous, however, whether he believed the king deserved this title. Indeed, he at least hinted in his closing remark not just that Louis XIV might not be fully qualified to regulate the kingdom but that perhaps the qualities required of the sovereign were simply beyond the capacities of any one individual.

La Bruyère's criticisms became widespread during the eighteenth century. Michel Foucault argued that the "monarchical super-power" came to be perceived as a "central excess" in the system of regulation and discipline.[107] The regulation of society was said to rest too much upon the arbitrary and unpredictable will of the king. At the same time, the king's powers were regarded as insufficient for effectively regulating society, allowing too many "illegalities." The reform movement was born, Foucault wrote, "at the point of junction between the struggle against the super-power of the sovereign and that against the infra-power of acquired and tolerated illegalities."[108] Reformers aimed to take power out of the hands of the king and spread it throughout society in order to make it "more regular, more effective, more constant and more detailed in its effects." In other words, they turned the king's regulatory ideology against him. The king's inability to live up to his regulatory ideals—governing as impartially and extensively as he would have liked—eventually helped to bring down the monarchy.[109] Paradoxically, Louis XIV prepared the way for the monarchy's obsolescence through the very propagation of his regulatory ideals.

Later reformers took important steps toward de-centering state regulatory powers, organizing them around an impersonal merit system, and extending them over a broader scope of social affairs. In this way, they carried out the designs of absolutist thinkers even while breaking from their form of government. In particular, they continued to depict the state administration as a super-rational and impartial entity composed of a corps of expert bureaucrats, and made the goal of creating a harmonious and unified nation-state one of the central aspirations of the state bureaucracy.[110] Hegel's state theory in particular comes to mind here. He envisioned a body of professional civil servants working to eliminate "contingencies" from civil society in order to unite individuals into the "universal" and "rational" ethical community.[111]

The ideas of Louis XIV, Colbert, and Bossuet thus help to explain the origins and development of state regulatory powers. They also highlight some problems with these powers in contemporary practice and theory. The legitimacy of state regulatory powers, like that of legislative sovereignty and executive prerogative, rests at base upon an exalted vision of the state. They presume a superlative degree of reason and impartiality among state functionaries. In fact, it is only because state officials are assumed to be impartial and expert representatives of the people that they are able legitimately to assert their broad regulatory authority over public affairs. Yet, state officials rarely are able to live up to the high ideals that justify their powers. As writers from Karl Marx to recent feminist theorists have pointed out, experts and bureaucrats are just as fallible and biased as kings.[112] Even if bureaucratic regulation is more rational and impartial than the rule of an absolute monarch, it is not necessarily rational and impartial enough to justify the broad regulatory powers of the state. "Impartiality is just as impossible for bureaucratic decisionmakers," Iris Marion Young has written,

> as it is for other moral agents. It is simply not possible for flesh-and-blood decisionmakers, whether in government or not, to adopt the standpoint of transcendental reason when they make decisions, divorcing themselves from the group affiliations and commitments that constitute their identities and give them a perspective on social life.[113]

State regulatory powers also presume the goal of creating a rational and predictable social order. But as Proudhon and Tocqueville pointed out, this goal stands in tension with the particularity and diversity of human existence. While all individuals might benefit from some state regulations, the broad scope of state regulatory powers exceeds individual interests. Under the modern state, individuals are subject to "a network of petty, complicated rules that are both minute and uniform," as Tocqueville wrote, that appear to serve the state's goal of rationalizing society rather than meeting the diverse interests of individuals. In sum, extensive state regulatory powers make sense only given the presumption of an impartial and rational state administration that has been authorized to impose a universal rational order upon society. This presumption made sense in the divine right ideology of Louis XIV and his supporters. But it is far from obvious why we should continue to apply this exalted vision of state powers to social affairs today.

CHAPTER FIVE

English State Theory

From Hooker's Ecclesiastical Polity to

Hobbes's Mortal God and Beyond

*I*n recent years scholars have begun to explore the ideological dimension of early modern English politics. While it was once assumed that nearly everyone in early modern England held a common law perspective, it is now recognized that there were several distinct and competing political ideologies in seventeenth-century England.[1] Johann Sommerville has led the revival of interest in early modern English ideologies. In his *Politics and Ideology in England, 1603–1640,* he argued that early Stuart England was dominated by three distinct political ideologies: the theory of royal absolutism, the theory of popular consent, and the theory of the ancient constitution.[2] Throughout the seventeenth century, political actors used these ideologies to defend or criticize royal policies, and eventually this ideological conflict contributed to the outbreak of the Civil War.

Critics of Sommerville's thesis have been especially dubious of his claim that royal absolutism represented an important ideology in early modern England.[3] They have argued that many of the theorists whom Sommerville identified as absolutist turn out on close inspection to have been fairly traditional supporters of the common law perspective. They have added that those theorists who were clearly absolutist, such as Hobbes, were without precedents or later adherents in England and formulated their ideas strictly in reaction to the events of the Civil War.

While Sommerville has done an admirable job of defending his thesis, his argument may be bolstered in important ways. Above all, his account of absolutist (a better term might be statist) ideas in England fails to recognize some of the distinctive philosophical assumptions of this ideology. Sommerville argued that royal absolutists shared with the proponents of popular consent and ancient constitutionalism an intellectual commitment to medieval natural law theory.[4] By his account, nearly everyone in early modern England believed that the universe was ordered into a hierarchical chain of being, that society and government were decreed by the natural law, and that the substantive principles of natural law were evident to human beings through their reason. Within this worldview, individuals disputed matters of detail such as whether the king or people rightfully held supreme power or whether the king's powers should be limited by the common law. But Sommerville has contended that there was consensus about the basic terms or framework of debate. In fact, it will be shown that the disagreements between absolutists and other thinkers were much more profound. Following their French counterparts, English absolutist thinkers challenged important elements of the medieval natural law tradition. They argued that social order was not immanent and natural but contingent and prone to dissolution. They claimed the natural law was vague in most matters and required clarification by the sovereign legislator. They portrayed absolute sovereignty as a principle of the divine and natural laws. In short, English absolutism, no less than French absolutism, was closely bound up with an assault on the medieval idea of order and an exaltation of the state.

This chapter examines the political philosophies of the three greatest English state theorists: James I (1566–1625), Robert Filmer (1588–1653), and Thomas Hobbes (1588–1679). Such a study has several objectives. First, it calls into question the supposed insularity of English political thinking.[5] All three of these writers were well versed in French statist literature. James I had a copy of Bodin's *Six livres de la république* in his library during his youth. The king's mature political writings resound with the Bodinian themes of theological voluntarism and legislative sovereignty.[6] Bodin's influence on Filmer was even more pronounced. Filmer copied vast portions of Bodin's *République* directly into his writings and published one work, *The Necessity of the Absolute Power of All Kings,* comprised of nothing but quotations from the 1606 English translation of the *République.*[7] Hobbes borrowed even more liberally from the French tradition. His political thought reveals the influence not only of Bodin but also of Montaigne, Charron, and French *raison d'état* theorists.[8] He further resided in Paris between 1640 and 1651, during which time he wrote *De Cive* and *Leviathan.*

A second objective is to explore the English absolutist ideology in more depth than Sommerville did. Sommerville focused on the forms of English absolutist arguments (for example, direct divine right, designation theory, patriarchalism).[9] Here the logic of these arguments will be outlined to show that the development of English state theory was closely bound up with the breakdown of the Tudor idea of order and a growing sensitivity to the contingency and disorder of human affairs. Stephen Collins has argued a similar point in his *From Divine Cosmos to Sovereign State,* but he associated the development of state theory with a secularization of politics.[10] The opposite is argued here: English state theorists (like the French) legitimized the state by portraying it as a metaphysically privileged institution specially designated to reinstitute a sanctified political community within the secularized temporal world. This chapter thus shows the relevance of the statist ideology discussed in earlier chapters to the Anglo-American tradition.

The third objective is to dispel the old Whig assumption—still prevalent in some circles—that English political thought lacks a statist tradition.[11] Even granting the existence of an English state tradition from James I to Hobbes, most scholars contend that this tradition was quashed by the Glorious Revolution and publication of Locke's *Two Treatises of Government.* The last section of this chapter challenges this assumption. Locke incorporated some of the central elements of absolutist state theory into his doctrine of liberal government.

The chapter begins with a brief discussion of Tudor political thought. Richard Hooker is studied as an example of a writer who espoused many of the assumptions of this tradition but adapted them to reflect the increased contingency of human affairs. It is then shown how James I and Filmer introduced state theory into English political thought by shifting the universal source of order from nature to the state and claiming the state was responsible for imposing a traditional moral order upon human affairs. The second half of the chapter provides a detailed reinterpretation of Hobbes's state theory. While Hobbes is usually studied in isolation from James I and Filmer, his arguments share the same metaphysical premises and goals. He legitimized state powers by portraying them as a logical deduction from the divine and natural laws and claiming they were necessary for restoring human beings to a moral and harmonious political order. In other words, Hobbes was no simple or straightforward "secularizer," as is so often assumed. The story ends with the Lockean reformulation of English statist ideas and a discussion of some of the problems his theory posed for the modern state tradition.

Tudor Political Thought and Richard Hooker

Tudor political thought was in many respects an extension of late medieval political theory.[12] Tudor theorists generally assumed that nature and society were suffused with God's eternal order. "Nature is nothing else but God himself, or a divine order spread throughout the whole and ingraft in every part of it," John Aylmer wrote.[13] References to the chain of being were commonplace. God was said to have ordered all of creation, including human society, into a perfect and harmonious hierarchy. Aylmer explained that God had ordained the social hierarchy of "one man over another: that some ruling and some obeying, concord and tranquillity might continue."[14] Within this hierarchy, every individual held a divinely ordained position and purpose; and all were morally obliged to uphold and fulfill their particular positions and responsibilities. The Elizabethan "Homily against Disobedience and Willful Rebellion" defined rebellion as "the unlawful and restless desire in men to be of higher estate than God hath given or appointed unto them" and denounced this desire as "the greatest ruin and destruction of all commonwealths."[15] Tudor theorists likewise held to a customary theory of law. The "good old law" was considered a supremely rational body of precepts that provided a tried and true application of the natural law to English society.[16] In sum, Tudor political thought was premised upon several assumptions characteristic of late medieval political thought. The first was that the universe was pervaded by an immanent divine order. The second was that human society was merely a particular manifestation of this universal order. The third was that the king was bound to respect and preserve the hierarchy and laws of society.

Although Tudor theorists built upon medieval premises, their thought was not rigid or static.[17] They adapted traditional ideas to meet new challenges and applied them in innovative ways. Richard Hooker provides a case in point. In his *Of the Laws of Ecclesiastical Polity,* Hooker synthesized a traditional Thomistic cosmology with elements of Augustinian thought in order to demonstrate the legitimacy of limited monarchy and the Anglican Church.[18] His thought represents an innovative defense of Tudor political institutions and hence may be taken as a fair barometer of Tudor political thought toward the end of the sixteenth century.

Hooker's *Of the Laws of Ecclesiastical Polity* was organized around a traditional medieval cosmology. The fundamental premise of this work was that God governed the universe according to a rational eternal law, defined as "that law which God from before the beginning hath set for himself to do all things by."[19] He clearly differentiated his position from the voluntarist theologies of the period: "They err therefore who think that of the will of God to do this or that, there is no reason besides the will" (LEP, 1:61). God ordered his actions and all affairs through a rational law that emanated from his very being. "The being of God is a kind of law to his working: for that perfection which God is, giveth perfection to that he doth" (LEP, 1:59). Issuing from the eternal law were a variety of other laws governing all dimensions of God's creation. Natural law governed the physical universe and nonrational creatures. The celestial law governed angels. The law of reason governed human beings in their natural affairs. Divine law guided them toward salvation. All of these laws were particular manifestations of God's eternal law and imbued the universe with rational and moral order. Hooker claimed any deviation from these laws spelled doom and disorder:

> Now the due observation of this law which reason teacheth us, cannot but be effectual unto their great good that observe the same. For we see the whole world and each part thereof so compacted, that as long as each thing performeth only that work which is natural unto it, it thereby preserveth both

other things, and also itself. Contrariwise, let any principal thing, as the Sun, the Moon, any one of the heavens or elements, but once cease or fail, or swerve, and who doth not easily conceive, that the sequel thereof would be ruin both to itself, and whatsoever dependeth on it? And is it possible that man being not only the noblest creature in the world, but even a very world in himself, his transgressing the law of his nature should draw no manner of harm after it? Yes, *tribulation and anguish unto every soul that doth evil.* Good doth follow unto all things, by observing the course of their nature, and on the contrary side evil by not observing it. (LEP, 1:93)

Hooker portrayed human society as an outgrowth of this universal order.[20] Following Aquinas, he claimed that human beings were "naturally inclined" to unite together in society by the law of reason (LEP, 1:95–96). He added that the laws governing human society were necessarily founded upon divine law and right reason (LEP, 1:95–134). He diverged from the traditional Thomistic framework, however, in two important ways. In the first place, he introduced a voluntaristic element into his account of the formation of human societies, claiming they owed their existence not only to human beings' natural instinct for association but also to their voluntary consent: "Two foundations there are which bear up public societies, the one, a natural inclination, whereby all men desire sociable life and fellowship, the other an order expressly or secretly agreed upon, touching the manner of their union in living together" (LEP, 1:96). Consent was necessary both in forming the original compact of society and also in ratifying the passage of all subsequent laws (except in the case—not much discussed by Hooker—of societies whose rulers were specially ordained by God). Hooker explained the need for consent by emphasizing the indeterminateness of natural law on many social questions. In contrast to Aquinas, he argued that the natural law did not mandate any one form of government "but leaveth the choice as a thing arbitrary" (LEP, 1:100). The same was true of many human laws, which Hooker divided into two sorts: "mixedly" and "merely" human. "Mixedly" human laws simply duplicated the principles of natural law (for example, "Thou shalt not kill") and provided sanction for them. "Merely" human laws consisted of all those particular matters about which the natural law gave no substantive guidance (LEP, 1:105–6). While Aquinas had argued that rulers might adapt the principles of natural law to particular situations, Hooker effectively portrayed human society as one step further removed from the divine and natural order. He claimed there was a whole realm of human laws—not to mention the form of the government—about which the natural law was indifferent. At least one scholar has seen in this assertion a heightened awareness of the contingency and variability of human affairs: "Hooker recognized beneath the towering and apparently stable architecture of the Thomist hierarchy of laws a movement in the affairs of men that all but denied that stability."[21] Since there was no naturally right form of government or best law in many circumstances,

Hooker asserted that the best means for determining these matters was the universal consent of the people (LEP, 1:81–84, 102–3). This was to his mind the most reliable method for indicating moral rightness and rationality in uncertain matters and preferable to the decisions of any single person.[22]

Hooker also departed from Aquinas by emphasizing the need for a strong coercive power in government. Aquinas had argued that government was necessary primarily to supply common direction to the particular wills of individuals.[23] Hooker claimed government was necessary just to compel individuals to obey the principles of natural law. His thought reflected something of the political Augustinianism that was becoming more prevalent during the late sixteenth century: "Laws politic, ordained for external order and regiment amongst men, are never framed as they should be, unless presuming the will of man to be inwardly obstinate, rebellious, and averse from all obedience unto the sacred laws of nature; in a word, unless presuming man to be in regard of his depraved mind little better than a wild beast" (LEP, 1:96). Hooker explained the unruliness of human beings by drawing a distinction between will and appetite. Will was the source of human conduct and "properly and strictly taken" followed reason toward natural ends. Appetite was the simple and immediate desire for sensible goods without consideration of natural ends. Since sensible goods were "most apparent, near and present," the appetite often overwhelmed the reason. "Reason therefore may rightly discern the thing which is good, and yet the will of man not incline itself thereunto, as oft as the prejudice of sensible experience doth oversway" (LEP, 1:77–80). As a result, there was need for a coercive government to discipline and compel individuals into behaving according to the natural law.

Drawing upon this modified Thomistic worldview, Hooker defended the traditional institutions and practices of Tudor England.[24] To begin with, he argued that the king was subject to all levels of the law: divine, natural, rational, and human. Despite the contingency and corruption of human affairs, Hooker still believed the polity existed in a rational and law-bound universe. If the king were to abandon the laws, he would, like the sun or the moon departing from the natural laws, cast himself and his subjects into ruin. "The axioms of our regal government are these, *Lex facit Regem*. The king's grant of any favor made contrary to the law is void. *Rex nihil potest, nisi quod jure potest*" (LEP, 3:342). Hooker laid particular emphasis on the king's subservience to the common law (LEP, 3:340).[25] The common law had not only received the universal consent of the community, but also had passed the test of time (LEP, 1:336–37). Lacking "some notable public inconvenience," Hooker therefore asserted that the common law ought to be maintained without change. There was a strong presumption in favor of its morality and rationality (LEP, 2:36–37). If the common law did need to be changed, Hooker added that the consent of the whole people was required, for such consent provided the most reliable means of identifying moral and rational laws. In England, the consent of the people was indicated by the decisions of the king in Parliament (LEP, 3:385, 404). In contrast to Bodin's argument in the *République,* Hooker thus placed human lawmakers under the common law and made their power dependent upon the actions of a coordinate body.[26] In the tradition of medieval legal theory, he claimed the law was sovereign and should be changed only rarely and with the consent of all.

By far the most significant element of Hooker's theory was his defense of the Church of England. Hooker defended the Anglican Church not only against proponents of universal Catholicism but also against Puritans who favored a more spiritual church.[27] He met both challenges by appealing to his theory of compact and consent. Contrary to Catholic doctrine, he suggested that the origin of the church was no different from the origin of political societies. Both were administrative organizations resting upon the consent of the people; the only difference related to their ends. Churches ministered to the spiritual well-being of human beings while political societies attended to their temporal well-being. "With us therefore the name of a Church importeth only a Society of men first united into some public form of regiment and secondly distinguished from other Societies, by the exercise of Christian religion" (LEP, 3:319). Yet even this distinction broke down in Christian societies. When political societies were composed solely of Christian citizens, they hardly differed from churches at all. For Christian governments existed to promote the good life of their citizens and the highest good for human beings was their spiritual salvation (LEP, 3:321). As such, Hooker argued that it was perfectly legitimate for the people to designate their temporal rulers as the heads of national churches just as they had done in England.[28]

Hooker's account of church law followed his discussion of civil law. He argued that there were certain doctrines of church law that were universal and inviolate because self-evidently spelled out in the Scriptures (LEP, 1:130–34). However, just as the natural laws allowed human beings some discretion in determining the form of their governments and their "merely" human laws, so also the Scriptures left the form of church government and ceremonies as "things accessory" (LEP, 1:212). These were matters that were rightfully decided by the members of the church as a whole. Since in England the king in Parliament (together with the convocation of bishops) represented the whole church, Hooker asserted that this body had rightful jurisdiction over the Anglican Church (LEP, 3:401–2). Turning next to address the Puritan reformers, Hooker asserted their duty to submit to the decisions of the church. While individual beliefs were often marred by ignorance and error, the decisions of the whole church were usually indicative of moral truth and reason. "To them which ask why we thus hang our judgement on the Church's sleeve," Hooker wrote most succinctly, "I answer with Solomon, 'because two are better than one'" (LEP, 2:33). It was sheer presumption for individuals to place their own consciences above the considered views of the community. Pointing to the unruliness and corruption of human beings, Hooker further argued that individual obedience to church authority was absolutely necessary for peace and order. "So that of peace and quietness there is not any way possible, unless the probable voice of every entire society or body politic overrule all private or like nature in the same body" (LEP, 1:34). In sum, Hooker defended common law monarchy and the Anglican Church by subtly integrating the main elements of the traditional Tudor worldview with a more contingent and corrupt vision of human society. His thought stands out as an innovative restatement of the central principles of Tudor political thought.

EARLY ENGLISH STATE THEORISTS: JAMES I AND FILMER

In the years following the publication of *Of the Laws of Ecclesiastical Polity,* an extensive literature developed in England commenting upon the contingency and corruption of human affairs.[29] The elements of will, appetite, contingency, and corruption that Hooker had incorporated into the Tudor worldview began to overwhelm it. Sir Richard Barckley's *A Discourse on the Felicitie of Man* (1598) was illustrative of this new perspective:

> And where all the mean causes of things even from the uppermost heaven, unto the lowest part of the earth, depended each upon other in such an exact order and uniformity to the production of things in their most perfection and beauty, . . . by the grievous displeasure, which God conceived against man, he withdrew the virtue which at the first he had given to things in these lower parts, and now through his curse the face of the earth, and all this elementary world, doth so much degenerate from his former estate, that it resembleth a chain rent in pieces, whose links are many lost and broken, and the rest so slightly fastened as they will hardly hang together; by means whereof the heavens and second causes do now far otherwise work in mans corrupt nature, and in this elementary world, then they did before.[30]

Barckley attributed the disorder of the world to humanity's original sin. But his practical point was to explain why the chain of being no longer held sway in present times. John Donne's "An Anatomy of the World" (1611) conveyed a similar sentiment:

> 'Tis all in pieces, all coherence gone;
> All just supply, and all Relation:
> Prince, Subject, Father, Son, are things forgot,
> For every man alone thinks he hath got
> To be a Phoenix, and that there can be
> None of that kind, of which he is, but he.[31]

Not everyone believed the old Tudor order was breaking down. Nor did everyone who perceived a breakdown believe that it meant the collapse of Tudor political ideas. Just as Hooker integrated elements of contingency and corruption into a traditional Tudor framework, so other writers pieced together a more dynamic vision of historical change with traditional ideas about politics and society. Yet more and more as the century progressed, writers began to look to new paradigms to address the uncertainty and variability of human affairs.

English millenarianism and classical republicanism represented two important responses to the breakdown of Tudor order.[32] A third important response (seldom recognized as such) was English state theory. The first whisperings of this theory were heard in the 1590s in England, as writers such as Hadrian Saravia began to articulate theories of sovereignty that, if not directly inspired by Bodin, at least closely resembled his ideas.[33] With the ascension of James I to the English throne in 1603, these ideas took center stage. In his speeches and books, James I asserted a new ideal of order that located the source of stability and justice not in the natural hierarchy of society or the common law but solely in the office of the king.

Recent interest in James I's thought may be traced to the work of W. H. Greenleaf. "James's political thought was neither so simple nor so foolish as it has often been made to appear," Greenleaf wrote. Rather, it represented an ingenious use of the Tudor idea of order to justify the theory of absolute sovereignty.[34] Central to Greenleaf's thesis, and indeed "central to an understanding of James I's political theory," is the following passage from a speech the king delivered before Parliament in 1610.

> The State of Monarchy is the supremest thing upon earth: For Kings are not only Gods Lieutenants upon earth, and sit upon Gods throne, but even by God himself they are called Gods. There be three principal similitudes that illustrate the state of Monarchy: One taken out of the word of God; and the two other out of the grounds of Policy and Philosophy. In the Scriptures Kings are called Gods, and so their power after a certain relation compared to the Divine power. Kings are also compared to Fathers of families: for a King is truly *Parens patriae,* the politique father of his people. And lastly, Kings are compared to the head of this Microcosm of the body of man.[35]

Greenleaf saw in this passage a perfect example of medieval correspondence theory. The king described his position in terms of a series of correspondences—to God, fathers, the head of a body—that legitimized his place within the natural hierarchy of beings. In other speeches and writings, too, James I made frequent references to notions of hierarchy, harmony, unity, and obedience, all of which were central to the traditional idea of order.[36]

More recently, Francis Oakley laid out a different interpretation of James I's thought.[37] In his speech of 1610, James I certainly did appeal to *an* idea of order. But it was not the traditional medieval or Tudor idea of order. Rather, it was the voluntarist idea of order first developed by Ockham and Scotus and applied so successfully to political affairs by Jean Bodin. Immediately following the quotation cited above, James I explained his correspondence to God in the following terms:

Kings are justly called Gods, for that they exercise a manner or resemblance of Divine power upon earth: For if you will consider the Attributes to God, you shall see how they agree in the person of a King. God hath power to create, or destroy, make, or unmake at his pleasure, to give life, or send death, to judge all, and to be judged nor accountable to none: To raise low things, and to make high things low at his pleasure, and to God are both soul and body due. And the like power have Kings: they make and unmake their subjects: they have power of raising, and casting down: of life, and of death: Judges over all their subjects and in all causes, and yet accountable to none but God only. They have power to exalt low things, and abase high things, and make of their subjects like men at the Chess; A pawn to take a Bishop or a Knight, and to cry up, or down any of their subjects, as they do their money. (*Speach, 1610,* 181)

James I's vision was hardly the image of Hooker's lawful God. Rather, it is the very image of the voluntarist God rejected by Hooker—creating and destroying, making and unmaking, as he saw fit. So, James I claimed, was the power of kings. They could make or unmake their subjects at will, accountable only to God. Nor was James I satisfied to rest his claim to authority upon a mere correspondence with God: he claimed kings were directly ordained by God and even "furnished with some sparkles of the Divinitie."[38] Robert Eccleshall observed that this "mystification" of royal power represented one of the most significant developments in English royalist theory between the sixteenth and seventeenth centuries.[39] While even the most committed of sixteenth-century royalist theorists claimed only that the king was the apex of a naturally ordered hierarchy, James I and other seventeenth-century writers portrayed the king as the omnicompetent authority specially ordained by God to bring order to the social hierarchy. Of course, all of this was quite consistent with developments in French state theory during the same period. Like French thinkers before and after him, James I portrayed the king as the sole mediator between God and political society. He made this point most explicitly in his speech to the Star Chamber of 1616:

So this ground I lay, that the seat of Judgement is properly Gods, and Kings are Gods Vicegerents; and by Kings Judges are deputed under them, to bear the burden of government. . . . Thus I speak, to show what a near conjunction there is between God and the King upward, and the King and his Judges downwards: for the same conjunction that is between God and the King upward; the same conjunction is between the King and his Judges downwards. As Kings borrow their power from God, so Judges from Kings: And as Kings are account to God, so Judges unto God and Kings.[40]

Greenleaf was correct when he observed that James I was obsessed with hierarchy and obedience. However, it was no longer obedience to the natural social hierarchy that concerned him. James I claimed that he stood directly below God as a sort of portal for channeling God's ordering power. He demanded (quite violently at times) that his subjects obey only him because he was the sole source of order within society.[41] Disobedience to him represented rebellion against God. Even the most "unruly and tyrannous" king was preferable to rebellion, he asserted, because without monarchical rule, the whole social order would collapse, "the reins being loosed to all the insolencies that disordered people can commit."[42]

Oakley concluded somewhat paradoxically that once the voluntaristic premises of James I's political thought are recognized, the king's speech of 1610 actually comes to appear "more conciliatory" and "less absolutistic" than it has usually been interpreted. For after comparing himself to the voluntaristic God, James I invoked the medieval theological distinction between God's absolute and ordinary powers to explain the power of kings:

> But now in these our times we are to distinguish between the state of Kings in their first original, and between the state of settled Kings and Monarchs, that do at this time govern in civil Kingdoms: For even as God, during the time of the old Testament, spoke by Oracles, and wrought by Miracles; yet how soon it pleased him to settle a Church which was bought, and redeemed by the blood of his only Son Christ, then was there a cessation of both; He ever after governing his people and Church within the limits of his revealed will. So in the first original of Kings, whereof some had their beginning by Conquest, and some by election of the people, their wills at that time served for Law; Yet how soon Kingdoms began to be settled in civility and policy, then did Kings set down their minds by Laws, which are properly made by the King only; but at the rogation of the people, the Kings grant being obtained thereunto. And so the King became to be *Lex loquens,* after a sort, binding himself by a double oath to the observation of the fundamental Laws of his kingdom. (*Speach, 1610,* 183)

Just as medieval theologians argued that God had chosen to bind his absolute will to the divine and natural laws, James I here expressed his willingness to subject his absolute powers to the law. James I's assertion of absolute powers, Oakley concluded, must be understood in light of this theological framework in order to understand their constitutionalist implications. Paul Christianson pushed this interpretation even further. Despite the king's absolutist rhetoric in some of his early writings, Christianson claimed he converted to a common law perspective after coming to England.[43] In the speech of 1610, James I articulated his mature theory of a "constitutional monarchy created by kings" in which kings were rightfully subject to the common law.

Oakley's and Christianson's arguments highlight an important theme in James I's writings: his sense of monarchical responsibility.[44] From his earliest writings, James I asserted that kings were ordained to rule not for their own benefit but according to God's law and the public interest.[45] This required that the king study both the Scripture and the civil laws of the kingdom, for the public interest required that the king rule by law.[46] "Albeit it be true," James I wrote, "that I have at length proved, that the King is above the law, as both the author and giver of strength thereunto; yet a good king will not only delight to rule his subjects by the law, but even will conform himself in his own actions thereunto."[47] Following his own advice, James I set himself the task after arriving in England to "learn my self the Laws of the Kingdom" (*Speach, 1616,* 207). He even admitted that he found the English laws to be in some ways preferable "even before the very Judicial Law of Moses," since they were specially suited to the character and circumstances of England (*Speach, 1610,* 185). Yet for Oakley and Christianson to conclude from these statements that James I supported a "constitutional monarchy governed by common law," or that his conception of government was anything less than "absolutist,"seems misguided. For if in one breath James I declared himself willing to subject himself to the fundamental laws, in the next he declared these laws to be "his own fundamental Laws and Orders" subject to his own approval (*Speach, 1610,* 182). In his later writings, too, he continued to maintain that the king was the sovereign lawmaker of the realm. In his Star Chamber speech of 1616, he demanded that the judges and lawyers of the realm give a strictly literal interpretation to the laws lest their judgments infringe upon his law-making prerogatives:

> As no King can discharge his account to God, unless he make conscience not to alter, but to declare and establish the will of God. So Judges cannot discharge their accounts to Kings, unless they take the like care, not to take upon them to make Law, but joined together after a deliberate consultation, to declare what the Law is; For as Kings are subject unto Gods Law, so they [judges] to mans Law. It is the Kings Office to protect and settle the true interpretation of the Law of God within his Dominions: And it is the Judges Office to interpret the Law of the King, whereto themselves are also subject. (*Speach, 1616,* 206)

James I may have been willing to subject himself to the law, but only after he had subjected the law to his own absolute will. He saw it as the primary responsibility of kings to settle the true interpretation of the laws within their dominions.

There is other evidence contradicting the notion that James I held to a common law perspective. Immediately after declaring his admiration for the common law in his speech of 1610, he added:

> But upon the other part, though I have in one point preferred our Common Law, concerning our use to the very Law of God; yet in another respect I must say, both our Law and all Laws else are far inferior to the judicial Law of God, for no book nor Law is perfect nor free from corruption, except only the book and Law of God. And therefore I could wish some three things specially to be purged and cleared in the Common Law. (*Speach, 1610,* 186)

James I went on to suggest that the common law should be written down in a "settled Text" since its existence in "old Customs, or else upon the

Reports and Cases of Judges" left too much to "the bare opinions of Judges, and uncertain Reports." Secondly, he claimed the common law should be written down in "our vulgar Language" so that it could be read by all the subjects. Thirdly, he asserted that all the "diverse contrary Reports, and Precedents" of the common law should be "reconciled" into one clear and concise body of law. James I justified these extensive reforms in his Star Chamber speech by pointing to the mutability and corruption of human affairs. "Nothing in the world is more likely to be permanent to our eyes then iron or steel, yet the rust corrupts it, if it be not kept clean: which showeth nothing is permanent here in this world, if it be not purged; So I cannot discharge my conscience in maintaining the Laws, if I keep them not clean from corruption" (*Speach, 1616,* 211). Christianson noted in relation to these and similar statements that "sensitive common lawyers may have perceived a threat" to the common law tradition.[48] No doubt! James I's proposals amounted to nothing less than the replacement of the common law tradition with a more rationalistic legal code based upon his own interpretation of the moral principles of divine law. While James I did invite Parliament to aid him in the reformation of the laws, he noted that he alone ultimately had to answer to God for the laws of England (*Speach, 1616,* 206, 211). Far from advocating a "constitutional monarchy," or even endorsing the notion of a monarchy ordinarily subject to law, James I outlined a theory of absolute monarchy subject only to divine law and the public interest.

What then remains of Greenleaf's thesis? Surprisingly much. Greenleaf may have misapprehended the nature of the order upon which James I built his state theory, but that theory did still have a great deal in common with the medieval idea of order. The very purpose of the state, by James I's account, was to impose something akin to the medieval idea of order upon a mutable and corrupt social and temporal world: hence all the references to harmony, unity, and obedience throughout his writings. He merely reoriented this traditional order around the king's will. In his earliest published work, *The Trew Law,* James I identified the king's duty as the maintenance of the moral and hierarchical order of society apart from change. Kings had "to maintain the Religion," "to maintain all the lovable and good Laws made by their predecessors," and "lastly, to maintain the whole country, and every state therein, in all their ancient Privileges and Liberties, as well against all foreign enemies, as among themselves."[49] In his Star Chamber speech, he explained why an absolutist king was necessary for this task:

> And as to maintain it, so to purge it; for else it cannot be maintained: and especially to purge it from two corruptions, Incertainty and Novelty: Incertainty is found in the Law it self, wherein I will be painful to clear it to the people; and this is properly to be done in Parliament by advice of the Judges. The other corruption is introduced by the Judges themselves, by Niceties that are used, where it may be said, *Ab initio no fuit sic.* (*Speach, 1616,* 211)

James I aimed to maintain and revitalize the "good old law" by actively reforming it. He saw his absolute powers as necessary to combat the disorder
and corruption of the times. He understood his task as comparable to that
of continually rebuilding a house that was constantly falling down in decay. It was upon these grounds that he justified the central principles of his
state theory: legislative sovereignty, a rationalistic reform of the laws, and
tighter state control over the judiciary.

A similar pattern of ideas may be discerned in Sir Robert Filmer's political thought. Greenleaf portrayed Filmer as another classic exponent of the
idea of order, arguing that he defended absolute sovereignty by developing
and extending the commonplace medieval correspondence between fathers
and kings.[50] Yet, as Gordon Schochet and James Daly have demonstrated,
Filmer's thinking actually departed from traditional patriarchal theory in
several key aspects.[51] Before the seventeenth century, patriarchal theories
were primarily of two types.[52] Since antiquity, writers had usually portrayed
families as precursors to political societies in a teleological or evolutionary
framework. Writers also regularly drew comparisons or correspondences between paternal and kingly powers, portraying the king as the father of his
people. During the seventeenth century, Filmer and a few other writers outlined a more abstract or "ideological" patriarchalism.[53] Ideological patriarchalism asserted the complete identity of paternal and regal authority and
associated both with the divine and natural law. Schochet related the appearance of this new form of patriarchalism to several factors; the increased
importance of the family in post-Reformation England and the development of new modes of historical thought both played a role.[54] But most importantly for our purposes, he claimed ideological patriarchalism emerged
in response to the breakdown of the Tudor idea of order and the differenti-
ation between state and society. John Daly concurred that Filmer's writings
show "no trace" of the familiar Tudor analogies—"the body politic and natural, the four humours and elements, and cosmic dance, and so on."[55]
Much like James I, Filmer used his patriarchal theory to identify a minimal
point of divine and natural order in an otherwise chaotic world and attempted to reconstruct a moral and harmonious political order around it.

Filmer premised his patriarchal theory primarily upon the book of Genesis. Genesis had the double advantage of being the word of God and a description of the origins of human society. Like many of his contemporaries,
Filmer regarded the origins of things to be decisive in determining their
true nature.[56] At the very origin of human society, Filmer claimed God gave
Adam an absolute power to rule over his wife and children.[57] This paternal
power was no different from political power: it included all "the chiefest
marks of sovereignty," including the power over life and death, of making
war and peace, and presumably (although Filmer did not explicitly mention it here) of making laws. This power also extended over a great multitude: "For Adam, living 930 years and seeing seven or eight descents from
himself, he might live to command of his children and their posterity a

multitude far bigger than many commonwealths or kingdoms" (P, 7, 16). God's original grant of power to Adam was not therefore merely a paternal authority but a paternal-political authority.

At his death, Adam's power passed to his sons and descendants, who ruled as patriarchs until the Flood. After the Flood, Noah divided his power among his three sons, who ruled their people each as a supreme father. Soon thereafter, human beings were divided into "seventy-two distinct nations" as a result of the confusion of Babel. Yet, Filmer noted, these nations "were not confused multitudes, without heads or governors, and at liberty to choose what governors or government they pleased, but they were distinct families which had fathers for rulers over them." Thus "God was careful to preserve the fatherly authority" even amid the confusion of Babel by establishing patriarchs at the head of each nation (P, 7–8).

The patriarchal succession continued through Abraham, Isaac, and Jacob down to the Egyptian captivity. But beyond this point, Filmer admitted that the direct line of succession from Adam was "quite lost" (P, 10). Contrary to the later assertions of Locke, Filmer never claimed existing kings were the direct lineal descendants of the original patriarchs. He openly acknowledged that most existing royal families came to power by election, donation, usurpation, or conquest (P, 10–11, 44). Indeed, he even maintained (at least prior to the execution of Charles I in 1649) that God sometimes sponsored usurpations and rebellions when he wanted to alter the royal line (P, 11).[58] His patriarchal theory was intended only to identify the ideal model of legitimate government and to justify those in power:

> In all kingdoms or commonwealths in the world, whether the prince be the supreme father of the people or but the true heir of such a father, or whether he come to the crown by usurpation, or by election of the nobles or of the people, or by any other way whatsoever, or whether some few or a multitude govern the commonwealth, yet still the authority that is in any one, or in many, or in all of these, is the only right and natural authority of a supreme father. There is, and always shall be continued to the end of the world, a natural right of a supreme father over every multitude, although, by the secret will of God, many at first do most unjustly obtain the exercise of it. (P, 11)

Filmer's approach to political theory was more rational than historical. He was not so much concerned with the historical transmission of patriarchal power from Adam to present-day kings; he looked rather to the patriarchal authority of the Old Testament to identify the universal form of political order. His argument was quite similar to Bossuet's in this respect. He claimed the patriarchal theory of the Old Testament revealed the original, true, and essential principles of political order.

Filmer used his argument to promote the full restoration of patriarchal (that is, absolute legislative, executive, and judicial) powers to the king. It was only by approximating the patriarchal ideal of government, he believed, that a just and orderly political society could be instituted. In this regard, he claimed that aristocracies and democracies hardly qualified as forms of government at all. They organized people into loose assemblages but failed to establish a truly virtuous and orderly society. Attempting to account for the empirical existence of aristocracies and democracies throughout history, he wrote: "Hereunto it may be answered that a people may live together in society and help one another, and yet not be under any form of government; as we see herds of cattle do, and yet we may not say they live under government. For government is not a society only to live, but to live well and virtuously."[59] Living well and virtuously consisted of two elements: "religion towards God and peace towards men" (AP, 256). The historical record of Rome and Venice showed that democratic and aristocratic governments were intrinsically opposed to the first of these goods: "This is the liberty that a popular estate can brag of, every man may be of any religion, or no religion, if he please" (AP, 257). As for peace, "it is well known that no people ever enjoyed it without monarchy" (AP, 257). The "disorders in popular states" were not "casual" but were "unavoidable" and "of necessity do follow" from the nature of these governments.

Similar difficulties accompanied mixed and limited monarchies. Filmer began his aptly titled *Anarchy of a Limited or Mixed Monarchy* by asserting that absolute sovereignty was a logical prerequisite of political order.

> We do but flatter ourselves, if we hope ever to be governed without an arbitrary power. No, we mistake. The question is not, whether there shall be an arbitrary power, but the only point is who shall have that arbitrary power, whether one man or many? There never was, nor ever can be any people governed without a power of making laws, and every power of making laws must be arbitrary.[60]

Drawing heavily from Bodin throughout this work, Filmer asserted that an absolute legislative power was a logical correlate of order. There was no law, he claimed, without someone to command it and hence no order without a supreme commander. Given these premises, it was not difficult for Filmer to demonstrate the anarchy of limited and mixed monarchies. Regarding limited monarchies, he queried, "who shall be judge whether the monarch transcend his bounds?" (A, 150) Either the sovereign authority was granted final judgment on all matters or it would have to be left to the conscience of each individual. "Thus at the last, every man is brought by this doctrine . . . to be his own judge. And I also appeal to the consciences of all mankind, whether the end of this be not utter confusion and anarchy" (A, 153–54). If the sovereign power were mixed between the king and Parliament, Filmer claimed similar problems arose. There would be no judge to decide disputes between them and government would teeter forever on the edge of anarchy (A, 150–57).

The only legitimate form of government was absolute monarchy (AP, 240–48, 255, 281). This was the form of government God bestowed upon

Adam and ordained for the ancient Hebrews (P,1–12; A, 7–8, 133). It was also the only form of government capable of establishing a virtuous and stable political order. While absolute monarchy was by definition "unlimited," this did not mean the king could do whatever he desired. All kings were bound as much as possible "to preserve the lands, goods, liberties and lives of all their subjects . . . by the natural law of a father" (P, 42). But these limitations took effect only insofar as they did not interfere with the king's primary responsibility of maintaining virtue and order within society. The "unlimited jurisdiction of kings," Filmer claimed, was "amply described by Samuel" in foretelling the rule of Saul (P, 35–37). The king could legitimately make his subjects serve in war, till his lands, pay taxes, or relinquish their fields if these actions were necessary for the public good; and it was, of course, the king's decision what was necessary for the public good. For God established kings to be his "speaking law" on earth (AP, 240). Without the king, there would be no law or order (P, 44). Even if the king should command his subjects to act contrary to the divine law, Filmer argued the subjects were still obliged to obey him.

> The sanctifying of the sabbath is a divine law, yet if a master command his servant not to go to church upon a sabbath day, the best divines teach us that the servant must obey this command, though it may be sinful and unlawful in the master; because the servant hath no authority or liberty to examine and judge whether his master sin or no in so commanding, for there may be a just cause for a master to keep his servant from church, as appears Luke xiv, 5. (P, 43)

The king was for Filmer the pivot between the universal order of God and the particular order of human society. He made manifest the divine and natural order within society. It was therefore both necessary and legitimate that he should possess absolute powers and that his subjects obey his every command.

While Filmer is best known for his patriarchal theory, he devoted much of his writing to refuting the other two dominant ideologies in early modern England: the theory of the ancient constitution and the theory of popular consent. His criticisms of these theories serve to clarify important aspects of his thought. His critique of the ancient constitution was a straightforward elaboration of his theory of absolute monarchy. Like Bodin, he portrayed legislative sovereignty as the source of all law and order within society. As such, he claimed there could be no such thing as unmade or immemorial law. The origin of every custom could be traced back to an act of the supreme legislator. Customs became law only by the command or consent of the legislative sovereign:

> Now concerning customs, this must be considered, that for every custom there was a time when it was no custom, and the first precedent we now have, had

no precedent when it began. When every custom began, there was something else than custom that made it lawful, or else the beginning of all customs were unlawful. Customs at first became lawful only by some superior power which did either command or consent unto their beginning. (P, 45)

By Filmer's account, the common laws were neither immemorial nor binding upon the sovereign but rather depended upon the sovereign will. In *The Freeholders Grand Inquest,* he developed this argument in more detail by examining various common law statutes and records pertaining to parliamentary privileges. He concluded that all these statutes originally stemmed from grants of the king. "But the truth is, the liberties and privileges of both houses have but one and the self-same foundation, which is nothing else but the mere and sole grace of kings."[61] Insofar as the king originally established the authority of the common law, Filmer argued he could rightfully disestablish it at will.

Some of the most compelling passages in Filmer's writings appear in his criticisms of consent theory.[62] These criticisms reveal, if only negatively, the premises of his state theory. In these passages, he demonstrated that consent theory could never justify even a limited territorial state power, and hence that it was necessary to resort to some transcendent principle (for example, patriarchalism) in order to establish the legitimacy of the state.

Filmer began his attack on consent theory by adopting what he took to be its central premise: the fundamental freedom and equality of all individuals. Given this assumption, he asserted that no group could claim the right to establish a commonwealth apart from other human beings "but by a mere usurpation upon the privilege of the whole world" (P, 20). Filmer's criticism might seem a mere quibble, but it actually points to a deep problem within consent theory. The very act of creating a nation-state represents an attempt on the part of some individuals to secure rights and protections apart from (and perhaps even against) others. It thus represents an infringement on the freedom and equality of all. Unless everyone consents to the formation of this community, it is nothing more than a coercive gang. "And therefore without a joint consent of the whole people of the world, no one thing can be made proper to any one man, but it will be an injury and an usurpation upon the common right of all others" (A, 140). Filmer's patriarchal theory avoided this theoretical difficulty. God had divided human beings into distinct nations after the Tower of Babel. The contemporary division of human beings into distinct nation-states was thus the result of divine ordination.

Setting aside this first objection and supposing "that the people of particular regions or countries have power and freedom to choose unto themselves kings," Filmer argued that consent theory was still mired in inconsistencies (A, 140–41). By its very premises, all individuals within a region or territory would have to consent to the government in order for it to be legitimate. In actual practice, however, few individuals ever actually consented to their governments. "It cannot truly be said that ever the whole people, or the major part, or indeed any considerable part of the whole people of any nation ever assembled to any such purpose" (A, 141–42). Some consent theorists attempted to address this problem by formulating the notion of tacit consent: although few individuals may have ever actually expressed their consent to government, all individuals could be said to have tacitly consented to it by peacefully living under it. Filmer disagreed. "If the silent acceptation of a governor by a part of the people be an argument of their concurring in the election of him," then it would follow "that every prince that comes to a crown, either by succession, conquest or usurpation, may be said to be elected by the people" (P, 21). The principle of tacit consent nullified the very notion of voluntary consent. It made the mere existence of an individual within the territory of a state an indication of his or her consent to it. It thus provided no basis for distinguishing legitimate from illegitimate authority and was an empty concept.

Filmer further pointed out that most consent theorists were unwilling to carry the premises of their theory to their logical conclusion. If all human beings were presumed to be naturally free and equal, then it made no sense to distinguish between the better and worse parts of the community, masters and servants, men and women, or even adults and children. All should logically possess the right to consent to government. The consent of the poor, servants, women, and children would have to be secured alongside that of propertied adult men (A, 142). In an attempt to avoid this outcome, consent theorists suggested that the votes of children and infants, at least, might be comprised in the votes of their parents. "This remedy may cure some part of the mischief," Filmer replied, "but it destroys the whole cause and at last stumbles upon the true original of government. For if it be allowed that the acts of parents bind the children, then farewell the doctrine of the natural freedom of mankind" (A, 142). Consent theory led logically back to patriarchy. Consent theorists countered that the rule of parents over their children lasted only during their minority, and that once children came of age they too became free to consent to government. Filmer retorted that "in nature there is no nonage. If a man be not born free she doth not assign him any other time when he shall attain his freedom" (A, 142). Consent theory provided only a very partial legitimacy for state authority, Filmer concluded, because only part of the people were ever given the opportunity to consent to government.

There were still other problems with consent theory. If all individuals had the right to consent to government, then there was no reason why they might not also withdraw their consent at any moment. There was likewise nothing to prevent them from giving their consent to some distant government. What right, after all, did any government have to exercise territorial sovereignty if its legitimate authority derived strictly from the wills of individuals? A government might legitimately rule over individuals who consented to it but not over the space in between them or nonconsenters. Filmer wrote on these points:

> Since nature hath not distinguished the habitable world into kingdoms, nor determined what part of a people shall belong to one kingdom and what to another, it follows that the original freedom of mankind being supposed, every man is at liberty to be of what kingdom he please. And so every petty company hath a right to make a kingdom by itself; and not only every city but every village and every family, nay, and every particular man, a liberty to choose himself to be his own king if he please. And he were a madman that being by nature free would choose any man but himself to be his own governor. (A, 140–41)

Consent theory did not establish a sound justification for territorial sovereignty or social cohesiveness, for by its premises any individual would be able at any time to transfer or withdraw his or her consent. The theory was contrary to the whole notion of a fixed and stable territorial sovereign state. Filmer claimed the only solid foundation for state legitimacy was the divine and natural laws. It could not be justified on mundane grounds. He formulated his patriarchal theory to provide a metaphysical, and hence certain, justification for territorial sovereignty.

Filmer's writings reflect an intellectual world in transition. He reformulated traditional patriarchal doctrines to legitimize the sovereign state and portrayed the state as a vehicle for reinstating a traditional moral order within an immanently disorderly world. The great weakness of his theory lay in the details. For all his seeming concern for scriptural truth, Filmer was a surprisingly careless interpreter of the Bible. He more or less assumed that his vision of patriarchal authority was found in the Bible and bent the text to fit his presuppositions. He thus left his argument easy prey for scriptural criticism. In his *First Treatise of Government*, Locke carried out just such a scriptural assault on Filmer's argument. He noted that in Genesis God gave Adam power not over other human beings but only over inferior creatures. Moreover, God granted dominion to "them," Adam and Eve, and not to Adam alone.[63] After the Flood, God granted dominion to "Noah and his sons." Filmer interpreted this passage to mean that Noah's sons exercised their dominion under and through their father. Locke remarked that Filmer would have us believe that "God must not be believed, though he speaks it himself, when he says he does any thing, which will not consist with Sir Robert's Hypothesis" (TT, 164). In a similar vein, Locke observed that the divine command to "Honour thy Father," which Filmer gave so much play, actually read, "Honour thy Father and thy Mother" (TT, 186). Nor was it even clear that God intended this command to apply to political matters since it was given to a people already under civil government (TT, 188). Locke continued in this manner page after page until by the end of the *First Treatise* he had utterly dismantled the scriptural foundations of Filmer's patriarchal theory. Filmer's patriarchal theory then fell into disrepute. Yet the theory of the state marched on, as we shall see, even in Locke's political theory of the *Second Treatise*.

HOBBES AND THE PSYCHOLOGY OF THE STATE

Hobbes's state theory is usually treated apart from the state theories of James I and Filmer. Whereas the latter outlined political theories based upon divine right theory, Hobbes is most often portrayed as a proponent of the modern secular state. Norberto Bobbio epitomized this view in his recent study of Hobbes:

> I mistrust recent interpretations which have attempted to place particular stress on the religious dimension of Hobbes's political thought. The essential part of his political theory, despite variations from work to work, is the rational justification of the origin of the state and its mission in this world. This enterprise represents a decisive moment in the process of the secularization of politics; the state ceases to be *remedium peccati* [a remedy for sin], and becomes the strongest and most reliable disciplinary authority of the passions.[64]

As Bobbio's statement indicates, there have been attempts to find a theological dimension to Hobbes's thought. Most famously, A. E. Taylor and Howard Warrender argued that the coherence of Hobbes's political philosophy hangs on his claim that God ordained and enforces the natural laws.[65] But the prevailing view is that Hobbes was an ardent secularizer and political realist.

Hobbes's state theory was undoubtedly more secular than James I's and Filmer's theories in one important respect: he premised his theory upon natural law rather than divine right. This one significant difference, however, has been allowed to obscure a whole host of similarities. Like James I and Filmer (as well as French absolutist thinkers), Hobbes portrayed the state as a metaphysically privileged institution resting upon an immutable basis—he simply shifted that basis from divine right to natural law.[66] Hobbes further looked to the state to elevate human beings above contingency and flux by instituting a static and harmonious order embodying universal moral principles. In other words, Hobbes proposed his state theory to restore human beings to some semblance of the Tudor ideal of order. His major innovation was to legitimize this moral vision of the state in terms of a materialistic psychological theory. In this way, he paved the way for the transmission of some of the sacred premises of absolute state theory into a more mundane political discourse.

Hobbes's state theory began from the proposition *"nosce teipsum*, read thy self"* (L, introduction, 4).[67] By reading oneself, one could learn to recognize "the similitude of the thoughts and passions of another," and thereby identify a universal foundation for morality and politics within human nature. It is perhaps easy to forget today just how innovative Hobbes's methodology was when he proposed it. In seventeenth-century England, most writers began their political tracts by discussing the principles of eternal and natural law—whether in the form of Hooker's all-encompassing vision of order or the divine right theories of James I and Filmer. Hobbes would have none of this. He rejected out of hand all suggestions of an immanent law and natural hierarchy, and gave only brief mention to the notion of direct divine right. Much like Descartes, Hobbes began his reconstruction of order by wiping the slate clean and turning inward to study the individual psyche.[68]

While Hobbes's psychological method has sometimes been portrayed as a reaction against the skepticism of Montaigne, Charron, and others, it actually represented a direct extension of their ideas.[69] Faced with the contingency of human affairs, Montaigne turned inward to discover a new ground of order within himself.[70] Charron applied Montaigne's method to discern a universal science of ethics. The opening chapter of *De la sagesse* even included the quotation: "Nosce teipsum."[71] Hobbes was almost surely familiar with Charron's work. In the early chapters of *Leviathan,* he even addressed many of the same issues discussed in the early chapters of the *Sagesse:* the generation of the senses; the origin of imagination, memory, and appetites; the nature of the will; and the definition of various passions such as love, ambition, hope, despair, envy, and fear.[72] The major difference between the *Sagesse* and *Leviathan* was that Hobbes started out from an even more skeptical premise than Charron. Charron maintained that human beings had an immediate and intuitive understanding of the principles of natural law through their reason. Hobbes argued, by contrast, that human reason was wholly instrumental and capable only of deducing conclusions from premises and vice versa (L, v, 22–23). He denied all innate or intuitive knowledge and premised his moral and political theory upon the natural desires of human beings.

Hobbes identified the fundamental principle of the human psyche as the vital motion—the internal life force within creatures "begun in generation, and continued without interruption through their whole life" (L, vi, 27). It consisted of the "course of the blood, the pulse, the breathing, the concoction, nutrition, excretion, etc.," and propelled all creatures to seek their self-preservation "no less than that whereby a stone moves downward" (DC, 8). Hobbes's discussion of the desire for self-preservation has often been associated with a narrow desire for immediate survival.[73] But Hobbes actually defined this desire more broadly in terms of the desire for long-term or perpetual survival. This point is important because it explains how Hobbes was able to trace all the complex passions and beliefs of human beings back to this one core desire. It is also essential for understanding his state theory. He most clearly described the broad scope of the desire for self-preservation in his discussion of happiness.[74] While admitting that individuals did not share any universal ends, Hobbes claimed they did share one underlying universal desire, the desire to perpetuate their pursuit of diverse goods indefinitely into the future. "Felicity is a continual progress of the desire, from one object to another, the attaining of the former being still but the way to the latter. The cause whereof is *that the object of man's desire is not to enjoy once only, and for one instant of time, but to assure forever the way of his future desire"* (L, xi, 57; emphasis added). Hobbes was quite explicit here about the core desire of human beings: individuals continually sought after the universal goal of self-perpetuation. They differed "only in the way" they attempted to fulfill this desire, "which ariseth partly from the diversity of passions in divers men, and partly from the difference of the knowledge or opinion each one has of the causes which produce the effect desired" (L, xi, 57).

In the final chapters of part 1 of *Leviathan,* Hobbes drew upon this universal desire for self-perpetuation to explain the roots of social disorder. These chapters introduced a whole new level of introspection into absolutist state theory. Whereas earlier absolutist thinkers had been content simply to characterize human beings as unruly and disorderly by nature, Hobbes attempted to explain why they were so by delving into the psychological causes of disorder. He claimed the primary cause of human disorder was the universal human desire for self-preservation. Because human beings desired above all else to perpetuate their existence into the future, they adopted all sorts of unruly behaviors and beliefs whenever the future appeared uncertain to them.

Hobbes began his discussion with an analysis of one of the most important sources of disorder among human beings: the desire for power. This drove individuals to seek a variety of different forms of power including wealth, honor, and command (L, x, xi, 50–58). Hobbes identified the source of this desire in temporal anxiety. Individuals pursued power as a means to assure themselves of their future well-being. Immediately after asserting that "Felicity is a continual progress of the desire," he next declared:

> So that in the first place, I put for a general inclination of all mankind, a perpetual and restless desire of power after power, that ceaseth only in death. And the cause of this is not always that a man hopes for a more intensive delight than he has already attained to, or that he cannot be content with a moderate power, *but because he cannot assure the power and means to live well, which he hath present, without the acquisition of more.* (L, xi, 58; emphasis added)

C. B. Macpherson saw in this statement evidence of an acquisitive or possessive sensibility underlying Hobbes's psychological theory.[75] Yet Hobbes explicitly stated in this passage that individuals did not seek power for the sake of "a more intensive delight" or the acquisition of more power. The reason individuals ceaselessly pursued power was because they were gripped by existential fear. They could not "assure the power and means to live well" in the future that they presently possessed "without the acquisition of more." They pursued power, in other words, to assure themselves against future contingencies and guarantee their continual well-being. Power represented a lien against future contingencies that individuals could discharge whenever they might need it.[76]

In chapter 12, Hobbes turned to consider the psychological roots of religious beliefs. At first glance, this chapter would seem to be out of place in the organization of *Leviathan*. It appears just after his discussion of power and just before his discussion of the state of nature. But two considerations seem to have guided Hobbes's decision to place this chapter here. First, Hobbes considered false religious beliefs, like the pursuit of power, to be an important source of disorder. In *Behemoth*, he even placed much of the blame for the Civil War on misguided religious doctrines (B, 1–2, 181). Secondly, Hobbes maintained that human beings' false religious beliefs were rooted in the same source as their desire for power: their anxiety about their future well-being.

Hobbes began chapter 12 by observing that since religious beliefs were unique to human beings, they must have their source "in some peculiar quality [in human beings], or at least in some eminent degree thereof, not to be found in any other living creatures" (L, xii, 63). This quality, he explained, was curiosity or the ability to discern the causes and effects of events stemming from human beings' superior memory and foresight. While memory and foresight allowed human beings to understand more of the world around them than animals, it also produced anxiety. "For being assured that there be causes of all things that have arrived hitherto or shall arrive hereafter, it is impossible for a man who continually endeavoureth to secure himself against the evil he fears, and procure the good he desireth, not to be in a perpetual solicitude of the time to come" (L, xii, 63–64). In one of his most colorful metaphors, Hobbes even compared the life of "everyman" to the fate of the mythic Prometheus:

> For as Prometheus (which, interpreted, is the prudent man) was bound to the hill Caucasus (a place of large prospect where an eagle, feeding on his liver, devoured in the day as much as was repaired in the night), so that man which looks too far before him, in the care of future time, hath his heart all the day long gnawed on by fear of death, poverty, or other calamity, and has no repose, nor pause of his anxiety, but in sleep. (L, xii, 64)

According to Hobbes, the very memory and foresight that allowed human beings more fully to control the world also made them more sensitive to the contingency of affairs.

In order to allay their anxiety, Hobbes claimed, human beings invented religion. "This perpetual fear, always accompanying mankind in the ignorance of causes (as it were in the dark), must needs have for object something. And therefore, when there is nothing to be seen, there is nothing to accuse, either of their good or evil fortune, but some power or agent invisible; in which sense, perhaps, it was that some of the old poets said that the gods were at first created by human fear" (L, xii, 64). Human beings invented the gods to explain the unintelligible causes of events and to provide themselves with some sense of assurance about the future. They likewise devised systems of worship in the hope that they could appease the gods and win their favor. In these respects, religious beliefs were not so very different from the desire for power.[77] They represented means for achieving some assurance over future affairs.

The first part of *Leviathan* culminates in Hobbes's famous description of the state of nature. The ideological significance of this chapter can hardly be overstated. Hobbes used his account of the state of nature both to debunk the idea of an immanent natural social order and to depict the behavior of human beings in a contingent social world. He began by asserting the natural equality of all human beings. By his account there was no natural hierarchy or chain of being within human society; the natural differences between individuals were inconsequential, and none had a natural right to rule over others. Because of their natural equality, individuals were naturally competitive and distrustful of one another. Instead of exhibiting any natural traits of sociability, Hobbes claimed individuals naturally tended to fear one another and undertake preemptive strikes to assure their own future security. Lacking some common power capable of imposing order upon them, human beings therefore naturally reverted to a state of war of all against all. Hobbes identified the primary cause of these disorderly behaviors, once again, as temporal anxiety:

> Hereby it is manifest that during the time men live without a common power to keep them all in awe, they are in that condition which is called war, and such a war as is of every man against every man. For war consisteth not in battle only, or the act of fighting, but in a tract of time wherein the will to contend by battle is sufficiently known. And therefore, the notion of time is to be considered in the nature of war, as it is in the nature of weather. For as the nature of foul weather lieth not in a shower or two of rain, but in an inclination thereto of many days together, so the nature of war consisteth not in actual fighting, but in the known disposition thereto during all the time there is no assurance to the contrary. All other time is peace. (L, xiii, 76)

Although scholars have not paid much attention to the role of "time" in Hobbes's state of nature, Hobbes himself gave it a central place. He defined the state of nature not as a state of perpetual battle but rather as a state of perpetual anxiety about battle. It was a "tract of time" during which the will to contend by battle was known; or stated more simply, it was a state of tremendous temporal uncertainty. The state of nature was what happened when individuals were confronted with a contingent social sphere. It was Hobbes's description of how individuals attempted to remain existentially stable within a stream of events conceived as essentially dangerous and destructive to their existence. Desiring above all to perpetuate their existence, they reacted to temporal uncertainty with anxiety and all sorts of antisocial behaviors that culminated in a war of all against all.

HOBBES'S NATURAL LAW THEORY

Hobbes proposed a traditional solution to the problem of disorder: natural law theory. He even described the natural law in terms strongly reminiscent of the traditional medieval theory. The natural law was "the dictate of right reason" (DC, 16). It was coterminous with the "law of God" and contained "immutable and eternal" moral principles applicable to all human beings at all times (L, xv, xliii, 99, 399). Hobbes's description of the substantive precepts of natural law, too, echoed the dictates of theologians and philosophers stretching back to St. Thomas Aquinas.[78] He condemned violence, theft, cruelty, slander, bias, dishonesty, and other traditional vices as contrary to the natural laws. He even summarized the principles of natural law with the Golden Rule: "Do not that to another, which thou wouldst not have done to thyself" (L, xv, 99).[79] Despite these similarities, there was one essential difference between Hobbes's natural law theory and the medieval theory: Hobbes grounded his natural law theory in human psychology rather than right reason and eternal law. He attempted to revitalize the basic principles of natural law theory in the face of skepticism and after the breakdown of the Tudor paradigm by rooting them in mundane human desires.

Hobbes began his account of natural law theory with a subjectivist explanation of values. He claimed individuals defined objects and actions as good or evil depending upon their perceptions of what contributed to or hindered their self-preservation (L, vi, 28–29). Because of their different life experiences, each individual defined goods and evils in different ways. Individuals also changed their value judgments over the course of their lives as they accumulated new and different experiences (L, xv, 100). In *De Homine*, Hobbes stated this position most clearly: "One cannot speak of something as being simply good; since whatsoever is good, is good for someone or other. . . . Therefore good is said to be relative to person, place, and time. What pleaseth one man now, will displease another later; and the same holds true for everyone else. For the nature of good and evil follows from the nature of circumstances" (DH, xi, 47).

From this passage and others like it, it has sometimes been assumed that Hobbes held a subjectivist view of human morality. But this was not his final word on the matter. Although he claimed individuals defined good and evil according to their own personal tastes, he added that some individuals were able to define real goods more accurately than others. In particular, more experienced individuals were usually more adept at discerning real goods than less experienced individuals. After having tasted a poisonous fruit, for example, an experienced individual would know not to eat it again. It hindered one's vital motion and caused a sensation of pain. But a less experienced individual, being unaware of the consequences of his or her actions, might still view this fruit as a good and desire to eat it. Based upon the objective outcome of actions, Hobbes asserted that goods and evils could actually be divided into apparent and real:

> Moreover, good (like evil) is divided into real and apparent. Not because any apparent good may not truly be good in itself, without considering the other things that follow from it; but in many things, whereof part is good and part evil, there is sometimes such a necessary connexion between the parts that they cannot be separated. Therefore, though in each one of them there be so much good, or so much evil; nevertheless the chain as a whole is partly good and partly evil. . . . Whence it happens that inexperienced men that do not look closely enough at the long-term consequences of things, accept what appears to be good, not seeing the evil annexed to it; afterwards they experience damage. And this is what is meant by those who distinguish good and evil as real and apparent. (DH, xi, 48)

As Hobbes carefully noted, an apparent good was still a type of good. A poisonous fruit could still appear good to an inexperienced individual. It might even temporarily satisfy his or her appetite. But apparent goods were shortsighted. They were pursued by inexperienced individuals unaware of the full consequences of their actions. Real goods, by contrast, were long-term goods. They were the sorts of goods that experienced individuals identified as beneficial to their self-preservation based upon their memories and foresight.

Hobbes added, however, that not even the most experienced individual could see all the consequences of every action. While acknowledging that "they shall conjecture best, that have most experience," he added that "experience concludeth nothing universally" (EL, 18). Even a very wise individual was always limited by considerations of time, place, and circumstance. In order to rise above these accidents of experience, Hobbes suggested that individuals had to leave the realm of experience and exercise their reason. Hobbes defined reason as a purely instrumental faculty for deducing consequences from causes and causes from consequences. "For reason, in this sense, is nothing but reckoning, (that is, adding and subtracting) of the consequences of general names agreed upon for the marking and signifying of our thoughts" (L, v, 22–23). The great value of reason by Hobbes's estimation was that it could carry human beings beyond experiential knowledge and toward a knowledge of all the possible causes and effects of any given phenomenon (L, v, 23). This knowledge was what Hobbes called "philosophy" or "science." It was the universal and eternal knowledge of causes and effects (L, v, 25).

Hobbes's natural law theory was his "moral philosophy" or "moral science." It was a rational deduction of human goods and evils based upon their core psychological desire. If one began from the basic desire of all human beings for self-preservation and examined the consequences of all actions, Hobbes claimed one could identify the real or universal good for all individuals:

> Every man by natural passion, calleth that good which pleaseth him for the present, or so far forth as he can foresee; and in like manner that which displeaseth him evil. And therefore he that foreseeth the whole way to his preservation (which is the end that every one by nature aimeth at) must also call it good, and the contrary evil. And this is that good and evil, which not every man in passion calleth so, but all men by reason. (EL, xvii, 109)

The real good for all individuals was whatever ensured the whole way to their future preservation; or, as Hobbes wrote in his discussion of felicity, it was whatever assured "forever the way of [their] future desire" (L, xi, 57). This was what everyone really wanted whenever they pursued any particular good. The desire for power, wealth, and honor were all short-term approximations of this good. So was belief in false religious ideas. The only absolutely true and long-term good was the natural law.

Hobbes defined the natural law as a set of rational rules describing all those actions that individuals were obliged to perform or omit in order to fulfill their fundamental desire for preservation. "A Law of Nature, *lex naturalis,* is a precept, or general rule, found out by reason, by which a man is forbidden to do that, which is destructive of his life, or taketh away the means of preserving the same; and to omit that, by which he thinketh it may be best preserved" (L, xiv, 79). The natural law prohibited individuals from performing all actions that secured only their short-term preservation while obliging them to perform all actions that promoted their long-term preservation. Its fundamental dictate was to pursue peace:

> As long as this natural right of every man to every thing endureth, there can be no security to any man, how strong or wise soever he be, of living out the time, which nature ordinarily alloweth men to live. And consequently it is a precept, or general rule of reason, that every man ought to endeavour peace, as far as he has hope of obtaining it. (L, xiv, 80)

Since Hobbes believed that all individuals by nature (or biologically) wished to perpetuate their existence to the greatest extent possible, he claimed they were obliged to pursue peace whenever it was attainable. To pursue some other end instead of peace was contrary to nature and their own desires.

Jean Hampton concluded her study of Hobbes's natural law theory by arguing that he intended the natural laws to be understood only as "hypothetical imperatives."[80] They were obligatory only for those individuals who desired peace above all other ends but were not obligatory for those who preferred other ends, such as glory or riches over peace. Yet what Hampton (and many others) failed to appreciate is that Hobbes regarded the desire for glory and riches and all other passions as merely short-term approximations of the true desire for peace. This is why he regarded the natural law as imperative for everyone. When an individual pursued honor or riches or attempted to dominate others, what he or she was really doing was attempting to ensure his or her future well-being. But these activities were shortsighted, securing only a temporary and partial security while provoking fear and hostility in others. It was in this respect that Hobbes made a number of deontological statements noticed by A. E. Taylor.[81] Any individual who violated the natural laws in peacetime for honor or riches or any other end "contradicteth himself" (EL, 85). Only a "fool" would risk the loss of public peace for a private gain (L, xv, 90–92), for to pursue the latter at the cost of the former was to choose a lesser good over a greater one. The natural laws outlined the "whole way" to an individual's preservation. They were not simply hypothetical imperatives but universal imperatives paving the way to the highest ends that every individual desired by nature.

In sum, Hobbes outlined a new foundation for natural law theory. With the breakdown of the medieval cosmology and the emergence of skepticism, it was no longer plausible to assert that universal moral principles were immediately apprehensible to all human beings through their reason. There was simply too much disagreement about the principles of natural law. Hobbes found a new prop for this theory in the universal desire of all human beings for self-perpetuation. Much of the old natural law theory could be reconstructed and defended upon this basis. But certain precepts of the old law had to be omitted.[82] The old natural law was part of a universal moral teleology pointing beyond nature toward salvation. Hobbes reconceptualized the natural law in more mundane terms. He claimed the highest end of human beings was perpetual self-preservation, and excluded all considerations about "eternal felicity after death" from his account of the natural laws (L, xv, 92). The natural law theory that Hobbes salvaged from the wreckage of the medieval worldview was similar to the old theory but stripped of higher religious ends. It was a natural law theory torn out of the context of the old moral cosmology and grounded in human biology and psychology.

HOBBES'S MORTAL GOD

Perhaps the most important difference between Hobbes's natural law theory and the medieval natural law tradition was the absence from Hobbes's theory of any self-enforcement mechanism. St. Thomas Aquinas argued that human beings naturally tended toward the fulfillment of the natural law by instinct and reason. Richard Hooker took a somewhat dimmer view of human nature but nonetheless still maintained that human beings understood the main principles of natural law through their reason. Hobbes, by contrast, argued that human beings were largely ignorant of the natural law and wholly incapable of enforcing it by themselves. He listed several reasons to explain his opinion.

Most fundamentally, he claimed the majority of individuals did not obey the natural law because they did not know it. It was not written into the human heart or immediately accessible to reason. Rather, it was an abstract rational deduction from the fundamental desire of all human beings for long-term preservation. Consequently, one had to have a well-developed capacity for scientific reasoning to understand it—a capacity that Hobbes claimed very few individuals possessed (L, xiii, 74). He wrote in his *Elements of Philosophy* that since "none hitherto have taught [the rules of moral philosophy] in a clear and exact manner," there were "but few in the world that have learned those duties which unite and keep men in peace" (EP, 8). Hobbes intended his own writings to be a revelation in this regard.

Even supposing the natural law were widely understood, Hobbes still did not think human beings would be able spontaneously to follow it. The passions made it difficult even for relatively rational individuals to agree about the precise meaning of the natural law. "Although men agree upon the laws of nature, and endeavor to observe the same, yet considering the passions of men, that makes it difficult to understand by what actions, and circumstances of actions, those laws are broken; there must needs arise many great controversies about the interpretation thereof, by which the peace must need be dissolved, and men return to their former estate of hostility" (EL, iv, 105). So deep-seated was this problem that Hobbes doubted whether individuals could ever spontaneously reach any objective definition of the natural law (EL, x, 225). Each individual defined the principles of natural law according to his or her own particular interests.

Hobbes added that even if individuals did come to an objective definition of the natural laws, they would still lack the self-discipline to obey them. On this point, at least, Hobbes was in agreement with Hooker. While individuals might understand on an intellectual level that they ought to perform or desist from certain actions, they frequently sacrificed long-term goods for short-term pleasures. The appetites, Hobbes wrote, "obstruct right reasoning in this, that they militate against the real good and in favor of the apparent and most immediate good, which turns out frequently to be evil when everything associated with it hath been considered" (DH, xii, 55). Finally, there was the problem of collective action. Unless an individual could be sure that others were going to behave peacefully (which was quite unlikely in the state of nature for all of the above reasons), Hobbes argued that it would be foolish to behave peacefully toward them (L, xv, 99). As long as there was no central body to coordinate and regulate individual behaviors, reason itself dictated that individuals should take whatever precautions were necessary to assure their continued preservation.

For Hobbes, therefore, the natural laws were strictly potential. The medieval vision of a self-enforcing natural law was by his estimation an illusion. Human society was naturally dominated by anxiety, ignorance, passion, and corruption. In order to actualize the principles of natural law, human beings had to institute a state authority to rule over them. The state was, for Hobbes, the necessary vehicle for imposing a moral and natural order upon human beings.

Hobbes located the theoretical origin of the state in the social contract. Hooker had of course anticipated this idea. But his "contract theory" remained inchoate and subsumed within the traditional natural law framework.[83] He believed consent was necessary only for those elements of the social order (for example, the form of the government and the "merely" human laws) that were not already ordained by divine and natural law. Hobbes, by contrast, claimed consent was necessary for all aspects of the social order. Indeed, it was the basis of the social order. There was by his account no preexisting natural or rational order. Individuals had to lay down their natural right to all things and establish a sovereign ruler to create an artificial order for them. Only then would they be able to fulfill their natural desire for long-term self-preservation. By basing his contract theory in the universal desire of individuals for self-preservation, Hobbes was able to avoid many of the pitfalls of consent theory identified by Filmer.[84] He was never very concerned, as Filmer assumed all contract theorists were, with the free will of the subjects. All that was necessary to legitimize a political regime, Hobbes argued, was the tacit consent of the subjects, and this could be assumed just as long as the state provided them with peace and security (L, xx, 127–28).

The purpose of the state was to restore human beings to the universal moral order of nature. It was supposed to manifest the principles of natural law and create a predictable and harmonious social order, thereby rescuing them from their inveterate anxiety about the future. "The final cause, end, or design of men" in establishing a state, Hobbes wrote, was "the *foresight* of their own preservation, and of a more contented life thereby" (L, xvii, 106 [my emphasis]). Hobbes argued that the state was responsible for instituting a highly predictable "state of peace" devoid of any "inclination" or "disposition" toward conflict (L, xiii, 76). The state was likewise supposed to forge "a real unity" of individuals, not simply "for one instant of time" but for "all the time of their life" (L, xi, xvii, 57, 107, 109). The state existed, in short, to bind human beings together into a static and moral political order consonant with the natural law. It relieved human beings of much of their temporal anxiety by uniting them into a predictable and safe social environment.

The principles of the state followed logically from this purpose. Following Bodin, Hobbes identified legislative sovereignty as the central principle of state power. Medieval writers had sharply circumscribed the legislative powers of rulers within the limits of natural law. Hobbes, however, adopted the position of Montaigne and other sixteenth-century skeptics in arguing that the principles of natural law were largely indeterminate (L, xxvi, 172–77). Even if all individuals were to agree that justice, gratitude, modesty, and equity were virtues, they would still disagree about the meaning of these terms. In order to establish a common definition of these virtues, it was therefore necessary to grant the sovereign ruler the authority to define the natural laws for the community as a whole. That is, the people had to authorize the sovereign ruler to stand in for right reason. "But this is certain," Hobbes wrote,

> seeing right reason is not existent, the reason of some man, or men, must supply the place thereof; and that man, or men, is he or they, that have the sovereign power . . .; and consequently the civil laws are to all subjects the measures of their actions, whereby to determine, where they be right or wrong, profitable or unprofitable, virtuous or vicious; and by them the use and definition of all names not agreed upon, and tending to controversy, shall be established. (EL, x, 225–26)

Regardless of whether the sovereign's laws were good or bad—indeed, precisely because there were no certain criteria for determining good or bad—Hobbes argued that the subjects had to treat his laws as if they were right reason itself. Dispensing with the traditional medieval distinction between natural and positive law, he asserted, "The law of nature and the civil law contain each other, and are of equal extent" (L, xxvi, 174). Hobbes even denied the validity of those few minimal limitations on the sovereign power endorsed by Bodin, such as the right to private property and the duty to obey the fundamental laws. There was to Hobbes's mind no defensible grounds for these limitations. All law and order depended solely upon the sovereign will.

In addition to these legislative powers, Hobbes argued that the state had to possess absolute and perpetual powers. All legislative, executive, judicial, and administrative powers had to be centralized in one source (L, xviii, 110–18). Ideally, Hobbes argued, these powers should be granted to a single monarch. But he acknowledged that they could just as well be vested in an aristocratic or democratic assembly (L, xix, 118–27). In any case, he claimed that any attempt to divide state powers between different branches of government was contradictory. It made the effectiveness of the state dependent upon the "accidental consent" of the legislative, executive, and judicial branches of government (L, xxix, 216). It thus defeated the very purposes for which the state was established. Hobbes made a similar point about limitations on the sovereign ruler's powers. The desire to place such limitations revealed a fundamental confusion about the nature of government (EL, 132–34, 168; L, xxix, 211). Limitations on the sovereign ruler's powers constrained his ability to address future contingencies and thus circumscribed the degree to which he could preserve the peace and security of society. They were equivalent to hiring a worker to build a house and then tying one arm behind his or her back. Finally, since individuals "did institute the commonwealth for their perpetual (and not temporary) security," it was necessary that the sovereign power be constituted as an "artificial eternity" (L, xix, 124). Otherwise the commonwealth would dissolve into disorder upon the death of each particular sovereign ruler. In all forms of government, the sovereign power thus had to be located in an abstract "seat of power" distinct from both the ruler and the ruled (L, letter dedicatory, 2). In monarchies, it was also necessary to establish a clear law of succession to ensure the instantaneous transfer of power from one ruler to the next (L, xix, 118–27). For Hobbes, therefore, the move toward a more abstract conception of state power was dictated by the purpose of the state. Before the state could raise the people above the contingent temporal world, the people first had to constitute the state as a super-temporal entity.

While Hobbes did not recognize any substantive limitations on the sovereign's powers, he did identify some formal obligations. Above all, he claimed the sovereign ruler was bound to secure "the safety of the people, to which he is obliged by the law of nature, and to render an account thereof to God, the author of that law" (L, xxx, 219). If the sovereign ruler failed in this duty, the people were no longer obliged to obey his commands (L, xxi, xxix, 142–44, 218–19). Bishop Bramhall regarded this element of Hobbes's state theory as an invitation to rebellion.[85] However, it also represented a standing justification for the expansion of state powers into all spheres of social activity. If the state's legitimacy rested upon the people's sense of security, then any and all contingencies legitimately fell within the purview of state regulation. Hobbes himself asserted the responsibility of the state to fulfill certain welfare functions. He claimed that it was contrary to the purposes of the state to leave the welfare of the subjects to the "hazard" of "uncertain charity" (L, xxx, 219, 228). The state was directly responsible for protecting each and every individual against social contingencies.

The sovereign ruler was also obliged to govern according to the natural law of equity.[86] Hobbes claimed the notion of equity was implicit to the social contract itself. In establishing the social contract, each individual agreed "to lay down his right to all things, and be contented with so much liberty against other men, as he would allow other men against himself" (L, xiv, 80). If the sovereign ruler made any law favoring some individuals over others, he thus contradicted the very terms of the contract. He effectively declared a preference for the well-being of some individuals over others (L, xv, 97). The rule of equity, then, provided an important formal constraint on the sovereign's powers:

> The safety of the people requireth further, from him or them that have the sovereign power, that justice be equally administered to all degrees of people, that is, that as well the rich and mighty as poor and obscure persons may be righted of the injuries done them, so as the great may have no greater hope of impunity when they do violence, dishonour, or any injury to the meaner sort, than when one of these does the like to one of them. For in this consisteth equity, to which, as being a precept of the law of nature, a sovereign is as much subject as any of the meanest of his people. (L, xxx, 226)

Hobbes's emphasis on equity more than anything else distinguished his vision of political order from the traditional Tudor ideal. Tudor writers envisioned order in terms of a natural hierarchy of superiors and inferiors. In Hobbes's state, all were equal under the sovereign ruler. The important exceptions were women, whom Hobbes claimed entered the social contract already subject to their husbands.[87] But otherwise, Hobbes reconstructed his universal polity on a new egalitarian basis. In his dealings with his subjects, the sovereign ruler was obliged to treat all in an equal and impersonal manner.

Hobbes summarized his discussion of the origin of the state in the following way: "This is the generation of that great Leviathan, or rather (to speak more reverently) of that Mortal God to which we owe, under the Immortal God, our peace and defence" (L, xvii, 109). "That the state is characterized as 'god,'" Carl Schmitt wrote, "has no particular meaning in Hobbes' construction of the state."[88] Most scholars have agreed with Schmitt's assessment. Yet in light of what has been said above, it seems hard to sustain this view. Hobbes proposed the state as a means to institute a political order akin to the universal moral order of God. He looked to the state to stand in for God in defining the principles of natural law and maintaining a static peace. The state was for Hobbes therefore very much a godlike power. It was the metaphysically ordained source of all order and morality within a temporal realm that had fallen away from the divine and natural law. It is perhaps only because we have become so familiar with this conception of the state that scholars have for the most part failed to recognize the peculiar metaphysical underpinnings of Hobbes's theory of the order. Yet Hobbes rather explicitly proposed his state theory to restore human beings to the static and universal political order associated with medieval political theories. His Leviathan resolved the most severe existential anxieties of human beings by establishing a universal political order standing apart from the irrational stream of temporal affairs.

HOBBES'S ECCLESIASTICAL STATE

Until recently, Hobbes's religious writings attracted little attention. In the early 1970s, J. G. A. Pocock observed that the general attitude of scholars toward the third and fourth books of *Leviathan* was "first, that they aren't really there, second, that Hobbes didn't really mean them."[89] The same cannot be said today. Over the past three decades, there has been an explosion of interest in Hobbes's religious thought.[90] A number of scholars have attempted to discern Hobbes's true religious beliefs and particularly whether he was a sincere Christian.[91] Others have set aside this thorny question and studied the ideological effect he was trying to produce through his religious arguments.[92] Pocock argued that Hobbes's religious arguments were designed to undermine the traditional authority claims of church powers and hence to lend independent historical support to his political ideas. David

Johnston suggested that Hobbes devised his religious writings to convince his readers to abandon their irrational religious beliefs and become the sort of self-interested rational actors "that had always been the inhabitants of his vision of political society."[93] In contrast to Johnston's views, S. A. Lloyd argued that Hobbes's theological arguments were intended not to rationalize away religious beliefs but rather to "redescribe" them into a new universal religion consistent with his state theory.[94]

All of these interpretations have some merit. But Hobbes intended far more in his religious writings than merely to undermine, rationalize, or redescribe traditional religious beliefs—he intended to transfer traditional religious loyalties away from the Catholic and Protestant clergy and to relocate them in the state. His religious writings were an integral part of his overall project to sacralize the state. They represented the final step in his project of making the state the sole mediator between God and humanity and the highest source of human loyalties.

Hobbes's theology begins with the assumption that God is an incomprehensible and arbitrary deity. He claimed human beings could know very little about God except that he existed and was the cause of all things. We could know God existed on the grounds that the stream of temporal events logically had to have one first cause or prime mover. This first cause or prime mover was what "men call God" (L, xi, 62). By the same logic, we could know that God was the cause of all actions and events within time because all actions and events could be traced back to their first cause (L, xxi, 137). But beyond these minimal deductions, Hobbes claimed there was very little we could know about God. We might say that God was "omnipotent" in order to indicate that he was the primary cause of all things (L, xxxi, 241). But it was utter nonsense to argue that God was eternal or infinite or to attribute any other characteristics to him. When we dubbed God infinite or eternal, we were really just admitting that "his greatness and power are unconceivable" (L, iii, 15). Indeed, Hobbes asserted that the most proper attitude for human beings to take toward God was one of pious incomprehension (L, xxxi, 240).

Hobbes accentuated the arbitrary or willful quality of God's rule in his commentary on Job—the same book of the Bible from which he took his image of the mighty Leviathan. The central question of the book of Job was "Why evil men often prosper and good men suffer adversity" (L, xxxi, 236). The answer Hobbes took away from this book was that God wills it that way. When Job questioned why he had been subjected to terrible misfortunes, his friends explained his fate in terms of his sinfulness. Job objected that he was a truly righteous man and undeserving of such treatment. Then God intervened in the argument, asserting that Job's fate was of no concern to anyone but him: "Where wast thou, when I laid the foundations of the earth[?]" (Job 38:4). Carrying Luther's and Calvin's voluntaristic theologies to the extreme, Hobbes implied here that it was not even proper to attribute the afflictions of human beings to their sinfulness.[95] God did just what he pleased to human beings when he pleased because he was God. Our existence in this world was utterly dependent upon his will.

While God's will was unknowable, Hobbes claimed human beings did have two sources for understanding what he expected of us: reason and Scripture. Hobbes began book 3 of *Leviathan* with his defense of reason: "Though there be many things in God's word above reason (that is to say which cannot by natural reason be either demonstrated or confuted), yet there is nothing contrary to it; but when it seemeth so, the fault is either in our unskillful interpretation or erroneous ratiocination" (L, xxxii, 245–46). Hobbes's argument here was orthodox.[96] He was following the long scholastic tradition that maintained the harmony of reason and revelation. He argued that God would not have given human beings reason unless he intended it to be the rule of their conduct (L, xxxii, 245; DC, 50–51). When coupled with his vision of a voluntaristic God, however, Hobbes's argument resulted in some very unorthodox conclusions. Specifically, it had the effect of subordinating divine law to natural law, faith to reason, religion to the state. But more on this below.

The other source for knowing God's intentions for human beings was Scripture. "The Old and New Testaments, as we have them now," Hobbes wrote, "are the true registers of those things which were done and said by the prophets and apostles" (L, xxxiii, 257). Moreover, they were purported "on all hands" to be the word of God (L, xxxiii, 259). Whether or not the Scriptures really were the word of God, however, was a matter of faith. It depended upon the belief that the prophets and apostles actually spoke with God and witnessed his actions (L, xxxii, xxxiii, 246–47, 259–60). Since individuals were likely to disagree about which books and passages of the Bible were authentic, Hobbes claimed it rightfully belonged to the sovereign authority to decide these points. For reason instructed us to establish an absolute sovereign power with the authority to establish peace and order. One of the necessary prerogatives of the sovereign ruler was the right to regulate and censor all doctrines and opinions within the commonwealth (L, xviii, 113–14). It thus followed logically that the sovereign ruler should have the authority to determine the canonical texts of Scripture just as he gave authoritative interpretation to the natural law. "Seeing, therefore, I have already proved that sovereigns in their own dominions are the sole legislators, those books only are canonical (that is, law) in every nation which are established by the sovereign authority" (L, xxxiii, 250). Here already we begin to see Hobbes's elevation of natural law over divine law, reason over faith. Since the divine law of Scripture was uncertain and open to various interpretations, he concluded that reason should be the authoritative guide in matters of public worship.

Hobbes proceeded from these premises to argue that the sovereign ruler was the supreme religious authority within the commonwealth, attempting to transfer traditional religious loyalties away from prophets and priests to the sovereign ruler. He began by acknowledging that God had indeed spoken directly to human beings in the past. Moses, Samuel, Elijah, Isaiah, and others were all divine prophets. Nonetheless, he warned his readers to be wary of self-proclaimed prophets. Prophecies were nothing more than the dreams, visions, or ardent passions that individuals experienced concerning God (L, xxxii, 246–48). Accordingly, most prophecies turned out to be delusions. Of the four hundred prophets who appeared before the king of Israel, only Micaiah was a true one (L, xxxii, 247). One way to distinguish true from false prophecies was through the appearance of miracles. But Hobbes asserted that miracles were only those strange events that human beings could not conceive "to have been done by natural means" (L, xxxvii, 273). The implication was that miracles were most likely to be seen (or at least thought to be seen) by inexperienced and ignorant individuals (L, xxxvii, 298). "For in these times," he wrote, "I do not know one man that ever saw any such wonderous work, done by the charm, or at the word or prayer of a man, that a man endued but with a mediocrity of reason would think supernatural" (L, xxxvii, 300). After the coming of Christ, Hobbes further observed that God no longer worked miracles. Christ had revealed to human beings all they needed to know to attain salvation. In the present epoch, the sole criterion for determining the authenticity of prophecies was their conformity to holy Scripture:[97]

> Seeing therefore miracles now cease, we have no sign left whereby to acknowledge the pretended revelations or inspirations of any private man, nor obligation to give ear to any doctrine farther than it is conformable to the Holy Scriptures, which since the time of our Savior supply the place and sufficiently recompense the want of all other prophecy, and from which, by wise and learned interpretation and careful ratiocination, all rules and precepts necessary to the knowledge of our duty both to God and man, without enthusiasm or supernatural inspiration, may easily be deduced. (L, xxxii, 249)

Hobbes never went so far as to deny the possibility of prophecy. But he did seriously circumscribe the possible range of its message. Any prophet who controverted the words of the Scripture was to be immediately judged a fraud. The Scripture was quite literally God's final word on human salvation. Hobbes then extended this teaching to apply to the sovereign ruler's interpretation of Scripture (L, xxxii, 248; xxxvi, 292–93). Just as the sovereign ruler was responsible for determining the canonical Scriptures, so also he was responsible for determining their authoritative interpretation. Any prophet who challenged the sovereign's interpretation of the Scriptures was therefore also to be judged a fraud. To suppose otherwise would be to suggest that God might contradict himself by sending a prophet to deliver a message contrary to the teachings of reason. Hobbes concluded that by divine precept the sovereign ruler was the supreme prophetic authority within the commonwealth:

Every man, therefore, ought to consider who is the sovereign prophet (that is to say, who it is that is God's vicegerent on earth, and hath next under God the authority of governing Christian men), and to observe for a rule that doctrine which, in the name of God, he hath commanded to be taught, and thereby to examine and try out the truth of those doctrines which pretended prophets (with miracle or without) shall at any time advance. . . . For when Christian men take not their Christian sovereign for God's prophet, they must either take their own dreams for the prophecy they mean to be governed by, and the tumor of their own hearts for the Spirit of God, or they must suffer themselves to be led by some strange prince or by some of their fellow subjects that can bewitch them, by slander of the government, into rebellion (without other miracle to confirm their calling than sometimes an extraordinary success and impunity), and by this means destroying all laws, both divine and human, reduce all order, government, and society to the first chaos of violence and civil war. (L, xxxvi, 293)

Contrary to what has sometimes been said about Hobbes's religious teachings, he did not destroy or undermine prophetic authority.[98] He merely relocated it in the "sovereign prophet." Hobbes did mean not to suggest by this term that the sovereign ruler actually spoke with God. But he did mean to say that the sovereign ruler's decisions could be assumed to be mandated by God. This much could be deduced through reason. God gave human beings reason to guide their conduct. Reason indicated that human beings should establish an absolute sovereign authority with the power to censor and regulate doctrines. Hence God indirectly ordained whatever the sovereign ruler proclaimed. The sovereign was a prophet in the sense that he spoke for God in a world where God no longer spoke directly to human beings.

Having transferred prophetic authority to the sovereign ruler, Hobbes next transferred the sacerdotal authority as well. He accomplished this theoretical move through a reinterpretation of the idea of the "Kingdom of God" (L, xxxiii, 261). The "greatest and main abuse of Scripture" and the one "to which almost all the rest are either consequent or subservient," Hobbes wrote, was the belief that the kingdom of God was a presently existing spiritual community (L, xliv, 412–13). "Consequent to this error" was the belief that "there ought to be some one man, or assembly, by whose mouth our Savior (now in heaven) speaketh, and giveth law, and which representeth his person to all Christians (or divers men or divers assemblies that do the same to divers parts of Christendom)." Hobbes's obvious target here was the papacy and its claim that the pope was the vicar of Christ on earth, "set between God and man," as Innocent III said, "lower than God but higher than man."[99] But Hobbes also meant to challenge the authority of Protestant ministers and Anglican clergy who claimed direct divine ordination (L, xlii, xliv, 368–69, 414).[100] Hobbes challenged these spiritual authorities with a careful reading of Scripture. Nowhere in the Scripture was there any indication that the

"Kingdom of God" was a spiritual or otherworldly realm. On the contrary, most scriptural passages portrayed the kingdom of God as "a kingdom properly so named," specifically the kingdom of the ancient Israelites under God (L, xxxv, 272). Alternatively, the kingdom of God also referred to the divine kingdom that Christ would establish on earth when he returned "to reign actually and eternally" (L, xxxviii, xliv, 305, 413). But in the interim there was no kingdom of God. There was therefore no independent spiritual basis upon which the pope and clergy could rest their authority. They were merely "schoolmasters" who proclaimed the kingdom of God and attempted to persuade individuals to follow Christian principles (L, xlii, 336). The true legitimate source of sacerdotal authority in each commonwealth was the sovereign authority. Hobbes once again defended this proposal through appeal to the natural law. Since the natural law identified the sovereign ruler as the supreme authority over opinions and doctrines, he was by extension the "supreme pastor" in every Christian commonwealth "to whose charge the whole flock of his subjects is committed" (L, xlii, 367). He had the right to appoint pastors, to preach, to baptize, to administer the sacraments, and to execute all other pastoral functions (L, xlii, 368–69). Indeed, whereas the authority of all pastors was *jure civili,* that is, derived from the authority of the civil sovereign, "the king and every other sovereign executeth his office of supreme pastor by immediate authority from God (that is to say, in God's right, or *jure divino*)" (L, xlii, 368). Hobbes thus collapsed all distinction between church and state. The state was the new church and the civil sovereign the new pope within his domain:

> Temporal and spiritual government are but two words brought into the world to make men see double and mistake their lawful sovereign. It is true that the bodies of the faithful, after the resurrection, shall be not only spiritual, but eternal; but in this life they are gross and corruptible. There is, therefore, no other government in this life, neither of state nor religion, but temporal; nor teaching of any doctrine, lawful to any subject, which the governor, both of the state and of the religion, forbiddeth to be taught. (L, xxxix, 316)

Some scholars have suggested that Hobbes attributed sacerdotal powers to the civil sovereign because he believed that human beings were too ignorant and superstitious to obey their ruler through a rational fear of death alone.[101] By this account, Hobbes ultimately based his political philosophy upon supernatural beliefs, superstitions, and myth. David Johnston rightly criticized this interpretation on the grounds that it fails to take into account the extent to which Hobbes's whole political project was intended to enlighten his readers and dispel religious superstitions.[102] But Johnston failed to recognize the extent to which Hobbes's rationalizing project was itself consistent with a transfer of religious loyalties to the civil sovereign. By undermining the superstitions and erroneous doctrines of the Catholic and Protestant clergy, Hobbes intended to show his readers that the true (that is, rational) path to salvation depended upon obedience to the civil sovereign and the state. He meant to awaken his readers to the religious significance of the state. The state for Hobbes was not only the *remedium peccati* but also the *sine qua non* of human salvation.

LOCKE'S STATE THEORY

The writings of James I, Filmer, and Hobbes represent the most important expressions of seventeenth-century English state theory. Each of these writers framed their state theories in different ways: James I was a pure divine right theorist; Filmer cast his divine right theory in terms of patriarchalism; Hobbes framed his argument in terms of natural law theory. Nonetheless, all set forth structurally similar arguments. All accentuated the disorderly nature of human affairs. They all claimed the state was decreed by divine and natural law to establish order among human beings. They all envisioned order in terms of a universal and static ideal. These common features not only tie together the political philosophies of James I, Filmer, and Hobbes, they also link their philosophies directly to the French state tradition. They demonstrate that even in England the state was originally conceived as an exalted institution ordained to impose a universal moral order upon human beings.

Locke's *Two Treatises of Government* are usually thought to mark a decisive break from this absolutist state tradition. In his *Two Treatises,* Locke first dismantled Filmer's divine right patriarchalism and then proceeded to defend a theory of limited and divided government. Locke is sometimes even said to have rejected the state tradition altogether in favor of a political philosophy based upon medieval natural law theory. But Locke's theory was not a rejection of absolutist state theory—only a revision of it. He drew upon the general assumptions of absolutist state theory in order to challenge some of its particular positions. He attacked the least plausible aspects of this theory and replaced them with a more palatable and consistent theory of state power.

Locke announced his absolutist convictions early in his career. In his earliest political writings, the so-called *Two Tracts of Government* (1660–1662), Locke articulated a classic absolutist position.[103] Setting aside questions of "whether the magistrate's crown drops down on his head immediately from heaven or be placed there by the hands of his subjects," Locke declared the "supreme magistrate of every nation what way soever created, must necessarily have an absolute and arbitrary power over all the indifferent actions of the people."[104] Indifferent actions included all those matters that were not explicitly commanded or forbidden by the divine and natural law.[105] As Locke made clear in the *Two Tracts,* he considered indifferent matters to cover a large field of activity. While acknowledging that it might seem dangerous or excessive to grant the sovereign authority so much power, Locke justified this arrangement by appealing to the old absolutist saw regarding the corruption and unruliness of the people.

> Nor will the largeness of the governor's power appear dangerous or more than necessary if we consider that as occasion requires it is employed upon the multitude that are as impatient of restraint as the sea, and whose tempests and overflows cannot be too well provided against. Would it be thought dangerous or inconvenient that anyone should be allowed to make banks and fences against the waves for fear he should too much encroach upon and straighten the ocean?[106]

The recent Civil War showed plainly enough for Locke the quarrels and hatred that arose when matters indifferent were left outside the authority of the sovereign power.[107]

The *Two Treatises* initially appear to chart a new course in Locke's thought. At the beginning of the *Second Treatise,* Locke proclaimed that "the State of Nature has a Law of Nature to govern it, which obliges everyone" (TT, 271). The law of nature is God's law made "plain and intelligible to all rational Creatures" (TT, 205, 271, 275, 351). The natural law imposes moral duties upon all individuals, including "that Obligation to mutual Love amongst Men" and "the Duties they owe one another . . . of Justice and Charity" (TT, 270). All these arguments were consistent with traditional natural law teaching—a point Locke himself emphasized by appealing to the authority of the "Judicious Hooker."

Yet while Locke may have believed that traditional natural law theory provided an attractive vision of order, his understanding of the actual condition of human affairs was quite different from traditional views.[108] He argued there was no natural hierarchy or political order among human beings. Rather, he set forth what he acknowledged to be a "very strange Doctrine" about the natural condition of human beings: that by natural right each was an executor of the law of nature (TT, 271–73). Since, moreover, "the greater part [are] no strict Observers of Equity and Justice," the natural condition of human beings was "very unsafe, very uncertain" and "full of fears and continual dangers" (TT, 350). Locke further explained that "though the Law of Nature be plain and intelligible to all rational Creatures; yet Men being biased by their Interest, as well as ignorant for want of study of it, are not apt to allow of it as a Law binding to them in the application of it to their particular Cases" (TT, 351). To make matters worse, human beings, "being partial to themselves," tended to carry their enforcement of the law too far. In actual fact, then, Locke understood the natural condition of human beings to be much the same as Hobbes portrayed it. God had implanted in human beings a natural desire for self-preservation. Through their reason human beings could identify moral rules based upon this instinct (TT, 204–5). But few individuals ever actually did so or applied their conclusions to their behaviors. As a result, the life of individuals outside organized society was very uncertain and dangerous, driving them "quickly" to seek refuge under government. Initial appearances aside, Locke's account of human existence in the *Two Treatises* was not all that different from his earlier position in the *Two Tracts*.

This is not meant to suggest that the opening chapters of the *Two Treatises* were inconsequential. They serve two important purposes in the argument of this work. First, they provide a new foundation of order to replace Filmer's divine right patriarchalism. Having dispensed with Filmer's patriarchal theory in the *First Treatise,* Locke began the *Second Treatise* by asserting that the true natural condition of human beings was one of freedom and equality under God (TT, 269–71). The important implication of this assertion was that the only legitimate basis of government was popular consent: "Men being, as has been said, by Nature, all free, equal and independent, no one can be put out of this Estate, and subjected to the Political Power of another, without his own Consent" (TT, 330). The second important function of Locke's early chapters was to define his ideal vision of order. In his description of the "State of Nature," Locke defined the universal moral condition of human beings under God.[109] In his later chapters, he described the political principles necessary to reestablish this universal moral condition amid the corruption and degeneracy of human affairs. His state theory was designed to guide individuals back to the peace and morality that reigned in the original natural condition.

The central principles of Locke's political theory were drawn straight out of absolutist state theory. He claimed the central source of order in every political community was the principle of legislative sovereignty. Much like Hobbes, he argued that a sovereign legislator was necessary to provide a common interpretation of natural law for human beings within each commonwealth. The legislature was responsible for providing "the Standard of Right and Wrong, and the common measure to decide all Controversies," since most individuals were "biased by their Interest, as well as ignorant for want of study of [the natural law]" (TT, 2:124, 351). The second main principle of Locke's state theory was executive prerogative. This was briefly discussed in chapter 3 in relation to the development of reason of state theory. Here it may be briefly revisited to demonstrate Locke's close connection with the absolutist state tradition. Locke argued that in every political order the legislative power had to be complemented by an executive officer with unlimited prerogative powers to do whatever was necessary for the public good. It was only through the actions of a willful executive authority that the moral order of society could be preserved amid the contingencies and viciousness of human affairs.

> This Power to act according to discretion, for the publick good, without the prescription of the Law, and sometimes even against it, is that which is called Prerogative. For since in some Governments the Law-making Power is not always in being, and is usually too numerous, and so too slow, for the dispatch

> requisite to Execution: and because also it is impossible to foresee, and so by
> laws to provide for, all Accidents and Necessities, that may concern the pub-
> lick . . . therefore there is a latitude left to the Executive power, to do many
> things of choice, which the Laws do not prescribe. (TT, 375)

Locke made no mention in his discussion of executive prerogative of the
not-so-judicious Gabriel Naudé. But as mentioned previously, he was reading Naudé's *Coups d'état* when he wrote his *Two Treatises* and appears to
have borrowed his notion of executive prerogative from him.[110] The two
foundational principles of Locke's political philosophy thus clearly bear the
marks of absolutist thought.

Locke is best known for his revisions of absolutist ideas, which are usually assumed to represent important departures from absolutist arguments.
But many of the revisions had precedents in absolutist thinking. Moreover, Locke justified his innovations by appealing to the premises of absolutist thought. Specifically, he argued that a limited and divided state
power could more effectively institute a stable and moral order than an
absolute prince.

Locke's first important innovation was anticipated by a number of absolutist theorists. Bodin, Bossuet, and even James I had suggested that as a
matter of prudence and right the sovereign ruler ought to govern according
to a body of standing laws. Locke simply formulated this idea into a cogent
principle. "Absolute Arbitrary Power, or Governing without settled standing
Laws," he wrote, "can neither of them consist with the ends of Society and
Government" (TT, 359). The purpose of government, according to absolutist theorist, was to establish a predictable social order in which individuals could exist without fear of contingencies. This purpose was defeated
when individuals were forced "to obey at pleasure the exorbitant and unlimited Decrees of [the rulers'] sudden thoughts, or unrestrain'd, and till
that moment unknown Wills without having any measures set down
which may guide and justifie their acts" (TT, 360). The rule of law thus represented a logical deduction from the premises of absolutist state theory.

Bodin anticipated Locke's second important innovation, too: his defense
of the right to private property. Bodin argued that this right was a divine
and natural law standing outside the legitimate scope of the sovereign
ruler. But he grounded this right rather loosely in scriptural proofs, and
later absolutist writers largely ignored his arguments on this point. Locke
defended the right to private property more rigorously. He claimed God in-
stilled in each individual a natural drive for self-preservation. As a correlate
of this drive, God granted each individual the right to appropriate as much
property as he or she could use before it spoiled (TT, 285–90). Anyone who
attempted to take the goods of others without their consent violated their
natural right and threatened their self-preservation (TT, 279–80). Since government was established to preserve and promote the well-being of the subjects, Locke argued that rulers should protect the private property of their

subjects and ought not to take it away without their consent. Locke's argument was certainly far from foolproof. Hobbes might have replied that the well-being of the community ought not to be made dependent upon the uncertain consent of property owners. But Locke at least made a persuasive case for private property rights.

Locke's third important innovation was his theory of the division of powers. The division of powers was anathema to absolutist theorists. Filmer and Hobbes, for example, both regarded it as tantamount to anarchy. But once again, Locke appealed to well-established absolutist assumptions to defend this innovation. Given the corruption and biases of human beings, he argued that it made no sense to vest all public powers in one person or assembly. Such a concentration of power was too great a temptation to tyranny. Many absolutist writers sidestepped this objection by claiming the king was divinely ordained and morally pure. Locke rejected these arguments. He took it as the task of human beings to construct a system of government suitable for the rule of corruptible human beings. His solution was the system of divided government, arguing it was more likely to yield impartial and rational rule than absolute government:

> And because it may be too great a temptation to humane frailty apt to grasp at Power, for the same Persons who have the Power of making Laws, to have also in their hands the power to execute them, whereby they may exempt themselves from Obedience to the Laws they make, and suit the Law, both in its making and execution, to their private advantage, and thereby come to have a distinct interest from the rest of the Community, contrary to the end of Society and Government: Therefore in well order'd Commonwealths, where the good of the whole is so considered . . . the Legislative and Executive Power come often to be separated. (TT, 364–65)

Once again Locke's argument was not foolproof. Hobbes claimed the ignorance and biases of human beings invariably led to conflicts whenever power was divided. But Locke at least suggested an alternative perspective on state theory by highlighting the dangers of an all-powerful sovereign prince.

Locke's most important innovation was his theory of popular consent. While Hobbes loosely based his state theory on popular consent, he ultimately anchored it in the universal desire of human beings for self-preservation. Locke, by contrast, based his state theory on the voluntary consent of individuals. He argued that individuals were obliged to obey the state authority only insofar as they had consented to it. In turn, then, he claimed individuals were justified in resisting the state whenever they felt it had overstepped its rightful powers. Filmer claimed that such a theory would lead to anarchy. But in the final chapter of the *Second Treatise,* Locke effectively answered this concern. Even if individuals had the right to oppose the government at will, they were unlikely to do so in most circumstances. Human beings were slow to change long-standing constitutions, reacted only to great mistakes and repeated abuses, and took action only if they already had the greater part of society on their side (TT, 414–18).

Locke's doctrine of consent and legitimate resistance represented the one dimension of his political philosophy that clearly departed from the absolutist state tradition. It was also the least successful part of his argument—at least when measured in terms of philosophical cogency. Although Locke may have answered Filmer's fears about the tendency of consent-based states to devolve into anarchy, he failed to explain how a state could ever be said to derive its legitimacy from the consent of the people. As Filmer so aptly pointed out, very few individuals ever actually expressed their consent to the state. Tacit consent, in turn, undermined the whole idea of voluntary agreement to governmental authority. Locke argued "that every Man, that hath any Possession, or Enjoyment, of any part of the Dominions of any Government, doth thereby give his tacit Consent, and is as far forth obliged to Obedience to the Laws of that Government, during such Enjoyment, as any one under it" (TT, 347–48). He then proceeded to explain that possession or enjoyment of the dominions of government included everything from the ownership of land within the jurisdiction of the state, to renting a lodging there for a week, to "barely traveling freely on the Highway," to "the very being of any one within the Territories of that Government." Hanna Pitkin has noted that we are likely to feel cheated by Locke's argument here: "why all the stress on consent if it is to include everything we do; why go through the whole social contract argument if it turns out in the end that everyone is automatically obligated?"[111] Julian Franklin has further argued that Locke's argument for tacit consent involves a philosophical sleight of hand.[112] The doctrine of "tacit consent through residence" already presupposes the right of the state to exercise supreme authority over a territory. But from where did this authority come? Locke argued that the state originally gained jurisdiction over a territorial area when the first citizens to the social contract consented to place their property under its rule. But in order to maintain the territorial integrity of the state, he then asserted that later generations could not inherit property without tacitly consenting to state authority. Locke thus subtly shifted the basis of state authority. If originally the state gained jurisdiction over property through the consent of individuals, it later secured the consent of individuals through their property. In other words, Locke implied that the original consent of the first inhabitants of a territory provided the state with a permanent and inalienable jurisdiction over this territory and all inhabitants within it. According to Franklin, a more consistent formulation of consent theory would have recognized the right of subsequent generations of individuals to terminate their membership from the community and remove their property from the jurisdiction of the state whenever they wanted. This was, of course, Filmer's point, too. Consent theory could never consistently legitimize the authority of the territorial sovereign state.

Locke did not address these problems. The aim of his consent theory was to rebut Filmer's divine right patriarchalism and to justify the people's right of resistance.[113] He thus did not very carefully explore the coherence of consent theory as a foundation for state legitimacy. As a result, he left to modern state theory a fundamental incongruity. While popular consent today is widely regarded as the foundation of state legitimacy, most scholars agree that it is logically incapable of justifying the legislative, executive, and administrative powers of the state.[114] In terms reminiscent of Filmer, they have pointed out the fundamental incompatibility between consent theory and the state form of organization. Consent theory assumes the existence of equal and free individuals subject only to the laws and decisions they have agreed to. State theory posits the existence of a central governing body responsible for making laws and decisions for all the people. Since it is virtually impossible to obtain the consent of all individuals for all the state's laws and decisions (or even for the state form of organization), the state must be said to rule for the most part illegitimately.

The principles of modern state theory were originally developed and legitimized by appealing to principles of divine and natural law. Very little has been made of this fact. Early modern divine and natural right theories are usually seen as merely a "transition stage between medieval and modern politics."[115] But there exists a more integral relationship between early modern divine and natural right theories and the state form of organization: these theories supplied the necessary foundations of state legitimacy. Liberal theorists discarded most of the metaphysical trappings of early modern state theory but retained its central powers and purposes. They failed, however, to identify a philosophically coherent mundane justification for these powers and purposes.[116] In fact, it is not clear that any exist. The legitimacy of state powers is integrally related to the metaphysical premises and purposes outlined by writers such as James I, Filmer, and Hobbes. Without the foundation of divine and natural right and the goal of instituting a universal moral order, there is no good reason to organize political power around the principles of modern state theory.

Conclusion

From Divine Sovereignty to the Secular State

*I*n *Political Theology* (1922), Carl Schmitt outlined one important and highly controversial thesis of the development of modern state theory. "All significant concepts of the modern theory of the state," he wrote, "are secularized theological concepts . . . transferred from theology to the theory of the state."[1] There exists, he explained, "a systematic structural kinship between theological and juristic concepts that obtrudes itself both in legal theory and legal practice."[2] Early modern theorists transferred theological ideas to the theory of the state. As a result, one cannot fully understand modern state theory without some knowledge of the theology behind it.

Schmitt's thesis appears plausible on a general level. Bodin clearly based his theory of legislative sovereignty upon the notion of a voluntarist God. Reason of state theorists compared the king's *coups d'état* to the miraculous interventions of God into nature. Bossuet used his theory of *providence particulière* to explain the new regulatory powers of the sovereign prince. Generally, all these theorists fit into Schmitt's account of the development of early modern state theory: "In the theory of the state of the seventeenth century, the monarch is identified with God and has in the state a position exactly analogous to that attributed to God in the Cartesian system of the world."[3]

The problem with Schmitt's thesis is its lack of theoretical precision. Modern state theory did not develop simply by transferring theological concepts to politics. It was also closely bound up with the emergence of historical consciousness and a new awareness of contingency and diversity. It likewise was built upon traditional political ideals about sacred monarchy and universal order. Moreover, the principles of modern state theory were not merely prefabricated theological concepts applied to political affairs. While reason of state theorists compared the king's executive prerogative to the extraordinary powers of God, for example, they developed this principle in unique ways. They defined executive prerogative as a special power belonging to the supreme executive officer of the state for protecting society from contingency and corruption. There was no precise equivalent to this idea in medieval theology.

Hans Blumenberg criticized Schmitt's thesis on similar grounds. He pointed out that the mere existence of a structural analogy between theological and political concepts is hardly sufficient to justify Schmitt's broad claims about the existence of a political theology of the state.[4] Instead, Blumenberg suggested an alternative explanation for the development of modern philosophy that can be fruitfully applied to the development of modern state theory. He argued that modern philosophy emerged as a new and distinctive alternative to ancient and medieval philosophy. It placed the concepts of contingency and self-assertion at the center of human existence. Individuals were called upon to assert themselves over and against a contingent temporal world. Within this new framework, however, Blumenberg observed that many writers still felt the need to "reoccupy" the "ideological" positions left vacant after the collapse of the medieval worldview. After modern thinkers abandoned the medieval eschatological interpretation of world history, for example, some thinkers still endeavored to outline a universal interpretation of history. The result was the grandiose philosophies of history and progress that were formulated during the eighteenth and nineteenth centuries. According to Blumenberg, these theories had the unfortunate effect of discrediting the whole modern project because they set overly high expectations for human self-assertion.

A similar framework can be applied to the development of modern state theory. Early modern theorists and statesmen proposed the principles of modern state theory to "reoccupy" the "ideological position" established by medieval Christian political thought and left open by the collapse of the medieval cosmology. Specifically, they looked to the state to restore human beings to some semblance of the static and moral political orders idealized by late medieval political theorists. They portrayed the state as a divinely and naturally ordained institution responsible for lifting human beings out of the realm of contingency and integrating them into a universal order. In short, state theory was invented as a grandiose theory of politics based upon medieval Christian ideals about order.

This thesis regarding the development of modern state theory stands outside the mainstream of Anglo-American scholarship. J. G. A. Pocock, Quentin Skinner, Richard Tuck, Maurizio Viroli, Stephen Collins, and others have all associated the development of modern state theory with the secularization of politics. In part, of course, they are right. The development of statist principles was made possible by the widespread perception among early modern writers that human affairs had fallen away from the divine and natural order and become more susceptible to contingency and change. Furthermore, early modern theorists did assert an independent political morality for the state apart from religion and universal law. But this is only part of the story. The other part involves early modern theorists' efforts to restore human beings to a universal and static political community. They did not tear the state away from the divine and natural laws but rather made the state the sole legitimate interpreter of these laws. They did not resign themselves to the contingency and corruption of temporal affairs but called upon the state to conquer these forces. Modern state theory was developed in the ambiguous space between the sacred and the secular. Victoria Kahn has argued in this regard that our notions of sacred and secular are much too rigid and simplistic, especially when applied to early modern European thought.[5] While early modern state theory was not a political theology, neither was it a wholly secular political philosophy. The principles of legislative sovereignty, reason of state, state regulatory powers, and rationalistic rule were all legitimized by appealing to the sacred nature and purpose of the state as well as the contingency and flux of the temporal world. The state was conceived as a sacred or metaphysically privileged institution for imposing universal order upon a secular temporal world.

Paul Monod has recently highlighted the importance of religious beliefs in the development of modern state theory.[6] Focusing largely on the rituals and images of rulership, he argued that sacred beliefs contributed in important ways to the legitimization of state power. They provided the charismatic underpinnings that bound people to the state until the state could stand on its own. For Monod, however, the conjunction of sacred beliefs and state authority was only a temporary stage on the road to the development of the secular and rational state. Yet the sacred underpinnings of the state run deeper than Monod recognized. Even after all the sacred rituals and images were stripped away from the state (and of course, they never were entirely stripped away), there still remained an exalted theory of politics. John Locke, for example, clearly contributed to the secularization of state theory by criticizing divine right theory and shifting the foundation of state legitimacy to popular consent. Yet the state remained in his philosophy a quasi-sacred entity closely associated with the natural law. It continued to be responsible for instituting a relatively static political order and manifesting the principles of natural law within society. It also retained its extraordinary legislative and executive powers. While Locke and other writers may have secularized the surface aspects of early modern state theory, they preserved many of its deep sacred presumptions.

What is the state? This is a notoriously difficult question to answer, and one that is susceptible to a variety of different approaches. This study suggests that the state is best understood as a remnant of an early modern worldview in which politics was given the task of imposing a static and universal order upon a contingent social world. The state was conceived as a god among human beings and delegated awesome powers and prerogatives to organize their lives according to divine and natural laws. The failure of Enlightenment thinkers to break decisively from the early modern origins of the state explains many of the problems of modern state legitimacy. Enlightenment thinkers did not give sufficient thought to the compatibility of state principles with the new mundane theories of state legitimacy which they outlined. Locke, for example, simply coupled the ideas of legislative sovereignty and executive prerogative with the notion of popular consent. But Rousseau effectively demonstrated that the notion of popular consent is logically incapable of justifying the broad powers of the state. He argued that individuals could not transfer legislative powers to representative officials without enslaving themselves. For although "it is not impossible for a private will to agree with the general will on a given point," he wrote, "it is impossible, at least, for this agreement to be lasting and unchanging."[7] Even if there were a temporary correspondence between the will of the people and their political representatives, they would diverge over time.[8] Then individuals would find themselves subject to laws and policies that they did not authorize.[9] "I say, therefore, that sovereignty, being only the exercise of the general will, can never be alienated, and that the sovereign, which is only a collective being, can only be represented by itself."[10] Rousseau argued that popular sovereignty logically pointed to a more participatory form of political organization than is possible within the state.

David Hume, Jeremy Bentham, and other utilitarian theorists attempted to re-found state legitimacy upon the basis of utility.[11] Hume pointed out that very few governments were founded upon an original contract or enjoyed the express consent of their subjects, and added that tacit consent provided a very dubious source of state authority.[12] Tacit consent supplied a legitimate source of authority only when individuals had the opportunity to remove themselves from the jurisdiction of a government they did not support. But few individuals had this opportunity.

> Can we seriously say, that a poor peasant or artisan has a free choice to leave his country, when he knows no foreign language or manners, and lives from day to day, by the small wages which he acquires? We may as well assert, that a man by remaining in a vessel, freely consents to the dominion of the master; though he was carried on board while asleep, and must leap into the ocean, and perish, the moment he leaves her.[13]

Hume claimed the real source of state legitimacy was the benefits it provided for the people, or in other words utility. "A small degree of experience and observation suffices to teach us, that society cannot possibly be maintained without the authority of magistrates, and that this authority must soon fall into contempt, where exact obedience is not payed to it. The observation of these general and obvious interests is the source of all allegiance, and of that moral obligation, which we attribute to it."[14] While utilitarianism initially appears to provide a more solid foundation for state legitimacy than consent theory, it too contains some problems. Individuals are obliged to obey the state authorities, according to utilitarian theory, only insofar as state policies serve their interests. Utilitarianism thus makes the legitimacy of legislative, executive, and administrative decisions dependent upon their conse-quences. Unless state officials govern in a rigorously utilitarian (or super-rational) manner, many state policies will therefore be illegitimate. More-over, it is not at all evident that the "general and obvious" interests of people justify the broad and arbitrary powers of the state. A strictly utilitar-ian political theory would seem to point to a much more restricted theory of governmental powers than that presumed by state theory—one based, for example, upon the enforcement of a few basic rights of all individuals rather than the broad law-making powers of elected officials who may or may not act in the people's interests on any given matter.

The theories of Rousseau and Hume serve to highlight some of the prob-lems of state legitimacy. The state originally rested upon the metaphysical foundations of divine and natural right. When these foundations were swept away, so were the justifications for state powers. Nonetheless, the state form of organization continued to exist; it is in fact the most pervasive and prominent form of political organization in the world today. In recent years, the problems of state legitimacy have become even more obvious and acute. While the literature on the contemporary nation-state is enormous, two recent critiques can serve to exemplify current views.[15] R. B. J. Walker has observed that contemporary political life is marked by "a widespread sense of accelerations, disjunctions and uncertainties."[16] The enhanced mo-bility of capital, new communication and transportation technologies, and other developments have increased the speed and fluidity of human inter-actions. Within this environment, the principle of state sovereignty appears increasingly problematic, for it rests upon the promise of "fixing temporal-ity within spatial categories," while the accelerations and disjunctions of contemporary political life make this goal impossible to achieve. As a result, Walker concluded that the state is gradually being stripped of its legitimacy: "If it is true that contemporary political life is increasingly characterized by processes of temporal acceleration, then we should expect to experience in-creasingly disconcerting incongruities between new articulations of power and accounts of political life predicated on the early-modern fiction that temporality can be fixed and tamed within the spatial coordinates of terri-torial jurisdictions."[17] For Walker, the state is in crisis because its powers and purposes are incongruous with the realities of contemporary political life. The traditional powers and purposes of the state, in turn, can be traced back to the universalist ideals of French and English state theorists. The goal of "fixing temporality within spatial coordinates," as Walker dubbed it, is the early modern aspiration of instituting and maintaining a sanctified political community free from contingency and corruption. As society be-comes more contingent and fluid, this goal appears increasingly antiquated.

If the state today is facing a crisis of legitimacy, it is at least in part because state theory remains tied to a sacred vision of politics.

Iris Marion Young has raised a similar set of criticisms but from a different perspective.[18] Rather than focusing on the accelerations, disjunctions, and uncertainties of contemporary political life, she has emphasized the diversity, heterogeneity, and particularity of groups and individuals within contemporary societies. From her perspective, the modern state's claim to represent a universal and impartial standpoint serves only to mask the particular biases of ruling groups.[19] There is no way, in her opinion, for the state to represent the universal interests of the public because there is simply no homogeneous public to represent: the public is composed of diverse individuals with heterogeneous interests. Nor is it possible for bureaucratic decision makers, "whether in government or not, to adopt the standpoint of transcendental reason when they make decisions."[20] The belief in a super-rational bureaucracy is in her estimation one of the central myths of the state. Like Walker, Young has thus challenged the legitimacy of the modern state. Focusing on the diversity and particularity of human beings, she has argueed that, the "universalist" state is ill-suited for governing contempory society. Young has traced statist ideals back to the Enlightenment notion of reason, but of course they have an older and more specific origin. The ideal of the universalist state standing above the particular interests and conflicts of civil society was defined and legitimized during the early modern period. This ideal was used during the eighteenth century to discredit absolute monarchy. The French Revolutionaries criticized the monarchy for being too irrational and arbitrary, and failing to attend sufficiently to peoples' needs. Today these arguments are being used to challenge the legitimacy of the state itself.

Contemporary criticisms of the state reinforce the critiques of modern theorists such as Rousseau and Hume. The state was never very well suited to mundane theories of legitimacy. It was conceived as a metaphysical institution resting upon divine and natural right and designed for the purpose of taming social contingency and imposing a harmonious order upon the people. Enlightenment thinkers only partially stripped away the mythic powers and purposes of the state. But they did not deeply interrogate state principles to test their validity against mundane theories of legitimacy. What they failed to do is the task facing us today. It is incumbent upon us to formulate a new political theory consistent with the presuppositions of a secular social environment. This task need not mean abandoning the state form of organization altogether, but it would seem to require denuding the state of its more excessive powers and goals. Scholars interested in international human rights and participatory democracy have already laid out two possible paths for developing alternative state theories. The former have looked to circumscribe the state's legislative, executive, and administrative prerogatives within the bounds of international legal norms. The latter have suggested possibilities for reorganizing political power so that individuals have more direct control over the legislative, executive, and administrative decisions of the state. There are of course many other possibilities for reforming the state; these are only suggestions. This book has simply analyzed the development of modern state theory in order to elucidate some of the problems of state legitimacy. It has been argued that modern state theory rests upon an exalted vision of political power that is incompatible with mundane theories of legitimacy. The task for the future is to develop a theory of political organization consistent with the premises of a mundane liberal society.

Notes

INTRODUCTION

1. Kenneth Dyson has drawn an important distinction between "the state apparatus" and the "idea of the state" that I follow throughout this study. I am concerned exclusively with the "idea" or "theory" of the state. *The State Tradition in Western Europe: A Study of an Idea and Institution* (New York: Oxford University Press, 1980), 2–3. There are countless books on the development of the state. In addition to the books mentioned below, see Perry Anderson, *Lineages of the Absolutist State* (London: Verso, 1974); Norbert Elias, *The Civilizing Process,* trans. Edmund Jephcott (Oxford: Blackwell, 1994); Anthony Giddens, *The Nation-State and Violence* (Berkeley: University of California Press, 1987); David Held, *Political Theory and the Modern State: Essays on State, Power, and Democracy* (Stanford: Stanford University Press, 1989); Michael Mann, *The Sources of Social Power* (Cambridge: Cambridge University Press, 1986); Christopher Pierson, *The Modern State* (London: Routledge, 1996); Gianfranco Poggi, *The Development of the Modern State: A Sociological Introduction* (Stanford: Stanford University Press, 1978); J. H. Shennan, *The Origins of the Modern European State, 1450–1725* (London, 1974); Joseph R. Strayer, *On the Medieval Origins of the Modern State* (Princeton: Princeton University Press, 1970).

2. Margaret Levi, *Of Rule and Revenue* (Berkeley: University of California Press, 1988); Hendrik Spruyt, *The Sovereign State and Its Competitors* (Princeton: Princeton University Press, 1994); Charles Tilly, ed., *The Formation of National States in Western Europe* (Princeton: Princeton University Press, 1975); Charles Tilly, *Coercion, Capital, and European States, AD 990–1990* (Cambridge: Basil Blackwell, 1990).

3. Jens Bartelson, *A Genealogy of Sovereignty* (Cambridge: Cambridge University Press, 1995); Anthony Black, *Political Thought in Europe, 1250–1450* (Cambridge: Cambridge University Press, 1992); Ernst Kantorowicz, *The King's Two Bodies: A Study in Medieval Political Theology* (Princeton: Princeton University Press, 1957); Quentin Skinner, *The Foundations of Modern Political Thought,* 2 vols. (Cambridge: Cambridge University Press, 1978); Richard Tuck, *Philosophy and Government, 1572–1651* (Cambridge: Cambridge University Press, 1993); Maurizio Viroli, *From Politics to Reason of State* (Cambridge: Cambridge University Press, 1992).

4. Weber identified rationalistic rule as one of the hallmarks of modern state authority. Max Weber, *Economy and Society,* ed. Guenther Roth and Claus Wittich (Berkeley: University of California Press, 1978), 1: 212–26, 2: 956–1005.

5. On the notion of a "language" of politics, see J. G. A. Pocock, "Languages and Their Implications: The Transformation of the Study of Political Thought," in

204 Notes to Pages 4–6

Politics, Language and Time: Essays on Political Thought and History (Chicago: University of Chicago Press, 1989), 3–41; Gordon Schochet, "Why Should History Matter? Political Theory and the History of Discourse," in *Varieties of British Political Thought, 1500–1800,* ed. J. G. A. Pocock, Gordon Schochet, and Lois Schwoerer (Cambridge: Cambridge University Press, 1993), 321–57.

6. This nonpartisan, nonpejorative definition of ideology is now widely accepted among scholars. Ian Adams, *Political Ideology Today* (Manchester: Manchester University Press, 1993), 1–8.

7. William Beik, *Absolutism and Society in Seventeenth-Century France* (Cambridge: Cambridge University Press, 1985); James Collins, *Fiscal Limits of Absolutism* (Berkeley: University of California Press, 1988); Sharon Kettering, *Patrons, Brokers, and Clients in Seventeenth-Century France* (New York: Oxford University Press, 1986); J. Russell Major, *From Renaissance Monarchy to Absolute Monarchy* (Baltimore: Johns Hopkins University Press, 1994); Roger Mettam, *Power and Faction in Louis XIV's France* (Oxford: Blackwell, 1988). Two recent articles that address particular elements of the revisionist thesis are Beth Nachison, "Absentee Government and Provincial Governors in Early Modern France: The Princes of Condé and Burgundy, 1660–1720," *French Historical Studies* 21 (spring 1998): 265–97; Guy Rowlands, "Louis XIV, Aristocratic Power and the Elite Units of the French Army," *French History* 13 (1999): 303–31.

8. Jay Smith, *The Culture of Merit* (Ann Arbor: University of Michigan Press, 1996), 5–10.

9. Richard Bonney, "Absolutism: What's in a Name?" *French History* 1 (1987): 93–117; D. Henshall, *The Myth of Absolutism* (London: Longman, 1992); Roger Mettam, "France," in *Absolutism in the Seventeenth Century,* ed. John Miller (New York: St. Martin's Press, 1990), 43–67.

10. Quentin Skinner, "The State," in *Political Innovation and Conceptual Change,* ed. Terrence Ball, James Farr, and Russell Hanson (Cambridge: Cambridge University Press, 1989), 90–131. See also more generally Istvan Hont, "The Permanent Crisis of a Divided Mankind: 'Contemporary Crisis of the Nation State' in Historical Perspective," in *Contemporary Crisis of the Nation State?* ed. John Dunn (Oxford: Blackwell, 1995), 166–231.

11. This is a fundamental tenet of Quentin Skinner's methodology. *Foundations of Modern Political Thought,* 1: x–xv.

12. Hans Blumenberg, *The Legitimacy of the Modern Age,* trans. Robert M. Wallace (Cambridge: MIT Press, 1983), 137, 139; Stephen Collins, *From Divine Cosmos to Sovereign State* (Oxford: Oxford University Press, 1989), 8, 200n.56, passim.

13. This is not to deny the diversity and complexity of medieval political thought, but only to suggest that there were certain general assumptions around which the different languages of medieval thought tended to be organized. Black, *Political Thought in Europe;* J. H. Burns, ed., *The Cambridge History of Medieval Political Thought, c.350–c.1450* (Cambridge: Cambridge University Press, 1988); Otto Gierke, *Political Theories of the Middle Age,* trans. F. W. Maitland (Boston: Beacon Press, 1958); Walter Ullmann, *A History of Political Thought: The Middle Ages* (Baltimore: Penguin, 1965); Michael Wilks, *The Problem of Sovereignty in the Later Middle Ages* (Cambridge: Cambridge University Press, 1963).

14. The classic account of this idea is Arthur Lovejoy, *The Great Chain of Being* (Cambridge: Harvard University Press, 1936). W. H. Greenleaf explored the relationship between the great chain of being and political theory in *Order, Empiricism, and Politics* (London: Oxford University Press, 1964).

15. Christine de Pizan, *The Book of the Body Politic,* tr. Kate Langdon Forhan (Cambridge: Cambridge University Press, 1994), 59.

16. St. Thomas Aquinas, *Summa Theologiae* (New York: McGraw-Hill, 1966), I–II, 93,5, 66–67.

17. Hans Baron, *The Crisis of the Early Italian Renaissance* (Princeton: Princeton University Press, 1966); Eugenio Garin, *Italian Humanism,* trans. Peter Munz (Westport, Conn.: Greenwood Press, 1965); J. G. A. Pocock, *The Machiavellian Moment: Florentine Political Thought and the Atlantic Republican Tradition* (Princeton: Princeton University Press, 1975); Quentin Skinner, *The Foundations of Modern Political Thought* (Cambridge: Cambridge University Press, 1978), 1: 69–189; Charles Trinkaus, *In Our Image and Likeness: Humanity and Divinity in Italian Humanist Thought,* 2 vols. (London: Constable, 1970).

18. John Donne, *The Complete English Poems of John Donne,* ed. C. A. Patrides (London: J. M. Dent and Sons, 1985), 276.

19. Collins, *From Divine Cosmos to Sovereign State,* 28–70, 114–48; James Daly, *Cosmic Harmony and Political Thinking in Early Stuart England,* Transactions of the American Philosophical Society, no. 69 (Philadelphia: American Philosophical Society, 1979), 31–38; Greenleaf, *Order, Empiricism, and Politics,* 26–32, 143–51.

20. Francis Oakley, *Omnipotence, Covenant, and Order: An Excursion in the History of Ideas from Abelard to Leibniz* (Ithaca: Cornell University Press, 1984).

21. Oakley, *Omnipotence, Covenant, and Order,* 113.

22. Michael Gillespie, "The Theological Origins of Modernity," *Critical Review* 13 (1999): 10.

23. Richard Popkin, *The History of Scepticism from Erasmus to Spinoza* (Berkeley: University of California Press, 1979).

24. Michel de Montaigne, *The Complete Essays of Montaigne,* trans. Donald Frame (Stanford: Stanford University Press, 1965), 437. Montaigne's ideas are further discussed in the first chapter.

25. Donald R. Kelley, *Foundations of Modern Historical Scholarship: Language, Law and History in the French Renaissance* (New York: Columbia University Press, 1970).

26. Greenleaf, *Order, Empiricism, and Politics,* 144; Daly, *Cosmic Harmony and Political Thinking in Early Stuart England,* 153.

27. Pocock, *Machiavellian Moment.* I further differentiate the statist confrontation with "time" from the republican approach in the first chapter of this book. Friedrich Meinecke similarly stressed the symbiotic relationship between reason of state and historical thinking in *Machiavellism: The Doctrine of Raison d'Etat and Its Place in Modern History,* trans. Douglas Scott (New Brunswick, N.J.: Transaction Publishers, 1998). I discuss Meinecke's work in chapter 3.

28. On the medieval tradition of sacred monarchy, see Marc Bloch, *The Royal Touch,* trans. J. E. Anderson (New York: Dorset, 1989); G. R. Elton, "The Divine Right of Kings," in *Studies in Tudor and Stuart Politics and Government* (Cambridge: Cambridge University Press, 1974), 193–214; Ralph E. Giesey, *The Royal Funeral Ceremony in Renaissance France* (Geneva: Librairie Droz, 1960); Kantorowicz, *The King's Two Bodies;* Jeffrey Merrick, *The Desacralization of the Monarchy in Eighteenth-Century France* (Baton Rouge: Louisiana State University Press, 1990), 1–26; Paul Monod, *The Power of Kings: Monarchy and Religion in Europe, 1589–1715* (New Haven: Yale University Press, 1999).

29. Blumenberg, *Legitimacy of the Modern Age,* 63–75.

30. As often noted, Cassirer was more concerned with rational and mythical techniques of statecraft than with the particular myth of the modern state. Ernst Cassirer, *The Myth of the State* (New Haven: Yale University Press, 1946).

31. Merrick, *Desacralization*.

32. Edmund Morgan, *Inventing the People* (New York: W. W. Norton, 1988).

33. Iris Marion Young, *Justice and the Politics of Difference* (Princeton: Princeton University Press, 1990).

34. Manuel Castells, *The Information Age: Economy, Society and Culture. Volume II: The Power of Identity* (Oxford: Blackwell, 1997), 243–308.

CHAPTER 1: THE MONTAIGNIAN MOMENT

1. Pocock, *Machiavellian Moment*.

2. Quentin Skinner has also argued this point. "The humanists first of all revert to claiming that, where man's capacity for action is limited, the controlling factor at work is nothing more than the capricious power of fortune, not the inexorable force of providence." *The Foundations of Modern Political Thought* (Cambridge: Cambridge University Press, 1978), 1: 96.

3. Pocock's thesis draws heavily upon Hans Baron, *The Crisis of the Early Italian Renaissance* (Princeton: Princeton University Press, 1966).

4. Pocock, *Machiavellian Moment*, viii.

5. Pocock, *Machiavellian Moment*, viii.

6. For an overview of criticisms of the Baron-Pocock thesis, see Albert Rabil, Jr., "The Significance of 'Civic Humanism' in the Interpretation of the Italian Renaissance," in *Renaissance Humanism: Foundations, Forms, and Legacy* (Philadelphia: University of Pennsylvania Press, 1988), 1: 141–74.

7. Victoria Kahn, *Machiavellian Rhetoric* (Princeton: Princeton University Press, 1994), 10. See also Harvey Mansfield, Jr., *Taming the Prince* (Baltimore: Johns Hopkins University Press, 1989), xxiii–xxiv. Charles Trinkaus argues a similar point in regard to Baron's civic humanist thesis. *In Our Image and Likeness: Humanity and Divinity in Italian Humanist Thought* (London: Constable, 1970), 1: 282–83, passim.

8. Kahn has discussed Montaigne's critique of classical humanist rhetoric in *Rhetoric, Prudence, and Skepticism in the Renaissance* (Ithaca: Cornell University Press, 1985), 115–51.

9. Richard Tuck has similarly portrayed Montaigne as a progenitor of early modern state theory. See *Philosophy and Government, 1572–1651* (Cambridge: Cambridge University Press, 1993), 45–64.

10. Niccolò Machiavelli, *The Prince*, trans. Harvey Mansfield, Jr. (Chicago: University of Chicago Press, 1985), 98. Hereafter this volume is cited as *Prince*.

11. Eugenio Garin identified this assumption as the "typical motif of the Renaissance." *Italian Humanism,* trans. Peter Munz (Westport, Conn.: Greenwood Press, 1965), 61.

12. Donald Kelley has noted, however, that there was also another side of Renaissance humanism that emphasized surrender to fortune and withdrawal from active or civic life. Montaigne may be placed in this often neglected tradition of humanist thought. *Renaissance Humanism* (Boston: Twayne Publishers, 1991), 53–54.

13. On this point, see especially Mario Santoro, *Fortuna, ragione e prudenza nella civiltà letteraria del Cinquecento* (Naples: Liguori, 1966); Skinner, *Foundations of Modern Political Thought,* 1: 113–89.

14. Myron Gilmore, "The Renaissance Conception of the Lessons of History," in *Humanists and Jurists* (Cambridge: Harvard University Press, 1963), 1–37; Felix Gilbert, *Machiavelli and Guicciardini* (Princeton: Princeton University Press, 1965), 89–93, 216–18.

15. Niccolò Machiavelli, *Discourses on Livy,* in *The Discourses,* trans. Harvey Mansfield, Jr., and Nathan Tarcov (Chicago: University of Chicago Press, 1996), I, preface, 5–6. Hereafter this volume is cited as *Discourses.*

16. The best analyses of the cosmological assumptions underlying Machiavelli's thought are Anthony Parel, *The Machiavellian Cosmos* (New Haven: Yale University Press, 1992)and Reinhart Koselleck, *Futures Past: On the Semantics of Historical Time,* trans. Keith Tribe (Cambridge: MIT Press, 1985), 4, 16, 114, 280.

17. Santoro, *Fortuna, ragione e prudenza,* 198.

18. *Discourses,* I, 39, 84.

19. Quentin Skinner, *Machiavelli* (New York: Hill and Wang, 1981), 77.

20. *Discourses,* II, 27, 193–95.

21. *Discourses,* II, 2, 129–33. In their introduction to Machiavelli's *Discourses on Livy,* Harvey Mansfield and Nathan Tarcov suggest that one important consequence of Christian culture in Machiavelli's eyes was to make stronger executive power an essential part of republican government (xvii–xlvi).

22. Several scholars have suggested that Machiavelli's methodology ultimately broke down under the weight of his qualifications and exceptions. See Peter Donaldson, *Machiavelli and Mystery of State* (Cambridge: Cambridge University Press, 1988), 183–85; Thomas Greene, "The End of Discourse in Machiavelli's *Prince,*" *Yale French Studies* 67 (1984): 57–71; John Lyons, *Exemplum: The Rhetoric of Example in Early Modern France and Italy* (Princeton: Princeton University Press, 1989), 35–71.

23. Skinner, *Foundations of Modern Political Thought,* 1: 128–38.

24. Skinner, *Foundations of Modern Political Thought,* 1: 126–28.

25. *Prince,* 15, 61.

26. *Prince,* 18, 70.

27. Gilbert, *Machiavelli and Guicciardini;* Santoro, *Fortuna, ragione e prudenza;* Skinner, *Foundations of Modern Political Thought,* 1:186–89. For a literary perspective on this same development, see Albert Ascoli, *Ariosto's Bitter Harmony: Crisis and Evasion in the Italian Renaissance* (Princeton: Princeton University Press, 1987).

28. Santoro has argued that Machiavelli grew increasingly pessimistic about human beings' ability to control fortune in his later works. *Fortuna, ragione e prudenza,* 228–31. Hanna Pitkin has more generally discussed Machiavelli's occasional ambivalence about the powers of virtue and fortune. *Fortune Is a Woman* (Berkeley: University of California Press, 1984), 143–60.

29. *Discourses,* II, 29, 197–99.

30. Francesco Guicciardini, *The History of Italy,* trans. Sidney Alexander (Princeton: Princeton University Press, 1969), 3–4.

31. Gilbert, *Machiavelli and Guicidardini,* 288–90.

32. I refer to all citations from Montaigne's *Essays* in the body of the text. I have used *The Complete Essays of Montaigne,* trans. Donald Frame (Stanford: Stanford University Press, 1965). Each citation lists book number, chapter, and page number.

33. Daniel Martin, who has most exhaustively studied Montaigne's theory of fortune, has argued that he saw it as a cosmological symbol representing all the instability, contingency, and disorder of human and temporal affairs. *Montaigne et la fortune* (Paris: Librairie Honoré Champion, 1977), 1–5, passim. See also R. A. Sayce, *The Essays of Montaigne: A Critical Exploration* (Evanston: Northwestern University Press, 1972), 99–112; Jean Starobinski, *Montaigne in Motion,* trans. Arthur Goldhammer(Chicago: University of Chicago Press, 1985).

34. For an excellent discussion of this essay, see Zachary Sayre Schiffman, *On*

the Threshold of Modernity (Baltimore: Johns Hopkins University Press, 1991), 53–55.

35. *Discourses,* III, 21, 262–64.

36. Kahn, *Rhetoric, Prudence, and Skepticism,* 116–51; Schiffman, *On the Threshold of Modernity,* 53–77.

37. *Prince,* 25, 99–101; *Discourses,* III, 9, 239–40.

38. Montaigne added in a later essay: "I will say more, that even our wisdom and deliberation for the most part follow the lead of chance. My will and my reasoning are moved now in one way, now in another, and there are many of these movements that are directed without me. My reason has accidental impulsions that change from day to day" (III, 8, 713).

39. Donald Frame, *Montaigne: A Biography* (New York: Harcourt, Brace and World, 1965), 217–18.

40. *Discourses,* I, preface, 5–6. See more generally Parel, *Machiavellian Cosmos.*

41. In his essay "Of Books," Montaigne added that his *Essays* were more composed by fortune than by himself. "I have no other marshal but fortune to arrange my bits. As my fancies present themselves, I pile them up; now they come pressing in a crowd, now dragging single file. I want people to see my natural and ordinary pace, however off the track it is" (II, 10, 297). See also II, 37, 574.

42. Several scholars have noted that there was an altogether new "notion of time" implicit in the *Essays.* Schiffman, *On the Threshold of Modernity,* 74; Starobinski, *Montaigne in Motion,* 85.

43. Montaigne's only other explicit reference to Machiavelli in the *Essays* appeared in his essay "Observations on Julius Caesar's Methods of Making War" (II, 34, 556). I follow David Schaefer in setting aside this reference as not very relevant for understanding Montaigne's opinion of Machiavelli's political ideas. *The Political Philosophy of Montaigne* (Ithaca: Cornell University Press, 1990), 348.

44. Sayce, *Essays of Montaigne,* 256. Other writers who have interpreted Montaigne in a similar fashion include Robert Collins, "Montaigne's Rejection of Reason of State in 'De l'utile et de l'honneste," *Sixteenth Century Journal* 23 (1992): 71–94; Géralde Nakam, *Les essais de Montaigne: Miroir et procès de leur temps* (Paris: Librairie A. G. Nizet, 1984), 252–55; Zachary Sayre Schiffman, "Montaigne and the Problem of Machiavellism," *Journal of Medieval and Renaissance Studies* 12 (fall 1982): 242–44; Pierre Villey, *Les sources et l'évolution des essais de Montaigne* (Paris: Librairie Hachette et Cie, 1908), 2: 357–62.

45. Schaefer, *Political Philosophy of Montaigne,* 347–96. An older defense of this position may be found in Alexandre Nicolai, "Le machiavélisme de Montaigne," *Bulletin de la société des amis de Montaigne* (1957–59): 4:11–21; 5–6:25–47; 7:2–8; 9:18–30. Hugo Friedrich has characterized Montaigne as a Machiavellian thinker who nonetheless believed moral action was a viable form of political action. *Montaigne,* trans. Dawn Eng (Berkeley: University of California Press, 1991), 148–51, 184–88.

46. Marcel Tetel is the only other scholar who, to my knowledge, has attempted to relate the differences between Machiavelli's and Montaigne's philosophies to their ideas about fortune. "Montaigne and Machiavelli: Ethics, Politics and Humanism," *Rivista di letterature moderne e comparante* 29 (September 1976): 165–81. However, his emphasis is less on these writers' different conceptions of fortune than on their different approaches to it: "Whereas Montaigne reacts in a passively active way toward [fortune], making the best of it, Machiavelli remains the ardent man of action who both battles it and seeks a confrontation with it" (172). Moreover, Tetel does not investigate the ways in which Montaigne's different understanding of fortune led him to articulate a different political philosophy.

47. Schaefer, *Political Philosophy of Montaigne,* 348.

48. *Discourses,* I, 39, 84.

49. Montaigne criticized Bodin's historical methodology from the *Methodus* in a similar manner. In his essay "Defense of Seneca and Plutarch," he first noted, "Jean Bodin is a good author of our day, equipped with much more judgment than the mob of scribblers of his time, and he deserves to be judged and considered" (II, 32, 546). However, he then went on to criticize his *"Method of History"* for taking an overly narrow view of human experience and for ruling out too many stories from antiquity as being fantastic and unbelievable.

50. Schaefer, *Political Philosophy of Montaigne,* 120–22.

51. This, in fact, was a common theme throughout the *Essays.* At the very beginning of his essay "Of Experience," Montaigne declared quite unambiguously: "The inference that we try to draw from the resemblance of events is uncertain, because they are always dissimilar: there is no quality so universal in this aspect of things as diversity and variety" (815). See also I, 37, 169; II, 14, 463.

52. As Schaefer has observed: "Given the unique quality of Machiavelli's ostensible advice to princes, as compared with the traditional 'mirrors' of princes, this passage can only be taken as a reference to *The Prince*—as commentators have generally recognized." *Political Philosophy of Montaigne,* 349.

53. Nakam, *Les essais de Montaigne,* 254–55; Sayce, *Essays of Montaigne,* 256; Villey, *Les sources,* 2: 357–62.

54. *Prince,* ch. 8, 37–38.

55. Machiavelli's riposte to this assertion was that the prince could always find new individuals to dupe and to mold to his will: "Alexander VI never did anything, nor ever thought of anything, but how to deceive men, and he always found a subject to whom he could do it" (*Prince,* 18, 70). Montaigne's counter-riposte: "It would be very naive for a man to let himself be taken in by either the face or the words of one who takes pride in being always different outside and inside, as Tiberius did" (II, 17, 491). Thomas Hobbes later took Montaigne's side in this debate, even phrasing his argument in terms strikingly similar to those used by Montaigne. In refuting the argument of the "fool" who claimed "there is no such thing as justice," Hobbes wrote: "He, therefore, that breaketh his covenant, and consequently declareth that he thinks he may with reason do so, cannot be received into any society that unite themselves for peace and defence but by the error of them that receive him; nor when he is received, be retained in it without seeing the danger of their error; which errors a man cannot reasonably reckon upon as the means of his security; and therefore, *if he be left or cast out of society,* he perisheth; and if he live in society, it is by the errors of other men, which he could not foresee nor reckon upon." *Leviathan,* ed. Edwin Curley (Indianapolis: Hackett Publishing, 1994), ch. 15, 91–92 (my emphasis).

56. For the evolution of Montaigne's thought, see Fortunat Strowski, *Montaigne* (Paris: Alcan, 1906); Villey, *Les sources;* Donald Frame, *Montaigne's Discovery of Man* (New York: Columbia University Press, 1955); Schiffman, *On the Threshold of Modernity,* 53–77.

57. Nannerl Keohane outlined Montaigne's different uses of the term "nature," but argued that he did not apply them to his theory of order. *Philosophy and the State in France* (Princeton: Princeton University Press, 1980), 103–5. See also James Beaudry, "Virtue and Nature in the Essais," in *Montaigne: A Collection of Essays,* ed. Dikka Bermen (New York: Garland Publishing, 1995), 4: 175–86.

58. Starobinski, *Montaigne in Motion,* 214–15, 234–35.

59. Hugo Friedrich has observed in this regard: "It is one of Montaigne's fundamental perceptions that the deliberate will is more likely to drive away than attract what it wants, and conversely, that it is more likely to attract what it fears than drive it away." *Montaigne,* 314.

60. Leo Strauss, *Natural Right and History* (Chicago: University of Chicago Press, 1950); Richard Tuck, *Natural Rights Theories* (Cambridge: Cambridge University Press, 1979).

61. Brian Tierney, "Origins of Natural Rights Language: Texts and Contexts, 1150–1250," *History of Political Thought* 10 (1989): 615–46.

62. Schiffman, *On the Threshold of Modernity,* 72.

63. Schiffman, *On the Threshold of Modernity,* 66–70.

64. This passage was added in the 1580s to the earlier essays. Montaigne's belief in the value of honest self-expression as a means of self-examination and character formation provides another clue to his aversion to dissimulation. Starobinski, *Montaigne in Motion,* 97–100.

65. See, for example, Keohane, *Philosophy and the State,* 98–116; Villey, *Les sources.*

66. J. G. A. Pocock, *The Ancient Constitution and the Feudal Law: A Study of English Historical Thought in the Seventeenth Century,* 2d ed. (Cambridge: Cambridge University Press, 1987), 1–29.

67. Keohane, *Philosophy and the State,* 108–11; Sayce, *Essays of Montaigne,* 233–36; Skinner, *Foundations of Modern Political Thought,* 2: 278–84; Starobinski, *Montaigne in Motion,* 251–56. While I disagree with Schaefer on many points, his comments on Montaigne's view of custom are quite enlightening. *Political Philosophy of Montaigne,* 170–71, 371–73.

68. The best work on Lipsius's life and ideas is Gerhard Oestreich, *Neostoicism and the Early Modern State,* trans. David McLintock (Cambridge: Cambridge University Press, 1982). The best works on Charron's life and ideas are J. B. Sabrié, *De l'humanisme au rationalisme: Pierre Charron (1541–1603)* (Paris: Alcan, 1913) and Renée Kogel, *Pierre Charron* (Geneva: Librairie Droz, 1972).

69. Quoted from Tuck, *Philosophy and Government,* 45.

70. Kogel, *Pierre Charron,* 18–21.

71. I refer to all citations from Lipsius's works in the body of the text. My citations from *De Constantia* (C) are from the English translation of 1594: *Two Bookes of Constancie,* trans. John Stradling (New Brunswick: Rutgers University Press, 1939). My citations from *Politicorum Sive Civilis Doctrinae Libri Sex* (P) are from the English translation of 1594: *Sixe Bookes of Politickes or Civil Doctrine,* trans. William Jones (New York: Da Capo Press, 1970). I have modernized the spelling.

72. Tuck, *Philosophy and Government,* 50.

73. While Lipsius did proceed to discuss the nature and limits of prudence, he did not attempt to identify precise historical precepts of the sort outlined by Machiavelli.

74. Schiffman makes a similar point about the differences between Montaigne and Charron. *On the Threshold of Modernity,* 85.

75. Oestreich, *Neostoicism,* 19, passim.

76. Oestreich, *Neostoicism,* 53.

77. Martin van Gelderen, "The Machiavellian Moment and the Dutch Revolt: The Rise of Neostoicism and Dutch Republicanism," in *Machiavelli and Republicanism,* ed. Gisela Bock, Quentin Skinner, and Maurizio Viroli (Cambridge: Cambridge University Press, 1990), 209.

78. Tuck, *Philosophy and Government,* 57–58.

79. I refer to all citations from Charron's *De la sagesse* in the body of the text. I have used the English translation of the revised 1604 edition of *De la sagesse.* Pierre Charron, *Of Wisdom,* trans. Samson Lennard (New York: Da Capo Press, 1971).

80. Kogel, *Pierre Charron,* 34–35.

81. Hobbes, *Leviathan,* 4–5; Paul Grendler, "Pierre Charron: Precursor to Hobbes," *Review of Politics* 25 (1963): 212–24.

82. Kogel, *Pierre Charron,* 138.

83. Charron's low opinion of the people did not prevent him (somewhat inconsistently) from repeating Montaigne's assertion that one could learn a great deal about the precepts of nature by observing the simple lives of the peasants (II, 3, 258–59).

84. Kogel, *Pierre Charron,* 138.

85. *Petit traicté de sagesse.* Quoted from Kogel, *Pierre Charron,* 138.

86. I have altered the translation of the final part of this passage. The Lennard translation renders the last part of this passage "or the gift of any person." The French reads: "elle consiste a pouvoir donner loy à tous en general, et à chascun en particulier, sans le consentement d'autruy, et n'en recevoir de personne."

CHAPTER 2: JEAN BODIN

1. I refer to all citations from Bodin's works in the body of the chapter. References to the *Methodus* (M) are from *Method for the Easy Comprehension of History,* trans. Beatrice Reynolds (New York: Columbia University Press, 1945). References to the *République* (R) are from *Les six livres de la république* (Paris, 1583; reprint, Aalen: Scientia, 1961). References to the *De la démonomanie des sorciers* (D) are from *On the Demon-Mania of Witches,* trans. Randy Scott (Toronto: Centre for Reformation and Renaissance Studies, 1995). References to the *Universae Naturae Theatrum* (T) are from *Universae Naturae Theatrum* (Paris, 1596). References to the *Colloquium Heptaplomeres* (C) are from *Colloquium of the Seven about Secrets of the Sublime,* trans. Marion L. D. Kuntz (Princeton: Princeton University Press, 1975). References to the *Paradoxon* (P) are to *Paradoxon* (Paris, 1596). References to the Latin edition of the *République* are from *De Republica Libri Sex* (Paris, 1586), and are listed in the notes.

2. Kenneth Pennington, *The Prince and the Law, 1200–1600* (Berkeley: University of California Press, 1993), 8–9, 276–84.

3. Pennington, *Prince and the Law,* 50–118, passim.

4. William F. Church, *Constitutional Thought in Sixteenth-Century France* (Cambridge: Harvard University Press, 1941), 43–73, 179–212; Julian H. Franklin, *Jean Bodin and the Rise of Absolutist Theory* (Cambridge: Cambridge University Press, 1973), 1–22.

5. See, for example, Pennington's discussion of Baldus's thought in *Prince and the Law,* 202–20.

6. Pennington, *Prince and the Law,* 78–79.

7. Claude de Seyssel, *The Monarchy of France,* trans. J. H. Hexter and Michael Sherman (New Haven: Yale University Press, 1981), 57.

8. Pennington, *Prince and the Law,* 283.

9. This point has been amply documented by Franklin, *Rise of Absolutist Theory,* 23–40, 54–69; J. H. M. Salmon, "Bodin and the Monarchomachs," in *Jean Bodin: Proceedings of the International Conference on Bodin,* ed. Horst Denzer (Munich: Verlag C. H. Beck, 1973), 359–78; Quentin Skinner, *The Foundations of Modern Political Thought* (Cambridge: Cambridge University Press, 1978), 2: 284–301.

10. Franklin, *Rise of Absolutist Theory,* vii, 41.

11. In a book review of *Jean Bodin: Proceedings of the International Conference on Bodin,* Michael Wilks noted that Christopher Baxter's essay depicted "the *République* in the unfamiliar guise of an exposition on the divine right of kings." *English Historical Review* 92 (1977): 142.

12. J. W. Allen, *A History of Political Thought in the Sixteenth Century* (London: Metheun, 1928), 415–16. For a more recent work, see Stephen Holmes, "Jean Bodin: The Paradox of Sovereignty and the Privatization of Religion," *Nomos* 30 (1988): 27.

13. Ann Blair, *The Theater of Nature: Jean Bodin and Renaissance Science* (Princeton: Princeton University Press, 1997); Simone Goyard-Fabre, *Jean Bodin et le droit de la "République"* (Paris: Presses Universitaires de France, 1989); Paul Lawrence Rose, *Bodin and the Great God of Nature: The Moral and Religious Universe of a Judaiser* (Geneva: Librairie Droz, 1980); Christopher Baxter, "Jean Bodin's Daemon and His Conversion to Judaism," in *Jean Bodin,* ed. Denzer, 1–21.

14. W. H. Greenleaf, *Order, Empiricism, and Politics* (London: Oxford University Press, 1964), 1–57, 125–41; W. H. Greenleaf, "Bodin and the Idea of Order," in *Jean Bodin,* ed. Denzer, 23–38. Bodin's theory of order is treated more generally in Preston King, *The Ideology of Order* (London: G. Allen and Unwin, 1974).

15. Greenleaf, *Order, Empiricism, and Politics,* 16.

16. Greenleaf, "Bodin and the Idea of Order," 27.

17. Francis Oakley, *Omnipotence, Covenant, and Order: An Excursion in the History of Ideas from Abelard to Leibniz* (Ithaca: Cornell University Press, 1984), 112–13, passim; Oakley, "The Absolute and Ordained Power of God in Sixteenth- and Seventeenth-Century Theology," *Journal of the History of Ideas* 59 (July 1998): 437–61; Oakley, "The Absolute and Ordained Power of God and King in the Sixteenth and Seventeenth Centuries: Philosophy, Science, Politics, and Law," *Journal of the History of Ideas* 59 (October 1998): 669–90.

18. Oakley suggested that Bodin held a voluntarist idea of order but made only passing reference to his ideas. *Omnipotence, Covenant, and Order,* 110; "Absolute and Ordained Power of God and King," 682–83. For a more extensive discussion of Bodin's voluntarism, see Margherita Isnardi Parente, "Le volontarisme de Jean Bodin: Maimonide ou Duns Scot?" in *Jean Bodin,* ed. Denzer, 39–51.

19. See also *De Republica Libri Sex,* 392–93; Jean Bodin, *The Six Bookes of a Commonweale,* ed. Kenneth McRae, trans. Richard Knolles (Cambridge: Harvard University Press, 1962), 436–37. Hereafter cited as *Six Bookes.*

20. Blair, *Theater of Nature,* 118–21.

21. "Quoniam futura mutabilia sunt, cum a Deo pendeant, qui non modo voluntates hominum flectere: quo velit, et unde velit reflectere possit, verumetiam belluarum impetus coercere, et exanimes naturas regere, ignes etiam quominus ardeant prohibere, ac naturae vim totam tollere, ac retinere." I would like to thank John Rundin of the University of Texas at San Antonio for helping me with the Latin translations from Bodin.

22. Blair, *Theater of Nature,* 119.

23. "M.: Quod scilicet nulla sit providentia si necessitate mundus stat: sed rerum universarum cura Deus absolvitur, ut Epicuro ac Stratoni Lampsaceno visum est. Th.: Cur non?

M.: Quia providentia duabus tantum in rebus cernitur, primum ut res una quaeque sit, deinde ut bene sit: at utrumque necessitas excludit: quia necessaria causarum series ordinem stabilem et immutabilem facit, ut aliter esse non possit, nec ordo rerum converti, ne flammis quis quam aut ullis praesentibus aut futuris periculis eripi. At providentia sublata Deus tollitur, quia cum ne vermiculus quidem frustra sit, ipse qui naturae moderator et arbiter esse debeat, servili necessitate coerceretur, nec ullam de rebus, quarum prima ac praecipua causa sit, statuendi potestatem haberet."

24. Oakley, *Omnipotence, Covenant, and Order,* 109–13.

25. Blair, *Theater of Nature,* 121–22.

26. Rose, *Bodin and the Great God of Nature,* 4, passim.

27. Blair, *Theater of Nature,* 18–30, 116–52.

28. Baxter, "Bodin's Daemon," 10–11; Janine Chanteur, "L'idée de loi naturelle dans la *République* de Jean Bodin," in *Jean Bodin,* ed. Denzer, 196–97; Rose, *Bodin and the Great God of Nature,* 4, 12.

29. This absence of a redemptive God from Bodin's thought has suggested to Rose a "judaizing" tendency in his religious doctrine. *Bodin and the Great God of Nature,* 67–148.

30. Since the *Colloquium* is written in dialogue format, one cannot always be sure that the opinions of the speakers are those of Bodin himself. However, he repeated this sentiment in several other works. Rose, *Bodin and the Great God of Nature,* 136–43, 180, 193.

31. Blair, *Theater of Nature,* 122–24.

32. "Quemadmodum mundi Procurator abundatem hominum multitudinem alere solet avium ac piscium legionibus derepente excitatis: sic quoque hominum arrogantiam ac superbiam castigat, cum vel suae largitioni modum facit, aut aquis, aut terris, aut aeri, aut animantibus foecunditatem propter hominum flagitia subtrahit."

33. This argument is extensively developed in Bodin's *De la démonomanie des sorciers.* See Rose, *Bodin and the Great God of Nature,* 100–2.

34. Franklin, *Rise of Absolutist Theory,* 41–53.

35. Franklin, *Rise of Absolutist Theory,* 49.

36. On the theme of divine retribution in Bodin, see Baxter, "Bodin's Daemon," 10–18.

37. Greenleaf, *Order, Empiricism, and Politics,* 19–20, 125–41; see also Greenleaf, "Bodin and the Idea of Order," 23–38.

38. See also the six letters relating to Bodin's league activities written toward the end of his life and discussed in Rose, *Bodin and the Great God of Nature,* 193–219.

39. Jonathan Pearl, introduction to *On the Demon-Mania of Witches,* Jean Bodin, trans. Randy Scott (Toronto: Centre for Reformation and Renaissance Studies, 1995), 9, 27.

40. *On the Demon-Mania of Witches,* 37. Bodin may also have presided as judge in a case of witchcraft in 1578 and condemned a woman to death, in which case the *Démonomanie* would also be his "apology." Marion L. D. Kuntz, introduction to *Colloquium of the Seven about Secrets of the Sublime,* Jean Bodin (Princeton: Princeton University Press, 1975), xxxiv.

41. The broad political and social context of Bodin's writings is discussed in Howell Lloyd, *The State, France, and the Sixteenth Century* (London: G. Allen and Unwin, 1983).

42. Julian H. Franklin, *Jean Bodin and the Sixteenth-Century Revolution in the Methodology of Law and History* (New York: Columbia University Press, 1963), 7–17.

43. Kelley, *Foundations of Modern Historical Scholarship,* 53–85.

44. Franklin, *Sixteenth-Century Revolution,* 46–58; Kelley, *Foundations of Modern Historical Scholarship,* 106–12.

45. François Hotman, *Antitribonian; ou, Discours d'un grand et renommé i urisconsulte de nostre temps sur l'estude des lois* (Université de Saint Etienne, 1980), 12.

46. Hotman, *Antitribonian,* 6–10.

47. Hotman, *Antitribonian,* 17.

48. Hotman, *Antitribonian,* 21–22.

49. Hotman, *Antitribonian,* 88–96.

50. Franklin, *Sixteenth-Century Revolution,* 54.

51. Franklin, *Sixteenth-Century Revolution,* 68; John Brown, *The "Methodus ad Facilem Historiarum Cognitionem" of Jean Bodin: A Critical Study* (Washington, D.C.: The Catholic University of America Press, 1939), 43–44; Beatrice Reynolds, *Proponents of Limited Monarchy in Sixteenth Century France: Francis Hotman and Jean Bodin* (New York: Columbia University Press, 1931), 108–9.

52. For a discussion of other writers' attempts to identify a new normative standard of law, see Zachary Sayre Schiffman, *On the Threshold of Modernity* (Baltimore: Johns Hopkins University Press, 1991), 25–52.

53. In 1578 Bodin published a short work (almost surely written in the 1550s or early 1560s) entitled *Juris universi distributio,* which contained what would seem to be the remnants of this work. He announced that his intention was to "collect in one body the best laws of those famous peoples who were most celebrated for their knowledge of ruling the state" and "arrange" them into an "order" with "definite limits and clarity." Yet Bodin seems never to have completed this work; it includes only his systematic arrangement of the Roman laws. Bodin, *Exposé du droit universel/Juris universi distributio,* trans. into French Lucien Jerphagnon (Paris: Presses Universitaires de France, 1985), 9–11.

54. Reinhart Koselleck, *Futures Past: On the Semantics of Historical Time,* trans. Keith Tribe (Cambridge: MIT Press, 1985), 21–38.

55. Bodin most clearly defined the subject of human history in chapter 6 (M, 153).

56. I have slightly altered Reynold's translation here. The original Latin reads: "At humana historia quod magna sui parte fluit ab hominum voluntate, quae semper sui dissimilis est, nullum exitum habet: sed quotidie novae leges, novi mores, nova instituta, novi ritus oboriuntur; atque omnino humanae actiones novis semper erroribus implicantur, nisi à natura duce, id est, à recta ratione...à quasi aberravimus, praecipites in omne dedecus labemur." *Œuvres philosophiques de Jean Bodin,* ed. Pierre Mesnard (Paris: Presses Universitaires de France, 1951), 115.

57. For Bodin's understanding of prudence, see Rose, *Bodin and the Great God of Nature,* 113–17.

58. Jean Moreau-Reibel, *Jean Bodin et le droit public comparé dans ses rapports avec la philosophie de l'histoire* (Paris: Librairie philosophique J. Vrin, 1933), 135.

59. Donald R. Kelley, "The Development and Context of Bodin's *Method,*" in *Jean Bodin,* ed. Denzer, 137–38.

60. Skinner, *Foundations of Modern Political Thought,* 2: 287–88; Church, *Constitutional Thought in Sixteenth-Century France,* 226.

61. Franklin, *Rise of Absolutist Theory,* 23–40; Church, *Constitutional Thought in Sixteenth-Century France,* 198–212.

62. At the end of this section on the human causes of changes in states, Bodin also "warns" rulers about several new sources of change that did not fit so well into his universalist framework: "the abolition of ancient slavery from the state, and in recent years the new religions, as well as the rights of vassalage and feudalism, have produced unbelievable opportunities for revolts unknown to the ancients" (M, 221–22).

63. In the Latin edition of the *République,* Bodin slightly altered his definition: "Sovereignty is supreme and absolute power over citizens and subjects." See Jean Bodin, *On Sovereignty,* ed. Julian Franklin (Cambridge: Cambridge University Press, 1992), 1n.

64. The *Theatrum* was probably written around 1590 but first published just a few months before Bodin's death. Blair, *Theater of Nature*, 11.

65. "Ex quo satis intelligitur cur ex omni memoria aetatum, temporum, civitatum illius disciplinae fines constitui non poterunt, cum ab hominum arbitrio ac erroribus ita pendeat, ut quae hi praemio, eadem illi supplicio digna iudicent. Quae certe me revocarunt ab instituto de legibus, quarum delectum ex omnibus fere omnium populorum moribus ac institutis inter se comparatis diuturno labore collegeram, ut certum aliquid constitueretur, reputantem omnia populorum edicta, decreta, leges ad hominum arbitrium ac libidinem temere ferri, nisi divinae, id est naturae lege velut in labirinto caeca filo regente vestigia nitantur."

66. Blair, *Theater of Nature*, 12.

67. Rose has also argued in this vein that Bodin came to emphasize much more strongly the arbitrariness of the human will in his later works. *Bodin and the Great God of Nature*, 126–33.

68. "ut quidem videmus leges innumerabiles de testamentis ac iure successorio nulla ratione rogari, abrogari, aut iis subrogari, obrogari, derogari, quae tamen uno capite divinae legis summa aequitate velut a stirpe convelluntur. At in natura nihil est incertum. Ignem apud Persas aeque ut apud Celtas urere, et candidam nivem unique, ratos etiam orbium coelestium cursus videmus, ut semper sui similia sint quae ab originis suae primordio decreta fuerunt: ac propterea naturam ducem, quasi numen aliquod ut sequamur, et oraculis, et sapientum omnium decretis ac vocibus admonemur."

69. Kenneth McRae, introduction to *The Six Bookes of a Commonweale*, by Bodin, A36; Kenneth McRae, "Bodin and the Development of Empirical Political Science," in *Jean Bodin*, ed. Denzer, 342; Myron Gilmore, *Humanists and Jurists* (Cambridge: Harvard University Press, 1963), 58.

70. Blair, *Theater of Nature*, 21–22.

71. Kuntz, introduction to *Colloquium*, xlii–xliii; Blair, *Theater of Nature*, 26, 48.

72. Rose, *Bodin and the Great God of Nature*, 96–100, 193–219.

73. McRae, "Bodin and the Development of Empirical Political Science," 342; see also McRae, introduction to *Six Bookes*, A35–36, where this claim is better supported.

74. *De Republica Libri Sex*, 356; see also McRae's edition of *Six Bookes*, 396.

75. *De Republica Libri Sex*, 350; *Six Bookes*, 389.

76. *De Republica Libri Sex*, 357; *Six Bookes*, 397.

77. *De Republica Libri Sex*, 360–62; *Six Bookes*, 400–2.

78. "Quanquam ignarus divinarum legum, non tamen earum quas ab ipsa natura arripuimus, et expressimus, nam si quis animi sui complicatas tabulas evolvere velit, iam se ipse doceat eum virum bonum esse qui prosit quidem quibus possit, noceat vero nisi lacessitus inuria nemini: quae nullis sunt populorum legibus comprehensa quinetiam multa pestifere, multa perniciose iuberi ac prohiberi videmus, quae non magis legum nomen merentur, quam si furiosus ea concessu suo sciscitat," *De Republica Libri Sex*, 630; *Six Bookes*, appendix, A155.

79. After demonstrating Bodin's more skeptical attitude toward law and history in the Latin *République*, McRae concluded: "Such remarks are scarcely to be found in any of the French editions." "Bodin and the Development of Empirical Political Science," 342n16; see also McRae's introduction to *Six Bookes*, A36.

80. Baxter, "Bodin's Daemon," 10–14.

81. In the *République*, Bodin further accorded new respect to the Roman law as a source of right. This did not mean that Bodin uncritically accepted the authority of Roman law on all points. On the contrary, he accepted or rejected the decrees of Roman

law based upon their conformity to the Old Testament and nature (R, 21–22). But he had come to see that Roman law embodied a good deal of what the divine and natural law prescribed. See Ralph E. Giesey, "Medieval Jurisprudence in Bodin's Concept of Sovereignty," in *Jean Bodin,* ed. Denzer, 178–79, passim.

82. This point will be illustrated further in the discussion of sovereignty below. For some indication of the central role of the Old Testament and nature in Bodin's argument, see Baxter, "Bodin's Daemon," 1–21; Greenleaf, "Bodin and the Idea of Order," 25–38; Michel Villey, "La justice harmonique selon Bodin," in *Jean Bodin,* ed. Denzer, 69–86.

83. "Quod si verum est rationi semper ac legi divine locum esse oportere, nec ipsam Palaestinae finibus concludi, cur non ubique terrarum lex illa de servitiis ac libertate tam utiliter, tam sapienter a Deo lata vim habitura sit, potius quam quae humanis ingeniis excogitata fuere?" *De Republica Libri Sex,* 45. This same statement appears in a condensed form in the French version of the *République,* 67.

84. Franklin, *Rise of Absolutist Theory,* 23–40, 54–69; Salmon, "Bodin and the Monarchomachs," 359–78; Skinner, *Foundations of Modern Political Thought,* 2: 284–301.

85. Blair has observed that the Old Testament was Bodin's highest authority in the *Theatrum. Theater of Nature,* 82, 88–89, 136.

86. As Blair has suggested, the *République* seems to be a sort of political "commonplace book" containing an overabundance of particular political examples loosely grouped under a few normative headings. *Theater of Nature,* 70–71.

87. Baxter, "Bodin's Daemon," 1–21; Rose, *Bodin and the Great God of Nature,* 164–65, passim.

88. *On the Demon-Mania of Witches,* 58–61, my emphasis.

89. That Bodin considered himself to be a prophet is attested by his letters written toward the end of his life. See Rose, *Bodin and the Great God of Nature,* 193–219.

90. Montaigne, *Essays,* III, ii, 790.

91. Allen, *History of Political Thought in the Sixteenth Century,* 415–16.

92. Jacques Maritain, *Man and the State* (Washington, D.C.: Catholic University Press, 1998), 34.

93. On the importance of change and contingency in the development of Bodin's theory of sovereignty, see Church, *Constitutional Thought in Sixteenth-Century France,* 212–23.

94. St. Thomas Aquinas, *Summa Theologiae* (New York: McGraw-Hill, 1966), I–II, q. 95, 2.

95. Julian Franklin, introduction to *On Sovereignty,* by Bodin, xx.

96. See, by contrast, Pennington's discussion of the variety of limitations that Baldus placed upon the prince's law-making authority. *Prince and the Law,* 202–20.

97. For this interpretation, see also Franklin, *Rise of Absolutist Theory,* 79. Bodin made a similar argument in regard to the variability of punishments (R, 152).

98. Skinner, *Foundations of Modern Political Thought,* 2: 302–48.

99. "Videmus saepe cives in principem armari, leges violari, iura omnia pessum ire, cur ita? Quia magistratus ipsi defectionis authores sunt, falsa iuris ac iustitiae opinione, At inquiunt, iniqua lex est, nec possumus, nec parere debemus: honesta quidem oratio, si non potes, sed illud quod non debeas unde didicisti? Quibus ex fontibus hausisti? Tu tibi privatos etiam iniusta praecipienti verberibus, carcere, mulcta, extremo denique supplicio parere cogas, nec tamen Imperanti principi obe-

dies? At negabis iniquum esse quod imperas: negat etiam princeps iniquum esse quod iubet: tune arbiter eris? Aut si te arbitrum feras, cur non idem de tuis erga privatos edictis ferendum putes?" *De Republica Libri Sex,* 297–98; *Six Bookes,* 323–24.

100. Pennington, *Prince and the Law,* 114, 120, 127, 152, 201.

101. Lionel Rothkrug outlined an argument regarding Bodin's economic theories with interesting parallels to his views on sovereignty and the law. In his *Réponse aux paradoxes de M. de Malestroit* (1568), Bodin argued that there existed an immanent divine and natural order within human affairs that encouraged cooperation and free exchange among people of different nations. In the *République,* he abandoned this argument and proposed a number of traditional mercantilist policies. The change in Bodin's attitude was due, according to Rothkrug, to his loss of faith in an immanent order within human affairs and his new belief that all justice and order in human affairs stemmed solely from the state: "Justice is inseparable from power. God, the unique source of Good, gave sovereigns the right to exercise the force necessary to impose peace and to govern according to His will. States were divinely instituted agencies consecrated for the establishment of Right Order. . . . Justice is possible only under the law of legitimate government; it cannot exist in the absence of this divinely ordained authority. Since God gave no Prince the right to impose His will on other rulers, no law existed to govern foreign relations. Therefore states should deal with one another in the absence of justice, for outside the consecrated limits of a prince's jurisdiction, sovereignty could not exist and conflict would be inevitable." *Opposition to Louis XIV: The Political and Social Origins of the Enlightenment* (Princeton: Princeton University Press, 1965), 22–29.

102. Allen, *History of Political Thought in the Sixteenth Century,* 410; for a more general discussion of these points, see Holmes, "Jean Bodin: The Paradox of Sovereignty," 9–12.

103. Franklin, *Rise of Absolutist Theory,* 79.

104. A. London Fell, *Origins of Legislative Sovereignty and the Legislative State* (Boston: Oelgeschlager, Gunn and Hain, 1987), 3: 119–87.

105. For various examples of this principle, see Greenleaf, "Bodin and the Idea of Order," 23–38.

106. "Nam si in rebus omnibus ordinem convenientem inquirimus et consectamur, confusione vero ac perturbatione nihil aspectu foedius ac deformius esse iudicamus, quanto magis in Republica enitendum est cives apta ac decenti collocatione sic constituere, ut primi postremis, medij utrisque, omnes omnibus nexu quodam ac vinculo inter se et cum Republica coniungantur? Est enim sapientus opinio vetus et contrita, supremum huius universitatis opificem ac parentem Deum in orbe condendo nihil maius ac milius praestitisse, quam quod permistas et confusas rudis materiae partes discreuit, certoque ordine suis quanque in sedibus collocavit," *De Republica Libri Sex,* 348; *Six Bookes,* 386–87.

107. Villey, "La justice harmonique selon Bodin," 69–86.

108. Rose, *Bodin and the Great God of Nature,* 134–48.

109. Greenleaf, "Bodin and the Idea of Order," 23–38.

110. Church, *Constitutional Thought in Sixteenth-Century France,* 243–46; Skinner, *Foundations of Modern Political Thought,* 2: 300–1.

111. The political philosophies of James I and Robert Filmer are discussed in chapter 5.

112. Church, *Constitutional Thought in Sixteenth-Century France,* 243–45; Allen, *History of Political Thought in the Sixteenth Century,* 442–43.

113. Church, *Constitutional Thought in Sixteenth-Century France,* 243–71; Myron

Gilmore, *Argument from Roman Law in Political Thought, 1200–1600* (Cambridge: Harvard University Press, 1941), 93–126.

114. Max Adam Shepard, "Sovereignty at the Crossroads: A Study of Bodin," *Political Science Quarterly* 45 (1930): 580–603.

115. Jean-Jacques Rousseau, *On the Social Contract with Geneva Manuscript and Political Economy,* tr. Judith Masters (New York: St. Martins, 1978), 49–55, 59–64, 101–4.

116. A. John Simmons, "Philosophical Anarchism," in *For and Against the State: New Philosophical Readings,* ed. John T. Sanders and Jan Narveson (New York: Rowman and Littlefield, 1996), 19.

117. A. John Simmons, *Moral Principles and Political Obligations* (Princeton: Princeton University Press, 1979).

118. This point is further discussed in the final section of chapter 5 and the conclusion of this work.

CHAPTER 3: CARDINAL RICHELIEU AND THE BIRTH OF MODERN EXECUTIVE POWER

1. Carl Schmitt claimed the power "to decide on the exception" was the central principle of modern state theory. *Political Theology: Four Chapters on the Concept of Sovereignty,* trans. George Schwab (Cambridge: MIT Press, 1985).

2. Harvey Mansfield, Jr., *Taming the Prince* (Baltimore: Johns Hopkins University Press, 1989).

3. Friedrich Meinecke portrayed reason of state as a timeless and universal principle in *Machiavellism: The Doctrine of Raison d'Etat and Its Place in Modern History,* trans. Douglas Scott (New Brunswick: Transaction Publishers, 1998), 1–22.

4. Mansfield, *Taming the Prince,* 23–85.

5. Maurizio Viroli, *From Politics to Reason of State* (Cambridge: Cambridge University Press, 1992), 1–125.

6. Gaines Post has argued that reason of state theory existed during the Middle Ages, citing as evidence that writers such as St. Thomas Aquinas admitted the legitimacy of otherwise immoral actions in a very few emergency situations. *Studies in Medieval Legal Thought* (Princeton: Princeton University Press, 1964), 241–308; see Viroli's rebuttal of this arguments in *From Politics to Reason of State,* 271–73.

7. Mansfield, *Taming the Prince,* 121–49; Meinecke, *Machiavellism,* 25–48; Viroli, *From Politics to Reason of State,* 126–77.

8. J. H. Hexter, *The Vision of Politics on the Eve of the Reformation* (New York: Basic Books, 1973), 150–78. See also Harvey Mansfield, Jr., "Machiavelli's Stato and the Impersonal Modern State," in *Machiavelli's Virtue* (Chicago: University of Chicago Press, 1996), 281–94.

9. Isaiah Berlin, "The Originality of Machiavelli," in *Against the Current: Essays in the History of Ideas* (New York: Viking Press, 1980), 46–49.

10. Viroli, *From Politics to Reason of State.*

11. Richard Tuck, *Philosophy and Government, 1572–1651* (Cambridge: Cambridge University Press, 1993), 31–119.

12. Meinecke, *Machiavellism;* a similar interpretation is outlined in Etienne Thuau, *Raison d'état et pensée politique à l'époque de Richelieu* (Paris: Armand Colin, 1966), esp. 411–19.

13. William F. Church, *Richelieu and Reason of State* (Princeton: Princeton University Press, 1972), esp. 8–12.

14. Mansfield, *Taming the Prince,* xxvii.

15. Meinecke, *Machiavellism,* 49; for a similar view, see Robert Bireley, *The Counter-Reformation Prince* (Chapel Hill: University of North Carolina Press, 1990).

16. Bireley, *Counter-Reformation Prince,* 17–18.

17. Jean Bodin, *Les Six Livres de la République* (Paris, 1583; reprint, Aalen: Scientia, 1961), ii–iv. Bodin also hesitated before the prospect of reason of state theory. Although he granted sovereign rulers wide latitude in formulating laws, he maintained that once they had declared their laws, they ought to govern the people by them. Meinecke, *Machiavellism,* 62–63.

18. Meinecke, *Machiavellism,* 117–18.

19. Bireley, *Counter-Reformation Prince;* Peter Burke, "Tacitism, Scepticism, and Reason of State," in *The Cambridge History of Political Thought, 1450–1700,* ed. J. H. Burns (Cambridge: Cambridge University Press, 1991), 480–82; Church, *Richelieu and Reason of State,* 56–72.

20. Giovanni Botero, *The Reason of State,* trans. P. J. Waley and D. P. Waley (London: Routledge and Kegan Paul, 1956), xiii.

21. Botero, *Reason of State,* 41.

22. Bireley, *Counter-Reformation Prince,* 46.

23. Church, *Richelieu and Reason of State,* 64–72. For a discussion of these and other writers, see Meinecke, *Machiavellism,* 65–116. On the anti-Machiavellian character of Spanish reason of state theory, see J. A. Fernández-Santamaría, *Reason of State and Statecraft in Spanish Political Thought, 1595–1640* (Lanham, Md.: University Press of America, 1983). For an analysis of Ribadeneyra's ideas, see also Bireley, *Counter-Reformation Prince,* 111–35.

24. Justus Lipsius, *Sixe Bookes of Politickes or Civil Doctrine,* trans. William Jones (Amsterdam: Da Capo Press, 1970), 115–23.

25. Charron, of course, adopted Lipsius's framework but more generously defended the prince's right to engage in light and medium forms of deceit. See the discussion in chapter 1.

26. Girolamo Frachetta, *Discorso della ragione di stato;* cited in Church, *Richelieu and Reason of State,* 65.

27. Ribadeneyra, *Príncipe cristiano;* cited in Bireley, *Counter-Reformation Prince,* 133.

28. Meinecke, *Machiavellism,* 90–116; Tuck, *Philosophy and Government,* 69–73.

29. This is not meant to deny that Richelieu and his supporters were influenced by Lipsius, Charron, and other earlier theorists. They merely moved beyond the position of these earlier writers by arguing that the justice of the king's actions could not be measured by any external moral values. On the influence of Lipsius and Charron on French *raison d'état* theory, see Anna Maria Battista, *Alle origini del pensiero politico libertino: Montaigne e Charron* (Milan: Giuffrè, 1966); Tuck, *Philosophy and Government,* 82–94.

30. Church, *Richelieu and Reason of State,* 93–97.

31. The two best surveys of French reason of state literature are Church, *Richelieu and Reason of State,* and Thuau, *Raison d'état et pensée politique.*

32. On Richelieu's propaganda efforts, see Church, *Richelieu and Reason of State,* 109–14; R. J. Knecht, *Richelieu* (New York: Longman, 1991), 169–89; Thuau, *Raison d'état et pensée politique,* 166–78.

33. Church, *Richelieu and Reason of State,* 128. For the sake of simplicity, I refer to Ferrier as the author of this work.

34. Church, *Richelieu and Reason of State,* 120–26.

35. Jérémie Ferrier, *Catholique d'éstat* (Paris, 1625). Hereafter referred to in the text as CE.

36. Allen, *History of Political Thought in the Sixteenth Century,* 367–93.

37. Peter Donaldson, *Machiavelli and Mystery of State* (Cambridge: Cambridge University Press, 1988); Ernst Kantorowicz, "Mysteries of State," *Harvard Theological Review* 47 (1955): 65–91.

38. "We do not at all condone the counsel of Machiavelli and the south for our kings," he wrote. "The counsel of God is always necessary, certain, useful, and followed by infinite blessings" (CE, 67–68).

39. Church has stated that the author of this portion of the *Catholique d'éstat* was probably Pierre de Bérulle. *Richelieu and Reason of State,* 135–38.

40. Jean Louis Guez de Balzac, *Le prince,* 2d ed. (Paris, 1632). Hereafter referred to in the text as P. Balzac was in correspondence with Richelieu throughout the 1620s and wrote his *Prince* partially at Richelieu's request. Church, *Richelieu and Reason of State,* 238.

41. Jean Louis Guez de Balzac, *Aristippe; ou, De la Cour,* in *Œuvres* (Paris, 1665), 173–74.

42. Mansfield, *Taming the Prince,* 121–35.

43. Church, *Richelieu and Reason of State,* 252–61.

44. Mathieu de Morgues, *Discours sur le livre de Balzac entitulé "Le Prince";* quoted in Church, *Richelieu and Reason of State,* 255.

45. Quoted in Church, *Richelieu and Reason of State,* 254.

46. Balzac, *Replique à la response de l'Apologie du Prince de Monsieur de Balzac;* quoted in Church, *Richelieu and Reason of State,* 258.

47. The first edition of this work contained only the first part, which is the focus here. The second and third parts were published in 1643 and 1661. I have used a later edition of this work: Jean de Silhon, *Le ministre d'éstat,* final ed. (Paris, 1665). Hereafter referred to in the text as ME.

48. Lionel Rothkrug, *Opposition to Louis XIV: The Political and Social Origins of the Enlightenment* (Princeton: Princeton University Press, 1965), 56.

49. Richard Popkin, *The History of Scepticism from Erasmus to Spinoza* (Berkeley: University of California Press, 1979), 161–71.

50. Richard Tuck observed that this "anti-scientific spirit" was a central tenet of French reason of state theory. *Philosophy and Government,* 93. Richelieu similarly observed in his *Testament politique*: "There is nothing more dangerous for the state than those who wish to govern kingdoms by the maxims they find in their books. They often ruin them by these means, since the past is not related to the present and the constitution of the times, places, and persons is different." *Testament politique,* ed. Louis André (Paris: Robert Laffont, 1947), 289. Hereafter referred to in the text as TP. See also the discussion of Silhon and others below.

51. As Church noted, Silhon did believe that "a knowledge of history was essential to statesmen." *Richelieu and Reason of State,* 262. But he did not look to history to provide statesmen with maxims or rules of conduct but only to provide them with a general sense of the mutability of temporal affairs so that they would not be shocked by sudden accidents or strange events (ME, 13).

52. Church, *Richelieu and Reason of State,* 265.

53. Aristotle, *Politics,* trans. Ernest Barker (Oxford: Oxford University Press, 1995), Bk. III, 15–18, 123–31.

54. Aristotle, *Politics,* Bk. III, 13, 117.

55. Thuau, *Raison d'état et pensée politique,* 45, 54, 59, 65, 68.

56. Rothkrug, *Opposition to Louis XIV,* 55–60.

57. Jansenius, *Mars Gallicus;* quoted in Church, *Richelieu and Reason of State,* 388.

58. Church, *Richelieu and Reason of State,* 393–401.

59. Daniel de Priézac, *Vindiciae Gallicae adversus Alexandrum Patricium Arma-canum Theologum;* quoted in Church, *Richelieu and Reason of State,* 396.

60. Daniel de Priézac, *Discours politiques* (Paris, 1652), 159–60. Hereafter cited in the text as D.

61. Francis Oakley, *Omnipotence, Covenant, and Order: An Excursion in the History of Ideas from Abelard to Leibniz* (Ithaca: Cornell University Press, 1984).

62. The authorship of the *Testament* has long been contested. Many of the doubts about Richelieu's authorship were put to rest in 1880 when Gabriel Hanotaux discovered a collection of Richelieu's personal papers that replicated almost verbatim some of the passages from the *Testament.* See Cardinal de Richelieu, *Maxims d'état et fragments politiques,* ed. Gabriel Hanotaux (Paris: Imprimerie Nationale, 1880). For a discussion of the debates concerning the authenticity of the *Testament,* as well as arguments supporting Richelieu's authorship, see Louis André, introduction to *Testament politique,* by Richelieu, 33–57; and Church, *Richelieu and Reason of State,* 480–85. Edmond Esmonin argued that by the standards of modern historical scholarship we cannot be certain that Richelieu was the author of all of the passages in the *Testament.* The work was in fact compiled and copied by his secretaries. "Sur l'authenticité du *Testament politique* de Richelieu," in *Etudes sur la France des XVIIe et XVIIIe siècles* (Paris: Presses Universitaires de France, 1964), 219–32. The weight of evidence nonetheless indicates that Richelieu at least oversaw the composition of this work and that the ideas within it reflect his thought.

63. Most famous in this regard was Richelieu's prosecution of the Marshal de Marillac. See Church, *Richelieu and Reason of State,* 225–31.

64. Richelieu made a similar point regarding venality of office (TP, 234–36).

65. Gabriel Naudé, *Considérations politiques sur les coups d'état* (Paris: Editions de Paris, 1988), 88. This work is referred to hereafter in the text as CP. Tuck has speculated that Naudé may have coined the term "coups d'état" (*Philosophy and Government,* 93), but Jean Sirmond published a book in 1631, several before Naudé's work, entitled *Coup d'état de Louis XIII.*

66. The importance of Naudé's reason of state theory has been widely recognized. See Peter Burke, "Tacitism, Scepticism, and Reason of State," 496; Nannerl Keohane, *Philosophy and the State in France* (Princeton: Princeton University Press, 1980), 171–74; Meinecke, *Machiavellism,* 196–204.

67. Church did not consider Naudé's reason of state theory in his *Richelieu and Reason of State* on the grounds that it was not "in any way related to Richelieu's ideas or policies" (416n.376).

68. This position has been most thoroughly developed by Donaldson, *Machiavelli and Mystery of State,* 141–85.

69. Battista, *Alle origini del pensiero politico libertino,* 206–7, 250–51, 259–65; Gerhard Oestreich, *Neostoicism and the Early Modern State,* trans. David McLintock (Cambridge: Cambridge University Press, 1982), 105–9; Tuck, *Philosophy and Government,* 93.

70. René Pintard has reported that Naudé had originally intended to give his *Coups d'état* the title of *De Arcanis Imperiorium.* René Pintard, *Le libertinage érudit dans la première moitié du XVIIe siècle* (Paris: Boivin, 1943), 615.

71. I disagree with Donaldson's claim that "Naudé wants to resist attempts to make politically necessary acts that violate the moral law respectable; wants to resist, that is, the moral alchemy of the reason of state school." *Machiavelli and Mystery of State,* 166.

72. Thuau wrote in this respect that "Naudé has a lively sense of the instability, and the mutability of things, what Montaigne called their 'voluability.'" He then

cites the following passage from Naudé's *Addition à l'histoire de Louis XII*: "all things in the world, without any exception, are subject to diverse revolutions, which render them much esteemed in one time, and then despised and ridiculed in another, make rise up today what will fall tomorrow, and turn this great wheel of the ages perpetually, that causes each to appear, die and be reborn in its turn on the theatre of the world." Thuau, *Raison d'état et pensée politique*, 330n.1.

73. Donaldson, *Machiavelli and Mystery of State*, 180.

74. *Discourses*, I, 58.

75. Naudé's reference to the Lesbian rule here is drawn from the *Nicomachean Ethics* (trans. Terence Irwin [Indianapolis: Hackett, 1985]), where Aristotle stated that, just as Lesbian builders adapt their standards to the shape of the stone, so ought rulers to adapt their decrees to fit the circumstances (Bk. V, 1137b).

76. Donaldson, *Machiavelli and Mystery of State*, 168–69.

77. Donaldson, *Machiavelli and Mystery of State*, 173, n.31.

78. Donaldson, *Machiavelli and Mystery of State*, 172.

79. Max Weber, *Economy and Society*, ed. Guenther Roth and Claus Wittich (Berkeley: University of California Press, 1978), 2: 956–84.

80. Meinecke, *Machiavellism*, 165–67.

81. Henri de Rohan, *De l'intérêt des princes et des états de la chrétienté*, ed. Christian Lazzeri (Paris: Presses Universitaires de France, 1995), 159. Hereafter referred to in the text as IP.

82. Richelieu's familiarity with Lipsius is discussed in Oestreich, *Neostoicism and the Early Modern State*, 105–9.

83. Mansfield, *Taming the Prince*, 181–246.

84. John Dunn, *The Political Thought of John Locke* (Cambridge: Cambridge University Press, 1969), 161–63.

85. John Locke, *Two Treatises of Government*, ed. Peter Laslett (Cambridge: Cambridge University Press, 1988), II, 14, 375.

86. Locke, *Two Treatises*, II, 13, 369.

87. Locke, *Two Treatises*, II, 12, 364–65.

88. Montesquieu, *The Spirit of the Laws*, ed. and trans. Anne Cohler, Basia Miller, and Harold Stone (Cambridge: Cambridge University Press, 1989), V, 11, 58.

89. Montesquieu, *Spirit of the Laws*, XI, 6, 156–57.

90. Montesquieu, *Spirit of the Laws*, XI, 6, 159.

91. Montesquieu, *Spirit of the Laws*, XI, 6, 161–62.

92. See, for example, the account of the evolution of executive power in Arthur Schlesinger, Jr., *The Imperial Presidency* (Boston: Houghton Mifflin, 1989).

93. Mansfield, *Taming the Prince*, xvii.

94. Kenneth Waltz, *Theory of International Politics* (Reading, Mass.: Addison-Wesley, 1979); John Mearsheimer, "The False Promise of International Institutions," *International Security* 19 (winter 1994/95): 5–49. For a critique of neorealism, see R. B. J. Walker, *Inside/Outside: International Relations as Political Theory* (Cambridge: Cambridge University Press, 1993).

CHAPTER 4: LOUIS XIV AND THE IDEOLOGY OF THE REGULATORY STATE

1. Michel Foucault, *Discipline and Punish*, trans. Alan Sheridan (New York: Vintage Books, 1977), 188–89. The medal is featured among the plates between pages 169 and 170. It is slightly different from the one presented in the official *Médailles*

sur les principaux événements du règne de Louis le Grand (Schaffhausen, 1704), which shows the inscription *Disciplina militaris restituta* across the top of the medal. The 1704 *Médailles* edition is a copy of the original one published in Paris in 1702 but includes German translations accompanying the French text.

2. *Discipline and Punish*, 215. See also Michel Foucault, "Governmentality," in *The Foucault Effect: Studies in Governmentality*, ed. Graham Burchell, Colin Gordon, and Peter Miller (London: Harvester Wheatsheaf, 1991), 87–104; and Michel Foucault, "Omnes et Singulatim," in *The Tanner Lectures on Human Values*, ed. Sterling McMurrin (Salt Lake City: University of Utah Press, 1981), 2: 225–54. While Foucault has pointed out that modern power-knowledge systems are diffuse and not always bound up with centralized state governments, he has also argued that the development and dissemination of these systems coincided with the expansion of state powers—the development of what he has called a new "pastoral technology."

3. Alexis de Tocqueville, *Democracy in America*, ed. J. P. Mayer, trans. George Lawrence (New York: Harper and Row, 1966), 680, 692.

4. P.-J. Proudhon, *General Idea of the Revolution in the Nineteenth Century*, trans. J. B. Robinson (London: Free Press, 1923), 294.

5. William Beik, *Absolutism and Society in Seventeenth-Century France* (Cambridge: Cambridge University Press, 1985); James Collins, *Fiscal Limits of Absolutism* (Berkeley: University of California Press, 1988); Sharon Kettering, *Patrons, Brokers, and Clients in Seventeenth-Century France* (Oxford: Oxford University Press, 1986); J. Russell Major, *From Renaissance Monarchy to Absolute Monarchy* (Baltimore: Johns Hopkins University Press, 1994); Roger Mettam, *Power and Faction in Louis XIV's France* (Oxford: Basil Blackwell 1988). Two recent articles that address particular elements of the revisionist thesis are Beth Nachison, "Absentee Government and Provincial Governors in Early Modern France: The Princes of Condé and Burgundy, 1660–1720," *French Historical Studies* 21 (spring 1998): 265–97 and Guy Rowlands, "Louis XIV, Aristocratic Power and the Elite Units of the French Army," *French History* 13 (1999): 303–31.

6. William F. Church, "Louis XIV and Reason of State," in *Louis XIV and the Craft of Kingship*, ed. John Rule (Columbus: Ohio State University Press, 1969), 362–406; James King, *Science and Rationalism in the Government of Louis XIV, 1661–1683* (Baltimore: Johns Hopkins University Press, 1949).

7. Jay Smith, *The Culture of Merit* (Ann Arbor: University of Michigan Press, 1996), 8–9.

8. Smith, *Culture of Merit*, 1–10, 125–90.

9. Orest Ranum, *The Fronde: A French Revolution, 1648–1652* (New York: W. W. Norton, 1993), 46. On the symbolic importance of the "royal touch," see Marc Bloch, *The Royal Touch*, trans. J. E. Anderson (New York: Dorset, 1989).

10. *Culture of Merit*, 184–85.

11. All citations from Louis XIV's *Mémoires* (M) appear in the body of the text and are taken from Louis XIV, *Mémoires for the Instruction of the Dauphin*, ed. and trans. Paul Sonnino (New York: Free Press, 1970).

12. Jean Longnon, introduction to *Mémoires*, by Louis XIV (Paris: Tallandier, 1978), 7–17; Orest Ranum, *Artisans of Glory* (Chapel Hill: University of North Carolina Press, 1980), 259–68; Paul Sonnino, introduction to *Mémoires for the Instruction of the Dauphin*, by Louis XIV, 7–10; Paul Sonnino, "The Dating and Authorship of Louis XIV's *Mémoires*," *French Historical Studies* 3 (1964): 303–37; Jean Louis Thireau, *Les idées politiques de Louis XIV* (Paris: Presses Universitaires de France, 1973), 9–31.

13. Andrew Lossky has argued that Louis XIV changed his thinking on several

matters over the course of his life. Some of these changes are discussed below. See Lossky, "The Intellectual Development of Louis XIV from 1661 to 1715," in *Louis XIV and Absolutism*, ed. Ragnhild Hatton (Columbus: Ohio State University Press, 1976), 101–29.

14. Andrew Lossky has provided a good synopsis of the basic elements of Louis XIV's thought in his "Intellectual Development of Louis XIV" and more recently in *Louis XIV and the French Monarchy* (New Brunswick: Rutgers University Press, 1994), 69–77. See also Thireau, *Les idées politiques de Louis XIV*.

15. Lossky, "Intellectual Development of Louis XIV," 112–13.

16. John Wolf, *Louis XIV* (New York: W. W. Norton, 1968), 560, 578, 608–13.

17. Pocock, *Machiavellian Moment*, 3–48.

18. Andrew Lossky examines this belief in "'Maxims of State' in Louis XIV's Foreign Policy in the 1680s," in *William III and Louis XIV*, ed. Ragnhild Hatton and J. S. Bromley (Liverpool: Liverpool University Press, 1968), 7–23.

19. Nannerl Keohane, *Philosophy and the State in France* (Princeton: Princeton University Press, 1980), 213–37, 262–311, 323–27; Anthony Levi, *French Moralists: The Theory of the Passions, 1585–1659* (Oxford: Clarendon Press, 1964). The theme of the passions and the interests is studied in depth in Albert O. Hirschman, *The Passions and the Interests: Political Arguments for Capitalism before Its Triumph* (Princeton: Princeton University Press, 1977).

20. Thireau has similarly observed: "Louis XIV has a realistic and pessimistic conception of human nature. This psychological pessimism is that of his age: Richelieu and Le Bret share it; it constitutes the foundation of the philosophical system of Hobbes, and Bossuet does not think otherwise. Left to themselves, men are dominated by their passions; incapable of obeying a superior reason, they fall fatally into anarchy and insecurity: man is a wolf for man." *Les idées politiques de Louis XIV*, 47.

21. Paul Sonnino, "The Sun King's Anti-Machiavel," in *Louis XIV and the Craft of Kingship*, ed. Rule, 345–61.

22. The similarity of Louis XIV's views of monarchy with the views of other seventeenth-century writers is discussed by Church, "Louis XIV and Reason of State," 362–406; and Georges Lacour-Gayet, *L'éducation politique de Louis XIV* (Paris: Librairie Hachette, 1923).

23. For a discussion of Louis XIV's divine right theory, see Paul Fox, "Louis XIV and the Theories of Absolutism and Divine Right," *Canadian Journal of Economics and Political Science* 26 (1960): 128–42.

24. Louis XIV's indoctrination into divine right theory is amply demonstrated by Lacour-Gayet, *L'éducation politique de Louis XIV*, 16–84, 192–208, 211–74.

25. Louis XIV's proprietary theory of kingship is discussed in Herbert Rowen, *The King's State: Proprietary Dynasticism in Early Modern France* (New Brunswick: Rutgers University Press, 1980), 75–82.

26. Hobbes made a similar argument in favor of monarchy in chapter 19 of *Leviathan:* "Now in monarchy the private interest is the same with the public. The riches, power, and honour of a monarch arise only from the riches, strength and reputation of his subjects. For no king can be rich, nor glorious, nor secure, whose subjects are either poor, or contemptible, or too weak (through want or dissension) to maintain a war against their enemies." *Leviathan*, ed. Curley, 120

27. On Louis XIV's views of legislative sovereignty and reason of state, see Fox, "Louis XIV and the Theories of Absolutism and Divine Right," 137–40.

28. This is from the official account of Louis XIV's announcement reported in Wolf, *Louis XIV,* 133.

29. F. Hartung, "L'état, c'est moi," in *Staatsbildende Kräfte der Neuzeit* (Berlin: Duncker and Humblot, 1961), 93–122.

30. Most of the actual reforms of the military were carried out by Michel Le Tellier and his son François-Michel Louvois. Louis XIV's ability to effect reform was constrained by cultural traditions and clientage networks. The king once remarked that he could not appoint someone from a new family to the command of a certain regiment because all of its officers were either relatives or clients of the current commander. James Collins, *The State in Early Modern France* (Cambridge: Cambridge University Press, 1995), 94. See also Rowlands, "Louis XIV, Aristocratic Power and the Elite Units of the French Army." It should be remembered that the discussion here is about the king's aspirations, not his accomplishments.

31. Smith provides a nice discussion of this point. *Culture of Merit,* 151–58.

32. James King, *Science and Rationalism in the Government of Louis XIV, 1661–1683* (Baltimore: Johns Hopkins University Press, 1949), 170; Lionel Rothkrug, *Opposition to Louis XIV: The Political and Social Origins of the Enlightenment* (Princeton: Princeton University Press, 1965), 106–8; Smith, *Culture of Merit,* 96–100.

33. Louis XIV did acknowledge later in the *Mémoires* the value of historical studies in strengthening the reasoning capacities of the king (M, 216). But he looked to history to gain a practical knowledge of "illustrious men and singular deeds" rather than to discover "maxims."

34. Louis XIV was notoriously distrustful of his ministers and officers. Lossky, "Intellectual Development of Louis XIV," 108.

35. Hirschman, *The Passions and the Interests,* 14–20.

36. Andrew Lossky, "The Nature of Political Power according to Louis XIV," in *The Responsibility of Power,* ed. Leonard Krieger and Fritz Stern (Garden City, N.Y.: Doubleday, 1967), 112, 116.

37. Foucault, *Discipline and Punish,* 141.

38. There are numerous studies of the propaganda under Louis XIV. A good summary of much of this literature is found in Peter Burke's *The Fabrication of Louis XIV* (New Haven: Yale University Press, 1992). One of the best studies of the printed literature during the early part of Louis XIV's reign is still Lacour-Gayet, *L'éducation politique de Louis XIV.* On printed literature during the last part of the king's reign, see Joseph Klaits, *Printed Propaganda under Louis XIV* (Princeton: Princeton University Press, 1976). Other important works include Jean-Marie Apostolidès, *Le roi-machine* (Paris: Les Editions de Minuit, 1981); Louis Marin, *Portrait of the King* (Minneapolis: University of Minnesota Press, 1988); Chandra Mukerji, *Territorial Ambitions and the Gardens of Versailles* (Cambridge: Cambridge University Press, 1997); Ranum, *Artisans of Glory.*

39. Burke, *Fabrication of Louis XIV,* 35.

40. "Louis to Louvois, July 26, 1676," in *Œuvres de Louis XIV* (Paris: Treuttel et Wurtz, 1806), 4: 91.

41. King, *Science and Rationalism in the Government of Louis XIV,* 116–46.

42. John Wolf, *Louis XIV,* 166.

43. Jean-Baptiste Colbert, *Lettres, instructions et mémoires,* ed. Pierre Clement (Paris: Imprimerie Imperiale, 1867), 4: 27–43.

44. The classic work on this topic remains Charles Woolsey Cole, *Colbert and a Century of French Mercantilism,* 2 vols. (New York: Columbia University Press, 1939). As Cole and others have pointed out, the basic tenets of mercantilism were developed by

English thinkers during the sixteenth century. Colbert's main innovation was his extensive regulation of domestic manufacturing.

45. Quoted from Cole, *Colbert and a Century of French Mercantilism,* 2: 378–79.

46. Colbert, *Lettres,* 2: 696. In another letter Colbert proclaimed that his mercantilist policies were aimed to restore France to its proper share of goods "in the natural order." *Lettres,* 2: 463–64.

47. See, for example, Colbert, *Lettres,* 2: 514–15, 694, 716–17, 726–27.

48. Cole, *Colbert and a Century of French Mercantilism,* 2: 363.

49. Cole, *Colbert and a Century of French Mercantilism,* 1: 333–35; King, *Science and Rationalism in the Government of Louis XIV,* 202–5.

50. Cole, *Colbert and a Century of French Mercantilism,* 2: 363–64.

51. Colbert, *Lettres,* 2: 728.

52. Colbert, *Lettres,* 2: 614–15.

53. See Cole, *Colbert and a Century of French Mercantilism,* 1: 338–39, 388–90.

54. Pierre Le Moyne, *De L'art de regner* (Paris, 1665), epistle to the king. Hereafter I refer to this work in the body of the text as AR.

55. Apostolidès, *Le roi-machine,* 47.

56. Aristotle, *Nicomachean Ethics,* Bk. I, 1094a–b.

57. Louis XIV was apparently pleased with the original version of *Tartuffe,* but temporarily prohibited its public performance in order to appease the *dévots* party. The revised version of the play that we possess today was first performed in 1669. For a discussion of these points, see Emanuel Chill, "Tartuffe, Religion, and Courtly Culture," *French Historical Studies* 3 (1963): 151–83.

58. Jean-Baptiste Molière, *Tartuffe and Other Plays,* trans. Donald Frame (New York: Penguin, 1967), 242.

59. Donald Frame, "Tartuffe," in *Tartuffe,* by Molière, 238.

60. Molière, *Tartuffe,* 311.

61. Ezechiel Spanheim analyzed the panegyrics to Louis XIV and concluded: "They present him as the sole author and inspiration of all the successes of his reign, attributing them entirely to his wisdom, his prudence, his courage and his direction." Quoted from Burke, *Fabrication of Louis XIV,* 26.

62. Paul Pellison, "Panegyrique du roy," in *Les panégyriques du roi,* ed. Pierre Zoberman (Paris: Presses de l'Université de Paris, 1991), 103.

63. *Médailles,* 119.

64. *Médailles,* 121.

65. *Médailles,* 123.

66. *Médailles,* 135, 139, 163, 171.

67. Mukerji, *Territorial Ambitions,* esp. 248–99; see also Guy Walton, *Louis XIV's Versailles* (New York: Viking-Penguin, 1986).

68. Norbert Elias, *The Court Society* (New York: Blackwell, 1983). See Smith's brief but insightful critique of Elias's thesis in *Culture of Merit,* 130–31.

69. See, for example, Rothkrug's discussion of Jean de Lartigue's thought, *Opposition to Louis XIV,* 86–130.

70. Keohane, *Philosophy and the State in France,* 21, 262–311.

71. A good survey of Bossuet's various literary feuds is provided by Patrick Riley, introduction to *Politics Drawn from the Very Words of Holy Scripture,* by Jacques-Bénigne Bossuet (Cambridge: Cambridge University Press, 1990).

72. Jacques-Bénigne Bossuet, "La providence divine," and "La divine providence," in *Œuvres complètes de Bossuet* (Bar-le-Duc: Louis Guérin, 1870), 2: 259–66, 537–47.

Patrick Riley has suggested that Bossuet developed his more particularistic theory of Providence only later in his life in his debates with Malebranche. Riley's introduction to *Malebranche's Treatise on Nature and Grace,* by Nicholas Malebranche (Oxford: Clarendon Press, 1992), 68–69. As evidence for his claim, Riley cites a passage from "La providence divine" in which Bossuet calls upon human beings to scorn the "particular" and embrace the "whole." Yet Bossuet's advice to human beings surely must be distinguished from his understanding of the nature of divine Providence. Moreover, in this same sermon, Bossuet asserted: God "does not conduct with less care the uneven accidents that entangle the life of individuals, than these great and memorable events that decide the fortune of empires" ("La providence divine," 260). He continued: "From the greatest to the most petite, his Providence spreads throughout" (262). Although Bossuet's confrontation with Malebranche may have sharpened his "particularist" theory of Providence, he already subscribed to this theory at least in inchoate form in his early sermons.

73. My discussion of Bossuet's debate with Malebranche is much indebted to Riley's introduction to Bossuet's *Politics Drawn from Holy Scripture* and his introduction to *Malebranche's Treatise on Nature and Grace.*

74. Malebranche, *Treatise on Nature and Grace,* 195.

75. Malebranche, *Treatise on Nature and Grace,* 196.

76. Malebranche, *Treatise on Nature and Grace,* 210–11.

77. Riley, *Politics Drawn from Holy Scripture,* xxiv.

78. Bossuet, "Oraison funèbre de Marie-Thérèse d'Autriche," in *Œuvres complètes,* 1: 447.

79. Bossuet, "Traité du libre arbitre," in *Œuvres complètes,* 8: 17.

80. Bossuet, "Lettre à Marquis d'Allemans," in *Correspondance de Bossuet* (Paris: Librairie Hachette, 1910), 3: 377–78.

81. All citations from Bossuet's *Discourse* (D) appear in the main body of the text and are taken from Bossuet, *Discourse on Universal History,* ed. Orest Ranum, trans. Elborg Forster (Chicago: University of Chicago Press, 1976).

82. In order to explain the apparent anomaly of the Jewish religion's continued existence in the Christian epoch, Bossuet explained: "But as they are one day to return to that Messiah whom they have disowned, and as the God of Abraham has not yet exhausted his mercies toward that patriarch race, despite its faithlessness, he has found a means, unprecedented in the world, to preserve the Jews outside their country and in their ruin, even longer than the nations that have conquered them" (D, 206).

83. Bossuet, "Histoire des variations des églises protestantes," in *Œuvres complètes,* 4: 719.

84. Bossuet, *Histoire des variations,* 4: 410; and "Lettre à Marquis d'Allemans," *Correspondance de Bossuet,* 3: 372–73.

85. All citations from Bossuet's *Politique* (P) appearing in the body of the text are taken from *Politics Drawn from the Very Words of Holy Scripture,* trans. Patrick Riley (Cambridge: Cambridge University Press, 1990).

86. In the *Discours,* Bossuet referred to political societies almost exclusively in terms of "empires." By contrast, in his *Politique,* he referred to political societies in terms of "States"—a term that he as well as Louis XIV always capitalized.

87. Quentin Skinner has observed that Bossuet's method was, paradoxically enough, based upon the "typically Lutheran assumption that all political principles must be derived from the pages of the Bible." *The Foundations of Modern Political Thought* (Cambridge: Cambridge University Press, 1978), 2: 113.

88. Jacques Truchet has observed that "it has not been sufficiently noticed

[that] this politics 'drawn from the very words of holy Scripture' is drawn essentially from [the books] of the Old Testament. Not that the author wanted to limit himself to it; but the Old Testament presents a series of historical books, as well as a mass of precepts touching on institutions, justice, government, war, etc., while the New offers only a few such texts to be considered." Jacques-Bénigne Bossuet, *La politique de Bossuet,* ed. Jacques Truchet (Paris: Armand Colin, 1966), 29.

89. Adrian Hastings has suggested that the idea of the Israelite nation of the Old Testament provided the model for the development of modern nationalism. *The Construction of Nationhood* (Cambridge: Cambridge University Press, 1997), 185–209.

90. In a letter addressed to Louis XIV, Bossuet wrote: "In proposing to oneself the good of the State for the end of one's actions, one practices the love of one's neighbor in the highest [*souverain*] degree, since in the good of the State is comprised the good and peace of an infinity of people." Bossuet, *Politique de Bossuet,* 293.

91. See also the discussion in chapter 3 of Naudé's use of this passage to justify reason of state.

92. So closely connected did Bossuet see "Church" and "State" that in his *Défense de la déclaration de l'assemblée du clergé de France* he felt compelled to pose the question: "But one will ask, if God is equally author of the sacerdotal and royal power, what is the difference between them?" He identified four main differences between the Church and State: (1) God directly established the Church through Christ but only generally established states; (2) God directly intervened in Church ceremonies such as the sacraments and consecration of priests, but did not intervene in state ceremonies; (3) God conjoined the true religion to the Church while he allowed states to adopt a variety of different religions; and (4) God explicitly chose the form of Church government but allowed states to adopt a variety of different forms of government. Aside from these institutional differences, Bossuet considered the Church and state to be essentially similar institutions. Bossuet, *Défense de la déclaration de l'assemblée du clergé de France,* trans. from Latin into French (Amsterdam, 1745), 1: 172.

93. Riley inserts here "[public] affairs." I have dropped the bracketed "public" because it is not clear that Bossuet meant to limit his meaning in this way.

94. Gordon Schochet, *Patriarchalism in Political Thought* (New York: Basic Books, 1975), 18–53.

95. Filmer's ideas are discussed in the next chapter.

96. For a discussion of the development of the more particularized care-taking functions of government, see Foucault, "Omnes et Singulatim."

97. King observed that "Bishop Bossuet pretended no difficulty in extracting from the Bible . . . a number of notions then common to mercantilist thought." *Science and Rationalism in the Government of Louis XIV,* 47.

98. Bossuet, *Politique de Bossuet,* 295–96.

99. See, for example, the sermons in Bossuet's *Politique de Bossuet,* 214–22, 247–53.

100. I have provided my own translation of this difficult passage. The original French reads: "Le prince est donc par sa charge à chaque particulier, 'un abri pour se mettre à couvert du vent et de la tempête, et un rocher avancé sous lequel il se met à l'ombre dans une terre sèche et brûlante.'"

101. Keohane, *Philosophy and the State in France,* 258.

102. Riley, *Politics Drawn from Holy Scripture,* lvi–lvii.

103. The most detailed study of the critics of Louis XIV's reign is Rothkrug, *Opposition to Louis XIV.* See also the brief but acute analysis of Keohane, *Philosophy and the State in France,* 312–57. The perpetuation of these criticisms into the eigh-

teenth century is studied in Jeffrey Merrick, *The Desacralization of the French Monarchy in the Eighteenth Century* (Baton Rouge: Louisiana State University Press, 1990).

104. *Les caractères* was first published in 1688 but was repeatedly revised, expanded, and reissued until La Bruyère's death in 1694.

105. Jean de La Bruyère, *Les caractères*, in *Œuvres complètes*, ed. Julien Benda (Paris: Gallimard, 1951), 282–83.

106. Bruyère, *Les caractères*, 286–88.

107. Foucault, *Discipline and Punish*, 78–80.

108. Foucault, *Discipline and Punish*, 128.

109. Commenting upon Louis XV's more discreet approach to governing, Smith has noted, "The systematic elaboration of personal government in the eighteenth century had made the prince's power so relentlessly impersonal that Louis XV understandably came to view the functioning of the monarchy and his own personal identity as being quite distinct." *Culture of Merit*, 237.

110. On the "ideology of expertism," "myth of impartiality," and "idea of the universalist state," see Young, *Justice and the Politics of Difference*, 66–121.

111. G. W. F. Hegel, *Elements of the Philosophy of Right*, ed. Allen Wood, trans. H. B. Nisbit (Cambridge: Cambridge University Press, 1991), 261–70.

112. Young, *Justice and the Politics of Difference*, 96–121.

113. Young, *Justice and the Politics of Difference*, 114.

CHAPTER 5: ENGLISH STATE THEORY

1. Johann Sommerville, *Royalists and Patriots: Politics and Ideology in England, 1603–1640* (New York: Longman, 1999); J. G. A. Pocock, Gordon Schochet, and Lois Schwoerer, eds., *The Varieties of British Political Thought, 1500–1800* (Cambridge: Cambridge University Press, 1993); Nicolas Phillipson and Quentin Skinner, eds., *Political Discourse in Early Modern Britain* (Cambridge: Cambridge University Press, 1993).

2. Johann Sommerville, *Politics and Ideology in England, 1603–1640* (New York: Longman, 1986). This work was revised and republished in a second edition as *Royalists and Patriots*, cited in the note above. My citations are all from the second edition of this work.

3. These points are discussed in the final historiographical chapter of Sommerville, *Royalists and Patriots*, 224–65. Important opponents to his views include Conrad Russell, *Unrevolutionary England* (London: Hambledon Press, 1990); Conrad Russell, *The Causes of the English Civil War* (Oxford: Clarendon Press, 1990); Glenn Burgess, *Absolute Monarchy and the Stuart Constitution* (New Haven: Yale University Press, 1996); Glenn Burgess, *The Politics of the Ancient Constitution: An Introduction to English Political Thought, 1603–1642* (University Park: Pennsylvania State University Press, 1992); Paul Christianson, "Royal and Parliamentary Voices on the Ancient Constitution, c.1604–1621," in *The Mental World of the Jacobean Court*, ed. Linda Levy Peck (Cambridge: Cambridge University Press, 1991), 71–95; Paul Christianson, *Discourse on History, Law, and Governance in the Public Career of John Selden, 1610–1635* (Toronto: University of Toronto Press, 1996); Kevin Sharpe, *The Personal Rule of Charles I* (New Haven: Yale University Press, 1992).

4. Sommerville, *Royalists and Patriots*, 15–20, 52–54.

5. On this point, see especially Johann Sommerville, "English and European Political Ideas in the Seventeenth Century: Revisionism and the Case of Absolutism," *Journal of British Studies* 35 (1996): 168–94. On the influence of French political thought on English ideas generally, see J. H. M. Salmon, *The French Religious Wars in English Political Thought* (Oxford: Oxford University Press, 1959).

6. Sommerville, introduction to King James VI and I, *Political Writings* (Cambridge: Cambridge University Press, 1994), xxviii.

7. James Daly, *Sir Robert Filmer and English Political Thought* (Toronto: University of Toronto Press, 1979), 21–22.

8. Quentin Skinner, "Thomas Hobbes and His Disciples in France and England," *Comparative Studies in Society and History* 8 (1966): 153–67; Quentin Skinner, *Reason and Rhetoric in the Philosophy of Hobbes* (Cambridge: Cambridge University Press, 1996), 426–37; Richard Tuck, *Philosophy and Government, 1572–1651* (Cambridge: Cambridge University Press, 1993), 279–345.

9. Sommerville, *Royalists and Patriots,* 9–54.

10. Stephen Collins, *From Divine Cosmos to Sovereign State* (Oxford: Oxford University Press, 1989).

11. Sommerville, "English and European Political Ideas in the Seventeenth Century," 168–73.

12. Collins, *From Divine Cosmos to Sovereign State,* 14–28; Daly, *Cosmic Harmony;* Robert Eccleshall, *Order and Reason in Politics* (Oxford: Oxford University Press, 1978); W. H. Greenleaf, *Order, Empiricism, and Politics* (London: Oxford University Press, 1964), 14–26; Whitney Jones, *The Tudor Commonwealth, 1529–1559* (London: Athlone, 1970); Donald R. Kelley, "Elizabethan Political Thought," in *The Varieties of British Political Thought, 1500–1800,* ed. Pocock, Schochet, and Schwoerer, 47–79; E. M. W. Tillyard, *The Elizabethan World Picture* (London: Chatto and Windus, 1943).

13. John Aylmer, *An Harborowe for Faithful and Trew Servants* (London, 1559). Quoted from Collins, *From Divine Cosmos to Sovereign State,* 16. I have modernized the spelling.

14. Aylmer, *Harborowe.* Quoted from Collins, *From Divine Cosmos to Sovereign State,* 17.

15. *Homilies* (London, 1817). Quoted from Collins, *From Divine Cosmos to Sovereign State,* 18–19.

16. Kelley, "Elizabethan Political Thought," 67–72. Pocock, *Ancient Constitution and the Feudal Law;* Pocock, *Machiavellian Moment,* 9–20.

17. The flexibility and dynamism of Tudor political thought is especially stressed by Collins, *From Divine Cosmos to Sovereign State,* 71–108. See also Eccleshall, *Order and Reason in Politics;* Kelley, "Elizabethan Political Thought."

18. Hooker's response to the Puritans is especially well handled by Eccleshall, *Order and Reason in Politics,* 126–50. Robert Faulkner stressed the degree to which Hooker's work was a response to the growing power of the monarchy. *Richard Hooker and the Politics of Christian England* (Berkeley: University of California Press, 1981), 151–84.

19. Richard Hooker, *Of the Laws of Ecclesiastical Polity,* in *The Folger Library Edition of the Works of Richard Hooker,* ed. W. Speed Hill (Cambridge: Harvard University Press, 1977), 1:58. All citations are given in the text with the abbreviation LEP. I have modernized the spelling.

20. Eccleshall, *Order and Reason in Politics,* 133.

21. Arthur Ferguson, "The Historical Perspective of Richard Hooker: A Renaissance Paradox," *Journal of Medieval and Renaissance Studies* 3 (1973): 19.

22. Eccleshall, *Order and Reason in Politics,* 134–50.

23. St. Thomas Aquinas, *On Politics and Ethics,* trans. Paul Sigmund (New York: Norton, 1988), 15.

24. W. D. J. Cargill Thompson, "The Philosopher of the 'Politic Society': Richard Hooker as a Political Thinker," in *Studies in Richard Hooker,* ed. W. Speed Hill

(Cleveland: Press of Case Western Reserve University, 1972), 47–50.

25. See more generally Eccleshall, *Order and Reason in Politics,* 144–48.

26. Thompson, "Philosopher of the 'Politic Society.'" 49.

27. Thompson, "Philosopher of the 'Politic Society,'" 57.

28. Thompson, "Philosopher of the 'Politic Society,'" 60–61.

29. Collins, *From Divine Cosmos to Sovereign State,* 28–70, 114–48; Daly, *Cosmic Harmony,* 31–38; Greenleaf, *Order, Empiricism, and Politics,* 26–32, 142–56.

30. Richard Barckley, *A Discourse of the Felicitie of Man* (London, 1598). Quoted from Greenleaf, *Order, Empiricism, and Politics,* 27. I have modernized the spelling.

31. John Donne, "An Anatomy of the World," in *Complete English Poems,* Patrides, 335. I have modernized the spelling.

32. See especially Pocock, *Machiavellian Moment,* 333–400. For an account of classical republican thought in England prior to the Civil War, see Markku Peltonen, *Classical Humanism and Republicanism in English Political Thought, 1570–1640* (Cambridge: Cambridge University Press, 1995).

33. Johann Sommerville, "Richard Hooker, Hadrian Saravia, and the Advent of the Divine Right of Kings," *History of Political Thought* 4 (1983): 229–45.

34. Greenleaf, *Order, Empiricism, and Politics,* 59, 67.

35. *A Speach to the Lords and Commons of the Parliament, March 21, 1610,* in King James VI and I, *Political Writings,* 181. All citations are given in the text with the abbreviation *Speach, 1610.* I have modernized the spellings of James I's speeches and writings.

36. Greenleaf, *Order, Empiricism, and Politics,* 60–64.

37. Francis Oakley, *Omnipotence, Covenant, and Order: An Excursion in the History of Ideas from Abelard to Leibniz* (Ithaca: Cornell University Press, 1984), 93–118.

38. *A Speach in the Parliament House, November 9, 1605,* in James VI and I, *Political Writings,* 147. Sommerville has stressed the importance of direct divine right theory to absolutist thought. *Royalists and Patriots,* 10–11 n.1, 35–36.

39. Eccleshall, *Order and Reason in Politics,* 76–96.

40. *A Speach in the Starre-Chamber, June 20, 1616,* in James VI and I, *Political Writings,* 205–6. All citations are given in the text with the abbreviation *Speach, 1616.*

41. Johann Sommerville, "James I and the Divine Right of Kings: English Politics and Continental Theory," in *Mental World of the Jacobean Court,* ed. Peck), 65–67.

42. James I, *The Trew Law of Free Monarchies,* in *Political Writings,* 79.

43. Christianson, "Royal and Parliamentary Voices," 72–78. For a similar view, see Burgess, *Absolute Monarchy and the Stuart Constitution,* 40–43.

44. See especially his *Meditation upon the 27th, 28th and 29th Verses of the 27th Chapter of Saint Matthew; or, A Patterne for a Kings Inauguration,* in *Political Writings,* 229–49.

45. James I, *Basilicon Doron,* in *Political Writings,* 12–49.

46. James I, *Basilicon Doron,* in *Political Writings,* 45.

47. James I, *Trew Law,* in *Political Writings,* 75.

48. Christianson, "Royal and Parliamentary Voices," 77–78.

49. James I, *Trew Law,* in *Political Writings,* 65.

50. Greenleaf, *Order, Empiricism, and Politics,* 89.

51. Gordon Schochet, *Patriarchalism in Political Thought* (Oxford: Basil Blackwell, 1975); Daly, *Sir Robert Filmer.*

52. Schochet developed this classificatory schema. Daly modified and clarified it. I follow Daly in defining Schochet's second category, "moral" patriachalism, in a more narrow sense as "analogical" patriarchalism. See Schochet, *Patriarchalism,* 10–17; Daly, *Sir Robert Filmer,* 71 n.49.

53. Schochet, *Patriarchalism,* 16, 18–53.

54. Schochet, *Patriarchalism,* 54–64.

55. Daly, *Sir Robert Filmer,* 34. Schochet nonetheless asserted that ideological patriarchalism "presupposed the chain of being." He even supplied a quotation in which Filmer appears to endorse the traditional idea of an immanent chain of being. *Patriarchalism,* 86, 145. The quotation, however, comes from a text, *A Discourse concerning Supreme Power and Common Right,* that is usually attributed to Sir John Monson. Schochet laid out his reasons for attributing this work to Filmer in "Sir Robert Filmer: Some New Bibliographical Discoveries," in *The Library,* 5th ser., 26 (1971): 135–60. Daly challenged Schochet's conclusions in *Sir Robert Filmer,* app. B, 194–98. The standard opinion today is that the *Discourse* was not written by Filmer. Johann Sommerville, introduction to *Patriarcha and Other Writings,* by Sir Robert Filmer (Cambridge: Cambridge University Press, 1991), xxx, xxxvi. My argument contributes to this debate in that it demonstrates the whole "chain of being" manner of thinking evident in the *Discourse* to be contrary to Filmer's cosmological presuppositions. This point further weighs against Filmer's authorship.

56. Schochet, *Patriarchalism,* 144; Daly, *Sir Robert Filmer,* 57–58.

57. Sir Robert Filmer, *Patriarcha,* in *Patriarcha and Other Writings,* 6–7. All citations are given in the text with the abbreviation P.

58. Filmer slightly revised his position on this matter after 1649. See Schochet, *Patriarchalism,* 157–58.

59. Sir Robert Filmer, *Observations upon Aristotles Politiques,* in *Patriarcha and Other Writings,* 255–56. All citations are given in the text with the abbreviation AP.

60. Sir Robert Filmer, *The Anarchy of a Limited or Mixed Monarchy,* in *Patriarcha and Other Writings,* 132. All citations are given in the text with the abbreviation A.

61. Sir Robert Filmer, *The Freeholders Grand Inquest,* in *Patriarcha and Other Writings,* 99.

62. For discussions of these criticisms, see J. W. Allen, "Sir Robert Filmer," in *The Social and Political Ideas of Some English Thinkers in the Augustan Age,* ed. F. J. C. Hearnshaw (London: G. G. Harrap, 1928), 32–38; Daly, *Sir Robert Filmer,* 82–103; Schochet, *Patriarchalism,* 115–35.

63. John Locke, *Two Treatises of Government,* ed. Peter Laslett (Cambridge: Cambridge University Press, 1988),156–61. All citations are given in the text with the abbreviation TT.

64. Norberto Bobbio, *Thomas Hobbes and the Natural Law Tradition,* trans. Daniela Gobetti (Chicago: University of Chicago Press, 1993), xii. Others who have expressed similar views include David Gauthier, *The Logic of "Leviathan": The Moral and Political Theory of Thomas Hobbes* (Oxford: Clarendon Press, 1969), 206; M. M. Goldsmith, *Hobbes's Science of Politics* (New York: Columbia University Press, 1966), 214–27; Michael Oakeshott, "Introduction to 'Leviathan,'" in *Rationalism in Politics and Other Essays,* ed. Timothy Fuller (Indianapolis: Liberty Press, 1991), 221–94; Richard Peters, *Hobbes* (Baltimore: Penguin Books, 1956), 225–48; Leo Strauss, *The Political Philosophy of Hobbes: Its Basis and Its Genesis,* trans. Elsa M. Sinclair (Chicago: University of Chicago Press, 1952), 59–78.

65. A. E. Taylor, "The Ethical Doctrine of Hobbes," *Philosophy* 13 (1938): 406–24; Howard Warrender, *The Political Philosophy of Hobbes: His Theory of Obligation* (Oxford: Clarendon Press, 1957). I discuss this interpretation in more detail below. Others who have argued that there exists an important theological dimension to Hobbes's thought include F. C. Hood, *The Divine Politics of Thomas Hobbes: An Interpretation of "Leviathan"* (Oxford: Clarendon Press, 1964); Tracy Strong, "How to Write Scripture: Words, Authority, and Politics in Thomas Hobbes," *Critical Inquiry* 20 (autumn 1993): 128–59;

Joshua Mitchell, "Hobbes and the Equality of All under One," *Political Theory* 21 (February 1993): 78–100; A. P. Martinich, *The Two Gods of "Leviathan": Thomas Hobbes on Religion and Politics* (Cambridge: Cambridge University Press, 1992). Martinich also proposed revisions to the Taylor-Warrender thesis in *Two Gods of "Leviathan,"* 71–135.

66. John Figgis emphasized in this regard the similarity between divine right and natural right theories: "Whether the theory be one of Divine Right in the older sense, or of natural rights as a proof of Divine sanction, the motives which lead men to adopt it are the same. It is the desire to find some immutable basis for politics and to lift them above considerations of mere expediency, that prompts men to elaborate systems of Divine or natural rights. They are haunted with the hope of finding a universal system, superior to time and circumstance, untrammeled by considerations of historical development or national idiosyncrasy." *The Divine Right of Kings* (Bristol: Thoemmes Press, 1994), 153.

67. All citations in this chapter to Hobbes's works are given in the body of the text. The capital letter designates the work, the Roman number designates the chapter, and the Arabic number is the page number. All citations from *Leviathan* (L), are from *Leviathan,* ed. Curley. For *De Homine* (DH), I have used the translation from Bernard Gert's edition, *Thomas Hobbes, Man and Citizen* (Indianapolis: Hackett, 1972). All other references are taken from *The English Works of Thomas Hobbes,* 11 vols., ed. Sir William Molesworth (London: John Bohn, 1966). The abbreviations and volume numbers for these works are as follows: *Elements of Philosophy,* volume 1 (EP); *De Cive,* volume 2 (DC); *Elements of Law,* volume 4 (EL); *Behemoth,* volume 6 (B).

68. Richard Tuck, "Hobbes and Descartes," in *Perspectives on Thomas Hobbes,* ed. G. A. J. Rogers and Alan Ryan (Oxford: Clarendon Press, 1988), 11–41. See also his *Philosophy and Government,* 279–348. I do not follow Tuck in all the particulars of his thesis. Skinner has recently suggested that Hobbes was reacting not to the problems posed by epistemological skeptics, as Tuck suggested, but rather to the skepticism that arose in the humanist tradition during the sixteenth and seventeenth centuries as a result of the *in utramque partem* method. Skinner, *Reason and Rhetoric in the Philosophy of Hobbes,* 8–10.

69. Strong, "How to Write Scripture," 143.

70. The "self" was of course only one of the sources of "nature" in Montaigne's philosophy. See Zachary Sayre Schiffman, *On the Threshold of Modernity* (Baltimore: Johns Hopkins University Press, 1991), 53–77.

71. Pierre Charron, *Of Wisdom,* trans. Samson Lennard (New York: Da Capo Press, 1971), 2.

72. Paul Grendler, "Pierre Charron: Precursor to Hobbes," *Review of Politics* 25 (1963): 212–24.

73. S. A. Lloyd has based her whole case for the logical incoherence of *Leviathan* upon the assumption that Hobbes could not possibly have deduced all the various attributes of human beings from the principle of self-preservation narrowly understood. *Ideals as Interests in Hobbes's "Leviathan": The Power of Mind over Matter* (Cambridge: Cambridge University Press, 1992), 1–47. Others who have interpreted Hobbes's account of self-preservation in terms of narrow self-interest include Gauthier, *The Logic of "Leviathan"*; Jean Hampton, *Hobbes and the Social Contract Tradition* (Cambridge: Cambridge University Press, 1986); and C. B. Macpherson, *The Political Theory of Possessive Individualism: Hobbes to Locke* (Oxford: Oxford University Press, 1962).

74. See also Hobbes's *The English Works of Thomas Hobbes, Elements of Law,* xvii, 109; *De Homine,* xi, 48; and *Leviathan,* xvii, xix, 106–7, 124.

75. Macpherson, *The Political Theory of Possessive Individualism Hobbes,* 34–46.

76. Hence Hobbes's definition of power: "The power of a man (to take it

universally) is his present means to obtain some future apparent good" (L, x, 50).

77. Hobbes carefully distinguished his own theistic religious beliefs from anxiety-based religions. Knowledge of God as the "one first mover," he wrote, "may more easily be derived from the desire men have to know the causes of natural bodies, and their several virtues and operations, than from the fear of what was to befall them in time to come" (L, xii, 64).

78. Johann Sommerville, *Thomas Hobbes: Political Ideas in Historical Context* (New York: St. Martin's Press, 1992), 47–51.

79. St. Thomas Aquinas, *Summa Theologiae* (New York: McGraw-Hill, 1966), I–II, 94, 4.

80. Jean Hampton, *Hobbes and the Social Contract Tradition* (Cambridge: Cambridge University Press, 1986), 42–51.

81. Taylor, "Ethical Doctrine of Hobbes."

82. Sommerville, *Thomas Hobbes,* 48–51.

83. Thompson, "Philosopher of the 'Politic Society,'" 35–50.

84. Filmer nonetheless criticized Hobbes for associating the origin and legitimacy of the state with consent. See "Observations concerning the Originall of Government," in *Patriarcha and Other Writings,* 184–97.

85. See Hobbes, *Leviathan,* 142n.22.

86. My argument here departs from the views of Norberto Bobbio. Bobbio has argued that the natural law served the sole purpose in Hobbes's political theory of providing a fundamental norm, or ground of legitimacy, for his legal system. Otherwise, he has claimed it did nothing to restrain the scope of the sovereign's positive legislative powers. Bobbio, *Thomas Hobbes and the Natural Law Tradition,* 114–71.

87. Carole Pateman, *The Sexual Contract* (Stanford: Stanford University Press, 1988).

88. Carl Schmitt, *The Leviathan in the State Theory of Thomas Hobbes* (Westport, Conn.: Greenwood Press, 1996), 32.

89. J. G. A. Pocock, "Time, History and Eschatology in the Thought of Thomas Hobbes," in *Politics, Language and Time: Essays on Political Thought and History* (Chicago: University of Chicago Press, 1989), 160.

90. In addition to the works cited below, recent works that have devoted significant attention to Hobbes's religious thought include Eldon Eisenach, "Hobbes on Church, State and Religion," *History of Political Thought* 3 (summer 1982): 215–43; R. J. Halliday, Timothy Kenyon, and Andrew Reeve, "Hobbes's Belief in God," *Political Studies* 31 (1983): 418–32; Patricia Springborg, "*Leviathan* and the Problem of Ecclesiastical Authority," *Political Theory* 3 (August 1975): 289–303.

91. A. P. Martinich's work is devoted to demonstrating that "Hobbes was a sincere, and relatively orthodox, Christian." *Two Gods of "Leviathan,"* 1. For the view that Hobbes was probably an atheist, see Edwin Curley, "'I Durst Not Write So Boldly'; or, How to Read Hobbes' Theological-Political Treatise," in *Hobbes e Spinoza, Scienza e politica,* ed. Daniela Bostrenghi (Naples: Bibliopolis, 1992), 497–593. See also Richard Tuck, "The Christian Atheism of Thomas Hobbes," in *Atheism from the Reformation to the Enlightenment,* ed. David Wooten (Oxford: Clarendon Press, 1992), 111–30; and Paul Cooke, *Hobbes and Christianity* (Lanham, Md.: Rowman and Littlefield, 1996).

92. Pocock has written, "The only recourse open to the historian is to examine, not Hobbes's sincerity of conviction, but the effects which his words seem designed to produce." *Politics, Language and Time,* 162.

93. David Johnston, *The Rhetoric of "Leviathan": Thomas Hobbes and the Politics of Cultural Transformation* (Princeton: Princeton University Press, 1986), 137, 129,

passim. For Johnston's criticism of Pocock, see 117–20. See also Johnston's, "Hobbes's Mortalism," *History of Political Thought* 10 (winter 1989): 647–63.

94. Lloyd, *Ideals as Interests in Hobbes's "Leviathan"*, 106–7. For Lloyd's criticism of Johnston, see 345–47n.12.

95. Curley has noted that Luther and Calvin claimed God was justified in condemning the wicked to damnation since all human beings were sufficiently evil to deserve this fate. *Leviathan*, 236–37n.6.

96. Sommerville, *Thomas Hobbes*, 105–7.

97. This point reflects Hobbes's belief that there was no contradiction between Christian beliefs and the new empirical science of the seventeenth century (L, xlvi, 468). Martinich has emphasized Hobbes's desire to reconcile Christianity with science in his *Two Gods of "Leviathan"*, 336–37, passim.

98. Johnston, *Rhetoric of "Leviathan,"* 162–63; Cooke, *Hobbes and Christianity*, 133–54.

99. Innocent III, *Patrologiae Latina*, vol. 217, ed. J. P. Migne (Paris, 1890), 657–58.

100. On these points, see Pocock, *Politics, Language and Time*, 180–81, 197–98; and Sommerville, *Thomas Hobbes*, 119–27.

101. Charles Tarlton, "The Creation and Maintenance of Government: A Neglected Dimension of Hobbes's *Leviathan*," *Political Studies* 26 (1978): 307–27; Eldon Eisenach, *Two Worlds of Liberalism: Religion and Politics in Hobbes, Locke, and Mill* (Chicago: University of Chicago Press, 1981), 13–71; Eisenach, "Hobbes on Church, State and Religion."

102. Johnston, *Rhetoric of "Leviathan,"* 110–13.

103. John Locke, *Two Tracts on Government*, ed. Philip Abrams (London: Cambridge University Press, 1967). Abrams has given these early writings their title.

104. Locke, *Two Tracts*, 122–23.

105. Locke, *Two Tracts*, 124–25.

106. Locke, *Two Tracts*, 158. Locke similarly argued in a Hobbesian vein that the want of sovereign power was more dangerous than the threat of tyranny. "To fight to support greatness and a dominion over himself, and rob his own necessities to maintain the pomp and pleasure of one that regards him not, to hold his life as a tenant at will and to be ready to part with his head when it shall be demanded, these and many more such are the disadvantages of government, yet far less than are to be found in its absence as no peace, no security, no enjoyments, enmity with all men and safe possession of nothing, and those stinging swarms of miseries that attend anarchy and rebellion" (156).

107. Locke, *Two Tracts*, 121.

108. Leo Strauss, *Natural Right and History* (Chicago: University of Chicago Press, 1950), 202–51.

109. John Dunn, *The Political Thought of John Locke* (Cambridge: Cambridge University Press, 1969), 96–119.

110. Dunn, *Political Thought of John Locke*, 161, 163.

111. Hanna Pitkin, "Obligation and Consent, I," *American Political Science Review* 59 (1965): 995.

112. Julian Franklin, "Allegiance and Jurisdiction in Locke's Doctrine of Tacit Consent," *Political Theory* 24 (1996): 407–22.

113. Dunn, *Political Thought of John Locke*, 143.

114. Pitkin, "Obligation and Consent, I," 990–99; Hanna Pitkin, "Obligation and Consent, II," *American Political Science Review* 60 (1966): 39–52; Carole Pateman, *The*

Problem of Political Obligation (New York: John Wiley and Sons, 1979); A. John Simmons, *Moral Principles and Political Obligations* (Princeton: Princeton University Press, 1979).

115. Figgis, *Divine Right of Kings,* 258.

116. A. John Simmons has demonstrated the incoherence not only of consent theory in justifying the powers of the state, but also of theories of utility, fairness, justice, and gratitude. *Moral Principles and Political Obligation.*

CONCLUSION

1. Carl Schmitt, *Political Theology: Four Chapters on the Concept of Sovereignty,* trans. George Schwab (Cambridge: MIT Press, 1985), 36.

2. Carl Schmitt, *Politische Theologie II* (Berlin: Duncken and Humboldt, 1970), 101n. Quoted from Hans Blumenberg, *The Legitimacy of the Modern Age,* trans. Robert M. Wallace (Cambridge: MIT Press, 1983), 94.

3. Schmitt, *Political Theology,* 46.

4. Blumenberg, *Legitimacy of the Modern Age,* 94.

5. Kahn, *Machiavellian Rhetoric,* 6–12.

6. Paul Monod, *The Power of Kings: Monarchy and Religion in Europe, 1589–1715* (New Haven: Yale University Press, 1999).

7. Rousseau, *On the Social Contract,* 59.

8. Hence Rousseau's comment that the English people "is free only during the election of the members of Parliament. As soon as they are elected, it is a slave, it is nothing," *Social Contract,* 102.

9. For a contemporary discussion of these same themes, see Carole Pateman, *The Problem of Political Obligation* (New York: John Wiley and Sons, 1979).

10. Rousseau, *Social Contract,* 59.

11. Jeremy Bentham, *A Fragment on Government,* ed. J. H. Burns and H. L. A. Hart (Cambridge: Cambridge University Press, 1988). David Hume, *Essays: Moral, Political and Literary,* ed. Eugene Miller (Indianapolis: Liberty Fund, 1985).

12. Hume, *Essays,* III, 12, 465–87.

13. Hume, *Essays,* III, 12, 475.

14. Hume, *Essays,* III, 12, 480.

15. The literature is enormous. The most comprehensive treatment of the topic is Manuel Castells, *The Information Age: Economy, Society and Culture,* 3 vols. (Oxford: Blackwell, 1996–1998). Other important works include Maryann Cusimano, ed., *Beyond Sovereignty: Issues for a Global Agenda* (New York: St. Martin's Press, 1998); Jean-Marie Guéhenno, *The End of the Nation-State,* trans. Victoria Elliott (Minneapolis: University of Minnesota Press, 1995); David Jacobson, *Rights across Borders* (Baltimore: Johns Hopkins University Press, 1996); Kenichi Ohmae, *The End of the Nation State* (New York: Free Press, 1995); Robert Reich, *The Work of Nations* (New York: Vintage Books, 1992); J. Rosenau, *Turbulence in World Politics* (Brighton: Harvester Wheatsheaf, 1990); Susanne Hoeber Rudolph and James Piscatori, eds., *Transnational Religion and Fading States* (Boulder: Westview Press, 1997).

16. Walker, *Inside/Outside,* 1.

17. Walker, *Inside/Outside,* 14.

18. Young, *Justice and the Politics of Difference.*

19. Young, *Justice and the Politics of Difference,* 96–121.

20. Young, *Justice and the Politics of Difference,* 114.

Works Cited

PRIMARY TEXTS

Aquinas, St. Thomas. *On Politics and Ethics*. Translated by Paul Sigmund. New York: Norton, 1988.

———. *Summa Theologiae*. New York: McGraw-Hill, 1966.

Aristotle. *Nicomachean Ethics*. Translated by Terence Irwin. Indianapolis: Hackett, 1985.

———. *The Politics*. Translated by Ernest Barker. Edited by R. F. Stalley. Oxford: Oxford University Press, 1995.

Balzac, Jean Louis Guez de. *Œuvres*. Paris, 1665.

———. *Le prince*. 2d ed. Paris, 1632.

Bentham, Jeremy. *A Fragment on Government*. Edited by J.H. Burns and H.L.A. Hart. Cambridge: Cambridge University Press, 1988.

Bodin, Jean. *Colloquium of the Seven about Secrets of the Sublime*. Translated by Marion L. D. Kuntz. Princeton: Princeton University Press, 1975.

———. *Exposé du droit universel/Juris universi distributio*. Translated into French by Lucien Jerphagnon. Paris: Presses Universitaires de France, 1985.

———. *Io. Bodini . . . De republica libri sex, Latine ab autore redditi, multo quam antea locupletiores*. Paris, 1586.

———. *Method for the Easy Comprehension of History*. Translated by Beatrice Reynolds. New York: Columbia University Press, 1945.

———. *Œuvres philosophiques de Jean Bodin*. Edited by Pierre Mesnard. Paris: Presses Universitaires de France, 1951.

———. *On the Demon-Mania of Witches*. Translated by Randy Scott. Toronto: Centre for Reformation and Renaissance Studies, 1995.

———. *Paradoxon*. Paris, 1596.

———. *The Six Bookes of a Commonweale*. Edited by Kenneth McRae. Translated by Richard Knolles. Cambridge: Harvard University Press, 1962.

———. *Les six livres de la république*. Paris, 1583. Reprint. Aalen: Scientia, 1961.

———. *On Sovereignty*. Edited by Julian Franklin. Cambridge: Cambridge University Press, 1992.

———. *Universae Naturae Theatrum*. Paris, 1596.

Bossuet, Jacques-Bénigne. *Correspondance de Bossuet*. 15 vols. Paris: Librairie Hachette, 1910.

———. *Défense de la déclaration de l'assemblée du clergé de France*. Translated from Latin into French. Amsterdam, 1745.

——. *Discourse on Universal History.* Edited by Orest Ranum. Translated by Elborg Forster. Chicago: University of Chicago Press, 1976.

——. *Œuvres complètes de Bossuet.* 12 vols. Bar-le-Duc: Louis Guérin, 1870.

——. *Œuvres oratoires.* Edited by J. Lebarq, C. Urbain, and E. Levesque. Vol. 1. Paris: Desclée, de Brouwer, 1914.

——. *Politics Drawn from the Very Words of Holy Scripture.* Translated by Patrick Riley. Cambridge: Cambridge University Press, 1990.

——. *La politique de Bossuet.* Edited by Jacques Truchet. Paris: Armand Colin, 1966.

——. *Politique tirée des propres paroles de l'Ecriture sainte.* Edited by Jacque Le Brun. Genève: Librairie Droz, 1967.

Botero, Giovanni. *The Reason of State.* Translated by P. J. Waley and D. P. Waley. London: Routledge and Kegan Paul, 1956.

Charron, Pierre. *Of Wisdom.* Translated by Samson Lennard. New York: Da Capo Press, 1971.

Colbert, Jean-Baptiste. *Lettres, instructions et mémoires.* Edited by Pierre Clement. Paris: Imprimerie Imperiale, 1867.

Donne, John. *The Complete English Poems of John Donne.* Edited by C. A. Patrides. London: J. M. Dent and Sons, 1985.

Ferrier, Jérémie. *Catholique d'éstat.* Paris, 1625.

Filmer, Sir Robert. *Patriarcha and Other Writings.* Cambridge: Cambridge University Press, 1991.

Guicciardini, Francesco. *The History of Italy.* Translated by Sidney Alexander. Princeton: Princeton University Press, 1969.

Hegel, G. W. F. *Elements of the Philosophy of Right.* Edited by Allen Wood. Translated by H. B. Nisbet. Cambridge: Cambridge University Press, 1991.

Hobbes, Thomas. *De Homine.* Translated by Charles T. Wood, T. S. K. Scott-Craig, and Bernard Gert. In *Thomas Hobbes, Man and Citizen,* edited by Bernard Gert. Indianapolis: Hackett, 1972.

——. *The English Works of Thomas Hobbes.* 11 vols. Edited by Sir William Molesworth. London: John Bohn, 1966.

——. *Leviathan.* Edited by Edwin Curley. Indianapolis: Hackett, 1994.

Hooker, Richard. *Of the Laws of Ecclesiastical Polity.* In *The Folger Library Edition of the Works of Richard Hooker.* 7 vols. Edited by W. Speed Hill. Cambridge: Harvard University Press, 1977.

Hotman, François. *Antitribonian; ou, Discours d'un grand et renommé iurisconsulte de nostre temps sur l'estude des lois.* Saint-Etienne: Université de Saint Etienne, 1980.

Hume, David. *Essays: Moral, Political and Literary.* Edited by Eugene Miller. Indianapolis: Liberty Fund, 1985.

Innocent III. *Patrologiae Latina.* Vols. 214–17. Edited by J. P. Migne. Paris, 1890.

James VI and I. *Political Writings.* Edited by Johann Sommerville. Cambridge: Cambridge University Press, 1994.

La Bruyère, Jean de. *Œuvres complètes.* Edited by Julien Benda. Paris: Gallimard, 1951.

Le Moyne, Pierre. *De L'art de regner.* Paris, 1665.

Lipsius, Justus. *Sixe Bookes of Politickes or Civil Doctrine.* Translated by William Jones. New York: Da Capo Press, 1970.

——. *Two Bookes of Constancie.* Translated by John Stradling. New Brunswick, N.J.: Rutgers University Press, 1939.

Locke, John. *Two Tracts on Government.* Edited by Philip Abrams. London: Cambridge University Press, 1967.

———. *Two Treatises of Government.* Edited by Peter Laslett. Cambridge: Cambridge University Press, 1988.

Louis XIV. *Mémoires.* Edited by Jean Longnon. Paris: Tallandier, 1978.

———. *Mémoires for the Instruction of the Dauphin.* Edited and translated by Paul Sonnino. New York: Free Press, 1970.

———. *Œuvres de Louis XIV.* Paris: Treuttel et Wurtz, 1806.

Machiavelli, Niccolò. *The Discourses.* Translated by Harvey Mansfield, Jr. and Nathan Tarcov. Chicago: University of Chicago Press, 1996.

———. *The Prince.* Translated by Harvey Mansfield, Jr. Chicago: University of Chicago Press, 1985.

Malebranche, Nicolas. *Malebranche's Treatise on Nature and Grace.* Translated by Patrick Riley. Oxford: Clarendon Press, 1992.

Médailles sur les principaux événements du règne de Louis le Grand. Schaffhausen, 1704.

Molière, Jean-Baptiste. *Tartuffe and Other Plays.* Translated by Donald Frame. New York: Penguin, 1967.

Montaigne, Michel de. *The Complete Essays of Montaigne.* Translated by Donald Frame. Stanford: Stanford University Press, 1965.

Montesquieu, Charles de Secondat. *The Spirit of the Laws.* Edited and translated by Anne Cohler, Basia Miller, and Harold Stone. Cambridge: Cambridge University Press, 1989.

Naudé, Gabriel. *Considérations politiques sur les coups d'état.* Paris: Editions de Paris, 1988.

Pellison, Paul. "Panégyrique du roy." In *Les panégyriques du roi,* edited by Pierre Zoberman. Paris: Presses de l'Université de Paris, 1991.

Pizan, Christine de. *The Book of the Body Politic.* Translated by Kate Langdon Forham. Cambridge: Cambridge University Press, 1994.

Priézac, Daniel de. *Discours politques.* Paris, 1652.

Proudhon, P. J. *General Idea of the Revolution in the Nineteenth Century.* Translated by J. B. Robinson. London: Free Press, 1923.

Richelieu, Cardinal de. *Maxims d'état et Fragments politiques.* Edited by Gabriel Hanotaux. Paris: Imprimerie Nationale, 1880.

———. *Testament politique.* Edited by Louis André. Paris: Robert Laffont, 1947.

Rohan, Henri de. *De l'intérêt des princes et des états de la chrétienté.* Edited by Christian Lazzeri. Paris: Presses Universitaires de France, 1995.

Rousseau, Jean-Jacques. *On the Social Contract with Geneva Manuscript and Political Economy.* Translated by Judith Masters. New York: St. Martin's Press, 1978.

Seyssel, Claude de. *The Monarchy of France.* Translated by J. H. Hexter and Michael Sherman. New Haven: Yale University Press, 1981.

Silhon, Jean de. *Le ministre d'éstat.* Final ed. Paris, 1665.

Tocqueville, Alexis de. *Democracy in America.* Edited by J. P. Mayer. Translated by George Lawrence. New York: Harper and Row, 1966.

Secondary Sources

Abercrombie, Nigel. *Saint Augustine and French Classical Thought.* Oxford: Clarendon Press, 1938.

Adams, Ian. *Political Ideology Today.* Manchester: Manchester University Press, 1993.

Allen, J. W. *A History of Political Thought in the Sixteenth Century.* London: Metheun, 1928.

———. "Sir Robert Filmer." In *The Social and Political Ideas of Some English Thinkers in the Augustan Age,* edited by F. J. C. Hearnshaw. London: G. G. Harrap, 1928.

Anderson, Perry. *Lineages of the Absolutist State*. London: Verso, 1974.

André, Louis. Introduction to *Testament politique,* by Cardinal de Richelieu. Paris: Robert Laffont, 1947.

Apostolidès, Jean-Marie. *Le roi-machine*. Paris: Les Editions de Minuit, 1981.

Ascoli, Albert. *Ariosto's Bitter Harmony: Crisis and Evasion in the Italian Renaissance*. Princeton: Princeton University Press, 1987.

Baron, Hans. *The Crisis of the Early Italian Renaissance*. Princeton: Princeton University Press, 1966.

Bartelson, Jens. *A Genealogy of Sovereignty*. Cambridge: Cambridge University Press, 1995.

Battista, Anna Maria. *Alle origini del pensiero politico libertino: Montaigne e Charron*. Milan: Giuffrè, 1966.

Baxter, Christopher. "Jean Bodin's Daemon and His Conversion to Judaism." In *Jean Bodin: Proceedings of the International Conference on Bodin in Munich,* edited by Horst Denzer. Munich: Verlag C. H. Beck, 1973.

Beaudry, James. "Virtue and Nature in the Essais." In *Montaigne: A Collection of Essays,* vol. 4, edited by Dikka Bermen. New York: Garland, 1995.

Beik, William. *Absolutism and Society in Seventeenth-Century France*. Cambridge: Cambridge University Press, 1985.

Berlin, Isaiah. *Against the Current: Essays in the History of Ideas*. New York: Viking Press, 1980.

Bireley, Robert. *The Counter-Reformation Prince*. Chapel Hill: University of North Carolina Press, 1990.

Black, Anthony. *Political Thought in Europe, 1250–1450*. Cambridge: Cambridge University Press, 1992.

Blair, Ann. *The Theater of Nature: Jean Bodin and Renaissance Science*. Princeton: Princeton University Press, 1997.

Bloch, Marc. *The Royal Touch*. Translated by J. E. Anderson. New York: Dorset, 1989.

Blumenberg, Hans. *The Legitimacy of the Modern Age*. Translated by Robert M. Wallace. Cambridge: MIT Press, 1983.

Bobbio, Norberto. *Thomas Hobbes and the Natural Law Tradition*. Translated by Daniela Gobetti. Chicago: University of Chicago Press, 1993.

Bonney, Richard. "Absolutism: What's in a Name?" *French History* 1 (1987): 93–117.

Brown, John. *The "Methodus ad Facilem Historiarum Cognitionem" of Jean Bodin: A Critical Study*. Washington, D.C.: Catholic University of America Press, 1939.

Burchell, Graham, Colin Gordon, and Peter Miller, eds. *The Foucault Effect: Studies in Governmentality*. London: Harvester Wheatsheaf, 1991.

Burgess, Glenn. *Absolute Monarchy and the Stuart Constitution*. New Haven: Yale University Press, 1996.

——. *The Politics of the Ancient Constitution: An Introduction to English Political Thought, 1603–1642*. University Park: Pennsylvania State University Press, 1992.

Burke, Peter. *The Fabrication of Louis XIV*. New Haven: Yale University Press, 1992.

——. "Tacitism, Scepticism, and Reason of State." In *The Cambridge History of Political Thought, 1450–1700,* edited by J. H. Burns. Cambridge: Cambridge University Press, 1991.

Burns, J. H. "The Idea of Absolutism." In *Absolutism in Seventeenth-Century Europe,* edited by John Miller. New York: St. Martin's Press, 1990.

Canning, J. P. "Law, Sovereignty and Corporation Theory, 1300–1450." In *The Cambridge History of Medieval Political Thought, c.350–c.1450,* edited by J. H. Burns. Cambridge: Cambridge University Press, 1988.

Carlyle, R. W., and A. J. Carlyle. *A History of Medieval Political Theory in the West.* 6 vols. New York: Barnes and Noble, 1903–1936.

Cassirer, Ernst. *The Myth of the State.* New Haven: Yale University Press, 1946.

Castells, Manuel. *The Information Age: Economy, Society and Culture.* 3 vols. Oxford: Blackwell, 1996–1998.

Chanteur, Janine. "L'idée de loi naturelle dans la *République* de Jean Bodin." In *Jean Bodin: Proceedings of the International Conference on Bodin in Munich,* edited by Horst Denzer. Munich: Verlag C. H. Beck, 1973.

Chauviré, Roger. *Jean Bodin, auteur de la "République."* Paris: Librairie Ancienne Honoré Champion, 1914.

Chill, Emanuel. "Tartuffe, Religion, and Courtly Culture." *French Historical Studies* 3 (1963): 151–83.

Christianson, Paul. *Discourse on History, Law, and Governance in the Public Career of John Selden, 1610–1635.* Toronto: University of Toronto Press, 1996.

———. "Royal and Parliamentary Voices on the Ancient Constitution, c.1604–1621." In *The Mental World of the Jacobean Court,* edited by Linda Levy Peck. Cambridge: Cambridge University Press, 1991.

Church, William F. *Constitutional Thought in Sixteenth-Century France.* Cambridge: Harvard University Press, 1941.

———. "Louis XIV and Reason of State." In *Louis XIV and the Craft of Kingship,* edited by John Rule. Columbus: Ohio State University Press, 1969.

———. *Richelieu and Reason of State.* Princeton: Princeton University Press, 1972.

Cole, Charles Woolsey. *Colbert and a Century of French Mercantilism.* 2 vols. New York: Columbia University Press, 1939.

Collins, James. *Fiscal Limits of Absolutism.* Berkeley: University of California Press, 1988.

———. *The State in Early Modern France.* Cambridge: Cambridge University Press, 1995.

Collins, Robert. "Montaigne's Rejection of Reason of State in 'De l'utile et de l'honneste.'" *Sixteenth Century Journal* 23 (1992): 71–94.

Collins, Stephen. *From Divine Cosmos to Sovereign State.* Oxford: Oxford University Press, 1989.

Cooke, Paul. *Hobbes and Christianity.* Lanham, Md.: Rowman and Littlefield, 1996.

Curley, Edwin. "'I Durst Not Write So Boldly'; or, How to Read Hobbes' Theological-Political Treatise." In *Hobbes e Spinoza, Scienza e politica,* edited by Daniela Bostrenghi. Naples: Bibliopolis, 1992.

———. Introduction to *Leviathan,* by Thomas Hobbes. Indianapolis: Hackett, 1994.

Cusimano, Maryann, ed. *Beyond Sovereignty: Issues for a Global Agenda.* New York: St. Martin's Press, 1998.

Daly, James. *Cosmic Harmony and Political Thinking in Early Stuart England.* Transactions of the American Philosophical Society, no. 69. Philadelphia: American Philosophical Society, 1979.

———. "The Idea of Absolute Monarchy in Seventeenth-Century England." *Historical Journal* 2 (1978): 227–50.

———. *Sir Robert Filmer and English Political Thought.* Toronto: University of Toronto Press, 1979.

Donaldson, Peter. *Machiavelli and Mystery of State.* Cambridge: Cambridge University Press, 1988.

Dunn, John. *The Political Thought of John Locke.* Cambridge: Cambridge University Press, 1969.

Dyson, Kenneth. *The State Tradition in Western Europe: A Study of an Idea and Institution.* New York: Oxford University Press, 1980.

Eccleshall, Robert. *Order and Reason in Politics.* Oxford: Oxford University Press, 1978.

Eisenach, Eldon. "Hobbes on Church, State and Religion." *History of Political Thought* 3 (summer 1982): 215–43.

———. *Two Worlds of Liberalism: Religion and Politics in Hobbes, Locke, and Mill.* Chicago: University of Chicago Press, 1981.

Elias, Norbert. *The Civilizing Process.* Translated by Edmund Jephcott. Oxford: Blackwell, 1994.

———. *The Court Society.* Translated by Edmund Jephcott. New York: Blackwell, 1983.

Elton, G. R. "The Divine Right of Kings." In *Studies in Tudor and Stuart Politics and Government.* Cambridge: Cambridge University Press, 1974.

Esmonin, Edmond. *Etudes sur la France des XVIIe et XVIIIe siècles.* Paris: Presses Universitaires de France, 1964.

Faulkner, Robert. *Richard Hooker and the Politics of Christian England.* Berkeley: University of California Press, 1981.

Fell, A. London. *Origins of Legislative Sovereignty and the Legislative State.* 5 vols. Boston: Oelgeschlager, Gunn, and Hain, 1983–1989.

Ferguson, Arthur. "The Historical Perspective of Richard Hooker: A Renaissance Paradox." *Journal of Medieval and Renaissance Studies* 3 (1973): 17–49.

Fernández-Santamaría, J. A. *Reason of State and Statecraft in Spanish Political Thought, 1595–1640.* Lanham, Md.: University Press of America, 1983.

Figgis, John. *The Divine Right of Kings.* Bristol: Thoemmes Press, 1994.

Foucault, Michel. *Discipline and Punish.* Translated by Alan Sheridan. New York: Vintage Books, 1977.

———. "Governmentality." In *The Foucault Effect: Studies in Governmentality,* edited by Graham Burchell, Colin Gordon, and Peter Miller. London: Harvester Wheatsheaf, 1991.

———. "Omnes et Singulatim." In *The Tanner Lectures on Human Values,* vol. 2, edited by Sterling McMurrin. Salt Lake City: University of Utah Press, 1981.

Fox, Paul. "Louis XIV and the Theories of Absolutism and Divine Right." *Canadian Journal of Economics and Political Science* 26 (1960): 128–42.

Frame, Donald. *Montaigne: A Biography.* New York: Harcourt, Brace, and World, 1965.

———. *Montaigne's Discovery of Man.* New York: Columbia University Press, 1955.

Franklin, Julian H. "Allegiance and Jurisdiction in Locke's Doctrine of Tacit Consent." *Political Theory* 24 (1996): 407–22.

———. *Jean Bodin and the Rise of Absolutist Theory.* Cambridge: Cambridge University Press, 1973.

———. *Jean Bodin and the Sixteenth-Century Revolution in the Methodology of Law and History.* New York: Columbia University Press, 1963.

———, ed. *On Sovereignty,* by Jean Bodin. Cambridge: Cambridge University Press, 1992.

Friedrich, Hugo. *Montaigne.* Translated by Dawn Eng. Berkeley: University of California Press, 1991.

Garin, Eugenio. *Italian Humanism.* Translated by Peter Munz. Westport, Conn.: Greenwood Press, 1965.

Gauthier, David. *The Logic of Leviathan: The Moral and Political Theory of Thomas Hobbes.* Oxford: Clarendon Press, 1969.

Gert, Bernard. Introduction to *Thomas Hobbes, Man and Citizen,* by Thomas Hobbes. Indianapolis: Hackett, 1972.

Giddens, Anthony. *The Nation-State and Violence.* Berkeley: University of California Press, 1987.

Gierke, Otto. *Political Theories of the Middle Age.* Translated by F. W. Maitland. Boston: Beacon Press, 1958.

Giesey, Ralph E. "Medieval Jurisprudence in Bodin's Concept of Sovereignty." In *Jean Bodin: Proceedings of the International Conference on Bodin in Munich,* edited by Horst Denzer. Munich: Verlag G. H. Beck, 1973.

———. *The Royal Funeral Ceremony in Renaissance France.* Geneva: Librairie Droz, 1960.

Gilbert, Felix. *Machiavelli and Guicciardini.* Princeton: Princeton University Press, 1965.

Gillespie, Michael. "The Theological Origins of Modernity." *Critical Review* 13 (1999): 1–30.

Gilmore, Myron. *Argument from Roman Law in Political Thought, 1200–1600.* Cambridge: Harvard University Press, 1941.

———. *Humanists and Jurists.* Cambridge: Harvard University Press, 1963.

Goldsmith, M. M. *Hobbes's Science of Politics.* New York: Columbia University Press, 1966.

Goyard-Fabre, Simone. *Jean Bodin et le droit de la "République."* Paris: Presses Universitaires de France, 1989.

Greene, Thomas. "The End of Discourse in Machiavelli's *Prince.*" *Yale French Studies* 67 (1984): 57–71.

Greenleaf, W. H. "Bodin and the Idea of Order." In *Jean Bodin: Proceedings of the International Conference on Bodin in Munich,* edited by Horst Denzer. Munich: Verlag G. H. Beck, 1973.

———. *Order, Empiricism, and Politics.* London: Oxford University Press, 1964.

Grendler, Paul. "Pierre Charron: Precursor to Hobbes." *Review of Politics* 25 (1963): 212–24.

Guéhenno, Jean-Marie. *The End of the Nation-State.* Translated by Victoria Elliott. Minneapolis: University of Minnesota Press, 1995.

Halliday, R. J., Timothy Kenyon, and Andrew Reeve. "Hobbes's Belief in God." *Political Studies* 31 (1983): 418–32.

Hampton, Jean. *Hobbes and the Social Contract Tradition.* Cambridge: Cambridge University Press, 1986.

Hartung, F. "L'état, c'est moi." In *Staatsbildende Kräfte der Neuzeit.* Berlin: Dunker and Humblot, 1961.

Hastings, Adrian. *The Construction of Nationhood.* Cambridge: Cambridge University Press, 1997.

Held, David. *Political Theory and the Modern State: Essays on State, Power, and Democracy.* Stanford: Stanford University Press, 1989.

Henshall, D. *The Myth of Absolutism.* London: Longman, 1992.

Hexter, J. H. *The Vision of Politics on the Eve of the Reformation.* New York: Basic Books, 1973.

Hinsley, F. H. *Sovereignty.* 2d ed. Cambridge: Cambridge University Press, 1986.

Hirschman, Albert O. *The Passions and the Interests: Political Arguments for Capitalism before Its Triumph.* Princeton: Princeton University Press, 1977.

Holmes, Stephen. "Jean Bodin: The Paradox of Sovereignty and the Privatization of Religion." *Nomos* 30 (1988): 5–45.

Hont, Istvan. "The Permanent Crisis of a Divided Mankind: 'Contemporary Crisis of the Nation State' in Contemporary Perspective." In *Contemporary Crisis of the Nation State?* edited by John Dunn. Oxford: Blackwell, 1995.

Hood, F. C. *The Divine Politics of Thomas Hobbes: An Interpretation of "Leviathan."* Oxford: Clarendon Press, 1964.

Huppert, George. *The Idea of Perfect History: Historical Erudition and Historical Philosophy in Renaissance France.* Urbana: University of Illinois Press, 1970.

Jacobson, David. *Rights across Borders.* Baltimore: Johns Hopkins University Press, 1996.

Johnston, David. "Hobbes's Mortalism." *History of Political Thought* 10 (winter 1989): 647–63.

――――. *The Rhetoric of "Leviathan": Thomas Hobbes and the Politics of Cultural Transformation.* Princeton: Princeton University Press, 1986.

Jones, Whitney. *The Tudor Commonwealth, 1529–1559.* London: Athlone, 1970.

Kahn, Victoria. *Machiavellian Rhetoric.* Princeton: Princeton University Press, 1994.

――――. *Rhetoric, Prudence, and Skepticism in the Renaissance.* Ithaca: Cornell University Press, 1985.

Kantorowicz, Ernst. *The King's Two Bodies: A Study in Medieval Political Theology.* Princeton: Princeton University Press, 1957.

――――. "Mysteries of State." *Harvard Theological Review* 47 (1955): 65–91.

Kavka, G. *Hobbesian Moral and Political Philosophy.* Princeton: Princeton University Press, 1986.

Kelley, Donald R. "The Development and Context of Bodin's *Method.*" In *Jean Bodin: Proceedings of the International Conference on Bodin in Munich,* edited by Horst Denzer. Munich: Verlag G. H. Beck, 1973.

――――. "Elizabethan Political Thought." In *The Varieties of British Political Thought, 1500–1800,* edited by J. G. A. Pocock, Gordon Schochet, and Lois Schwoerer. Cambridge: Cambridge University Press, 1993.

――――. *Foundations of Modern Historical Scholarship: Language, Law and History in the French Renaissance.* New York: Columbia University Press, 1970.

――――. *Renaissance Humanism.* Boston: Twayne Publishers, 1991.

Keohane, Nannerl. *Philosophy and the State in France.* Princeton: Princeton University Press, 1980.

Kern, Fritz. *Kingship and Law in the Middle Ages.* Translated by S. B. Chrimes. Oxford: Blackwell, 1948.

Kettering, Sharon. *Judicial Politics and Urban Revolt in Seventeenth-Century France.* Princeton: Princeton University Press, 1978.

――――. *Patrons, Brokers, and Clients in Seventeenth-Century France.* Oxford: Oxford University Press, 1986.

King, James. *Science and Rationalism in the Government of Louis XIV, 1661–1683.* Baltimore: Johns Hopkins University Press, 1949.

King, Preston. *The Ideology of Order.* London: G. Allen and Unwin, 1974.

Klaits, Joseph. *Printed Propaganda under Louis XIV.* Princeton: Princeton University Press, 1976.

Knecht, R. J. *Richelieu.* New York: Longman, 1991.

Kogel, Renée. *Pierre Charron.* Geneva: Librairie Droz, 1972.

Koselleck, Reinhart. *Futures Past: On the Semantics of Historical Time.* Translated by Keith Tribe. Cambridge: MIT Press, 1985.

Kuntz, Marion L. D. Introduction to *Colloquium of the Seven about Secrets of the Sublime,* by Jean Bodin. Princeton: Princeton University Press, 1975.

Lacour-Gayet, Georges. *L'éducation politique de Louis XIV.* Paris: Librairie Hachette, 1923.

Lamont, William. *Godly Rule: Politics and Religion, 1603–1660.* London: Macmillan, 1969.

Lanson, Gustave. *Bossuet.* Paris: Lecéne, Oudin et Cie., 1891.

Levi, Anthony. *French Moralists: The Theory of the Passions, 1585–1659.* Oxford: Clarendon Press, 1964.

Levi, Margaret. *Of Rule and Revenue.* Berkeley: University of California Press, 1988.

Lloyd, Howell. *The State, France and the Sixteenth Century.* London: G. Allen and Unwin, 1983.

Lloyd, S. A. *Ideals as Interests in Hobbes's "Leviathan": The Power of Mind over Matter.* Cambridge: Cambridge University Press, 1992.

Longnon, Jean. Introduction to *Mémoires,* by Louis XIV. Paris: Tallandier, 1978.

Lossky, Andrew. "The Intellectual Development of Louis XIV from 1661 to 1715." In *Louis XIV and Absolutism,* edited by Ragnhild Hatton. Columbus: Ohio State University Press, 1976.

———. *Louis XIV and the French Monarchy.* New Brunswick: Rutgers University Press, 1994.

———. "'Maxims of State' in Louis XIV's Foreign Policy in the 1680s." In *William III and Louis XIV,* edited by Ragnhild Hatton and J. S. Bromley. Liverpool: Liverpool University Press, 1968.

———. "The Nature of Political Power according to Louis XIV." In *The Responsibility of Power,* edited by Leonard Krieger and Fritz Stern. Garden City, N.Y.: Doubleday, 1967.

Lovejoy, Arthur. *The Great Chain of Being.* Cambridge: Harvard University Press, 1936.

Lyons, John. *Exemplum: The Rhetoric of Example in Early Modern France and Italy.* Princeton: Princeton University Press, 1989.

McIlwain, Charles Howard. *The Growth of Political Thought in the West.* New York: Macmillan, 1932.

Macpherson, C. B. *The Political Theory of Possessive Individualism: Hobbes to Locke.* Oxford: Oxford University Press, 1962.

McRae, Kenneth. "Bodin and the Development of Empirical Political Science." In *Jean Bodin: Proceedings of the International Conference on Bodin in Munich,* edited by Horst Denzer. Munich: Verlag G. H. Beck, 1973.

———. Introduction to *The Six Bookes of a Commonweale,* by Jean Bodin. Edited by Kenneth McRae. Translated by Richard Knolles. Cambridge: Harvard University Press, 1962.

Major, J. Russell. *From Renaissance Monarchy to Absolute Monarchy.* Baltimore: Johns Hopkins University Press, 1994.

Mann, Michael. *The Sources of Social Power.* Cambridge: Cambridge University Press, 1986.

Mansfield, Harvey, Jr. *Machiavelli's Virtue.* Chicago: University of Chicago Press, 1996.

———. *Taming the Prince.* Baltimore: Johns Hopkins University Press, 1989.

Marin, Louis. *Portrait of the King.* Minneapolis: University of Minnesota Press, 1988.

———. "Pour une théorie baroque de l'action politique." In *Considérations politiques sur les coups d'état.* Paris: Editions de Paris, 1988.

Maritain, Jacques. *Man and the State.* Washington, D.C.: Catholic University Press, 1998.

Martin, Daniel. *Montaigne et La fortune.* Paris: Librairie Honoré Champion, 1977.

Martinich, A. P. *The Two Gods of "Leviathan": Thomas Hobbes on Religion and Politics.* Cambridge: Cambridge University Press, 1992.

Mearsheimer, John. "The False Promise of International Institutions." *International Security* 19 (winter 1994/95): 5–49.

Meinecke, Friedrich. *Machiavellism: The Doctrine of Raison d'Etat and Its Place in Modern History.* Translated by Douglas Scott. New Brunswick, N.J.: Transaction Publishers, 1998.

Merrick, Jeffrey. *The Desacralization of the French Monarchy in the Eighteenth Century.* Baton Rouge: Louisiana State University Press, 1990.

Mettam, Roger. "France." In *Absolutism in the Seventeenth Century,* edited by John Miller. New York: St. Martin's Press, 1990.

———. *Power and Faction in Louis XIV's France.* Oxford: Blackwell, 1988.

Mitchell, Joshua. "Hobbes and the Equality of All under One." *Political Theory* 21 (February 1993): 78–100.

Monod, Paul. *The Power of Kings: Monarchy and Religion in Europe, 1589–1715.* New Haven: Yale University Press, 1999.

Moote, A. Lloyd. *Louis XIII, the Just.* Berkeley: University of California Press, 1989.

———. *The Revolt of the Judges.* Princeton: Princeton University Press, 1971.

Moreau-Reibel, Jean. *Jean Bodin et le droit public comparé dans ses rapports avec la philosophie de l'histoire.* Paris: Librairie philosophique J. Vrin, 1933.

Morgan, Edmund. *Inventing the People.* New York: W. W. Norton, 1988.

Mukerji, Chandra. *Territorial Ambitions and the Gardens of Versailles.* Cambridge: Cambridge University Press, 1997.

Murat, Inès. *Colbert.* Charlottesville: University Press of Virginia, 1984.

Nachison, Beth. "Absentee Government and Provincial Governors in Early Modern France: The Princes of Condé and Burgundy, 1660–1720." *French Historical Studies* 21 (spring 1998): 265–97.

Nagel, Thomas. "Hobbes's Concept of Obligation." *Philosophical Review* 68 (January 1959).

Nakam, Géralde. *Les essais de Montaigne: Miroir et procès de leur temps.* Paris: Librairie A. G. Nizet, 1984.

Nicolai, Alexandre. "Le machiavélisme de Montaigne." *Bulletin de la société des amis de Montaigne* 4–7, 9 (1957–1959).

Oakeshott, Michael. "Introduction to *Leviathan.*" In *Rationalism in Politics and Other Essays,* edited by Timothy Fuller. Indianapolis: Liberty Press, 1991.

Oakley, Francis. "The Absolute and Ordained Power of God and King in the Sixteenth and Seventeenth Centuries: Philosophy, Science, Politics, and Law." *Journal of the History of Ideas* 59 (October 1998): 669–90.

———. "The Absolute and Ordained Power of God in Sixteenth- and Seventeenth-Century Theology." *Journal of the History of Ideas* 59 (July 1998): 437–61.

———. *Omnipotence, Covenant, and Order: An Excursion in the History of Ideas from Abelard to Leibniz.* Ithaca: Cornell University Press, 1984.

Oestreich, Gerhard. *Neostoicism and the Early Modern State.* Translated by David McLintock. Cambridge: Cambridge University Press, 1982.

Ohmae, Kenichi. *The End of the Nation State.* New York: Free Press, 1995.

Pagden, Anthony, ed. *The Languages of Political Theory in Early Modern Europe.* Cambridge: Cambridge University Press, 1987.

Parel, Anthony. *The Machiavellian Cosmos.* New Haven: Yale University Press, 1992.

Parente, Margherita Isnardi. "Le volontarisme de Jean Bodin: Maimonide ou Duns Scot?" In *Jean Bodin: Proceedings of the International Conference on Bodin in Munich,* edited by Horst Denzer. Munich: Verlag G. H. Beck, 1973.

Pateman, Carole. *The Problem of Political Obligation.* New York: John Wiley and Sons, 1979.

———. *The Sexual Contract.* Stanford: Stanford University Press, 1988.

Pearl, Jonathan. Introduction to *On the Demon-Mania of Witches,* by Jean Bodin. Toronto: Centre for Reformation and Renaissance Studies, 1995.

Peltonen, Markku. *Classical Humanism and Republicanism in English Political Thought, 1570–1640.* Cambridge: Cambridge University Press, 1995.

Pennington, Kenneth. *The Prince and the Law, 1200–1600.* Berkeley: University of California Press, 1993.

Peters, Richard. *Hobbes.* Baltimore: Penguin Books, 1956.

Phillipson, Nicolas, and Quentin Skinner, eds. *Political Discourse in Early Modern Britain.* Cambridge: Cambridge University Press, 1993.

Pierson, Christopher. *The Modern State.* London: Routledge, 1996.

Pintard, René. *Le libertinage érudit dans la première moitié du XVIIe siècle.* Paris: Boivin, 1943.

Pitkin, Hanna. *Fortune Is a Woman.* Berkeley: University of California Press, 1984.

———. "Obligation and Consent, I." *American Political Science Review* 59 (1965): 990–99.

———. "Obligation and Consent, II." *American Political Science Review* 60 (1966): 39–52.

Pocock, J. G. A. *The Ancient Constitution and the Feudal Law: A Study of English Historical Thought in the Seventeenth Century.* 2d ed. Cambridge: Cambridge University Press, 1987.

———. "The Concept of a Language." In *The Languages of Political Theory in Early-Modern Europe.* Cambridge: Cambridge University Press, 1987.

———. *The Machiavellian Moment: Florentine Political Thought and the Atlantic Republican Tradition.* Princeton: Princeton University Press, 1975.

———. *Politics, Language and Time: Essays on Political Thought and History.* Chicago: University of Chicago Press, 1989.

Pocock, J. G. A., Gordon Schochet, and Lois Schwoerer, eds. *The Varieties of British Political Thought, 1500–1800.* Cambridge: Cambridge University Press, 1993.

Poggi, Gianfranco. *The Development of the Modern State: A Sociological Introduction.* Stanford: Stanford University Press, 1978.

Popkin, Richard. *The History of Scepticism from Erasmus to Spinoza.* Berkeley: University of California Press, 1979.

Post, Gaines. *Studies in Medieval Legal Thought.* Princeton: Princeton University Press, 1964.

Quilet, Jeannine. "Community, Counsel and Representation." In *The Cambridge History of Medieval Political Thought, c.350–c.1450,* edited by J. H. Burns. Cambridge: Cambridge University Press, 1988.

Rabil, Albert, Jr. "The Significance of 'Civic Humanism' in the Interpretation of the Italian Renaissance." In *Renaissance Humanism: Foundations, Forms, and Legacy,* vol. 1. Philadelphia: University of Pennsylvania Press, 1988.

Ranum, Orest. *Artisans of Glory.* Chapel Hill: University of North Carolina Press, 1980.

———. *The Fronde: A French Revolution, 1648–1652.* New York: W. W. Norton, 1993.

Reich, Robert. *The Work of Nations.* New York: Vintage Books, 1992.

Remer, Gary. *Humanism and the Rhetoric of Toleration.* University Park: Pennsylvania State University Press, 1996.

Reynolds, Beatrice. *Proponents of Limited Monarchy in Sixteenth Century France: Francis Hotman and Jean Bodin.* New York: Columbia University Press, 1931.

Riley, Patrick, ed. and trans. *Malebranche's Treatise on Nature and Grace,* by Nicolas Malebranche. Oxford: Clarendon Press, 1992.

———. *Politics Drawn from the Very Words of Holy Scripture,* by Jacques-Bénigne Bossuet. Cambridge: Cambridge University Press, 1990.

Rose, Paul Lawrence. *Bodin and the Great God of Nature: The Moral and Religious Universe of a Judaiser.* Geneva: Librairie Droz, 1980.

Rosenau, J. *Turbulence in World Politics.* Brighton: Harvester Wheatsheaf, 1990.

Rothkrug, Lionel. *Opposition to Louis XIV: The Political and Social Origins of the Enlightenment.* Princeton: Princeton University Press, 1965.

Rowen, Herbert. *The King's State: Proprietary Dynasticism in Early Modern France.* New Brunswick: Rutgers University Press, 1980.

Rowlands, Guy. "Louis XIV, Aristocratic Power and the Elite Units of the French Army." *French History* 13 (1999): 303–31.

Rudolph, Susanne Hoeber, and James Piscatori, eds. *Transnational Religion and Fading States.* Boulder: Westview Press, 1997.

Ruggie, John. "Territoriality and Beyond: Problematizing Modernity in International Relations." *International Organization* 47 (1993): 139–74.

Russell, Conrad. *The Causes of the English Civil War.* Oxford: Clarendon Press, 1990.

———. *Unrevolutionary England.* London: Hambledon Press, 1990.

Sabrié, J. B. *De l'humanisme au rationalisme: Pierre Charron (1541–1603).* Paris: Alcan, 1913.

Salmon, J. H. M. "Bodin and the Monarchomachs." In *Jean Bodin: Proceedings of the International Conference on Bodin in Munich,* edited by Horst Denzer. Munich: Verlag C. H. Beck, 1973.

———. *The French Religious Wars in English Political Thought.* Oxford: Oxford University Press, 1959.

Santoro, Mario. *Fortuna, ragione e prudenza nella civiltá letteraria del Cinquecento.* Naples: Liguori, 1966.

Sayce, R. A. *The Essays of Montaigne: A Critical Exploration.* Evanston: Northwestern University Press, 1972.

Schaefer, David. *The Political Philosophy of Montaigne.* Ithaca: Cornell University Press, 1990.

Schiffman, Zachary Sayre. "Montaigne and the Problem of Machiavellism." *Journal of Medieval and Renaissance Studies* 12 (fall 1982): 237–58.

———. *On the Threshold of Modernity.* Baltimore: Johns Hopkins University Press, 1991.

Schlesinger, Arthur, Jr. *The Imperial Presidency.* Boston: Houghton Mifflin, 1989.

Schmitt, Carl. *The Leviathan in the State Theory of Thomas Hobbes.* Westport, Conn: Greenwood Press, 1996.

———. *Political Theology: Four Chapters on the Concept of Sovereignty.* Translated by George Schwab. Cambridge: MIT Press, 1985.

Schochet, Gordon. *Patriarchalism in Political Thought.* Oxford: Basil Blackwell, 1975.

———. "Sir Robert Filmer: Some New Bibliographical Discoveries." *The Library,* 5th ser., 26 (1971): 135–60.

———. "Why Should History Matter? Political Theory and the History of Discourse." In *Varieties of British Political Thought, 1500–1800,* edited by J. G. A. Pocock, Gordon Schochet, and Lois Schwoerer. Cambridge: Cambridge University Press, 1993.

Sharpe, Kevin. *The Personal Rule of Charles I.* New Haven: Yale University Press, 1992.

Shennan, J. H. *The Origins of the Modern European State, 1450–1725.* London: Hutchinson, 1974.

Shepard, Max Adam. "Sovereignty at the Crossroads: A Study of Bodin." *Political Science Quarterly* 45 (1930): 580–603.

Simmons, A. John. *Moral Principles and Political Obligations*. Princeton: Princeton University Press, 1979.

———. "Philosophical Anarchism." In *For and Against the State: New Philosophical Readings,* edited by John T. Sanders and Jan Narveson. New York: Rowman and Littlefield, 1996.

Skinner, Quentin. *The Foundations of Modern Political Thought.* 2 vols. Cambridge: Cambridge University Press, 1978.

———. *Machiavelli.* New York: Hill and Wang, 1981.

———. *Reason and Rhetoric in the Philosophy of Hobbes.* Cambridge: Cambridge University Press, 1996.

———. "The State." In *Political Innovation and Conceptual Change,* edited by Terrence Ball, James Farr, and Russell Hanson. Cambridge: Cambridge University Press, 1989.

———. "Thomas Hobbes and His Disciples in France and England." *Comparative Studies in Society and History* 8 (1966): 153–67.

Smith, Jay. *The Culture of Merit.* Ann Arbor: University of Michigan Press, 1996.

Sommerville, Johann. "English and European Political Ideas in the Seventeenth Century: Revisionism and the Case of Absolutism." *Journal of British Studies* 35 (1996): 168–94.

———. Introduction to *Patriarcha and Other Writings,* by Sir Robert Filmer. Cambridge: Cambridge University Press, 1991.

———. Introduction to *Political Writings,* by King James VI and I. Cambridge: Cambridge University Press, 1994.

———. "James I and the Divine Right of Kings: English Politics and Continental Theory." In *The Mental World of the Jacobean Court,* edited by Linda Levy Peck. Cambridge: Cambridge University Press, 1991.

———. "Richard Hooker, Hadrian Saravia, and the Advent of the Divine Right of Kings." *History of Political Thought* 4 (1983): 229–45.

———. *Royalists and Patriots: Politics and Ideology in England, 1603–1640.* New York: Longman, 1999.

———. *Thomas Hobbes: Political Ideas in Historical Context.* New York: St. Martin's Press, 1992.

Sonnino, Paul. "The Dating and Authorship of Louis XIV's *Mémoires.*" *French Historical Studies* 3 (1964): 303–37.

———. Introduction to *Mémoires for the Instruction of the Dauphin,* by Louis XIV. New York: Free Press, 1970.

———. "The Sun King's Anti-Machiavel." In *Louis XIV and the Craft of Kingship,* edited by John Rule. Columbus: Ohio State University Press, 1969.

Springborg, Patricia. "Leviathan and the Problem of Ecclesiastical Authority." *Political Theory* 3 (August 1975): 289–303.

Spruyt, Hendrik. *The Sovereign State and Its Competitors.* Princeton: Princeton University Press, 1994.

Starobinski, Jean. *Montaigne in Motion.* Translated by Arthur Goldhammer. Chicago: University of Chicago Press, 1985.

Strauss, Leo. *Natural Right and History.* Chicago: University of Chicago Press, 1950.

———. *The Political Philosophy of Hobbes: Its Basis and Its Genesis.* Translated by Elsa M. Sinclair. Chicago: University of Chicago Press, 1952.

Strayer, Joseph R. *On the Medieval Origins of the Modern State.* Princeton: Princeton University Press, 1970.

Strong, Tracy. "How to Write Scripture: Words, Authority, and Politics in Thomas Hobbes." *Critical Inquiry* 20 (autumn 1993): 128–59.

Strowski, Fortunat. *Montaigne.* Paris: Alcan, 1906.

Tarlton, Charles. "The Creation and Maintenance of Government: A Neglected Dimension of Hobbes's *Leviathan.*" *Political Studies* 26 (1978): 307–27.

Taylor, A. E. "The Ethical Doctrine of Hobbes." *Philosophy* 13(1938): 406–24.

Tetel, Marcel. "Montaigne and Machiavelli: Ethics, Politics and Humanism." *Rivista di letterature moderne e comparante* 29 (September 1976): 165–81.

Thireau, Jean Louis. *Les idées politiques de Louis XIV.* Paris: Presses Universitaires de France, 1973.

Thompson, W. D. J. Cargill. "The Philosopher of the 'Politic Society': Richard Hooker as a Political Thinker." In *Studies in Richard Hooker,* edited by W. Speed Hill. Cleveland: Press of Case Western Reserve University, 1972.

Thuau, Etienne. *Raison d'état et pensée politique a l'époque de Richelieu.* Paris: Armand Colin, 1966.

Tierney, Brian. "Origins of Natural Rights Language: Texts and Contexts, 1150–1250." *History of Political Thought* 10 (1989): 615–46.

Tilly, Charles. *Coercion, Capital, and European States, AD 990–1990.* Cambridge: Basil Blackwell, 1990.

———, ed. *The Formation of National States in Western Europe.* Princeton: Princeton University Press, 1975.

Tillyard, E. M. W. *The Elizabethan World Picture.* London: Chatto and Windus, 1943.

Trinkaus, Charles. *In Our Image and Likeness: Humanity and Divinity in Italian Humanist Thought.* 2 vols. London: Constable, 1970.

Truchet, Jacques. Introduction to *La politique de Bossuet.* Edited by Jacques Truchet. Paris: Armand Colin, 1966.

Tuck, Richard. "The Christian Atheism of Thomas Hobbes." In *Atheism from the Reformation to the Enlightenment,* edited by David Wooten. Oxford: Clarendon Press, 1992.

———. "Hobbes and Descartes." In *Perspectives on Thomas Hobbes,* edited by G. A. J. Rogers and Alan Ryan. Oxford: Clarendon Press, 1988.

———. *Natural Rights Theories.* Cambridge: Cambridge University Press, 1979.

———. *Philosophy and Government, 1572–1651.* Cambridge: Cambridge University Press, 1993.

Ullmann, Walter. *A History of Political Thought: The Middle Ages.* Baltimore: Penguin, 1965.

van Gelderen, Martin. "The Machiavellian Moment and the Dutch Revolt: The Rise of Neostoicism and Dutch Republicanism." In *Machiavelli and Republicanism,* edited by Gisela Bock, Quentin Skinner, and Maurizio Viroli. Cambridge: Cambridge University Press, 1990.

Villey, Michel. "La justice harmonique selon Bodin." In *Jean Bodin: Proceedings of the International Conference on Bodin in Munich,* edited by Horst Denzer. Munich: Verlag G. H. Beck, 1973.

Villey, Pierre. *Les sources et l'évolution des essais de Montaigne.* 2 vols. Paris: Librairie Hachette et Cie, 1908.

Vincent, Andrew. *Theories of the State.* Oxford: Basil Blackwell, 1987.

Viroli, Maurizio. *From Politics to Reason of State.* Cambridge: Cambridge University Press, 1992.

Walker, R. B. J. *Inside/Outside: International Relations as Political Theory.* Cambridge: Cambridge University Press, 1993.

Wallace, Robert M. Translator's preface to *The Legitimacy of the Modern Age,* by Hans Blumenberg. Cambridge: MIT Press, 1983.

Walton, Guy. *Louis XIV's Versailles.* New York: Viking-Penguin, 1986.

Waltz, Kenneth. *Theory of International Politics.* Reading, Mass.: Addison- Wesley, 1979.

Walzer, Michael. *The Revolution of Saints.* Cambridge: Harvard University Press, 1965.

Warrender, Howard. *The Political Philosophy of Hobbes: His Theory of Obligation.* Oxford: Clarendon Press, 1957.

Watkins, J. W. N. "Philosophy and Politics in Hobbes." In *Hobbes Studies,* edited by K. C. Brown. Cambridge: Harvard University Press, 1965.

Weber, Max. *Economy and Society.* 2 vols. Edited by Guenther Roth and Claus Wittich. Berkeley: University of California Press, 1978.

Wilks, Michael. *The Problem of Sovereignty in the Later Middle Ages.* Cambridge: Cambridge University Press, 1963.

———. Review of *Jean Bodin: Proceedings of the International Conference on Bodin in Munich,* edited by Horst Denzer. *English Historical Review* 92 (1977): 142–43.

Wolf, John. *Louis XIV.* New York: W. W. Norton, 1968.

Young, Iris Marion. *Justice and the Politics of Difference.* Princeton: Princeton University Press, 1990.

Index

and Lipsius, 38; and Louis XIV,
118–19, 127; and Montaigne, 17;
and Richelieu, 98–99; and Silhon, 93

Reformation, the, 7, 8, 140–41
religious wars, 7, 17, 38, 48, 53, 65, 69
republicanism, 7–8, 13, 19, 158
Ribadeneyra, Pedro de, 85–86
Richelieu, Armand Jean du Plessis, cardinal de, 6, 11–12, 83, 84, 89, 90,
114, 116, 117, 221n.62, 221n.63,
221n.64; and Balzac, 93, 98,
220n.50; and Bossuet, 145; and
Charron, 219n.29; on fortune,
98–99; and the French court, 86–87;
and Lipsius, 219n.29; and Louis XIV,
127, 129; and Montesquieu, 112–13;
and Naudé, 104, 106; on rationalistic rule, 109–11; on reason of state
theory, 97–100; and Silhon, 95
Riley, Patrick, 226n.72
Roman law, 7, 47–48, 56–58
Rose, Paul Lawrence, 213n.29, 215n.67
Rothkrug, Lionel, 217n.101
Rousseau, Jean-Jacques, 10–11, 30, 80,
199, 200, 201, 236n.8

Samuel, 166, 186
Santoro, Mario, 15, 207n.28
Saravia, Hadrian, 158
Saul, 166
Sayce, R.A., 21
Schaefer, David, 21, 22, 23, 208n.43,
209n.52, 218n.1
Schiffman, Zachary, 208n.42
Schmitt, Carl, 183, 196–97
Schochet, Gordon, 163, 232n.55
Scipio, 18, 94
Scotus, Duns, 7, 158
Sebond, Raymond, 27, 29
Seneca, 19, 66, 108
Servin, Louis, 80
Seyssel, Claude de, 47–48, 50, 62
Silhon, Jean de, 12, 83, 93–95, 97, 98,
220n.51
Simmons, A. John, 80, 236n.116
Sirmond, Jean, 100
skepticism, 8; and Bodin, 49, 69; and
Hobbes, 171, 175, 178; and reason

of state theory, 83, 93
Skinner, Quentin, 197, 206n.2,
227n.87, 233n.68
Smith, Jay, 116–17, 123, 229n.109
Socrates, 31
Solomon, 156
Sommerville, Johann, 150–51
Starobinski, Jean, 208n.42

Tacitus, 85, 94
Tarcov, Nathan, 207n.21
Tarquin, 103
Taylor, A. E., 170, 178
Tetel, Marcel, 208n.46
Thireau, Jean Louis, 224n.20
Thomas Aquinas, St., 7, 73, 141–42,
153, 154, 155, 175, 178
Thuau, Etienne, 221n.72
Tierney, Brian, 29
Tocqueville, Alexis de, 115–16, 149
Tribonian, 57
Trois-eschelles, 55
Truchet, Jacques, 227n.88
Tuck, Richard, 42, 83, 197, 206n.9,
220n.50, 233n.68

Ulpian, 61

Versailles, 137
Villey, Michel, 78
Viroli, Maurizio, 83, 197
virtue: Lipsius's theory, 39, 40, 41;
Louis XIV's theory, 119–20, 130;
Machiavelli's theory, 14–15, 16–17,
20, 24–25; Montaigne's theory,
24–26, 28, 35–36
voluntarist theologies, 7; Bodin's theory, 49, 50–56, 69, 138, 158;
Bossuet's theory, 138–39; Hobbes's
theory, 184–85; and Hooker, 153;
James I's theory, 151, 158–60

Walker, R. B. J., 200–201
Warrender, Howard, 170
Weber, Max, 106, 203n.4
Wilks, Michael, 212n.11
Wolf, John, 131

Young, Iris Marion, 149, 201